FUTURE
WEAPONS

KEVIN DOCKERY

BERKLEY CALIBER, NEW YORK

THE BERKLEY PUBLISHING GROUP
Published by the Penguin Group
Penguin Group (USA) Inc.
375 Hudson Street, New York, New York 10014, USA
Penguin Group (Canada), 90 Eglinton Avenue East, Suite 700, Toronto, Ontario M4P 2Y3, Canada
(a division of Pearson Penguin Canada Inc.)
Penguin Books Ltd., 80 Strand, London WC2R 0RL, England
Penguin Group Ireland, 25 St. Stephen's Green, Dublin 2, Ireland (a division of Penguin Books Ltd.)
Penguin Group (Australia), 250 Camberwell Road, Camberwell, Victoria 3124, Australia
(a division of Pearson Australia Group Pty. Ltd.)
Penguin Books India Pvt. Ltd., 11 Community Centre, Panchsheel Park, New Delhi—110 017, India
Penguin Group (NZ), 67 Apollo Drive, Mairangi Bay, Auckland 1311, New Zealand
(a division of Pearson New Zealand Ltd.)
Penguin Books (South Africa) (Pty.) Ltd., 24 Sturdee Avenue, Rosebank, Johannesburg 2196,
South Africa

Penguin Books Ltd., Registered Offices: 80 Strand, London WC2R 0RL, England

This book is an original publication of the Berkley Publishing Group.

The publisher does not have any control over and does not assume any responsibility for author or third-party websites or their content.

First edition: March 2007

Library of Congress Cataloging-in-Publication Data

Dockery, Kevin.
    Future weapons / Kevin Dockery.
        p.   cm.
    Includes bibliographical references and index.
    ISBN-13: 978-0-425-21215-8
    1. Military weapons.   2. Military weapons—United States.   3. Weapons systems.
    4. Weapons systems—United States.   I. Title.
    UF500. D68   2007
    623. 4—dc22   2006032450

PRINTED IN THE UNITED STATES OF AMERICA

10   9   8   7   6   5   4   3   2   1

CONTENTS

INTRODUCTION: THE PAST INTO THE FUTURE

What might be the weapons of the near future makes a fascinating subject path that is filled with the potholes of public perceptions. Many times the items that have been seen in the hands of the black-suited ninja soldiers are little more than the results of imaginative speculation. They are basically mock-ups of wood, plastic, and metal to show the public what might be, rather than what is probably going to be.

What might be the weapons of the future should not be examined before knowing what came before them. Nothing is created in an absolute vacuum. The new designs of today are based on the familiar weapons of yesterday. There is the rare flash of insight, the genius of innovation that results in something truly new in the world. But in the conservative military world of firearms, that is a very rare thing, and when it happens, it has to prove itself to what is a very skeptical audience. Thomas Edison, probably the most prolific inventor of the modern age, said that genius is 2 percent inspiration and 98 percent perspiration. The development of a new weapon fits these parameters; it's the result of a lot of hard work.

When examining the weapons that may be used in the conflicts of the coming years, it is easy to get lost in the fascination of big, impressive hardware. The new missiles have us looking to the skies where we can also see the exotic aircraft that are practically invisible to everything but the naked eye. In the dark of the night, their batlike silhouettes would become indistinct, except for a fleeting shadow blotting out the stars. Satellites look down across the earth from high up in orbit with very little escaping their views. Flashing beams of directed energy can rip an incoming missile from out of the sky. These are the stuff of science fiction become reality.

In all of the glamour of the big, high-tech hardware, it is easy to lose sight of the simpler, but much more common, individual weapons of warfare. Those are the pieces of hardware carried in the arms of the individual soldier, the tools of personal war. Though air and sea power can dominate a battlefield and heavy armor rush across the land while the space assets are there to tell us about it, it is the individual soldier who must finally stand and hold the ground.

It is the boots of the troops on the ground that go into harm's way that is the final statement of the will of a people and their fighters. It is the weapons that the soldier fights with, those personal arms that are held in the hands of the troops facing the enemy, that he depends on. They provide the means for that soldier to project his will across the last few hundred meters of the battlefield.

On these pages are the weapons that are being built today and in the years to come. These are not imaginary pieces of hardware. They are the weapons that will be used to fight the immediate conflicts of today and the wars of tomorrow. They are not of a grand scale—each of them can be held in the hands of a single soldier—but they are what that soldier will use to fight and survive. The soldier is the end of the kill chain, that sequence of events and decisions that resulted in him facing an enemy. The weapons in the hands of those shooters are the cutting edge of that chain.

Some of the weapons shown are so new that they are still in the prototype stage. They exist only as a few specimens at most. Others were successfully developed and demonstrated but never issued in numbers due to the political or economic situation of their time acting against them. Others, no matter how promising, simply disappeared due to the personal tastes and opinions of the people in charge of their adoption.

There are a handful of small arms described here that have been issued to only a select few special military units. They are so rarely seen that the only place the public has been able to view them has been in popular entertainment such as the *Stargate* science fiction series.

These entertaining shows are the result of creative minds coming up with ideas that may not have been thought of before. The special effects people who produce the writer's ideas visually and the props people who have built them into three-dimensional objects are very good at their craft. There has been more than one occasion where something seen only in a movie raised the interest of a high-ranking officer. He has gone back to the technical people, the ordnance experts, and told them to build him that. Sometimes, they have.

RIFLES

CARRYING A RIFLE

1918

It had been long weeks since Private John Stormer had stepped off the troop ship and onto the soil of France. The spring was supposed to be a beautiful time in the French countryside, or at least that's what he had been told it used to be. In the spring of 1918, there was little enough worth looking at, at least in the area where he found himself.

As far as the French soil went, John had seen, slept in, shoveled, and eaten enough of it to last him the rest of his life. He had yet to see real combat, but what he had seen had already terrified him. The ground in front of the trenches was churned mud covered with lumps, ripped trees, tangles of barbed wire, and the remains of the dead.

Both sides had pretty much cleared out the remains of their fellow soldiers when they could. But the bloated bodies of what few horses had still been around proved that the machine gun and the artillery shell splinter didn't care who or what it ripped open or killed. The nightly rattle of machine guns up and down both sides of no-man's-land made sure that what little sleep you received was fitful at best. He was tired, had been tired, didn't remember what it was like not to be tired. But his thoughts about what they were going to do that early spring morning had kept him from sleeping much the night just past, even when he had the chance.

As his hands gripped his Springfield rifle more tightly, he twisted at the long rifle to keep those hands from shaking off the wrists they were attached to. Suddenly, he felt another person's hand grasp his shoulder. He opened his eyes and looked at the sarge.

Sergeant Kinsey knew what was going through Stormer's mind as he had watched the soldier. Fear could grip a man and freeze him in place if he thought about it too much. The sergeant had been a veteran of other campaigns on other battlefields, and he had seen the signs often enough.

"Okay, Stormer?" Kinsey asked

"Okay, Sarge," Stormer said in a voice stronger than he felt at the moment. He knew that Kinsey had been through a lot in his twenty years in the service. The stories told in the barracks had said that the sarge had been a volunteer for the Spanish-American War and had even gone up San Juan Hill with Roosevelt and the Rough Riders. He had seen action in the Philippines and Mexico. The huns would be nothing new for him. Just the solid presence of the man was reassuring to a scared soldier.

"Okay, keep your rifle clean," Kinsey said. "Listen for the signal. We go over the top at the sound of the lieutenant's whistle. We move right after the bombardment is over."

Stormer's eyes went wide as he remembered about the bombardment. Even as he realized what they were about to go through, there was the sound of whistling through the air followed by a distant thunder. The new artillery in the rear put a shell out that traveled so fast you heard it go by before the sound of the cannon fire even reached you. The ground shook with the thudding impact of the artillery. Then there was a solid wall of noise as the heavy rounds just kept passing overhead.

The noise just went on and on for what seemed like forever. Then, after not even a full hour had passed, they suddenly stopped. The thud of his heart was heavy in his chest as Stormer listened for the whistle. He turned and faced the parapet of the trench. Normally, just sticking your head up for even a moment past the protection of the trench could get you killed from a sniper's bullet. But the hun snipers should be badly shaken up, maybe even killed, by the bombardment. It was something to hope for.

Even though he was expecting it, the shrill blast of the whistle startled Stormer. He jerked up as the command, "Over the top!" went up and down the line. Clambering up the side of the trench, Stormer reached the top and started down the other side. Before he had even moved a foot away from the trench, the German machine guns started up. The stitching sound of the German Maxim guns had been something he had listened to every day on the front. But this time there wasn't a wall of dirt between him and the guns. Bullets snapped past him as he continued to advance. Williams took a slug in the chest not ten feet from where Stormer was moving. He just stared at the man as he lay moaning in the mud. Then a sharp shove in his back broke the spell of sudden death.

"Get moving there, Stormer!" Sergeant Kinsey said as he struck the frozen man in the back with the butt of his rifle. "You stand still, and you'll be the next one! Keep going!"

It was only a few hundred yards between where Stormer had been and where the Germans were waiting. How he crossed that horrible width of no-man's-land he would never be able to say. His tongue was stiff in his dust-dry mouth. Fear had sucked all the moisture from him and left only the taste of copper in his mouth. Then he saw them, the Germans, the hated huns. And there was nothing else to do but jump into the trenches and take them on.

Even as he struck out with the long bayonet on his rifle, a small bit of Stormer's mind watched what was going on in front of him. The man who was trying to stab at him with another long, black bayonet looked just as young and scared as Stormer felt. Then he was into the trench, and there wasn't time for even a piece of him not to concentrate on fighting and trying to stay alive.

It was a confusing hell of shouting men, firing guns, and flashing blades. Sergeant Kinsey had his Springfield in his hands and a trench knife flopping in its scabbard in his belt on the side opposite of his pistol holster. They all had fought their way along the trench until they had come up to the remains of a bunker that had been partially knocked down by the bombardment. Stormer didn't even know how many of the men from his platoon were still in the trench with him. The whole world had settled down into a series of jabs with his bayonet, working the bolt, and firing a shot. Mechanically, he had stuffed new stripper clips into his rifle as the bolt stopped closing against an empty magazine. The training he had gotten in the States and again in France had helped give him something to concentrate on as the world fell into a mass of confusion all around him.

As Kinsey jabbed his bayonet into a German soldier who had just come around the fallen bunker, someone inside the ruin shoved against a wall of sandbags. The heavy bags tumbled down onto Kinsey as Stormer looked on in horror. Slammed down into the muck at the bottom of the trench, Kinsey was pinned under the weight of the sandbags as a big German soldier came out of the gaping hole that had closed off the bunker he had been trapped in. In the man's hands was an odd, short little weapon with a perforated barrel and an odd-looking handle sticking out the side of it. It was some kind of gun—that was something Stormer was sure of—as the nasty little weapon started to stutter and spit lead.

There wasn't any time to think, only act. The Springfield rifle that had served Stormer so well that morning now acted against him. As he swung the weapon around to strike at the German, the bayonet on the long rifle hit the far side of the trench wall, struck it, and stuck against some woven reeds holding up the dirt. Only the fact that the German was half blinded by dust and dirt gave Stormer any time to save himself and his pinned sergeant. Letting go of his rifle completely, Stormer charged at the German, screaming as he snatched at the brim of his own helmet.

Pulling the steel hat from his head, Stormer swung it hard at the German in front of him. The stamped flat edge of the helmet smashed into the other man's face just before Stormer rammed into him hard. Stunned, the big enemy soldier fell back against the ruins of the bunker behind him. He never let go completely of the odd little gun he held in his hands, but at least he had stopped firing it.

Bending down, Stormer grabbed at a dull shine of brass he saw in the welter of sandbags and muck at the bottom of the trench. It was Sergeant Kinsey's trench knife. Yanking it from the scabbard, Stormer swung back at the German, who was starting to wave his short weapon around again. The man was badly hurt from the looks of the blood streaming across his face, but the gash that Stormer had put there with the edge of his helmet had not been enough to stop the man completely.

Driving himself forward, Stormer struck out with the double-edged dagger blade of the trench knife. He felt the blade strike something hard and then slip past into something softer and more yielding. As he grappled with the German to keep the short gun away from himself, Stormer felt the man's stinking breath in his face. There were some kinds of words the man was trying to say and he struggled against the weight of the American soldier, weight that was driving a blade deep into his chest. Later, all Stormer thought he had heard was something like "Gut," repeated over and over. Then there was a gurgling noise from the enemy soldier, and the man slumped back against the ruins of the trench he had probably been in for months.

Gasping for breath, Stormer stood back up and then fell against the far wall of the trench. There wasn't any time for rest as he saw his sergeant struggling underneath the weight of the sandbags and rubble that had knocked him down. Bending over, Stormer pulled up at a sandbag, uncovering Kinsey, who was still alive.

"Get this crap off of me," Kinsey growled.

As Stormer smiled and bent to pull at another sandbag, he heard a smack nearby. It had been a small sound, and there was no reason for him to have heard it, but he had. Looking up, the dribbling sandbag in his hands, Stormer saw the black-painted metal can and wooden handle of a German hand grenade lying in the mud not five feet from where he stood. And there was a thin stream of smoke rising up from the end of the hollow handle.

1970

"Damn, this place stinks," Corporal Pete "Stormy" Stormer grumbled as his boots caused a big bubble of gas to belch up from the mud and burst on the oily surface of the filthy water.

"Small wonder, Stormy," Petersen said from a few feet behind him. "Papa-san and Mama-san fertilize these paddies with their toilets."

"Can it," Sergeant Brower said, "we're not to the boats yet."

The platoon of American infantry soldiers was close to finishing a patrol through the hot, humid Mekong Delta area of South Vietnam. They had responded to a report of a suspected Vietcong supply cache and so far had found nothing to justify their efforts. Nineteen seventy was a good year for a lot of things, but slogging through the rice paddies of I Corps was not one of them. The Mekong Delta was the rice bowl of Southeast Asia. The fertile, stinking mud produced more rice per acre than almost anywhere else on earth. And Corporal Stormer felt he had walked through so much of it that he may never want to eat rice again in his life.

Clambering up on the dike, the men left the rice paddies behind them as they entered an area of relatively dry land covered with a spotting of banana trees. It was another grove, and beyond that would be the riverbank and an extraction boat. It was not a time for anyone to let up on their vigilance. With the end of their long slog in sight, it was human nature for the men to start to relax a bit. Stormy was guilty of that himself. But he was the third generation of Stormer men to serve their country, and he made a vow that if he ever had a son back in the World, he wouldn't have to. He could grow up and be a fireman, cop, farmer, garbageman, anything he wanted to, but not another generation of soldier. Grandfather had been wounded by a German grenade during World War I and received the Silver Star for saving a bunch of people in some unnamed trench in France. His father had landed on Omaha Beach, lived through that, and received the Bronze Star for heroism in the hedgerow country of Normandy. The family luck had to run out eventually!

The sarge stuck up his fist and brought the patrol to a halt. At another signal, Stormy moved up front to rotate with Rankle in the point position. Up front was a dangerous place to be, but Stormy preferred it, as he was on his own and could let himself just concentrate on the jungle and the area surrounding him. He actually relaxed and let his senses pick up on the terrain around him. There was the all-pervasive smell of South Vietnam, a cross between a barnyard and a sewer at the moment. A warm breeze blew across his face and he listened to . . . nothing.

Everything went on high alert as stormy realized there wasn't a sound from the area all around them, no birds, certainly no people. The short XM177E2 felt slick in his hands as he unconsciously felt for the safety with his thumb. The switch was already set on auto, and there were eighteen rounds in the magazine with one locked in place in the chamber. With his weapon secured firmly in his firing hand, Stormy held up his left in a clenched first. The patrol stopped at the warning signal, and everyone crouched down into a squat. Everyone had their weapons out and covering the area around them. Platoon Sergeant Brower had instilled, beaten may be a better word, the value of a clean weapon into the men under him. Their uniforms were spotted with mud and sweat-stained, but their M16A1 rifles were spotless and lubricated on the inside. This was the sarge's third tour in Vietnam, and he swore there would never be a jammed weapon in his platoon because some newbie hadn't cleaned his rifle.

The worst thing about the situation wasn't that they were in the middle of a combat zone. No; the newest guy in the platoon had to be the lieutenant. Some shavetail second who felt he knew how the war was going to go under his command. After only a few moments had gone by while everyone else scanned the area, the lieutenant came up to where Stormy crouched down in the almost nonexistent cover.

"What the hell is it, Corporal?" Lieutenant Carmichael asked in a loud whisper.

As Stormer turned to speak, he heard a sharp metallic *clack* from off to his left. It was a sound that you never forgot once you heard it, if you survived the encounter. It was the infamous "AK clack"—the sound of the safety coming off on an AK-47 and the weapon ready to fire.

"Gooks on the flank!" Stormy shouted as he turned and saw the ground seem to lift up a few dozen feet away. It was the grass-covered woven bamboo cover of a VC spider hole. And the pajama-clad Cong underneath it was holding an AK-47.

Time seemed to slow as Stormer swore he could see each individual flash of the muzzle as the VC fired at him on full automatic. Sound became dull, and he moved as if deep in tar, trying to swing his weapon and bring it to bear on the man trying to kill him. There was a grunt to his side as the startled lieutenant stopped a round and slumped down. The ground all around the patrol erupted in Vietcong as they came up out of their holes. There must have been a dozen men firing in at the American patrol as the soldiers fired back.

The deep booming sound of the AK-47s was interrupted by the staccato crack of the M16 rifles putting out their high-velocity slugs. The rifles were feared by the Vietcong, who had named them the Black Rifle years ago. But they had gotten over their fear of the tall Yankees armed with the light little gun. Now that the bugs had been worked out of the vicious aluminum and plastic weapon, the Vietcong were once again learning a healthy respect for it.

This particular group of Uncle Ho's little brown brothers must have been waiting for just such a group of soldiers as Stormer's to come walking along. They may have detected the unit earlier and planned the attack on the run. He had detected the ambush without really noticing it. And his warning may have saved the platoon he had served with for the last eight months. Well, maybe not the lieutenant.

There was a thump as Petersen popped off a high-explosive round with his XM203. The launcher was brand-spanking-new, and the company only had one of them. It had gone to the best grenadier in the outfit, and Petersen was demonstrating why.

Having already emptied the magazine in his M16A1, Petersen had pulled the trigger on the 40 mm XM203 grenade launcher underneath the barrel of the rifle. The fat little gold-colored egg sailed through the air and burst on the ground among the spider holes. Even before the first grenade had hit, Petersen had jacked the barrel of the XM203 open and was stuffing another round into the chamber.

Rounds were tearing into the grass all around them as the platoon took heavy fire from the Vietcong. Then the jungle beyond also opened up with enemy fire. The platoon had no idea how many Vietcong were out there, but it was obvious they had stumbled into a hornet's nest.

"Lieutenant's down!" Stormer shouted as he dumped the now-empty magazine from his weapon. An instant later, he had reloaded, and the loud boom of his short-barreled weapon roared out once more. A ball of fire appeared in front of the muzzle of his well-used XM177E2 with every shot it fired. The muzzle flash moderator had become crapped up over the months, and there was no way to properly clean it. But the handy little weapon was great when on point, and the reassuring thunder from the gun let the platoon know that Stormy was still in the fight. The lieutenant lying next to him wasn't, and the radio he had strapped to his back had taken a couple of rounds from that first enemy burst. The metal had ripped open, and wires were sticking up out of the dull green box.

"Commo's down!" Stormy shouted as he continued to return fire. He saw one Vietcong go down, his head disappearing in a splash of gore as the high-velocity 5.56 mm slugs from the XM177E2 smashed into him.

"Pull out for the river!" Brower shouted over the noise of the battlefield. Several men had been hit and gone down. If the platoon stayed where they were, they would just get cut to pieces. The edge of the banana grove was just a handful of yards away, and there was the cover of the riverbank beyond.

The return from the Americans seemed to grow in volume as everyone opened up on full auto to cover their withdrawal. The Vietcong slowed their own fire as men took cover from the volume of bullets coming their way. As the men passed him, Stormer kept up a heavy return fire until the last man had gone by. Stuffing another magazine into his smoking weapon, he smacked the bolt release catch with the palm of his left hand, finishing the loading process with a scraping clack as the bolt rammed a round into the hot chamber.

"Incoming fast movers!" Brower shouted as he threw out a green canister. "Danger close!"

The platoon sergeant had gotten to one of the other radios in the patrol and contacted a pair of Navy jets flying nearby. The smoke grenade he had thrown out to mark their position started spewing violet smoke as the sound of the jets started to grow in the air.

"Come on, Stormy," Petersen shouted, "time to go!"

As he started to get up, the lieutenant lying on the ground groaned.

"Shit!" Stormer exclaimed as he bent down to the fallen officer.

Hoisting the barely moving man to his left shoulder, Stormer kept firing with his weapon in his right hand. When the bolt locked back on an empty magazine, he turned away from the Vietcong and just started to run to where the platoon was under cover beyond the riverbank.

Suddenly, he felt a hammer blow to his side and another on his left leg. Falling to one knee, Stormer struggled to get back up as the sound of the jets screaming in roared out around him. He suddenly felt as if he had been kicked in the ass by his sergeant as another AK bullet struck him in the left butt cheek. Gritting his teeth, he got back up and started to run, or at least stagger quickly. Blood was streaming from his side, butt, and leg as he finally got away from the grove. Stumbling over the riverbank, he felt the heat spread across the back of his head from the jungle exploding behind him. Falling down into the mud, he lay there, trying to keep from passing out as the world spun around him.

2005

Captain Randall Stormer kept watch as the men from First Platoon moved up the road. The other two platoons from Company E, First of the Third, his command, were moving on either side of the block they were sweeping. While the Marines and other American forces were kicking ass in Fallujah, there were still other parts of Iraq that had to be cleaned out of insurgent forces. He hated giving the terrorists they were fighting even the honor of that name, but the media had called the miserable fanatics that for so long that the habit had just kind of grown.

It seemed the habit of serving with the military had also grown with the Stormer clan. His dad hadn't wanted him to serve but wouldn't talk him out of it. As the son of a Medal of Honor recipient from the Vietnam War, Randall had been able to take his pick of appointments to any of the military academies. His sister Sandy had gone on to the Air Force Academy in Colorado, while Randall had taken on the discipline and tradition of West Point and the Army. But he never forgot that his father, grandfather, and great-grandfather had always been enlisted men. Graduating from the academy could put a man's nose in the air, but he would never be a ring-knocker; the commandant of the academy himself had made certain that the freshly minted Lieutenant Randall Stormer never forgot where he had come from. It was easy for General Carmichael to speak to Cadet Stormer; he had known the boy all his life. It was then-Lieutenant Carmichael who had been carried by his wounded father away from a Vietcong ambush, endangering his own life in the process as fighter jets ripped up the jungle behind him.

The influence of the officer stayed with the family long after Sergeant Peter Stormer stood up at the White House as President Nixon placed the piece of watered blue silk around his neck. The story of the incoming jets was what had pushed Sandy to the Air Force Academy. Randall felt he should be a ground-pounder like his father before him. After the World Trade Center had fallen on 9/11, he had only been one of the many young cadets at West Point who had wanted to strike back at those who had attacked their country.

There was no question in his mind that what they were doing in Iraq was the right thing. Along with his men, he had seen the stockpiles of weapons and ammunition Saddam had built up. The world was eventually going to learn about the VX Nerve Gas artillery shells that had been found, but not yet. Only the story about the one round that had been used as an IED had ever gotten out. And even that had been ignored by most of the press back home.

"Snipers reported in the area, sir," Platoon Sergeant Rexall said as he walked up to where the captain stood in momentary reflection.

"Have the men stay sharp, Rex," Stormer said. "In this heat even the best of us can make mistakes."

"Roger that, sir," Rexall said with a grin. "This place is hot even compared to Texas. And there isn't—"

Stormer actually heard the bullet hit the sergeant standing next to him as the air left the man's lungs with a grunt. His Kevlar pot had taken the hit as the 7.62 mm bullet from an ex-Soviet sniper rifle smacked into it. The sergeant went down hard, his M14 rifle tumbling into the dirt. Rexall had liked the big rifle for the power and range it had given him. But the weapon hadn't done him any good from what had apparently been the carefully aimed bullet of an insurgent sniper.

"Sniper on the right flank!" Stormer shouted as he took cover against a building. He heard his men responding as they fell into position. The mostly young men of the platoon moved as the carefully drilled force that they were, as they assaulted in the direction of the unseen shooter. Their platoon sergeant had gone down, and somebody was going to pay a lot.

As the medic trotted up to where Rexall lay in the dirt, Stormer bent down and picked up the fallen man's weapon. He knew that the M14 was loaded with tracer rounds. The platoon sergeant habitually kept a magazine full of the orange-tipped rounds locked in place to mark targets. The proof of that habit was going to show itself in a moment, but the hammer blow Stormer felt against his chest knocked him to the ground first.

He never even heard the shot that had struck him dead center of his chest. It must have been time for the Stormer family combat luck to finally run out. Only it wasn't gone yet. The 7.62 mm slug from the SVD sniper rifle had struck dead center of the captain's chest, right in the middle of the center plate of his Interceptor body armor.

The heavy armor was a bother to wear in the heat of Iraq, but it was a bother Stormer had been glad to get used to. He had gotten the wind knocked out of him, but that was the worst of his wound, other than the big-ass bruise he knew would be coming along by tomorrow. What was important was that he had seen the flash and smoke of the shot. There hadn't been much, but it was enough.

The insurgent was firing from the fourth floor of a tall building half a block down the road. The distance was a few hundred meters, well inside the range of Stormer's M4A1 carbine. But he could barely speak as the medic rushed over to him. That didn't matter as he waved the man away and toward where Rexall lay. The platoon sergeant had given him a very good means of directing his men.

Dropping the M4A1 down against its sling, Stormer pulled up the M14 and pushed the safety off with his trigger finger. He hadn't taken his eyes off the spot where he had seen the sign of the sniper's shot. There was a balcony with a short cement wall covering the front of it. The bottom of the wall ended about six inches above the floor of the balcony. That was where the sniper had fired, and as Stormer watched, another round snapped out toward his men in the street.

Yanking up the M14, he settled the big rifle in his hands, and he peered through the sight. Lying on his back was an odd position to be shooting from, but it was good enough as the big rifle bucked and roared in his hands.

The Army had brought back the M14 for the additional range and power it gave a squad's base of fire. Most of the weapons had been mounted with telescopic sights, but Rexall didn't have one on his. That didn't matter; Stormer had used the

The Landwarrior, with all of his modern communications, computer, sighting, and navigation equipment is still at the bottom of it all—a soldier with a rifle.
U.S. Army

M14 a lot back at the academy, where it was still the weapon they drilled with.

Round after round of 7.62 mm tracers pounded the area of the balcony as Stormer pulled the trigger. The recoil of the big weapon wasn't important; showing his men where the enemy was, that was the significant effect. As tracers bounced off the concrete, other rounds from the platoon in front of him also started to smash into the building. The men concentrated their fire, and suddenly there was an explosion bursting out from the enclosed balcony area. One of the men had pumped a 40 mm grenade into the area of the sniper, the round exploding with a cloud of dirty black smoke and hundreds of speeding steel shards. If the sniper was still on that balcony, he was finding out if the virgins were really there right about now. If he wasn't there, the rest of the platoon going in to the building to clear it out would find him soon enough. Second Platoon on the next street over had already moved up to surround the rest of the structure.

"Give that man a cigar," Stormer said as he laid the heavy rifle down.

"Got one waiting for him," Rexall said as he sat up with a wince.

The medic had removed the sergeant's Kevlar. The pointed bullet fired by the sniper could still be seen, sticking out from the inside of the helmet. The sergeant wasn't even bleeding, but he had a hell of a headache.

"Isn't armor wonderful?" Stormer said as he looked down at the torn front of his own vest.

THE HISTORY

Every Soldier a Rifleman . . .
General Peter J. Schoomaker, Army Chief of Staff

Every soldier is a rifleman, and he will be a wolf . . .
Colonel Robert Gryms, Third Infantry Division

The longtime mission of the foot soldier has been and remains ultimately to close with the enemy and destroy him. The means used to complete this mission have changed over the millennia that mankind has been involved in battle, but in the final analysis, it has always been fire and movement that made up the formula to win the day. Those two aspects of combat are as important today on the streets and mountains of Iraq and Afghanistan as they were with Leonidas and the Spartans at Thermopylae or with Napoleon at Waterloo. The difference has become the range and destructive power that can be projected by a single soldier and how well he is able to apply it. It has been the individual weapon that has been the last application of fire in that classic military equation.

For thousands of years, it was the range of muscle-powered weapons that determined the distance between armies just prior to battle. The arrow, the spear, and the sword can only reach so far before they lose their ability to seriously damage the opposing force. Even with the adoption of gunpowder weapons, the final lines at an open battle were still only a relatively short distance apart.

Since the middle of the 1700s, it has been the rifle, evolving from the musket, that has allowed the soldier to project his will across the final few hundred meters of the battlefield before he closed with the enemy. Linear formations made up of long lines of men would face each other, spread out as far as their numbers and terrain would allow. Distances between musket-armed combatants could be so close that one side could see the expressions on the faces of the men who were opposing them. Then orders would be shouted, and the volleys would thunder out from the ranks. In quick order, roiling banks of thick, stinking powder smoke would fill the areas in front of the opposing lines, blocking one side from viewing what carnage its fire was producing on the other. And the smoke clouds would thicken as they were pierced with the orange-red lances of additional musket fire. Those sudden spears of fire could be the only indication of just where the enemy ranks might be as the battle continued.

The poor accuracy of the individual weapon, combined with an almost complete lack of marksmanship training in any army at the time, made volley fire the only way to effectively rain destruction into the enemy ranks from shoulder-fired weapons. After relatively few rounds had been fired, training would have the ranks of men advance to close with one another to conduct their final battle at the point of a bayonet.

This was the "thin red line" of classic military literature. It required a heavy measure of discipline to conduct warfare successfully with such weapons and general tactics. It also expended men even more than matériel, though the battle consumed both. For decades, officers would direct their men into the fight, and the noncommissioned officers—the sergeants—would make sure that the drill and iron-hard discipline it took to conduct war under such conditions remained intact. Training for combat centered on complete and utter obedience to orders, constant drill to make actions not require thought, and the ability to understand the simple commands that could be transmitted through the ranks by drums or bugle calls. Then the American Civil War took place.

Technology made its first real impacts on the conduct of warfare during the American Civil War. The adoption of the rifled bore and the hollow-based minié ball made the weapons of individual soldiers able to kill and maim over impossible distances when compared to the battle implements of just a few decades earlier. But tactics did not change as fast as technology required. Men would charge with fixed bayonets to close with a dug-in enemy to force them out of their positions, only to have their numbers decimated by the rapid and accurate rifle fire from the enemy that covered hundreds of meters. On both sides of that conflict, the ability to advance in the face of consistent and accurate fire was proved to be possible, but only at a terrible cost. It took thousands of lives for the officer corps to change their application of tactics to account for the new technology of killing, and even then they did so reluctantly.

Ordnance officers took great pains to halt or change the adoption of new weapons during the American Civil War with their intention to be the economy of supplies, among other reasons. As new forms of breech-loading and repeating rifles were brought forward from the inventors of the Northern states, most were dismissed out of hand by the chief of ordnance for the Union Army, General James Wolfe Ripley.

Ripley had fought in the War of 1812 and other engagements with the muzzle-loading musket as the predominant shoulder arm. He was used to the general line infantryman being issued eighteen rounds of ammunition for his musket since the soldier was expected to fire only as many as six volleys before advancing with the bayonet. As a stickler for regulations, he saw little reason to exceed the allowances of ammunition or other supplies for a battle. As the chief of ordnance, the idea of a weapon that would hold as many as seven rounds (the Spencer rifle) and could fire as quickly as a soldier could work the action was extremely wasteful. Such a weapon would allow a lowly infantryman to expend all of his ammunition in wild, ineffective fire.

To an ordnance chief, ammunition was a precious commodity. It was heavy, expensive, difficult to produce in vast numbers, and hard to move in volume with the limited transportation of the day. Even as seemingly as important an invention as a breech-loading rifle (the Sharps) that could be even more accurate than the muzzle-loader/minié ball standard of the day was suppressed by Ripley to the best of his ability. That fact that a man could reload such a weapon while remaining prone was offset by his corresponding higher rate of fire. Only carefully aimed fire from the rifle at selected targets or volley from ranks prior to a charge was an acceptable method of warfare to men like General Ripley, who was eventually forced out of his position by an enraged President Abraham Lincoln.

The Sharps breech-loader and the Spencer lever-action repeater got into the hands of the combat soldiers, who quickly learned how to apply them. The volume of fire produced by such weapons proved influential at a number of battles. The demand for such weapons grew well past the ability of the manufacturers to produce them. But the supply columns were able to expand and absorb the increased demand for ammunition. And the average soldier was found not to excessively waste the ammunition he had. Ripley was proven wrong, but that didn't matter.

The opinion held by General Ripley during the American Civil War has had its proponents to the present day. The term used for such individuals is a generally derogatory one; they are called *gravel-bellies*.

The gravel-belly philosophy is a simple one, and it has remained in the background of American small arms development for almost as long as the country has existed. In general, it is the attitude that the only way an individual soldier can be truly effective with his rifle is by his careful aim at a distinct target and only deliberately shooting. The trooper was to lie down with his belly in the dirt and gravel, shoulder his weapon, and squeeze off a single shot at a visible enemy, not just pull the trigger and work the action as quickly as he could. If there was a large number of the enemy visible, then the men would move into the proper formation, as the terrain allowed. It was only through volley fire by command that a proper application of force could be made of infantrymen and their shoulder weapons as a group. That fire would then be followed with a traditional bayonet charge to drive the enemy from his positions. Any other course of action would simply be an extravagant and unnecessary waste of valuable ammunition. The average soldier could not be expected to properly comprehend this, so the only sure way to control the excessive firing of his weapon during the heat of battle was to mechanically limit its ability to fire.

This opinion was only reinforced by members of the military who knew marksmanship very well, much better than the average soldier did. These experts were often championship shooters who gathered their tactical knowledge from their personal experiences on the rifle range; the tradition-bound, carefully managed, ridged, and regulated rifle range. What was missed for long decades was the fact that a bull's-eye target rarely ever existed on a battlefield. And the targets that were found in combat were very often shooting back.

Experiencing the significant fact of return fire for the first time often made it very difficult for even the most accomplished target shooter to take a careful aim toward a target among the enemy ranks. And the ever-increasing volume of fire on a battlefield as the 1800s came to an end had eliminated the traditional linear tactic of the bayonet charge from ever being an effective tool of war again, though a large number of men would die before that lesson sank home among some of those in command.

At the beginning of the twentieth century, the United States military was just starting to face major changes in the tools of war—the munitions and the weapons—that it employed. There were still large numbers of veterans in the country who remembered fighting with muzzle-loading rifles they had charged with paper cartridges filled with black powder. The standard U.S. military rifle for most of the latter part of the 1800s had been a single-shot breech-loader, the Springfield Model 1873, little more than a conversion of the standard Union Civil War rifle.

After the Civil War, repeating weapons had been withdrawn from service, in spite of their having served with distinction in a number of significant engagements. The reason for this action was twofold. First, there were more than a million muzzle-loading rifles in storage after the war, and Congress did not want to see them go to waste. And the new chief of ordnance for the U.S. Army, General Alexander Brydie Dyer, wanted a single-shot weapon to conserve ammunition. This was in spite of the fact that the war just past had proven that soldiers in the field would conserve the ammunition they had, either by training or experience. During the three days of one of the greatest battles of the Civil War, the average Union soldier at Gettysburg fired only ten rounds a day. Running out of ammunition could get you killed, a lesson combat soldiers tended to learn quickly.

General Dyer reluctantly accepted a new metallic cartridge for military service but insured that the new weapon was a single-shot to conserve ammunition. The breech-loading modification of the new Springfield rifle was changed from a .57 caliber to a .45 caliber in 1873, and the weapon remained in production at the Springfield Armory until June 1893. In its final version, the weapon launched a 500-grain lead slug pushed by 70 grains of black powder to a muzzle velocity of 1,315 feet per second. It was to be the last black-powder rifle in major front line military service in the world.

In 1892, the United States military, only thirty years earlier considered a world leader in military technology, finally adopted a small-bore, bolt-action repeating rifle. At the time, *small-bore* meant in the .30 caliber range, something allowable by the Frenchman Paul Vielle's invention of smokeless powder in 1884. The French had adopted the bolt-action Model 1886 Lebel repeating rifle in 1886, immediately making every black-powder military gun in the world obsolete.

It was not as major an undertaking to outfit the U.S. military with a .30-caliber bolt-action rifle as it would have been in wartime. Since 1869, the standing regular U.S. Army consisted of only 25,000 officers and men. They accepted the Model 1892 Krag-Jørgensen with modifications being made to the basic design in 1896 and again in 1898. These modifications, refitted to earlier specimens, included improvements indicated by field use. One of the improvements placed on the weapon by the experts at ordnance was a magazine cutoff switch.

The soldier was expected to use the Krag as a single-shot weapon, working the bolt and hand-loading a new round into the breech. The five-round internal magazine that stuck out so distinctively from the right side of the receiver was to be held in reserve. It was another result of the expert proponents of single-shot, slow, aimed, long-distance fire, only now in a repeating rifle firing a 220-grain metal-jacketed round-nosed .30-caliber bullet at a muzzle velocity of 2,000 feet per second. It was not the last showing of outmoded military opinions and methods of employing men in combat.

Less than fifty years after the American Civil War, the new tactics dictated by new weapons were still changing slowly. The application of fire had been changed; marksmanship was being taught to the soldier with much greater emphasis than had been given in the years leading up to the Great War. Uniforms were changed to reflect the fact that it was more important to blend in with a battlefield rather than to stand out so that commanders could more easily observe the movements of their troops from a nearby vantage point. Dull, drab cloth and blackened metal were replacing the bright colors, white leather, and polished brass of earlier years, much to the dismay of the traditional officer corps. The time was also fast approaching when the volume of fire put out on the battlefield would dictate much greater changes in the thinking of the officer corps than simply concerns about uniforms.

The rimmed .30-40 round fired by the U.S. Krag rifle, as well as the weapon that used it, had proven to be lacking in a number of crucial areas. The side-mounted magazine was difficult to load quickly, and the round was lacking in power when compared to the equivalent caliber of European military ammunition of the day. Another factor working against it was that it simply wasn't an American design. The Krag-Jørgensen was a Norwegian weapon. The United States was so far behind the rest of the world in arms development by the late 1800s that when the call went out for submissions to meet the requirement for a new .30-caliber smokeless powder repeater, there were no American rifle designers familiar with the needs of such a design.

A demonstration of the flaw in the gravel-belly philosophy that forced the Krag on the U.S. military came in Cuba during the short Spanish-American War. Many of the American state militia and volunteer forces were still armed with the single-shot, black-powder Springfield rifle, little more than a modified breech away from still being the main rifle of the American Civil War. Every time an American soldier discharged his Springfield, the big plume of smoke quickly drew fire from any Spanish observers.

The Spanish forces were armed with the newest of the Mauser rifles, a 7 mm bolt-action, magazine-fed repeater. The high-velocity, jacketed bullets from the Mausers snapped through the air like the sound of angry hornets—hornets that would quickly close in on a plume of smoke.

The regular U.S. Army forces as well as a few of the volunteer units, including the famous Rough Riders under Theodore Roosevelt, did not fare a great deal better when they pitted their Krag rifles against the Spanish weapons. While struggling to load their side-mounted magazines that would only accept loose, individual rounds—after all it did save ammunition—the Krag-armed Americans would have to operate while under a hail of Spanish bullets.

The Mauser rifle developed in Germany had an internal five-round magazine. That magazine was charged from five-round stripper clips. All a man had to do to reload his magazine was leave the bolt open from the last shot, place a full clip into the loading slot, and push the rounds home with the pressure of his thumb. Tossing away the stripper clip and closing the bolt gave the shooter a fully-loaded weapon. Against the slow-loading Krags, the Spanish Mausers appeared to have four to six times the rate of fire. Against the Springfields, there wasn't even a realistic basis for comparison. In practical terms, the Mauser rifle allowed 500 Spanish soldiers to equal the firepower of a least 2,000 American troops.

By the turn of the century in 1900, the intent of the U.S. military Ordnance Department was a new bolt-action rifle in another new caliber. It would again be a .30-caliber round, but rimless and including some of the newest advances in ballistics. The rifle adopted was the soon-to-be-famous Springfield M1903. It was chambered for the also new M1903 ball cartridge, which launched a cupronickel-jacketed bullet at 2,300 feet per second. One of the men who had been pushing for the new weapon was the president of the United States himself. This was not the first time that the chief executive of the country would get directly involved in the adoption of a new military small arm, but President Teddy Roosevelt had not forgotten what it was like to face those Spanish Mausers down in Cuba only a few years earlier.

The proposed cartridge was a new design, but the projectile wasn't. The bullet used in the M1903 ball round was the same 220-grain round-nosed, lead-cored slug that had been fired by the M1892 Krag. The new M1903 round was not going to prove as good as the rifle that was intended to fire it. The hot gases of the early nitroglycerin-based smokeless powder, pushing the heavy 220-grain bullet, severely eroded the barrels of the new rifles. Even when the velocity was reduced to 2,200 feet per second in 1904, the barrels still only had an unacceptable service life of between 1,200 to 1,400 rounds, only 100 rounds if it was rapid-fire, before accuracy was destroyed by the rifle being eroded in the first few inches of the bore.

The French had adopted a sharp-pointed solid-bronze *Balle D* bullet with a boat-tailed base in 1898. The German military followed suit with the adoption of a 7.92 mm pointed-nosed spitzer (from the German *Spitzgeschoss* or "pointed bullet") 154-grain projectile with a flat base in 1904. Military ballistics experts in the United States could see the advantages of the lighter, pointed bullet over the heavier, round-nosed designs as the foreign militaries fielded their new weapons. The lighter bullets could be pushed to a higher velocity, the pointed nose passed through the air with less resistance, and new powder developments from DuPont looked to eliminate much of the erosion problems of the earlier round.

In 1906, a new round was adopted in the United States military that would become famous in combination with the Springfield M1903 rifle. It was a round of ammunition that would help the United States win out across the battlefields of more than a half century. That round was the .30-caliber, M1906 Ball, far more commonly known as the .30-06. The M1906 Ball round put out a 150-grain, pointed, flat-based, full-jacketed bullet at the then amazing velocity of 2,700 feet per second from a twenty-four-inch barrel. In the M1903 Springfield, the round had an extreme range of 3,400 yards. And it was accurate. It was a gravel-belly's dream.

The upcoming war that ravaged Europe and affected most of the world was no one's dream. The instigation of World War I was the assassination of Archduke Ferdinand of Austria by Bosnian Serbs seeking freedom for their country. But the high conflagration that followed that relatively small incident was the culmination of years of ethnic hatreds; economic gains, losses, and jealousies; national pride; and massive ambitions.

Archduke Franz Ferdinand, heir to the throne of the Austro-Hungarian Empire, was killed by Serbian nationalist Gavrilo Princip on June 28, 1914. The match had been struck, and the powder keg that was Europe soon exploded. The majority of the countries of Europe soon declared war on each other. The countries that did not get directly involved of their own accord were quickly swept up by the maelstrom.

Germany was the first to move, smashing through Belgium, ostensibly a neutral country, on August 3, 1914. The next day, Britain declared war on Germany in order to protect Belgian neutrality. The German thrust into Belgium involved the destruction of border fortresses with heavy artillery such as the world had never seen before. It was only the first of many new weapons of that great conflict that would affect the conduct of warfare well into the future. France reacted quickly to the onslaught, maneuvering its forces to counter the threat to its own borders, but the speed of the German Army was astonishing.

On August 20, Brussels fell to the invaders. The Germans then moved on into France, and the French military as well as the newly formed British Expeditionary Force drew back from the Belgian border to dig in deeper inside

France. The German advance was held up, and they were forced into a short re-treat at the Battle of the Marne that ran from September 5 to 10.

Both sides of the conflict now slowed their movements and began to estab-lish solid lines of defense. Shallow indentations in the ground that were barely capable of hiding one man were dug deeper and enlarged. The depressions be-came ditches, then trenches, and then layers of trenches interconnected with each other and spotted with bunkers and other fortifications. The weapons fired, artillery roared, and the men dug into the ground. By the end of 1914, the front had formed into solid lines of trench works. The lines of combat had been drawn more distinctly than at any other time in military history.

The trench system on both sides of the conflict ran for 400 miles, extending from the Swiss border to the North Sea shore of Belgium. Two huge gatherings of military force faced each other across a no-man's-land of ground plowed into thick mud by artillery and explosives, spotted with craters, and laced with barbed wire.

The average width of no-man's-land, the distance between the lines of the two faction's trenches, was typically 100 to 300 yards. At some points along the lines, such as at Vimy Ridge, only thirty yards separated the two foes. Com-manding the open areas of the front was the still relatively new machine gun.

The war machine that was being observed by the world had several new gears in its makeup. The worst of these new cogs to make itself known early in the con-flict was the machine gun. It was a weapon that reached out and consumed men like a harvester running through a ripe cornfield. The Germans, having adopted the Maxim machine gun in 1908, had spent the time to incorporate the effects of the weapon into their tactics. France and England scrambled to develop new de-signs and build them in numbers. Within a short time, the United States joined in the rush to adopt the new class of weapon.

The basic firepower of World War I, the shoulder weapon of the infantry-man, was fairly evenly matched on all fronts. Almost all of the combatants dur-ing World War I were armed with a bolt-action, magazine-fed, repeating rifle of .256 to .315 caliber firing a jacketed bullet at an average velocity of slightly less than 2,500 feet per second. These were all weapons capable of engaging targets accurately from at least 600 to 800 yards, depending on the training and skill level of the shooter. Some of these guns could take down an individual target at much longer ranges.

This situation was one to put joy and justification in a gravel-belly's heart. Here was a war where all of the basic infantry weapons were long-range, relatively slow-fire rifles. The only problem was that the distances between opponents weren't usually very far. Often combatants were so close that an expert pistol shot could successfully engage an opposing trench, resulting in return artillery fire from a riled enemy. The rifle simply wasn't in a dominant position overlooking no-man's-land. That was the realm of the machine gun and quick-firing artillery.

The war had now bogged down into a stalemated battle of attrition. A soldier exposing himself to the enemy trenches during an unguarded moment had a very strong chance of becoming the target of a sniper. Offensive operations consisted of generals still trying to live the glory days of the charge and the bayonet, refusing to accept or even understand the new mechanics of war. From their positions safely in the rear, commanders ordered their juniors to lead the charge "over the top." That meant get up out of the safety of the trenches and charge across no-man's-land into and through the barbed wire entanglements that more often than not had only been made more impassable by the explosive action of the preattack artillery bombardment. And the machine gun sprayed across the oncoming men. For years, the front lines moved barely miles back and forth.

On April 6, 1917, the United States officially entered the conflict and finally declared war on Germany and her allies. The battles had bled the combatants badly by the time U.S. troops entered the fray. The French and British forces felt that they had the upper hand in experience and felt they could utilize the American forces as reinforcements for their own style of tactics. This didn't sit well with most of the American commanders or the troops they led.

During the battle at Belleau Wood on June 2, 1918, the French were rapidly retreating from the oncoming German forces when the U.S. Fourth Marine Brigade made its presence known among the enemy. Refusing the join in the French withdrawal, the Marines, part of the U.S. Second Division, demonstrated the long-range marksmanship that they had been competing with for the last dozen years or so.

Following the orders of their sergeants in setting the range on the sights of the Springfield M1903 rifles, the Marines opened fire on the Germans at the astonishing (to the French) range of 800 yards. Round after round of lethally accurate fire from the Marines dropped German soldiers at what they had previously thought was a safe range. The German advance was halted, and the Marines led the counterattack. It was a horrendous battle with the Marines suffering more losses that day (1,087 casualties) than they had received in their entire history up to that point. Their position in the history of the corps was assured, as was the example they had set, which was held up as proof of the viability of the gravel-belly's concept of what the rifle should do: long-range, aimed fire.

World War I finally drew to a close at 11:00 a.m., November 11, 1918. The German forces had not been able to regain the momentum of the first months of the war. It was also impossible for their industrial base to match the incredible out-pouring of war material from the United States. The manpower of Europe had also come close to running out. Estimated deaths from the fighting over the four years of the war were: 1,357,800 French, 908,370 British (which included Canadian and other Commonwealth losses), 1,700,000 Russians (not including a horrendous es-timated 2,000,000 civilian deaths), 462,390 Italians, 50,585 Americans, 13,715 Bel-gians, 45,000 Serbians, 3,000 Montenegrins, 335,700 Romanians, 5,000 Greeks, 7,222 Portuguese, 300 Japanese, 1,808,546 Germans, 922,500 Austro-Hungarians, 325,000 Turks, and 75,844 Bulgarians. The map of Europe and the world was per-manently changed by the fighting that cost these 8,000,000-plus lives. The number of wounded men on all sides exceeded 22,000,000, and the civilian deaths are esti-mated to have been over 6.5 million. It was called "the war to end all wars."

Of course, it wasn't. And the tools of war would continue to evolve in effi-ciency and lethality. The tank, aircraft, machine gun, submachine gun, poison gas, and quick-firing artillery had all made their introduction on the World War I battlefield. The hand grenade, mortar, flamethrower, shotgun, automatic pistol, automatic rifle, and other weapons had been reintroduced and greatly improved over the course of the war. In the United States, it was a matter of only a decade or so for the lessons to result in a new infantry rifle, among other im-provements in ordnance.

THE BEGINNINGS OF THE MODERN ERA

The search for greater individual firepower in the form of increased volume of fire had not begun during World War I. In spite of the disapproval of many mil-itary officers who agreed with the gravel-belly approach to an individual sol-dier's weapon, the search for a self-loading rifle was put forward well before the United States entered that conflict. In 1909, the following list of features was issued in a call for military submissions by inventors (as excerpted from *U.S. Rifle M14 from John Garand to the M21* by R. Blake Stevens):

A simple, strong, and durable mechanism, composed of as few parts as pos-sible, readily dismounted and mounted with as few tools as practicable, and assembled with the minimum number of springs, screws, or pins. The mechanism should be as compact as practicable.

The caliber should be about .30.

The magazine or other attachment for holding cartridges to have a capacity of not less than eight. The department [Ordnance] will, however, consider a design submitted with a view of modifying or adapting the present service rifle to a semi-automatic rifle, in which case a capacity of five cartridges will be sufficient.

The weight of the bullet to be not less than 150 grains.

The initial velocity to be not less than 2650 feet per second.

The bolt to be locked or in its firing position before the firing mechanism can be operated.

The breech-block to remain open when the last cartridge in the magazine has been fired.

The trigger pull (measured at the middle point of bow of trigger), to be not less than three or more than 4½ pounds.

A magazine cut-off, and a safety or locking device permitting arm to be carried cocked and with cartridge in barrel without danger.

A minimum limit of fire, considering time for motion of parts, for reloading, etc., of 90 rounds per minute, when firing as rapidly as possible.

(a) Must be capable of use as a single loading arm, magazine in reserve.

(b) Must be capable of use as a magazine rifle, fed by hand, with semi-automatic feature entirely cut out.

Recocking the piece without moving bolt in case of Mis-Fire.

Reasonable certainty of action in automatic loading and ejection.

Comparatively easy action in ejecting by hand in case of Mis-Fire or Jam.

Good balance and shape, adapted to endurance firing. Not to be [full] automatic.

Weight not to exceed 11 pounds. This does not include cartridges or bayonet.

THE FOLLOWING FEATURES ARE CONSIDERED DESIRABLE

In the construction, such separation of parts that each part may be readily replaced in case of repair. Parts riveted together or more or less permanently joined are objectionable.

Vertical in preference to side ejection of cartridge case.

No special tools for dismounting or assembling.

An automatic indicator of the number of cartridges in the magazine, the mechanism to be so arranged as to prevent the entrance of dust, etc.

Cartridges of length over all not more than three inches. The use of shorter cartridges will allow for reduction in length of receiver, and will facilitate feeding. This will be considered a very desirable feature.

THE FOLLOWING FEATURES ARE PREFERABLE
A bolt securely locked to the barrel until the bullet has left the bore.
Interchangeability of parts between rifles of the same model.
A bolt in one piece, to a bolt with a separate head.

Some of the 1909 characteristics desired of a semiautomatic rifle are very interesting on reflective examination. The magazine cutoff aspect is an example of the gravel-belly opinion slipping into a weapon that would "waste" ammunition at a rate that would make an 1800s-era ordnance officer swoon. The extra consideration that would be given to a modification of the service rifle of the time, the bolt-action M1903 Springfield, is an example of the frugality of the military. Modifying the millions of Springfield rifles that had been produced during World War I into a semiautomatic rifle would be a money-saving prize that would easily be worth the smaller magazine capacity—to the Ordnance Department.

The .30 caliber M1918 Browning Automatic Rifle had been adopted during World War I, relatively few specimens making it to Europe before the fighting ended. In spite of the weapon's limited use in combat, it had impressed a large number of people. The sixteen-pound weight of the empty BAR was considered acceptable for something that was used as a light machine gun, but it would be excessively heavy for a standard infantryman's weapon. In addition, the full automatic fire capability of the BAR was considered to be tactically too much of an ammunition supply problem to issue the weapons in bulk. It was also a relatively expensive item to produce.

The search for an efficient semiautomatic rifle was continuing worldwide, particularly in the United States. The thought of a large number of engineers was that the full-powered rifle round, the .30-06, was too powerful to be operated in a light shoulder weapon such as a nine-pound rifle. The suggestion was put forward that a lighter caliber, .276 instead of .30, be adopted, and the .30-06 be retained for use in machine guns. That opinion lasted well into the 1930s as several designs for semiautomatic weapons were developed and tested. Economic considerations were topmost in the mind of Army Chief of Staff General Douglas MacArthur in 1932 when he finally killed the planned adoption of a .276-caliber rifle cartridge. The country was in the Great Depression, and there would be no money from Congress for a new rifle and new ammunition. There was barely any money to develop a new rifle, no matter how good it was. With millions of rounds of .30-06 ammunition in storage, MacArthur ordered that any new rifle be chambered for the standard military round.

A design genius name John C. Garand had foreseen that the Army would not accept a new round of lighter ammunition. Working quietly at Springfield Armory along with his other duties, Garand did what other noted engineers of the day said couldn't be done; he made a working semiautomatic rifle chambered for the full-power service cartridge. Garand's rifle was available for testing within months of MacArthur's order. Examined thoroughly and found satisfactory, on January 9, 1936, Garand's weapon was officially adopted by the U.S. military as the "U.S. Rifle, Cal. .30, M1" and replaced (on paper at least) the M1903 Springfield. The United States military was the first country in the world to have as general issue a semiautomatic rifle that could put out aimed rounds at more than 2.5 times the rate of the fastest bolt-action weapon.

By January 1940, new mass production techniques and equipment were in place, and the production facility at Springfield Armory was producing about 100 M1 rifles a day. When the United States actively entered World War II on December 8, 1941, many military units were still armed with the bolt-action M1903 Springfield in one variation or another. This situation changed fairly rapidly as "Arsenal America" moved into a wartime production footing. Production of M1 rifles at the armory doubled to 200 per eight-hour day and multiplied several times over the months leading to war. During the first six months of 1944, Springfield Armory alone produced 2,000,000 M1 rifles among other weapons, and there were other manufacturers. During World War II, Springfield Armory and Winchester Repeating Arms Company together produced over 4,000,000 M1 rifles.

The design and production of the M1 Garand was a stellar achievement and proved itself a decisive factor in some of the combat situations of World War II. The weapon performed in all environments, from the steaming jungles of the South Pacific to the dusty sands of North Africa. Operating in the field of summertime Europe, the cold of a freezing Belgian winter, the ice of Alaska, or the smothering sand of a volcanic Pacific island, the M1 fought and served. It was the death knell of the bolt-action military rifle and no less a personage than General George S. Patton called it in writing, "The greatest battle implement ever devised." To the average infantry soldier who fought in all the theaters of combat of World War II, it was simply his rifle—the rifle—and it served him well.

GERMANY, WORLD WAR II, AND A NEW BREED OF RIFLE

It was in the choked confines of the trenches of World War I that the demand for compact individual firepower developed and grew. When soldiers fought each other between the dirt walls of a stormed trench, the traditional rifle, even of carbine length, was too long to be quickly handled. It was when the enemy forces came over the parapets that the fighting became close-quartered and vicious. The hand grenade, pistol, and knife were more easily used than a rifle, except perhaps as a clumsy club or spear when the bayonet was fitted.

When the U.S. expeditionary forces arrived in France in 1917 and faced the realities of trench warfare, they soon adopted an old American traditional close-quarters weapon, the short shotgun. When the Germans faced the devastating blasts of a pump-action shotgun, they made official protests against its use, to the point of threatening summary execution of any soldier caught using a fighting shotgun. The German threat was diplomatically dealt with when the American Expeditionary Force commander suggested that any such actions by the Germans would draw serious punishments against any of their own troops who might be captured. And it was pointed out that poison gas, the flamethrower, and other such weapons of war first used by the Germans were far more injurious than the lead shot of a shotgun blast. The German forces were not known to have carried out their threat. But they had already devised their own form of close-combat firepower in the form of the submachine gun.

The submachine gun was an automatic weapon used by an individual rather than as the normally mounted gun the rest of the world had become familiar with. The first true submachine gun was the Maschinenpistole (machine pistol) 18/I, otherwise known as the MP18. Designed by Hugo Schmeisser and produced at the Theodor Bergmann Waffenfabrik factory in Suhl, Germany, the MP18 was a very short, rifle-pattern weapon that fired the common German pistol cartridge, the 9 mm Parabellum (9×19 mm) from a 32-round specialized Luger pistol magazine. The simple operating mechanism of the MP18 fired at full automatic, the rounds cycling through the action at a rate of 350 to 400 rounds per minute. The new weapon made a substantial impact on all of those opposing forces who faced it in combat. After World War I, the submachine gun concept was quickly copied by the rest of the military forces in the world.

The volume of fire that could be put out by the submachine gun was noted, as was its quick handling characteristics. The German military was soon to seriously incorporate the submachine gun into their military organization and tactical planning. But the individual firepower offered by a full-automatic weapon was also noted by another farseeing German officer who had a different application for it.

First Lieutenant Piderit of the German Army wrote a memorandum in 1919 where he put forward the idea of an automatic weapon chambered for a round more powerful than that used by a pistol but less so than a full-sized rifle cartridge. With such a weapon, gunners would be able to engage targets at a very practical range of 300 meters, interestingly enough, the common maximum distance across no-man's-land during World War I.

Piderit's ideas were not immediately put into effect, but neither were they irretrievably lost in the archives. What he had suggested was an intermediate round of ammunition, lighter than the standard rifle round but much more powerful than a pistol round. By the 1930s, there was a new power in Germany that would eventually prove to be very interested in the idea of an automatic weapon and an intermediate round.

In existence for little over a dozen years, the Nazi Third Reich of Germany left an imprint on warfare and weapons design that is still echoing loudly today. And it will continue to do so well into the future. The concept of the assault rifle was first formed into metal in the workshops of Germany during and shortly prior to World War II. The classic definition of the assault rifle comes from the German design: that of a shoulder-fired rifle of compact (carbine) length chambered for an intermediate-power cartridge loaded into a large-capacity magazine and capable of semiautomatic and full automatic fire. This gave a light, quick-handling weapon that could fire semiautomatically for individual target accuracy but put out an overwhelming volume of automatic fire when necessary.

The intermediate cartridge is the portion of the definition that separates the assault rifle from the submachine gun or automatic rifle, though it has characteristics of both. The round would be less powerful than the standard rifle round, and that meant a shorter cartridge with a lighter projectile and probably lower muzzle velocities.

The standard German military rifle and machine gun caliber during World War I and II was eight millimeters in a long cartridge case, identified as the 7.92 × 57 mm round. This round was known in the United States as the 8 mm Mauser, and aspects of it were used to develop the original .30-caliber U.S. round commonly called the .30-06. The standard-issue loading for the 7.92 × 57 mm round was the schweres Spitzgeshoss (s. S.-heavy pointed ball), which put out a 0.312-inch diameter, 197-grain, full-jacketed projectile at a nominal velocity of

2,575 feet per second (785 meters per second) from a twenty-four-inch (61 cm) barrel. This makes it a very powerful round, the general equivalent of the U.S. military .30 M2 round, capable of accurate long-range fire.

The ballistic power of a cartridge centers on its ability to launch a heavy projectile at high velocities. That power also means that it generates noticeable recoil in a light weapon and operates at high internal pressures. The recoil and pressure of the propellant gases can be harnessed to operate an automatic weapon. To control such forces, the device that fires the round must be equally strong, and that usually means heavy. The use of the traditional rifle-caliber round of ammunition would prevent the concept of the assault rifle from being met in any practical manner.

In the middle 1930s, German industry had come up with a number of new cartridge concepts that met the *intermediate* definition of a rifle round. Several experimental weapons were chambered for the various new rounds, proving that the idea had serious merit. The German war machine was already more openly gearing up for an upcoming war, and resources could prove limited during a time of conflict. An intermediate round could substantially save in casings, brass, bullet materials, and propellants when compared to a normal full-power rifle round. This would prove very important if such things became harder to get. Even the weapons that used such ammunition could be designed so that they could be made more easily than even the bolt-action Mauser rifle that much of the German army carried. And the increased firepower of a select fire weapon, capable of either semi- or full-automatic fire, spoke for itself.

The final cartridge that was to have the new weapon designed for it was a light 8 mm rifle-style bullet in a shortened case. The caliber was 7.9 mm and the case length 33 mm, about half the size of the standard rifle rounds. The 7.92 × 33 mm ball round, also known as the 7.9 mm Kurz Patrone (short cartridge), as developed by Polte-Werke of Magdeburg, fires a 122-grain, full-jacketed projectile at a nominal muzzle velocity of 2,250 feet per second from a sixteen-inch barrel. Ready in 1938, contracts were issued by the German Ordnance Department to design a suitable weapon for it. The design was to be for a select-fire short rifle with an effective range of 800 meters. The weapons firms of Haenel, and in 1940 Walther, both received contracts to design the new MKb and produce prototypes for testing.

World War II began officially on September 1, 1939, at 0445 hours when Plan White went into effect for the German Army. Fifty-three divisions of German forces swept into Poland, invading the country with a new form of warfare, the blitzkrieg, or lighting war. In a combined arms attack with airpower, armor, and infantry forces working in mutual support of each other, the German military eliminated any resistance from the Polish forces. The fighting was over in a few weeks with the final surrender of the last Polish military units on October 1,1939.

The German infantry forces were armed with a mix of bolt-action Mauser rifles (the KAR 98), 9 mm submachine guns (primarily the MP38), and 7.92 mm light machine guns (the MG34). There was no thought given to the intermediate round or the weapon that would fire it. But design work continued on by the staffs at Haenel and Walther.

Weapons were ready for testing by 1942. To facilitate easy manufacture, the new designs were built primarily of stampings. As few precision parts as possible were intentionally included in their design so that they could be produced quickly, easily, and cheaply from subassemblies made by other, smaller companies. The final results from the two companies were too late for the initial stages of the war, but there would be a great deal of combat yet to go. The new weapons also had a new designation. Since it was to be more powerful than a standard submachine gun, it would be the sMP42, for schwere Maschinenpistole 42 (heavy machine pistol 42). The name was changed again; since it was smaller than a standard rifle but so much larger than a submachine gun, the new weapon would be a Maschinenkarabiner (MK). The short designation was later changed to MKb to distinguish it from the already-used MK that stood for Maschinenkanone (automatic cannon). Identified by the designator MKb, the two weapons were further known by the year of their manufacture and the company that designed them. The Haenel design had the designation MKb42(H); the Walther weapon was the MKb42(W). Both guns had an extremely futuristic appearance, one that would be copied in large numbers over the decades to come.

Testing in late March 1942 showed an advantage to the Walther design over that of Haenel. The Haenel design fired from the open bolt. An open-bolt weapon has the bolt assembly drawn to the rear when cocked and held in place by the firing mechanism. When the trigger is pulled, the bolt is released and slid forward, stripping a round from the feed system, chambering it, and then firing it. The system keeps the action as open as possible to allow cooling air to circulate in the barrel and receiver between shots. Commonly used in automatic weapons, the open bolt is also harder to fire accurately, since the bolt is slammed shut on the first round, the jar moving the weapon and altering the aim of the firer.

The Walther design fired from the closed bolt, a much more accurate means of initiating semiautomatic fire. But only one specimen of the Walther design was available for testing, while fifty of the Haenel guns were already on hand. Further testing and evaluation of the MKb42(H) continued while the first 200 Walther guns were not expected to be delivered until July 1942.

The whole idea of the intermediate cartridge and the weapon firing it was almost eliminated in April. On April 14, 1942, an MKb42(H) was demonstrated for the supreme commander of the (German) Armed Forces and commander in chief of the Army, the German führer, Adolf Hitler.

After an explanation of the idea behind the MKb, how it would increase the firepower of the infantry squad and replace a large number of weapons already in use, Hitler refused to grant his approval of the program. He didn't think that the range of 500 meters would be long enough for use in the desert where a 1,200- to 1,500-meter range would be needed—in spite of the fact that the standard infantry rifle and soldier couldn't engage a target at such ranges. The führer also stated that the reequipping of the military would result in a massive logistics problem with two completely different primary weapons in use for a fairly long time while the MKb guns were being produced in numbers. And lastly, he didn't want the six billion rounds of 7.92 mm rifle ammunition already produced to be wasted because they couldn't be fired in the new carbines.

In spite of not having Hitler's approval, the German Ordnance Department continued with the development and trials of the MKb rifles, since much of the machinery of testing was already moving forward. Of the fifty weapons already produced by Haenel, twenty-five underwent trials at the Infantry School beginning on April 15, 1942. Of the 300,000 rounds of 7.92 × 33 mm ammunition that had been produced to date, 50,000 rounds of it went to the trials. In regards to much of the rest of the ammunition and the other twenty-five MKb42(H) weapons, something of a legend has grown up about them.

On the eastern front fighting the Soviets was a German battle group known as Kampfgruppe Scherer after their commander, General Major Theodor Scherer. When the German offensive in Russia ground to a halt in December 1941, the Soviet forces quickly launched a counterattack. In northwestern Russia, Soviet forces encircled a large group of German troops at the small town of Cholm, about 100 kilometers southwest of Demjansk. These troops numbered 5,500 men and were ordered by Hitler to "hold to the last man."

From January 21, 1942, to May 5, that German battle group held on at what became known as Fortress Cholm. Their only source of resupply during the 105-day-long siege was by air. In early May, with the horrible Russian winter over, the surviving men of Kampfgruppe Scherer fought their way out of Cholm, breaking through the surrounding Soviets. In one of the later airdrops of supplies were reported to be the twenty-five MKb42(H) rifles that had not gone to the trials at the Infantry School, along with a supply of ammunition. The firepower of the new rifles has been credited by a number of knowledgeable people with having aided in the breakout. It may have also greatly impressed the Soviets who faced the new weapon concept in battle. There was reportedly an MKb42(H) captured by the Soviets at Cholm, but the serial number of a Russian museum specimen does not match up with the time period of the battle. In spite of that possible error in timing, it was not long before the Soviets were facing the new weapon in much greater numbers.

The Haenel design was chosen over that of Walther with modifications. The weapon had its internal firing mechanism changed over to include a hammer, much like that of the Walther, and the system was converted to fire from a closed bolt to increase the accuracy of semiautomatic fire. By January 1943, there were 500 of the original MKb42(H) model weapons ready for further testing and issue with a total of 2,000 weapons ready for shipment by April 21, 1943. The Walther version was finally dropped after several thousand had been made, and production commenced in numbers on the Haenel weapon.

Hitler still did not approve of the new weapon, so a nomenclature change was used to help hide its existence while it was developed. The modified MKb42(H) became the MP43/1, which was put into limited-series production in July 1943. Numbers of the MP43/1 were sent on to combat units desperate for the increase in individual firepower. Their evaluations were taken into consideration in further improvements of the design. Changes to allow a standard type of rifle grenade launcher were incorporated, and the MP43/1 became the MP43. Both weapons are distinctly different from the original MKb42(H). The very long gas tube of the MKb42(H), extending nearly to the muzzle of the weapon, is much shorter on the MP43 series.

By 1944, the production of the new weapon was reaching reasonable quantities. The nomenclature was once again changed, this time to the MP44. The Soviet military had switched from issuing bolt-action rifles to submachine guns for many of their soldiers. Entire Soviet units would face the German army equipped with relatively short-range submachine guns. The volume of fire put out by those units might have not had much of an accurate range, but its effect was staggering. The only real competition the Germans had for it was the MP43 and MP44. Even Hitler finally saw the error in his earlier opinion and ordered the production of the new rifles to go forward.

Around October 22, 1944, Hitler ordered the last nomenclature change of the MP44. The weapon was to be made standard issue in all of the German military. The new designation was Sturmgewehr 44 or StG44 for short. The designation directly translates into "storm rifle" but has been interpreted to mean assault rifle and was the first of its kind.

It was far too late in the war for the StG44, or whatever name it may be called, to have an appreciable effect on the outcome of World War II. It was significant in that it fought on both fronts of the war, directly against the Allies in the east as well as the Soviets to the west. Many European countries recognized the significance of the new type of rifle, with the notable exception of the American Ordnance Department. In what would very soon be the Soviet Union, the impressions that had been made in combat by the new weapons were not lost and were anything but ignored.

THE RUSSIAN RIFLE

The AK-47 design is not, as has been popularly believed, simply a redesign of the German concept of an assault rifle, the Sturmgewehr. Kalashnikov had been removed from combat on the front due to injuries long before the Weremacht had begun fielding even the first of their new rifle. Instead of working on a new rifle, his experiences and input from others had Kalashnikov trying to develop a new submachine gun.

The ultimate realization of the Kalashnikov assault rifle was a classic example of the "form follows function" rule of design. The end result was a weapon that externally resembled the German Sturmgewehr series but was internally completely different.

The Soviet military had only two primary calibers of small-arms ammunition in inventory as they entered World War II. The standard pistol round was the 7.62 × 25 mm Tokarev, a bottlenecked cartridge that resembled a shrunken rifle shell, close to being a direct copy of the German .30 caliber Mauser pistol round introduced in 1893. The Tokarev ammunition served well in both pistols and submachine guns as a light-recoil round with the Type P ball loading putting out an eighty-six-grain projectile at 1,493 feet per second.

The Soviet standard rifle and machine gun round was the 7.62 mm Mosin-Nagant (7.62 × 54R), a large-rimmed cartridge adopted by the Russians in 1893 when they entered the smokeless powder era. The Type LPS light ball load of the 7.62 × 54R cartridge has a 147-grain, pointed, full-jacket projectile that is fired at a muzzle velocity of 2,886 feet per second. It is a very powerful, traditional type of rifle cartridge, one of the few still issued today that has a prominently rimmed case.

The exact source of the Soviets' new rifle round they report as having developed during World War II is hidden by story, time, and propaganda. It is thought that the Soviets may have learned of the experiments done to produce a shortened rifle round in prewar Germany. What is well-known is that the Soviet forces obtained quantities of the German MP43/44 series weapons and ammunition during and after the war. The standing claim is that the new Soviet round was a native invention, distinct from that of the Germans. The timing of events as the Great Patriotic War, what the Soviets and now Russians called World War II, unfolded match the claim of a Soviet design of a then-new intermediate round.

The 7.62 mm Tokarev round performed well in a submachine gun, but it was underpowered for use in a carbine or rifle. The 7.62×54R ammunition, like so many military rounds of the era, was too powerful to be practical in a shoulder-fired automatic weapon. Even designing a semiautomatic rifle for the big-rimmed round was a difficult undertaking. The Soviet concept for an intermediate round was a nominally .30-caliber (7.62 mm) projectile in a 39 mm–long cartridge case. Adopted by the Soviets in 1943, the 7.62×39 mm round was known as the M43. The standard Type PS ball loading of the 7.62×39 mm has a 123-grain projectile fired at a muzzle velocity of 2,330 feet per second. Since its adoption, and with the weapons family designed to use it, the 7.62×39 mm round has become one of the most successful military cartridges in the world.

It was during the battle for Bryansk that a young Soviet tank commander named Mikhail Timofeyevich Kalashnikov faced combat for the first time, and things did not go well for him. When a German artillery round struck his T34, Sergeant Kalashnikov was severely wounded in the left shoulder by a piece of spall broken off from the inside of the tank's armor. Though his injury was bad, that was not the worst of the situation for Kalashnikov. Along with a number of his comrades, he was now well behind German lines. It was a long, seven-day trek before the tough sergeant and the men with him, dodging German patrols along the way, finally reached Soviet lines and relative safety. His wound very bad by this time, the twenty-three-year-old Kalashnikov was hospitalized, which became the turning point of his life.

Having been mechanically minded for a long time, Kalashnikov had already developed a tank running aid that had earned him a certain amount of acclaim in his unit. While in the hospital, Kalashnikov listened to his fellow soldiers, and their comments made a lasting impression on him. The bolt-action rifles that fired the powerful 7.62×54R round had long range but little in the way of firepower, especially when compared to the Germans' prolific use of submachine guns. Another soldier commented that they had submachine guns, but they were few and far between.

Immediately putting his mind to work on the problem, Kalashnikov decided to try to develop a new weapon to fulfill the needs of his fellow soldiers. He read everything that was available to him on weapons and their design. He was lucky in that Vladimir Federov, a very noted Soviet weapons engineer, had written a book on ordnance titled *Evolution of Small Arms* and that there was a copy available to him. Decorated for his actions and ordered to a six-month-long convalescence, Kalashnikov was able to connect with a train driver who also worked as a machinist and had tools available to him. The man and his superiors agreed to help Kalashnikov in his desire to come up with a new submachine gun to augment the weapons already being produced for the Soviet Army.

In three months, Kalashnikov and his fellows were able to build a working model of a new gun. The weapon was not adopted but did bring the young soldier to the attention of party officials who were on the lookout for people with an inventive and technical bent. This kind of designer was badly needed in the Soviet Union at a time when it was fighting for its very existence. Though his submachine gun wasn't adopted for manufacture, Kalashnikov showed a lot of promise. He was soon put to work as a technician at the military small arms proving ground at Ensk. His active combat days were over.

Guided away from submachine guns, Kalashnikov was eventually directed to set his talents to designing a carbine to fire the very new 7.62×39 mm M43 cartridge. Kalashnikov knew that the design should combine the characteristics of both a submachine gun and a rifle. It is not known if he ever saw one of the German MP43/44 series of weapons, but this is very likely. The first weapon to be issued that chambered the M43 cartridge was the Simonov semiautomatic carbine, the SKS. Adopted in 1945, the small, light, ten-shot carbine helped establish a technical base for the further development and manufacture of the M43 family of ammunition. While the SKS was being manufactured, Kalashnikov continued in his design efforts. His first weapon was the prototype AK46, a short, select-fire rifle that was chambered for the experimental 7.62×41 mm round. Though unsuccessful, the weapon bore a striking resemblance to a design Kalashnikov was going to end up with. That was going to be a rifle that proved to be very successful.

After several further developmental models, Kalashnikov perfected the Avtomat Kalashnikova in 1947. The final design was modified in 1948 to accept the final version of the M43 round, the 7.62×39. Thoroughly tested and examined, the new weapon was adopted to become the new primary shoulder arm of the Soviet Army, the AK-47.

There were three models of AK-47 that were all known under the same name to the world at large. The first weapon that Kalashnikov had designed was intended to be made primarily of sheet metal stampings. The Soviet Army had been practically saved when they had adopted a stamped-steel submachine gun during World War II. The PPSh41 (Pistolet-Pulemet Shpagina 1941) and PPS43 (Pistolet-Pulemet Sudaeva 1943) had both been designed with mass production and conservation of critical materials in mind. The PPSh41 was by far the more common of the two and was very recognizable by its perforated barrel shroud and short wooden stock. The PPS43 was produced completely out of metal except for the wooden pistol grip. It had a folding metal stock and was designed for use with a thirty-five-round box magazine, while the PPSh41 could use the same box magazine but was more often seen loaded with a seventy-one-round drum. Both weapons fired the 7.62 × 25 mm Tokarev round and had armed hundreds of thousands of Soviet fighters during the war.

With the success of the World War II submachine guns, it was suggested that Kalashnikov use as much of their manufacturing techniques in his new weapon as was practical. The fact that the German assault rifles had all been primarily made from metal stampings may have also influenced Kalashnikov's design. The final result of this all was a supremely functional weapon with relatively smooth sides but for two of the rivets holding the mechanism in place being plainly visible above the magazine well. The long safety/selector switch on the left side of the weapon closed off the opening where the bolt handle moves, keeping the mechanism covered when on safe as well as holding the bolt locked in the forward position. Pressing the selector lever down puts the weapon first on fully automatic fire and, when pressed all the way down, sets the AK-47 to semiautomatic fire.

Intended for use on the assault with the tactical employment of a high volume of automatic fire, a system that had served the Soviets well during the latter part of World War II with their submachine guns, the AK-47 went into volume production from 1948 to 1951. During that time, a second model was produced with a metal folding stock for use by paratroopers, armored forces, and other troops who had to operate in tight confinements. Both weapons became very noticeable by their distinctive silhouettes and long, curved magazine.

The second model AK-47 was produced from roughly 1951 to 1954. It was a switch back to the more traditional way of making a rifle, machining the receiver from a block of metal or forging. This may have been done to make a stronger receiver or to relieve the pressure on the limited number of skilled tool and die makers still left in the Soviet Union. One factor in the second model of the AK-47 design that did not prove satisfactory was the method of attaching the stock. This was through a socket that was keyed and pinned to the machined receiver and was a weak point in the design. By 1954, the machine receiver AK was once more modified, this time with a stronger stock attachment point. Both of the machined AK-47 rifles are recognized by the long, machined groove in the receiver, just above the magazine well. The folding stock design of the original pattern was also incorporated in the second and third models of the AK-47. The production of all of the first three AK models exceeded 5 million weapons, the bulk of these being the third model. Copied extensively, the third-model AK-47 has been encountered all over the world.

The design is tough and resilient to battlefield conditions. It was used to arm thousands of "freedom fighters" and client states of the Soviets all around the world. The basic weapon is simple to operate and relatively easy to maintain. It has been said that the AK-47 could be given to a fighter who was used to the technology level of a rock, and he could soon work the weapon effectively. Many of the internal parts that would be exposed to the dirty gases of the fired cartridge, such as the gas piston, were hard-chromed to increase their resistance to dirt and corrosion. The heavy bolt carrier combined with the dirt-clearing grooves in the gas system allow the AK-47 to operate in the worst conditions on the planet. Covered in mud or wet sand, the weapon has continued to fire when the trigger was pulled. The relatively heavy bullet gave good terminal effects and could punch through materials that could stop lighter projectiles. Such were some of the strengths of the basic AK-47 design.

Modifications of his design were not finished, and further demands were put on the skills of Mikhail Kalashnikov and his design bureau. A modernized version of the AK-47, identified as the AKM-47, was introduced in 1959. The AKM had reverted back to a stamped sheet metal receiver, relieving over a pound of weight from the forged and machined model. Manufacturing techniques and skilled-worker shortages had been improved or eliminated, and the AKM-47 took advantage of all of the ten years of experience and feedback developed from the use of the earlier versions.

The relatively smooth sides of the AKM had a single noticeable dimple on both sides of the receiver, right above the magazine well. These depressions helped act as magazine guides for loading and were in place of the long, machined groove in the same position on the AK-47. Also missing were the rows of four gas vent holes along the upper tube of the AK-47 that guided the piston assembly. Internal changes in the mechanism made for a smoother and more accurate operation of the weapon. This increase in accuracy was reflected in the change on the rear sight. For the AK-47 series, the rear sight was graduated out to 800 meters. On the AKM weapons, the rear sight was graduated to 1,000 meters. These numbers are well in excess of what could be considered accurate shooting ranges for such a rifle, but they do indicate a greater expectation of the new weapon.

Ribbing of the top cover, magazines, and other parts of the AKM increased the strength of the sheet metal construction. A folding-stock AKMS version was also produced, with the two legs of the stock assembly also being made of stamped metal rather than the machined parts that were used in the AKS-47. At the muzzle of the AKM series, a simple compensator, made up of a threaded extension with an angular cut across it, aided in holding the muzzle of the weapon down, especially when fired on full automatic.

Manufacture of the 7.62×39 mm AK-47 series continues all around the world in a number of ex-client states of the Soviet Union, Warsaw Pact, and other countries. It has been modified into a number of other weapons, all of which are internally the same basic design. Overall, the number of AK-47 rifles and variants produced is staggering. It has become the most common military weapon in the world, with estimates of the numbers of weapons produced to date ranging from 50 to 90 million.

THE UNITED STATES, NATO, AND THE M14

While the United States sat complacent on what was thought to be the world's only nuclear weapons, the Soviet Union continued to consolidate power among the territories it controlled since World War II. The M1 Garand rifle had proven itself any number of times during the fighting of World War II. Experiments had been conducted during the latter part of the war to make the M1 Garand capable of both semiautomatic and full automatic fire as well as increasing the magazine capacity. John Garand had said that the modification of his design to such capabilities could be done but that it wasn't practical. Some modifications, such as adding a round bearing to the bolt and operating rod interface, were very worthwhile. But overall, the old problem of too powerful a cartridge in too light a weapon was thought to prevent the M1 from ever evolving into a full-automatic-capable weapon.

The answer from the Ordnance Department was to design a new cartridge, taking advantage of newly developed propellant powders and manufacturing. The T65 cartridge had been under development since shortly before the end of World War II. Evolving originally from a sporting rifle round, the .300 Savage, eventually the T65 had the same ballistics and power of a .30-06 ball round but in a cartridge half an inch shorter. Instead of having a cartridge case 63 mm long, as the .30-06 did, the new light-rifle round finally had a case length of 51 mm. There were no weapons designed to use it during the first years of its existence. All developments of a new family of small arms had been down-graded in priority following the end of World War II. There just was not an immediate need for greater firepower for the American soldier in the atomic age.

When the Soviet Union tested their first atomic bomb in August 1949, the United States knew that it no longer held a monopoly on the most powerful weapons on earth. Nuclear war was still an unthinkable option, and the threat of annihilation from the weapons of the U.S. was still considered strong enough to prevent conventional war. When North Korean forces invaded South Korea in June 1950, it was obvious that the nuclear deterrent was not strong enough to stop a ground war.

The United States led the fight in defending South Korea from Communist invasion. American troops were armed with the same small arms as they had fought World War II with only five years earlier. Without a new rifle design being available, the M1 Garand went back into production.

Prior to the breakout of the Korean War, the development of a light rifle capable of automatic fire had been ongoing at a relatively low level. Colonel René R. Studler, chief of Small Arms Research and Development for the U.S. Army Ordnance Department, had specimens of the German StG44 and the 8 mm Kurz ammunition. Glowing reports regarding the effectiveness of the rifle had come in from American combat forces in the field, starting when the U.S. troops first encountered the weapon in the snows of Belgium during the Battle of the Bulge. The American Ordnance Department had no real idea as to the developments in the Soviet Union and the designs of a simple armored unit sergeant. Studler denied the usefulness of the assault rifle concept outright; he considered the StG44 as having too short a combat range, too light a projectile, and too low a muzzle velocity for effective ballistics. It wasn't a long-range combat rifle and didn't fit the gravel-belly approach to warfare. About the only thing he didn't say publicly was that the concept wasted ammunition. That would have been hard to explain, given that his department was trying to issue each soldier with a weapon that would be a form of light machine gun.

What Studler wanted was a select-fire rifle with a twenty-round magazine that would chamber the new T65 cartridge. The Korean War was fought with the weapons of World War II, but development of the new rifle and other small arms were given a new priority because of the combat. Soldiers in Korea commented on the human-wave attacks by the Communist forces. They could be beaten back with the weapons available, but at a high cost. The new AK-47 rifle had not yet made an appearance on the battlefield, but the Communists had large numbers of the submachine guns that the Soviets had fought World War II with. The range of such weapons was still limited, but their volume of fire when the troops holding them grew near to American lines could come close to overwhelming the defenders.

Select-fire M1 Garands were converted to use the new T65 round in the early 1950s. In a few years, the T44 rifle had been developed and was undergoing testing. The T44 was at its heart an M1 Garand with a new gas system, a twenty-round removable box magazine—which could be loaded with stripper clips while on the rifle—and a flash hider. Combat studies from both World War II and later Korea had shown that men armed with automatic weapons tended to fire at the enemy considerably more often than those riflemen who carried semiautomatic weapons. Those same studies showed that combat ranges were practically far less than those the military trained and planned for. Instead of shooting at a thousand yards with their capable M1 Garand rifles, nearly all soldiers waited until they could see the enemy clearly before engaging him. This meant a practical range of only a few hundred yards at most—much like what Lieutenant Piderit of the German Army had said in his writings just after World War I. The world was thirty-five years older, but the facts of warfare hadn't changed that much as far as the foot soldier was concerned. For the most part, the American ordnance experts would supply him with the weapons they felt he needed, not what he wanted.

The British had developed a new rifle of their own as the Americans were designing the T44 series in the early 1950s while the Korean War was raging. The British weapon was a bullpup design, which is where the trigger mechanism was in front of the magazine and receiver. The bullpup pattern allowed a weapon to have a long barrel for accuracy and ballistic efficiency while still being much more compact than a conventional rifle. The name of the new British weapon was the EM-2, and the unique layout of the weapon wasn't the only new thing about it; it was chambered for a new cartridge.

The new British round had resulted from their studies of what had actually happened during World War II, and the results of the German developments in small arms. The .280 Enfield was the result of the British study, a short, midrange cartridge that put out a 130-grain projectile at 2,400 feet per second, ballistically almost a match for the .276 Pedersen with its 120-grain projectile at 2,550 feet per second. Except for the orders of General MacArthur, the .276 Pedersen would have been the caliber of the M1 Garand.

The close match to what had almost been the U.S. Army–issue rifle round was ignored during tests at Aberdeen Proving Grounds in 1952. The caliber, light weight, and odd appearance of the EM-2 all worked against it in the opinion of the American ordnance experts. The new round of ammunition that all of the North Atlantic Treaty Organization (NATO) forces would use would be a .30-caliber round. And it would be based on the T65 cartridge.

NATO was a new organization, only having been officially formed in 1949. One of the ideas behind the organization was to standardize all of the weapons and their calibers for all signatories. The high-handed approach to the idea by the Americans, the insistence on a round of their design, and a .30-caliber, full-powered one, did not sit well with the other countries. But many of them were already armed with American weapons from World War II, and the United States was the big dog at the party. Simply put, their economies were very dependent on the billions of dollars that the United States was spending as part of the Marshall Plan to rebuild Europe. They reluctantly agreed to the acceptance of the .30-caliber round.

It was the T44E4 that was considered the final step to a new U.S. Army rifle, one that would last for years to come. It would replace the M1 Garand, the Browning Automatic Rifle, the M1 carbine, and the M3A1 submachine gun all in one stroke, eliminating the need for three different rounds of ammunition at the same time. In May 1957, the T44E4 rifle was adopted as the new 7.62 mm M14 rifle. The T65 cartridge had already become the 7.62 mm NATO round. But in spite of the M14 rifle being adopted, there were still a number of problems to be overcome in producing it in large enough numbers for the U.S. military. The weapon resembled the M1 Garand a great deal, but it couldn't be built on the same machinery and with the same tooling that had made six million Garands since 1937. The pilot production of M14 rifles at Springfield Armory was 15,669 weapons and was started in April 1958. Commercial contracts were released to a number of rifle companies, several of whom had already been producing M1 Garands during World War II, the Korean War, or both. But the rifles just weren't being made in the numbers needed.

Problems in production of the M14 included the tooling and machines, much of which had to be scrapped and the whole line set up again. Other difficulties centered on the steel and heat treatment of the parts to the weapon. Guns shattered, components cracked, and interchangeable parts didn't. By June 30, 1961, 133,386 acceptable M14 rifles had been produced by three makers including Springfield Armory (52,706 units). The weapon was liked by a number of the soldiers who were issued it, but it proved to have a number of drawbacks. Production continued to grow, problems and all, as the difficulties with the design and basic concept of the weapon were being discovered.

The M14 was normally issued with a small selector lock placed on the receiver to keep the weapon firing in the semiautomatic mode only. The lock could be easily exchanged for a selector switch by an armorer at the unit level. This lock and switch system kept each soldier from actually having an automatic weapon, just one capable of it. It was unit commanders who would make the decision as to just how many select-fire M14s would be in their command. This was another way of controlling ammunition expenditure by the supply people in ordnance. They still had a fear of soldiers wasting ammunition with wanton, ineffective automatic fire.

One of the problems with the M14 was that most automatic fire with it was wasteful. Aimed fire with the weapon at the shoulder was relatively easy on semiautomatic. On full automatic, aimed fire was almost impossible; the recoil of the powerful round would drive the muzzle of the M14 up and off target even before the second round of a burst had been fired. Fired from the hip, the weapon could be braced, and automatic fire allowed a soldier to rake rounds across an enemy position. The volume of fire may not have been as accurate as desired, but it would prove more than enough to drive an enemy to cover. The powerful 7.62 mm NATO round would chop through cover, walls, bunkers, and light vehicles just as the earlier .30-06 round had done. But it could not be easily controlled on full automatic from a rifle-weight weapon.

Automatic riflemen in an infantry squad would have earlier been armed with a BAR. With a select-fire M14, they were still expected to carry out their assigned mission. The only difference between the M14 used by the automatic riflemen and the regular foot soldier was the addition of a few accessories. A folding bipod helped support the M14 when used as an automatic rifle. In addition, there was a modified stock for the weapon that had a much more straight-line recoil, a folding vertical forward grip, and a pistol grip. Lastly, a muzzle stabilizer could be locked down over the flash hider to help hold the barrel down during automatic fire. Fully equipped for the automatic rifle role, the new model was the M14E2.

The rifle that was intended to be in service for decades would still prove to be so, but not in the way that the designers would ever have foreseen. As a frontline service rifle in the United States military, the days of the M14 were very numbered.

SPECIAL-PURPOSE INDIVIDUAL WEAPON: THE NEEDLE GUN

Concerned about how to fight in a future nuclear war, in September 1948, the U.S. Army General Staff established the Operations Research Office (ORO), staffed with civilians and given the task to supply scientific advice to the Army in regards to the future conduct of combat. In one of their first major projects, ORO was to develop new views on how to improve body armor for the soldier. The group decided to first compile information on just how soldiers were wounded, what weapons were used, and how they were applied.

The ORO study resulted in several reports, none of which pleased the traditional-minded commanders of the Army. Compiling and analyzing data from both World War II and Korea, ORO scientists found that the actual range of engagements, where the soldiers not only fired but also hit their targets, was much, much shorter than previously accepted. Most effective rifle and machine gun fire—80 percent of it—took place at ranges of less than 200 yards. Above 300 yards, the chances of a soldier hitting his target in combat dropped to negligible.

One way to increase the effectiveness of the individual soldier, who already "wasted" most of the rounds he fired, was for him to use a high-velocity, small-caliber weapon that quickly launched three projectiles. The small projectile would help minimize recoil, the high velocity would make the light projectile more lethal, and the three rounds would make a pattern where it was much more likely that at least one of them would strike the target.

The result of this research was the creation of a series of exotic weapons and ammunition with multiple projectiles that started in the mid 1950s and extended through the 1960s and into the '70s and beyond. One result of what was called Project SALVO was a round of 7.62 mm ammunition that had two projectiles. The M198 Duplex Ball had two bullets loaded one on top of the other. The lead bullet weighed eighty-four grains and the rear eighty-five. The lead bullet left the barrel at 2,750 feet per second, while the rear projectile left the muzzle at 2,200 feet per second. It was thought that the dispersion of the two projectiles would help increase the hit probability of the M14 rifle.

The other system that came out from the new studies involved a very small projectile, the smallest the military has ever considered for combat. The flechette is a needlelike projectile that is much longer than its diameter. This gives the flechette-style projectile a very high penetration into a target. During World War I, French pilots would drop flechettes (little arrows) down onto the enemy trenches. The fin-stabilized projectile would reach a good velocity if they were tossed out at a high altitude. Inexpensive projectiles would rain down point first, penetrating steel helmets with ease. German soldiers had been completely penetrated by a flechette going all the way through their body from the top down.

Seizing on the flechette concept was the Advanced Aircraft Armaments Company (AAI) of Maryland. Their idea was first for a shotgun shell loaded with a number of flechettes. The flechettes were about the size of finishing nails and were made on modified nail production machinery. The finned flechettes were 0.087 inches in diameter, weighed eight grains, and were slightly over an inch long. The shotgun shell studies continued with a number of experimental designs, but AAI had what they considered a better idea. The AAI concept was for a discreet flechette to be launched at a very high velocity in bursts from an automatic weapon. AAI received a developmental contract from the Army for their flechette rifle concept in 1956. They continued with their studies and made a number of discoveries regarding the flechette as a projectile.

One of the things discovered about the single flechette was that it could be much more destructive to a target than was suspected. Above a certain critical high velocity, depending on the design of the flechette, the small projectiles would bend when they hit a target, producing a semicircular hook. The hooking phenomenon took place as the projectile also spun around itself. This action caused tremendous damage to a target, especially a soft one such as human flesh would be.

The very light weight of the flechettes also caused very little recoil when they were fired, even at speeds of over 3,500 feet per second. Weapons could be designed that held a large number of flechette rounds, fired them in mechanically controlled bursts at very high cyclic rates, and would have such a flat trajectory that a soldier could use the same aiming point on the target at long range as he did close in. It was an ideal solution for many of the difficult aspects of combat.

In the early 1960s, the Special Purpose Individual Weapon (SPIW) program was initiated. A number of military and civilian weapons designers were asked to submit weapons firing a standardized single flechette round. The Army Ordnance Department was already being pressured to adopt a new rifle to replace the M14, which had been proving difficult to produce. The upcoming AR-15 rifle that fired what was a high-velocity .22 bullet controllably on full automatic was drawing an increasing amount of attention. In an attempt to prevent the embarrassment of eliminating a rifle that had just been produced, the Ordnance Department pointed to the SPIW program as being the source of what would be a new Army weapon.

To increase the value of the new SPIW rifle, the army added a grenade launcher attachment to their list of requirements. The launcher was to fire the new 40 mm grenade cartridge as a repeater. The system requirements included a sixty-round capacity of flechette rounds, a three-round 40 mm ca-

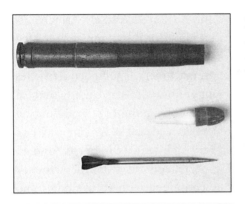

The XM645 flechette round broken down into its componets. At the center is the fiberglass sabot that pulls the flechette through the barrel. At the bottom is the finned flechette "needle."
Kevin Dockery

pacity, and be short, handy, and of minimum weight. The SPIW had evolved from being a simple rifle to both a point target weapon (the rifle) and an area target weapon (the grenade launcher). The project never worked.

The idea of a flechette rifle was a good one, but putting in into a physical form was very difficult. The only company to produce a weapon that looked at all practical was AAI. But the flechette ammunition and the weapon that fired it would prove to be far too expensive to produce. Manufacturing techniques of the 1960s could not economically make the tiny precision flechettes needed for a high-velocity weapon in the numbers that would be required for Army use. The weight of the multiple-round 40 mm launcher never proved acceptable. The final weapon produced for the SPIW project was the AAI XM70. It was a "simplified serial flechette rifle" that worked to a limited extent, but only a single specimen was ever produced. The discreet flechette, a lethal steel needle moving through the air at thousands of feet per second, was an idea whose time had not come—yet.

THE BIRTH OF THE BLACK RIFLE

In 1952 at the height of the Korean War, then Chief of Staff General J. Lawton Collins stated what the common opinion of many Army officers was. The general said that having every soldier armed with an automatic weapon might be occasionally useful, and that there certainly should be a light automatic weapon (in his era, a Browning Automatic Rifle) in every squad. But that arming every soldier with such a weapon would be a mistake and a waste of too much ammunition.

Following original lines of research rather than just listening to popular military opinion, the Operations Research Office (ORO) reported what proved to be almost the complete opposite of what General Collins had said. And the researchers could back up their findings with fact. ORO stated that a practical investigation of combat shootings showed that most shots were fired at ranges of fewer than 150 meters; power at long ranges just wasn't generally needed. The researchers also said that infantrymen using special high-rate-of-fire automatic weapons could be expected to have a greater hit and kill probability on a target.

Smaller calibers would allow for the development of the kind of weapons that would give the soldiers the capabilities that would make them more effective; that was ORO's findings. And they matched the findings of the .276 Pedersen studies done after World War I. It was not a new idea, just a well-researched one.

The ORO study, ORO-T-160, *Operational Requirements for an Infantry Hand Weapon*, was authored by Norman A. Hitchman et al. The conclusion of the report was that an automatic weapon of less than .30 caliber should be considered for the future army. At the time that the report came out, Army Ordnance was pushing ahead on the development and adoption of the .30-caliber NATO rifle, what would eventually be the M14. They were the technicians and experts; their opinion was that they would tell the infantry what it needed, not some scientists who simply crunched numbers and wrote reports. Nothing else would be considered for the infantry but a full-powered rifle.

Other officers not quite so set in their opinions also read the Hitchman report as well as other studies that stated generally the same thing. They came to different conclusions as to what would make a good infantry weapon. So did individuals and engineers outside of the military who had read the same reports.

One set of experiments was done with a small, light automatic weapon firing a high-velocity, .22-caliber cartridge even prior to the release of the Hitchman report. This was part of the small-caliber, high-velocity (SCHV) concept conducted at Aberdeen Proving Grounds and not the Springfield Armory. It was a ballistics study, and one of the weapons looked at was the M2 carbine. The M2 carbine was capable of selective fire, but the very low-powered .30-caliber cartridge it fired had poor terminal effects. The weapon had proved popular because it was light and handy, but the results of its use in combat, especially in the Korean environment, left a great deal to be desired.

An M2 carbine was converted to fire a shortened .22-caliber cartridge based on the commercially available .222 Remington round. The final round could put out a thirty-five-grain bullet at about 3,000 feet per second, or forty-one-grain projectiles at 2,700 to over 2,800 feet per second. It was thought that developing a load that could exceed 3,000 feet per second with a forty-one-grain bullet was practical. Results from range testing such a combination of projectiles, weapons, and loads resulted in the .22 M2 carbine comparing favorably to the M1 Garand rifle at ranges of up to 300 yards. The full-power infantry rifle program and the 7.62 mm cartridge it would use was far too advanced for it to be derailed by a single short rifle and a study done around it. But additional studies of high-speed, small-caliber rounds would continue under the SALVO programs. With the promising examinations of the .22-caliber M2 carbine conversion, Project SALVO would be given a higher priority, much to the chagrin of the traditionalists at Ordnance.

An early 1950s meeting between an ordnance dealer and an aircraft engineer/patent attorney resulted in the combination of two different sets of experiences into one very significant idea. The weapons broker, Monsieur Jacques Michault of Brussles, and George Sullivan of California joined the knowledge of a man who had fully examined the German assault weapons concepts with someone familiar with the alloys and plastic used in the aircraft industry. The seed of an idea was created and germinated quickly.

Another meeting furthered the creation of a new style of weapon. Sullivan met with Richard S. Boutelle, the president of Fairchild Engine and Airplane Works, during a 1953 conference. Sullivan described to Boutelle what he and Michault had started to develop in their rented making shop facilities. Fascinated with the idea of combining aircraft technology with firearms design, Boutelle put forward the idea of a new company being spun off from Fairchild. The new company was named ArmaLite, a division of the Fairchild Corporation. The mandate for the new company would be the design, development, and production of prototype weapons. The weapons thus developed would be produced under license by other companies already in the arms manufacturing business.

The president of ArmaLite was George Sullivan, who hired his brother-in-law, Charles Dorchester, as the plant manager of their new facility. The two men had come up with a very lightweight bolt-action rifle design that had an aluminum receiver and barrel, fitted with rifled steel bore liner and barrel extension. The action assembly was fitted to a fiberglass stock shell that was filled with hardened foam. The new weapon was the first design from the ArmaLite company and was designated the AR-1 for ArmaLite Rifle #1. It was neither commercially or militarily successful as a sniping rifle, but it gave the new company a great deal of practical experience.

Two additional people added a very great deal to the possible future success of the fledgling weapons company. Within a year of the creation of ArmaLite, they hired an ex-Marine from World War II and previous Army ordnance technician, Eugene M. Stoner, to be the chief engineer for small arms projects. In addition, ArmaLite brought Melvin R. Johnson into the fold as he was working with Fairchild as a consultant and publicist. With Johnson came his patents for a multilugged bolt that he had developed prior to World War II as a possible competitor for the M1 Garand.

With Johnson's locking system, Sullivan's ideas for incorporating modern plastics and alloys, and Stoner's mechanical genius and ideas of his own, the stage was set for some very new and innovative designs to come out of the ArmaLite offices. A number of designs were built and tested, including a survival rifle, a very lightweight autoloading shotgun, and a traditional-appearing lightweight military rifle. None of these weapons were directly either a commercial or military success. Then Stoner combined a number of ideas into a truly innovative new rifle, the AR-10.

Stoner's idea was to keep everything in line to make a 7.62 NATO chambered automatic rifle controllable, even when fired on full automatic. To have everything in line meant that the line of recoil from the barrel went directly back into the shooter's shoulder. It also meant that the operation of the weapon, the basic working mechanism, was also in line with the bore. To accomplish this, Stoner developed a novel new idea.

Instead of having a gas-operated piston pushing a rod or other mechanical contrivance above or below the barrel, Stoner had the propellant gas from firing tapped directly from the barrel and guided back into the mechanism held in the receiver of the weapon. There, the gases were guided into the bolt carrier where there was a small expansion chamber behind the bolt itself. The propellant gas expanded, driving the bolt carrier away from the bolt while it was still locked to the barrel extension. The eight lugs of the bolt had to rotate only a short distance over an arc to lock or unlock the bolt. With the bolt carrier acting as the cylinder to the bolt's pistol, the expanding propellant gases drove the two pieces apart until a cam action rotated the bolt and unlocked it.

By the time the bolt had unlocked, the bullet had left the barrel and the remaining gas pressure had dropped to a safe level. Remaining gases in the bolt carrier were vented to the outside through a number of holes made for the purpose. The action of locking and unlocking was simple and remained in line with the barrel, minimizing any deflection to the action during functioning and increasing the inherent accuracy of the system. The only drawback of the design, as had been found by Melvin Johnson himself during his developmental work in the late 1930s, was that there was no primary extraction for the cartridge case. Once the bolt unlocked, the inertia of the bolt carrier kept the whole assembly moving to the rear, drawing the bolt and the fired cartridge case along with it. Testing didn't show any real difficulty with the system, and it worked.

The only parts in the weapon that had to be able to withstand the highest pressure of firing were the barrel and bolt. The barrel extension was made of high-strength steel, as was the bolt. With those two parts locked together with the multiple lugs of the bolt, the rest of the weapon only had to support them. This meant that the bulk of the AR-10 design could be made of light plastics and aluminum forgings. The final design of the weapon was a full two pounds lighter than the M14 candidate, and it was considerably more controllable on full automatic fire.

To keep the recoil in line with the shoulder of the firer and help keep the muzzle from climbing on automatic fire, the top of the stock was directly in line with the barrel. The large bolt carrier assembly recoiled back into a large tube the stock was mounted on, compressing a mainspring that would drive it back forward to complete the cycling of the action. The tube helped keep the stock rigid and give it strength. So that the shooter could aim the weapon effectively with such a low mounted receiver, the sights were raised up well above the line of the barrel. The rear sight was placed at the back end of a carrying handle that extended the length of the upper receiver. Underneath the carrying handle was the triggerlike cocking handle. A prominent pistol grip was underneath the weapon, and a twenty-round magazine went into the receiver just in front of the trigger guard.

Though a very light and controllable weapon when it was introduced, the AR-10 did not fare well in competition with the M14. When the AR-10 was introduced in 1956, the rifle that would become the M14 was well along in its development. The AR-10 still had a number of bugs that had to be worked out of the design, and by the time these were completed, the rifle trials were nearly completed. Offered for sale internationally, the AR-10 was not a great commercial success. About 6,000 military weapons were produced, most of these made under license in the Netherlands. Production was completed in 1961, but by then the AR-10 had led the way to a considerably more successful design by ArmaLite and Eugene Stoner.

A number of military personnel had witnessed the testing and comparisons of the AR-10 in the various weapons tests. One of these officers was Willard G. Wyman, commanding general of the Continental Army Command (CONARC). General Wyman had been impressed with the AR-10 and the capabilities the design showed. He also knew that it wasn't about to beat a design that Springfield Armory had come up with and would never be adopted in its present form.

General Wyman had worked with the Infantry Board, who was examining the SCHV concept with considerable interest. He had also seen a classified "confidential" document that had outlined the .22 M2 carbine experiments, the recommendations from those tests, and the request for funding to continue the program. That request had been turned down by the same arsenal personnel who were so adamant in the adoption of a full-powered, select-fire rifle for the infantry. In early 1957, General Wyman approached Gene Stoner and made a

One of the original ammunition boxes for the experimental .22 Special ammunition that became the .223 Ball around.
Kevin Dockery

suggestion that would impact the U.S. military for the balance of the twentieth century and into the foreseeable future. Using the outlines in the documents he had, General Wyman suggested that the AR-10 be redesigned to accept a new cartridge, one that was of .22 caliber and fired a fifty-five-grain projectile at a high velocity. It was the establishment of the idea that would become the M16 rifle.

There was still the problem of range, a subject that the gravel-bellies in ordnance held dear. As initially proposed to Stoner, the practical combat range of the new weapons and ammunition should be 300 yards. That was also the range accepted by the Infantry Board when general Wyman approached them with a formal request that a high-velocity, small-caliber rifle be developed and tested. General military politics suggested that a combat range of 400 yards would be more acceptable to the general officer corps. The final proposal from the Infantry Board was for the submission of a six-pound, .22-caliber weapon capable of both semi- and full automatic fire with a conventional stock and a magazine capacity of at least twenty rounds. The new round of ammunition, which didn't exist yet, was to be capable of matching the trajectory of the M1 rifle and penetrate a steel helmet (0.135 inches of steel) at a range of 500 yards. The final range had been decided on as a number that would be easy to remember and acceptable in the halls of the Pentagon.

The request that General Wyman had initiated was approved and funds allocated. Ten new .22-caliber ArmaLite rifles would be procured for testing along with 100,000 rounds of ammunition. There would be other weapons developed to meet the board's requirements. The ArmaLite weapon would have competition.

The first ArmaLite design intended to meet the Infantry Board parameters was a straightforward rifle design chambered for the commercial .222 Remington round. The high rate of fire of the weapon, combined with a light weight from alloys and plastics, as well as a conventional-style rifle stock made the weapon difficult to control on full automatic fire. The standard rifle outline just didn't work for such a weapon, even if it would be more acceptable to traditionally minded military officers. Only one such weapon was made by ArmaLite before the project centered on the use of the AR-10 layout.

Gene Stoner was developing an additional 7.62 mm design (the AR-16) at ArmaLite at the time and did not see a lot of military interest in the proposed .22-caliber round. He concentrated on his new rifle project and left the bulk of the .22-caliber work to his staff. Two other engineers at ArmaLite, Robert Fremont and L. James Sullivan, took up the project of modifying the design of the AR-10 to match the new specifications. Fremont had been Stoner's chief design assistant and was very familiar with the AR-10 design. The involved project was more than just rescaling the AR-10 and reducing it to accept a new round, it was a redesign of the concept in order to operate with the very high pressures required to meet the range and penetration demands put forward by the Infantry Board.

After meeting with Army officials at Fort Benning to learn just what was desired for the new .22-caliber round, Stoner spent some time examining the problems. To meet the required penetration characteristics and the nearly doubled range requirements, Stoner decided that there would have to be a case design change from the .222 Remington in order to meet the necessary powder volume the new round would have to have. In addition to the new case, Stoner had decided that DuPont Improved Military Rifle Powder, specifically IMR4475, would need to be loaded behind a fifty-five-grain bullet of his devising to make the new round, designated the .222 Special. By 1959, Remington Arms was running into some difficulty with the multiple cartridges all identified as the .222. They declared that the Stoner .222 Special round would be renamed the .223 Remington.

It was the AR-15 that was the most successful weapon tested by the Infantry Board at Fort Benning. Gene Stoner had witnessed the tests and considered them complete and exhaustive, especially the combat simulations. Changes suggested by the testing were included in the AR-15 design, and it was declared safe for further testing by the Infantry Board. In March 1958, extensive Army testing was conducted on the AR-15 by a group of ordnance people who had just been involved with the adoption of the M14 rifle. The bias of the ordnance people caused them to seize on a problem with the AR-15 noticed in the testing. The original barrel of the .22-caliber weapon had split open when fired after exposure to simulated rain. A simple change by Stoner, adding a few ounces in weight to the barrel, prevented the malfunction from happening again. But the situation was grabbed up by the Army Ordnance community who had put so much behind the development of the M14.

The final report of the Infantry Board on the AR-15 was to continue supplemental trials of the AR-15 and Winchester weapons after the inclusion of suggested modifications. An earlier recommendation that enthusiastically recommended the potential replacement of the M14 with the AR-15 had been changed.

Invited to attend the Fort Benning tests, Gene Stoner had been allowed to examine all of the weapons being tested and supervise any repairs or parts changes. In December 1958, he traveled to Fort Greeley, Alaska, to supply some needed spare parts and repairs to the AR-15 specimens that were being tested in arctic conditions. What the engineer found when he examined the weapons shocked and angered him. They had been badly mishandled, to the point where some parts that were considered permanent assemblies had been removed for no known reason. The front sights of several of the guns had been taken off and placed back on the barrels loosely. Hardened tapered steel pins that had been pressed into place at the factory had been driven out and then misassembled. One rifle had no steel pins at all but just pieces of soft welding rod ground down to fit and hammered into place. After Stoner's arrival, the weapons were scheduled for an arctic accuracy test, and he could see that the loose sights would prevent them from coming even close to their capabilities.

The engineer was told that the tests would only go ahead with corrected weapons, and he returned to ArmaLite. What Stoner hadn't been told was that the tests had been concluded prior to his arrival, and the weapons had shown poor accuracy at best. Even though the AR-15 was shown to be the best of the weapons tested at the Infantry Board and elsewhere, the cards were stacked against the weapon ever seeing military adoption. Only the M14 was considered acceptable for Army use, as was declared by General Maxwell Taylor, chief of staff, in February 1959. The general formally directed that there be no further purchases of the AR-15 by the Army.

ArmaLite was out nearly 1.5 million dollars for the development and manufacture of the AR-15 rifle with now no military sales expected to materialize. In December 1959, the rights to manufacture the AR-15 were sold to Colt Firearms for $75,000 in cash and a 4.5 percent royalty on any future sales of the weapon. The next year, ArmaLite underwent a significant reorganization ordered by the parent company, and Gene Stoner left the organization. The patent for the heart of the AR-15 weapon, the gas-operated bolt and carrier system, was awarded patent number 2,951,424 on September 6, 1960, after ArmaLite had gone out of the AR-15 business.

Colt Firearms was desperate for a commercially successful weapons design in the early 1960s. The military and sporting arms market had flattened as far as sales were concerned in the post–Korean War world. The thought at Colt was that the AR-10 and maybe the AR-15 could draw enough foreign military sales to make the licensing purchase worthwhile. While Colt was tooling up to produce the new weapons, Bobby Macdonald of Cooper-Macdonald, the brokers of the licensing agreement between ArmaLite and Colt, was on a sales trip throughout the Far East in 1959. Still part of ArmaLite at the time, Gene Stoner accompanied him through the Philippines, Burma, Malaysia, Indonesia, Thailand, Singapore, and India.

The general physical stature of the Southeast Asian people is smaller than that of Europeans and Americans. It wasn't very long into the trip that Macdonald got rid of the ammunition he was transporting for the AR-10; none of the prospective customers he was meeting wanted to fire it. The popular weapon for the trip was one of the very early AR-15 rifles, serial number 000004. That single weapon fired an estimated 8,000 rounds flawlessly. The only malfunction was traced back to a damaged feed lip on a magazine. Contacting Colt, Macdonald told them to stop all production work on the AR-10 and get the AR-15 into full production as soon as possible.

The first 300 AR-15 rifles were completed by Colt in December 1959. Sales of limited test quantities, twenty-five weapons or so, were sent out, the first sale being made on September 30, 1959, to Malaysia. But there still were no orders coming from the U.S. military, the customer who could single-handedly put Colt back in the red. During a Fourth of July weekend at Richard Boutelle's farm in Maryland, Air Force General Curtis LeMay was invited to a celebration of the holiday and Boutelle's birthday. One of the highlights of the shoot at one of the farm's several ranges was punching rounds from an AR-15 into a watermelon at 50 and 150 yards. When LeMay saw the high-velocity .223 projectiles blow two melons apart, he suggested saving the third for eating. A short time later, General LeMay was suggesting that the AR-15 be adopted by the Air Force as a replacement for their aging M1 and M2 carbines. He followed his suggestion with an eventually approved order for 8,500 weapons for use by the Air Force security elements at Strategic Air Command bases.

With the AR-15 in production and improved with experience, shortly before LeMay was experiencing the AR-15, Colt was formally requesting another test of the weapon by Army ordnance. The request was turned down as there was no stated need for such a weapon in the military. Then came the request that the AR-15 be examined as a replacement for the M2 carbine by the Air Force, and suddenly there was a military demand for such a weapon. The Air Force had been using their old carbines for so long that the Army no longer stocked replacement parts for them. When Congress started looking into the reluctance of Army ordnance to examine the AR-15, testing was scheduled for September 1960.

In the early summer of 1962, 1,000 AR-15 rifles were purchased by the Advanced Research Projects Agency (ARPA) for use by South Vietnamese troops. With the beginning of the Kennedy administration in 1961, the idea that ground troops would be of little use in a nuclear war had been supplanted by the recognition that there would be a lot of combat in the brushfire or guerrilla wars that were occurring all over the world. President Kennedy had recognized the growing threat, and so did his new secretary of defense, Robert McNamara. Having been established in 1958 to provide defense research, ARPA found its field of responsibility expanded from primarily one of ballistic missiles to aiding foreign allies of the United States in their struggles against guerrilla war. For the slight-statured South Vietnamese, ARPA saw the AR-15 as a much superior weapon to the M1 Garand, M2 Carbine, and M1818A2 BAR.

ARPA was not the only organization to recognize the value of the new rifle. The Air Force ordered an additional 19,000 AR-15 rifles soon after a glowing report was released from ARPA regarding the effectiveness of the AR-15 in Vietnam. The Navy in the form of the officer in charge of the fledgling SEAL Team Two in Little Creek, Virginia, purchased a little over 120 AR-15 rifles to arm the very new and still highly classified SEAL teams.

Under the direct order of the secretary of defense, the Army Ordnance Corps ceased to exist as they had since well before the Civil War. In place of the organization was the new Army Materiel Command, where individuals with personal biases would find it more difficult to put roadblocks in the way of innovative ideas. A study done around the same time as the ending of the Ordnance Corps served to illustrate one of the reasons the organization had to be rebuilt. Known as the Hitch Report, the document compared the M14 rifle, the AR-15 rifle, and the AK-47. It stated in no uncertain terms that the AR-15 was the superior weapon in many respects, and that the M14 wasn't superior in any respect.

The Hitch Report was at its core a comparison of assault rifles, which the

M14 was never expected to be. But the increasing level of combat around the world, and particularly in Vietnam, was showing the value of the assault rifle and the need for controllable individual automatic fire in sudden combat situations. That was something the AR-15 supplied very well.

In 1963, the Army Materiel Command finally issued a purchase order for 85,000 AR-15 rifles to be supplied over a three-year period. Production of the M14 rifle had been ordered ceased by Robert McNamara in January earlier that year. The SPIW flechette-launching weapon was expected to be perfected and ready for issue to the Army inside of three years, a timetable that was never met. With the big military order, Colt went into full production of the AR-15 rifle. The modifications insisted upon by the Army, all 130 of them, had to be included on the weapons before they would be accepted as the M16A1 rifle. One of these modifications affected one aspect of the AR-15 that had impressed those people who had seen its use in combat, the terrible lethality of the high-velocity .223 projectiles.

The rifling twist chosen by Stoner to stabilize the new projectiles was one full turn in fourteen inches of barrel. That spin rate was not the result of a careful study but was the adoption of the rifling used by Remington in their commercial .222 hunting weapons. As it turned out, the rate of spin given to the projectiles by the one-in-fourteen twist was just enough to stabilize the flight of the bullet through the air. When the projectile penetrated a target that was denser than air, such as flesh, the bullet became unstable, rapidly turning end over end and dumping all of its energy into the target.

This tumbling action resulted in terrible wounds being attributed to the tiny .223 projectile and the rifle that fired it. Limbs were reported as almost blown off the targets, and bodies appeared to almost explode. Only a small percentage of the AR-15 rifles used in the U.S. military were showing these terrible, almost explosive wound effects. One of the modifications the Army had insisted upon was the change of the rifling rate from one turn in fourteen inches to one turn in twelve inches. The reason was that they had found in testing that at subzero temperatures, the projectiles became unstable, and accuracy suffered as a result. The trade-off in lesser lethality of the more stable projectiles was considered acceptable by the Army. Their opinion was that it was better to hit a target with a stable projectile than miss one with a more destructive bullet.

Another modification that the Army insisted upon was the design and inclusion of a bolt-closure device for the new XM16E1 rifle. This action could be taken on the M1 and M14 rifles by just striking the bolt handle with the heel of the hand. But the idea of basically pounding a bolt closed on a dirty chamber or damaged round is not a good one among shooters. Such an action can take a bad jam and make it an almost-impossible-to-clear one. The Air Force would not wait for the adoption of a bolt-closing device that they, and Gene Stoner, considered useless and possibly dangerous. In a compromise, the Army allowed the XM16 to be produced without a bolt-closure device, but only for the Air Force. For the Army, the XM16E1 would have to include the device.

The M14 rifle was proving unwieldy in combat in South Vietnam, where it was being used by U.S. forces. The rifle was long and heavy, barely controllable on automatic fire, and the ammunition was also bulky and heavy for the number of rounds that could be carried. The XM16E1 rifle was the Army's answer to this problem as they began issuing the weapon in numbers to airborne units in 1965. It was when the Army started ordering ammunition in huge amounts that the real problem with the M16 arose.

The IMR powder the AR-15 had been designed to use burned cleanly and completely in the tight bore and small cartridge case of the compact weapon. That allowed the AR-15 to be fired continually with little or no cleaning. When the Army adopted the weapon as the M16A1, they did not include an order for sufficient maintenance materials for the weapons. To make what could be a bad situation worse, they changed the powder that was used to load the .223 Remington, now known as the 5.56 mm round.

As infantry soldiers began using the XM16E1 rifle in numbers in Vietnam, stoppages and malfunctions began to be reported in increasing numbers. That was something that hadn't happened with other units using the new weapons. In 1966, a study was done of the weapons in the field and the soldiers using them. It was found that the XM16E1 rifles in Vietnam were corroding in the hot, humid environment. In addition, the new ammunition, filled with ball powder rather than IMR, was much dirtier than the original. The rifles needed more cleaning, not less, than the M14 and M1 Garand that had preceded them.

Changes in the instruction on the maintenance of the XM16E1 helped a great deal in lowering the malfunction rate. So did the design and issue of cleaning equipment in large volume. Chrome-plating the bore and chamber of the barrel cut down on corrosion in these critical areas of the weapon. On February 28, 1967, the XM16E1 rifle was accepted as the standard military weapon of the Army and was renamed the 5.56 mm M16A1 rifle. The Vietcong who had faced the early versions of the M16 back in 1965 had another name for it; they called the weapon the Black Rifle.

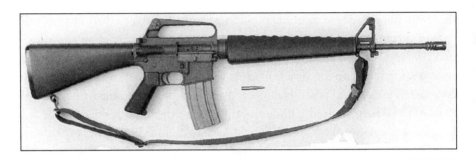

The M16A1 rifle.
Kevin Dockery

As experience in using the M16A1 in Vietnam grew, further improvements were included in the weapon. By March 1970, the announcement was made that the M16A1 rifle would become the standard weapon of all U.S. military forces, including those in NATO. This action shocked and angered many NATO countries who still remembered how the 7.62 mm round had been forced on them by an adamant U.S. Ordnance Department. The British were particularly angry as their own smaller round had been rudely rejected by the same military that was now bringing forward an even smaller round. Soon there would have to be a new set of standardization agreements made within NATO to agree on a new lighter round of ammunition.

COLT AUTOMATIC RIFLE

To increase the sales potential of the AR-15 rifle, Colt developed a number of variations of the basic weapon within a few years of receiving the license to the design from ArmaLite. Most of the AR-15 variations were not successful, and few of them were ever produced. One set the stage for a new class of weapons that is still growing today.

The overall name of the new weapons family was a derivative of the original AR-15 by adding Colt to the name, resulting in CAR-15. The letters now stood for Colt Automatic Rifle. The CAR-15 weapons system consisted of the AR-15 rifle and five variations. The variations included:

The CAR-15 Carbine, with a fifteen-inch barrel on an otherwise standard weapon

The CAR-15 Heavy Assault Rifle M1, with a standard-length, thick barrel for extended automatic fire

The CAR-15 Heavy Assault Rifle M2, with a belt feed mechanism turning the weapon into a sustained-fire light machine gun

The CAR-15 submachine gun

The CAR-15 survival rifle

In addition, the Colt Grenade Launcher Model 4 (CGL-4) was also offered as part of the weapons system. Of the five rifle designs, only the submachine gun was successful as it was developed into an issued military weapon.

The CAR-15 submachine gun, identified as the Colt Model 607, had a ten-inch barrel, half the length of the standard rifle barrel. The short barrel reduced the muzzle velocity of the 5.56 mm round by several hundred feet per second from that of the rifle, but the projectile was still considered an effective one. In addition to the short barrel, the Model 607 also incorporated a sliding stock in the design.

The bolt carrier assembly of the basic AR-15 rifle recoiled back into the receiver extension tube inside of the stock, compressing the mainspring as it moved. Because of this aspect of the AR-15 design, a major portion of the entire stock assembly had to remain in line with the upper receiver of the weapon. This greatly complicated fitting the weapon with any form of stock that would fold up underneath or along the side of the weapon.

The only practical way to reduce the size of the stock was to shorten the interior components and then slide the main part of the stock along the remaining length of the receiver extension tube. With the stock locked in the fully forward (collapsed) position, the CAR-15 could still be easily handled and fired. With the stock extended, the weapon was able to be shouldered and aimed in the same manner as a standard AR-15 rifle.

With the modifications, the Model 607 CAR-15 submachine gun was an extremely compact weapon, capable of all of the firepower of the full-sized AR-15 but at a reduced effective range. Not being chambered for a pistol-caliber cartridge, the Model 607 did not fit the classic definition of a submachine gun. But that was the designation Colt placed on the weapon, and it was accepted as such. This was to be the weapon that would permanently blur the line between assault rifles and submachine guns.

One problem with the Model 607 was the tremendous muzzle blast and noise of firing the 5.56 mm cartridge in such a short barrel. A lot of unconsumed propellant made it out of the muzzle only to finish burning in the open air. The short barrel also changed the pressure-time curve that was so essential to the proper functioning of the basic AR-15 design. A short flash and noise suppressor was added to the muzzle of the Model 607 to reduce the firing signature of the weapon and to increase the time that the back pressure of the propellant gas had to operate the action.

A small number of the Colt Model 607 CAR-15 weapons were acquired by special operations units such as the Navy SEALs and Army Special Forces. The quick-handling and powerful little weapon soon became a favorite of those special operations soldiers who had to work in tight areas or be transported with limited room for equipment. Reports from the men using the compact weapon reached Army staff officers, and interest was raised in obtaining a number of the new weapons. In November 1965, an Army staff study in Vietnam showed the desirability of using the CAR-15 submachine gun to replace a number of secondary weapons, such as the M1911A1 pistol, the .38 revolver, and the M3A1 .45 caliber submachine gun, as well as some XM16E1 rifles in certain specialists' hands.

The Army staff suggested that the CAR-15, as it was now commonly called, had greater range, power, and automatic fire capability over pistols and some submachine guns. It would be a better choice of weapon to arm combat soldiers who needed to have their hands free to conduct their primary mission. This included dog handlers, radio operators, point men working in front of a patrol, and field commanders. Using the same ammunition and having a large commonality of parts with the XM16E1 rifle made the CAR-15 an excellent choice for adoption from a logistical viewpoint.

As the Army was deciding what to do in regards to the compact weapon, Colt had modified the design of the Model 607, changing the layout of the stock and simplifying the locking system used to secure it. The front hand guards had been made cylindrical, and internal changes incorporated into the action made the weapon function more reliably. The Air Force wanted a number of the compact weapons as soon as they were available. The Army again wanted the bolt closure device, the forward bolt assist, to be included on the weapon they wanted to order.

Authority was issued for a purchase of 2,050 Colt submachine guns on March 15, 1966. The first weapons produced to the specifications of the contract were to be delivered by September 1966, with the balance due two months later in November. The Army weapons were to have the forward bolt assist and would be identified as the XM177E1. Weapons without the forward bolt assist would be known as the XM177 and be used primarily by the Air Force. To add to the confusing of nomenclature, the Air Force would assign their own names to the weapon series, beginning with GAU-5, and Colt was referring to the design as the Commando.

By November 1966, the first of the new XM177E1 weapons were starting to arrive in South Vietnam, and their distribution was completed by March 1967. The bulk of the new weapons were used by officers in the field with their platoons. Over half of the users reported not carrying the weapon by the sling, with a number of times the sling having been removed completely. Operators were using the XM177E1 as if it were a large pistol, holding the weapon by the pistol grip and allowing the buttstock to rest underneath their armpit. This made the weapon fast, easy to handle, and left the left hand free for other use.

The weapon was received enthusiastically by the users in the field. Over 90 percent of the men who carried one considered the CAR-15 to be an adequate and effective weapon. Few thought it made excessive noise or had too bright a muzzle flash, especially at night. A new, longer noise and flash suppressor had been developed by Colt and placed on the XM177 and XM177E1 weapons that had been sent to Vietnam. The new model numbers of these weapons were the Model 609 (XM177E1) and Model 610 (XM177).

Though well-received, there was still room for improvement in the CAR-15 series. The XM177E1 was modified by the addition of 1.5 inches to the overall length of the barrel. A stamped metal washer the width of the noise and flash suppressor was added and was held against the muzzle of the weapon by the suppressor. The washer was referred to as the launcher spacer by Colt, and it helped secure a 40 mm grenade launcher when it was mounted underneath the barrel. The additional barrel length also increased the dwell time for the back pressure in the barrel, aiding in the reliable operation of the weapon. This new weapon, the Colt Model 629, was used by the Army as the XM177E2. It was only the ending of the Vietnam War that caused the CAR-15 series to be ended. But the compact weapon had made a tremendous impression on the users who had carried it in combat. Specimens in the arms rooms of the Navy SEALs and Army Special Forces were used until they were literally worn out. Barrels and parts unique to the CAR-15 series had ceased being produced at Colt after 1970, and remaining weapons were cannibalized to keep others operating. The idea was too good to die, and a further development in the series would come up as the demand increased.

NATO TOWARD THE TWENTY-FIRST CENTURY

AUSTRIA

When the United States made the announcement that the 5.56 mm M16A1 rifle would become the standard arm of all of its forces, many of the NATO allies took it as a slap in the face at worst, bluntness and lack of consideration at best. Other countries could see that the industrial base of the United States would make anything adopted by the U.S. military something to be very seriously considered. The best idea would be simply to adopt the 5.56 mm cartridge and develop native designs that employed it.

One of the earliest and most striking of the new European 5.56 mm rifles was produced in Austria by Steyr-Daimler-Puch with work commencing on the new design even before the United States had stopped conducting ground combat in Vietnam. The Steyr designers had studied the reports that had come their way on the effectiveness of the 5.56 mm round used in the fighting in Southeast Asia. The light weight, limited recoil, and compact size of the cartridge fit in very well with a Steyr concept for a drastically new rifle. By 1977, testing had been completed, and the new weapon was adopted by the Austrian Army as the Sturmgewehr 77 or StG77. To the rest of the world, the new Austrian weapon was the AUG, the Armee Universal Gewehr (Universal Army Rifle).

The AUG was built as a bullpup design, the first military weapon to be accepted as such since the dropped British Enfield EM-2. The bullpup pattern generally allows for a 25 percent reduction in the overall length of a weapon. With the action behind the trigger mechanism, the AUG had a very compact and unusual silhouette. But it still retained a long barrel for accuracy and velocity. The design did not stop there. The AUG was the first accepted rifle that was made extensively out of synthetic polymer materials. The receiver of the AUG is made from a precision aluminum die casting with steel parts only used for critical applications. The stock body, grips, and magazine are all formed from tough, durable plastics. The waffle-surfaced magazine was translucent, and the rounds remaining inside of it could be seen at a glance. Most versions of the AUG also came equipped with a raised optical sighting system. The tube extended up above the receiver and kept the recoil of the weapon in line with the shoulder to help hold the muzzle down under full automatic fire. The very limited magnification of the optical sights (normally only 1.5 power) along with a circular reticle, made the sights fast and clear to use, increasing the hit probability of the weapon.

One serious drawback with the bullpup layout is that the weapon is very difficult to use by left-handed shooters. At best, a left-handed shooter can switch to firing the bullpup from his weak side; at worst, he can try to fire the weapon left-handed, usually with bad results as the ejected brass strikes him in the face. The designers of the AUG could see that the weapon would be a problem for left-handed firing, so they included a selectable ejection system. By

The AUG receiver and barrels that make up the AUG weapons family.
Steyr Mannlicher

changing the bolt for a left-handed version, and switching the ejection port cover from the left side of the stock to the right, the AUG becomes a dedicated left-handed weapon.

Another new aspect of the AUG involved the mechanics of the design. Through a straightforward gas-operated piston system, the barrel of the AUG could be removed easily by the operator without tools. Different-length barrels could be installed that changed the tactical applications of the weapon. A long barrel with an attached bipod turned the AUG into a light machine gun. For this role, Steyr designed a forty-two-round magazine for use with the weapon. A short barrel could be mounted to make the weapon a carbine, or a shorter still barrel was available for situations where the maximum in compactness is demanded.

The housing assembly that goes into the stock to secure the major internal components also supports the optical sight assembly. The housing is removable and can be exchanged for a different model with iron sights, a mounting rail for telescopic or electronic sights, or other components as required. After placing the AUG on the world arms market, Steyr produced a semiautomatic-only version for civilian and law enforcement sales. Since the introduction of the weapon in 1977, a number of police and military organizations around the world have adopted the AUG. The plastic receiver has proved strong in both desert heat and arctic cold. The bullpup design does prove slower to reload than more conventional weapons, such as the M16A1, but it has been accepted as a reasonable trade-off for the compact size and accuracy of the AUG design. One unique aspect of the polymer plastic body of the AUG is that it can be manufactured in different colors. Initially only made in green, the AUG has been seen in desert (coyote) brown and UN blue. The appearance of the AUG on the international arms scene gave a number of designers pause and forced them to rethink their conventional layouts.

FRANCE

In the 1960s, the French had been in the process of developing a new full-powered rifle chambered in 7.62 mm NATO when the success of the American 5.56 mm round in Vietnam gave them pause. The fighting in Vietnam was of national interest to the French, since they had been holding it as Indochina until the defeat of the French forces by the Communists in the mid-1950s. The advantages of the new 5.56 mm ammunition were not lost on the French, and they didn't bother modifying it in any way. Instead, they simply accepted the round, abandoned their 7.62 mm design work, and looked at developing a whole new army rifle.

As the Austrians were doing at the time, the French centered their development on a bullpup layout for the compactness of the overall package. The final design was available for testing in 1972 and resembled no other weapon available at the time. The odd-looking Fusil d'Assaut de la Manufacture d'Armes de St-Etienne had a bulbous stock that necked down to the magazine well and extended into a slim fore section of the stock. Reminiscent of the AR-10 rifle, the cocking lever resembled an upside-down trigger on the top of the receiver. To protect the cocking lever and raise the sight plane, a long carrying handle stretched the length of the weapon ahead of the action. Finally, the protruding section of barrel was stepped with raised rings behind a cylindrical slotted flash hider.

The rings around the barrel were intended to be an aid when firing rifle grenades, something the FAMAS was intended for from its inception. There was a single-cartridge magazine holder for the rifle that would not accept a ball round, only a crimp-nosed grenade launching blank. Along the side of the upper part of the receiver were the folding legs of a bipod that came as standard equipment on the FAMAS. A cheek piece was snapped in place on the stock and, when used in combination with the bipod, made the FAMAS a very accurate rifle, particularly for its size. The FAMAS was the same length as the

American XM177E2 with the stock retracted but still had a full-length, twenty-inch barrel, thanks to the bullpup layout.

To eliminate the left-handed shooting problem with the bullpup design, the builders of the FAMAS had included a simple way of changing the direction of ejection for the weapon. Any trained operator could simply strip the rifle down and remove the bolt. Switching the locations of a plug and the extractor in the face of the bolt changed the action to one that would now eject on the opposite side. The cheek piece snapped into the ejector slot on the action. By switching the parts in the bolt and moving the cheek piece to the opposite side of the weapon, the FAMAS could be changed from a right- to a left-handed weapon, an even simpler and more economical system than that used in the Steyr AUG.

Training operators on the FAMAS was made simpler by the inclusion of a controlled-burst firing mechanism. The firing system of the FAMAS could be set for safe, semiautomatic, full automatic, and controlled three-round bursts. It was recognized by the French that one of the hardest things to teach recruits is trigger control on full automatic fire. The simplest way to teach this is to just make the weapon fire one three-round burst for a single pull of the trigger. The system allowed for a maximum hit probability and minimum ammunition wastage. But the French also recognized that there is definitely a place for full automatic fire in combat and wisely included the mechanism for that capability in the action of the FAMAS.

Adopted by the French military as their standard-issue weapon in 1978, the odd shape of the FAMAS F1 (Fusil 1) caused the weapon to be nicknamed *Le Clarion* (the bugle) for its resemblance to that traditional military musical instrument.

UNITED KINGDOM

Moving into the future of the assault rifle for their own military, Great Britain resurrected their own bullpup design for the 1950s-era Enfield EM-2 that had been soundly rejected by the Americans. Intended from the beginning as a purely combat weapon, the new Enfield XL 64 Individual Weapon was short enough for soldiers to easily handle within the tight confines of an armored troop transport while still having a reasonable range and lethal terminal effects.

After careful study of the situation and borrowing from the studies that had been conducted previously, the British designers developed a new cartridge for the Enfield weapon that would consist of a rifle and light machine gun. By October 1970, the ordnance production facility Radway Green had received an order to produce a new round of ammunition based on the 5.56 mm cartridge case as used by the Americans. The 5.56 mm case would be shortened from its normal 45 mm and necked down to hold a 5 mm projectile. In March 1972, the nomenclature of the new round was changed to 4.85 mm with no other change in the design. By August that same year, the length of the cartridge case used in the 4.85 mm was lengthened from 44 mm to 49 mm. The cartridge was now known as the 4.85 × 49 mm and was produced beginning in February 1973.

As the round was being developed, so was the weapon that would fire it. Several other 5.56 mm weapon designs, significantly the Stoner 63 and AR-18 rifles, were converted to fire the 4.85 mm round as well as being changed over to a bullpup configuration. The receiver extension tube in the stock of the M16 rifle prevented it from being easily converted to a bullpup configuration, but the Stoner 63 rifle and the AR-18 both had easily removable stocks. It was a simple matter to convert them to firing a cartridge that was based on the 5.56 mm round they had originally chambered. There had been AR-15 rifles converted to the new caliber but only for ballistic studies of the round.

Experiments with the converted weapons proved out the concept, and the Enfield design team went ahead with the development of a purpose-built weapon for the 4.85 mm round. The final rifle was a stamped metal design that was fairly easy and inexpensive to produce. A long-barreled version of the design, with an attached folding bipod, was also developed as the light support weapon (LSW) of the new weapons system. An optical sight was intended for use with the new weapons. The sight unit small arms trilux (SUSAT) sight was a very rugged, compact device that mounted on the top rail of the receiver, just ahead of the ejection port.

Toward the end of the 1970s, the pressure was on for NATO to examine new weapons and decide on a secondary standard round of ammunition. Field trials of weapons and ammunition were begun in June 1978 at the German Infantry School in Hammelburg. A number of countries sent weapons and ammunition to the trials, with Britain pushing forward with their 4.85 mm Enfield Weapons System consisting of the individual weapon and the light support weapon. Most of the other weapons being examined were chambered for the 5.56 × 45 mm round, with the noteworthy exception of an exotic German entry, the Heckler & Koch caseless G11 rifle. There was still a good deal of development necessary to make the caseless ammunition concept work as well or better than the M16A1 standard it was being compared against. The G11 did not do particularly well in the trials.

The control weapons for the rifle study were the M16A1 loaded with standard-issue M193 ball and M196 tracer ammunition. The other weapon used as a control was the German Heckler & Koch G3 rifle in 7.62 mm NATO. It was only five months into the study when the British decided that the 4.85 mm round would not succeed against the 5.56 mm round. The only way to save their weapons program was to switch the caliber of the guns over to the standard 5.56 mm round. The design of the Enfield weapons system included the ability to be converted over to the American caliber, and the 4.85 mm program came to an end. The new 5.56 mm Enfield weapons were designated as "Small Arms for the 1980s" and commonly called the SA80.

Along with switching the Enfield system over to 5.56 mm, the guns were redesigned to use the standard M16 magazine. This magazine was soon declared a NATO standard so that each member country would have their weapons use the same caliber and the same magazines, greatly simplifying supply in time of conflict. None of the weapons tested in the trials were considered so superior that they should be adopted by all NATO countries. One standard that was agreed on was STANAG 4179 for the M16-style magazine. The other winner of the trials was the Belgian FN-designed SS109 ball and L110 tracer rounds.

The 5.56 mm SS109 projectile was heavier than the original bullet designed by Eugene Stoner in the late 1950s, sixty-three grains to Stoner's fifty-five grains. The interior of the SS109 projectile was also considerably more complex, with a steel core and lead filler contained within a full-metal jacket. The rifling twist to stabilize the new rounds at one turn in seven inches was nearly twice as fast as the standard one-in-twelve twist in the M16A1. The faster twist gave the SS109 projectile more stability and a greater range, with a loss of some of the wounding power that was inherent in the 5.56 mm round. Accepting the NATO findings, the United States adopted the new round as the XM855 ball and XM856 tracer rounds.

The 5.56 mm conversion of the Enfield weapon had been designated the XL70E3 when it was finally adopted in 1985. The British army finally had a bullpup-style service rifle, something they had been trying to do for decades. Only known commercially as the SA80, the new service rifle was officially known as the L85A1 but still referred to as the individual weapon or IW.

THE NEW AK

The adoption of the 5.56 mm cartridge and the rifle that fired it interested more people than just the members of NATO. Intensely interested in any military developments in the West, but particularly those of the United States, the Soviet Union wanted to closely examine the M16 rifle and its ammunition. With North Vietnam as one of their revolutionary client states they were supplying arms to, the Soviet Union was supplied with captured specimens of the M16 and its ammunition.

The low-impulse (recoil), high-speed, small-caliber projectile fascinated the Soviets, and they had no difficulty seeing the advantages it would give their AK-47 weapons platform. The Soviet project to develop a small-caliber round began in 1964 and continued into the 1970s. During the design stage of the ammunition, it was compared to the samples of the M16 and ammunition that had been captured in Southeast Asia. The round as finally designed was slimmer overall than the 7.62 × 39 mm round but very close to the same overall length. The lacquered steel case of the round was inexpensive to make and utilized little in the way of critical materials. But the true effectiveness of the ammunition lay in its complex projectile.

Examined in the West publicly for the first time in 1980, the 5.45 mm bullet is a long, slender, full-jacketed projectile that is stable in flight. The flight stability gives the 5.45 mm bullet good accuracy but would work against it in the terminal ballistics that take place after it hits the target. It is the internal construction of the projectile that makes the 5.45 mm ball one of the most lethal of the small-caliber rifle bullets.

Inside the mild-steel jacket of the 5.45 mm projectile is a small empty space in the tip of the bullet. A steel core and lead alloy filler make up the balance of the interior components of the projectile. When the projectile hits tissue or any other target or obstacle, the nose of the jacket crushes down on the air cavity. The change in the center of gravity for the projectile causes it to immediately start to yaw. The bullet tips end for end, tumbling through the target and quickly dumping its energy. It is tremendously destructive to tissue, so much so that the Afghans who faced it in the Afghan War of the 1980s referred to it as the "poison bullet."

In spite of the benefits of the new ammunition, Mikhail Kalashnikov did not like the idea of a new round for his rifle. The old veteran was centered on his 7.62 mm round, just as Stoner had been on the 7.62 mm NATO round when he was first told to change the AR-10 to a smaller caliber. Kalashnikov did not rest on his reputation and tackled the new project, but he also followed Stoner's example and handed off a good amount of the work in the new design to his staff people.

The changeover of the AK-47 pattern to the new 5.45 × 39 mm round was a great deal more than simply swapping out the barrel. The high operating pressure of the new round caused bulged barrels and damaged receivers as strength had to be balanced against weight in order to gain the most advantage from the lighter ammunition.

Adopted as the AK-74, the new rifle was seen in the West in the hands of specialized troops during the annual May Day parades in Moscow. Externally, the rifle greatly resembled its predecessor, the only obvious difference being the large cylindrical muzzle break and recoil compensator on the muzzle. The large gap in the muzzle break is visible at some distance and serves to identify most of the AK-74 series of weapons and their derivatives. A large groove is cut lengthwise into the plywood butt of the AK-74 to also help identify the weapon by touch. Internally, the basic mechanism of the AK-47 remained unchanged in the new rifle. Primarily, the bolt had been changed and an improved extractor design installed. The stamped-metal magazine had been changed to one made of dull orange fiberglass with steel components. For the most part, the AK-74 was an improved AKM and was still produced from steel stampings.

AKS-74U

The small-caliber round made the new AK-74 more accurate on both semi- and full automatic fire than was its 7.62 mm predecessor. The muzzle break helped cut back on the lesser recoil of the light projectile, making the weapon much easier to hold on target, even while firing a long burst. This increased accuracy more than doubled the effective range of the AK-74 over that of the AK-47. And there was no new training needed for a veteran soldier to be able to pick up the AK-74 and immediately be familiar with its operation. The weapon and its derivatives have proved extremely successful with over seven million specimens having been made during the 1980s in the Soviet Union. It was astonishing to Western analysts when the Soviets completely changed over their military from the 7.62 mm AK-47 to the 5.45 mm AK-74. It was an amazing logistical feat.

The advantages of the small-caliber, high-velocity cartridge was not the only thing the Soviets learned from the United States and the weapons they employed in Vietnam. The tactical advantages of the CAR-15/XM177 family of weapons also weren't lost on them. Development of a CAR-15 equivalent version of what would become the AK-74 began in the late 1960s with a working specimen available in 1970. The first model had a folding stock that looked a lot like the stock from the old PPS 43 submachine gun in that it folded up and over the top of the weapon. The 1973 version had an underfolding stock like that of the AKMS, another had a triangular-shaped stock that folded up against the right side of the weapon, and the final version of the short AK-74 was produced with a triangular metal stock that folded up against the left side of the weapon.

All of the guns had several new design aspects in common. The top cover of the weapon was hinged so that it opened up but was still attached to the weapon by the front. This hinged aspect of the top cover helped ensure that the short rifles had accuracy as the rear sight had been moved back from its normal position where it would have been located on the full-sized rifle.

The rear sight of the short AK was a simple L-shaped flip sight. It had been moved back onto the top cover, since the barrels of the shortened weapons were less than half the length of the standard AK-47 models. The hand guard had been shortened, and the front sight block, with its gas port and forward section of the gas system, remounted on the barrel. With the rear sight moved to the top cover, the weapon still had a reasonable sight radius that would give fair accuracy.

To prevent some of the same problems that had occurred with the CAR-15 series, the shortened Kalashnikov had an unusual muzzle device attached to the barrel just ahead of the front sight. The large cylinder acted as an expansion chamber for the propellant gases, maintaining a high pressure curve to ensure the proper operation of the gas system. The muzzle device also cut back on the large blast and muzzle flash that is very characteristic of the shortened weapons that are firing a cartridge designed for a much longer barrel. A large cone is at the very muzzle of the weapon, also cutting down on the flash of firing.

Intended for specialists, vehicle crews, and others who had missions that required that they work in close quarters, the shortened AK-74 was officially adopted by the Soviet military in 1979, and deliveries of the weapon started in 1980. Officially, the weapon is known as the AKS-74U, U for *ukorochennyj* (shortened) but has picked up a number of nicknames. In the Soviet military and police units (where it has become very popular), the weapon is also known as the *Ksysusha*, a feminine nickname, and *Okurok* (cigarette stub). In the West, the weapon has been called the AKR80 by the U.S. military and the Krinkov by a number of popular gun writers. Probably the most famous user of the short, very handy little weapon is Osama bin Laden, who is almost always shown in pictures and videos with an AKS-74U within close reach.

Whoever the user and whatever the name, the AKS-74U has filled the same niche that the compact assault rifle has in the West. It is very popular among Russian special operations units and counterterrorist teams for its quick handling characteristics and reasonable power.

FURTHER CHANGES IN THE M16: THE M16A2

The adoption by NATO of the Belgian SS109 round as the standard 5.56 mm round did cause some problems for the U.S. military. The U.S. troops in Europe who were still armed with M14 rifles needed to be rearmed to meet the requirement stated by the Pentagon. But the new NATO round would not operate well with the rifling twist rate in the M16A1 rifle. When fired with the one-in-twelve-inch twist rate, the SS109 projectile lost accuracy badly. This alone was enough to cause a replacement of the barrels that were already in use in the Army. A new rifling rate of one turn in seven inches would stabilize the new projectile, and the weapon could still operate with the earlier fifty-five-grain M193 ball round, which the U.S. military had large stockpiles of.

It was the U.S. Marine Corps that pushed forward with a request for a new infantry rifle. The Marines had maintained their tradition of long-range marksmanship training established prior to World War I. With the design now considered very reliable, the M16A1 was grudgingly accepted as a good combat weapon, but the Marines wanted something better. In December 1981, they put their requirements down on paper when the USMC issued a "statement of need" for a better rifle. They would settle for an improved version of the M16A1 as long as it matched a number of their requirements. A Joint Service Rifle Product Improvement Program was established, and fifty rifles were ordered from Colt to be delivered in November 1981.

The new weapons included a number of improvements Colt already had available. These included a heavier barrel (with the new rifling twist needed for the SS109 round), improved sights, stronger parts, and something that was straight from the gravel-belly's opinion sheet, removal of the full-automatic capability of the weapon.

The new weapons, designated the M16A1E1, did not have a position on the selector for full automatic. Instead, a limiter mechanism had been built into the weapon that restricted them to three-round bursts only. Round handguards replaced the triangular ones of the Vietnam era, eliminating the need for right and left parts. The flash hider was modified for the fourth time, this one eliminating the slots along the bottom of the device so that it also acted as a compensator and would not kick up material when the weapon was fired in the prone position. The stock was slightly longer and made of a stronger material. The pistol grip was changed for a firmer and more comfortable hold, especially when wearing gloves, and the sights were greatly changed.

The front sight post of the M16A1E1 had been changed from the round version, which had been used on the weapon since the first AR-15s, to a square post that made for a sharper sight picture. The biggest change in the sighting system was in the rear sight. The simple flip-over peep sight of the A1 had been replaced with a large, movable sight base placed above a range drum that would allow it to be adjusted out to 800 meters. There was also a large windage knob on the right side of the sight to allow for more precise adjustments than had ever been possible with the M16A1.

Outside of other changes and modifications to make the weapon easier to operate and maintain, the M16A1E1 had a heavy barrel option for greater rigidity and accuracy. The changes made the new, improved version of the M16 a heavier weapon than the earlier model. The supposedly "heavier" barrel on the new weapon turned out to be something of a sham. Only the front part of the barrel, that section ahead of the front sight, was actually thicker. In order for the new weapon to mount the M203 40 mm grenade launcher, the barrel underneath the handguards was the same diameter as that of the M16A1. There was little improvement in the characteristics of the barrel on the new weapon over that of the old, outside of the new rifling twist.

Having been built almost exactly to Marine Corps specifications, the M16A1E1 was enthusiastically recommended as a replacement for the M16A1. The weapon had performed well, especially on the firing ranges, where the adjustable sights could be used to their greatest advantage. There were still disadvantages to the weapon, but it was the best available. In September 1982, the new rifle was officially accepted for issue as the M16A2 rifle.

The Marine Corps began accepting the M16A2 in 1983, while the Army remained fixed on the M16A1 for the time being. NATO standardization and the issue of the M855 ball and M856 tracer rounds started to eliminate the practical use of the M16A1. The Army finally switched to the M16A2 in 1985.

As Colt put the M16A2 into production, engineers at the company adopted the aspects of the A2 rifle to a complete family of weapons. Among the new models produced as part of the Colt M16A2 Weapon System were the M16A2 Carbine (Model 723) and the M16A2 Commando (Model 733). The carbine version of the weapon was produced in part to meet a 1985 request from the Army Research and Development Center for forty prototype weapons for evaluation. The new weapons, to be delivered in February 1986, would be the first of the XM4 carbines. The popularity of the CAR-15/XM177 weapons had not been forgotten.

The new Carbine had a 14.5-inch barrel and the Commando an 11.5-inch barrel, while both weapons also had the sliding stock and round hand guards from the CAR-15 days. The stocks were modified over the development of the XM4 to where they were made from tough nylon and other

The Colt Modular Weapon System, a family of weapons all based on the basic M16 action.
Kevin Dockery

polymers and had four different lengths the stock could be locked into. The stock could now be adjusted by the user to fit comfortably when shouldered over body armor or load-carrying gear. The longer barrel on the Carbine gave it an improved reliability over the old XM177E2 while eliminating any need for the flash and noise suppressor of the earlier weapon. The Carbine originally had a thin barrel with the same contour as the original M16A1 barrel but including the new faster twist rate. It was also capable of full automatic fire, though the three-round burst system could be installed by Colt at a customer's request. Both the Carbine and the Commando were in Colt commercial literature in 1985.

The Carbine model was of particular interest to the Army Special Forces and other special operations units. For five years, Colt was making and selling commercial versions of the Model 723, with 15,000 weapons going out into the international marketplace. The Special Forces were not left behind as Colt sold over 5,000 Carbines to them over the same time period. Finally, the XM4 was developed enough to meet the Army's standards. The barrel had been made thicker with a noticeable step, a reduction in diameter, about midway between the front sight assembly and the flash hider. This step was to allow the Carbine to mount the M203 grenade launcher. In 1993, Colt received an order for 18,597 of the new Carbines, to be identified as the M4. The weapons were the Colt Model 720 with the three-round burst mechanism. The planned procurement of the new weapon was for 52,000 M4s along with their needed spare parts.

PICATINNY RAIL

During the 1970s, an engineer designed an upper receiver for the M16A1 sniper rifle variation that did not have the normal carrying handle. Instead, there was a rear sight but also a mounting rail that could accept an optical sight. The design did not develop further, but it was the first time a flat-top receiver with a mounting surface had been produced. This action was repeated at Picatinny Arsenal in 1982 when a Marine officer and an arsenal engineer machined off the handle from the upper receiver of an M16A1. On the flat surface that was created on the upper receiver, the men secured a commercial Weaver telescopic sight rail. The weapon could now accept a number of different optical sights as long as they could be mounted to a Weaver rail.

The Weaver scope mounting system had been a commercial success for a number of years before it was used at Picatinny on that modified M16A1 upper receiver. The Weaver mounting system centered on a variety of base mounts that could fit a wide variety of commercial firearms. The common factor among the mounts was a flat top of specified width with angular edges. Along the surface of the mount were cut grooves that went from side to side. A standard mounting ring would clamp down on the angular edges of the mount with the clamping screw fitting into one of the grooves. The system also had long mounting rails that could be machined to fit a custom weapon and give a mounting surface where a sighting device could be moved forward or backward to suit a particular shooter.

The general idea of the Weaver rail was taken by the engineers at Picatinny and modified to better suit military applications. Dimensions and cross sections were standardized. The diagonal grooves across the surface of the rail were cut to a square cross section and evenly spaced out. The final result was a standard rail that could be used to securely mount a wide range of accessories, sights, and other devices. The rail system was known as the MIL-STD-1913 and was a standard set of dimensions that could be issued by the military to suppliers and manufacturers. The common name of the device came from the place where it was developed; it is called a Picatinny rail.

THE ADVANCED COMBAT RIFLE

From 1986 to 1990, the U.S. Army again tried to come up with a major leap in firearms technology, a leap that would produce the combat rifle for the twenty-first century. The program was known as the ACR, for Advanced Combat Rifle. It was also referred to as the Advanced Individual Weapons System (AIWS) program. By either name—ACR was far the more common—the idea was to come up with something really new in firearms or at least demonstrate a major improvement over the M16 series.

Development programs that had already been awarded some years earlier to weapons companies were to have their results submitted to the ACR tests. The basic requirement of the program was to come up with a weapon that was a 100 percent improvement on the hit probability, terminal effects, and other capabilities of the M16A2 rifle. The U.S. Army Infantry School felt that the rifle had already reached the peak of its destructive potential and that the only way to go forward from that would be to utilize energetic projectiles, another term for explosive-filled warheads.

COLT ACR

The most traditional-appearing of the weapons tested in Phase III of the ACR program in the late 1980s was the Colt ACR candidate. The candidate was based on an M16A2 with a significant number of modifications to the layout of the design. Most striking of these changes was a long aiming/pointing rib along the upper part of the handguards. The long, flat surface of the aiming/pointing rib was to take advantage of the natural characteristics of the eye. The long plane of the rib could be easily drawn up and quickly pointed at a fleeting target, much like the rib on a shotgun barrel is used.

For more precision aiming, the top of the upper receiver of the Colt had been machined into a flat mounting surface where an optical sight could be mounted. A removable handle assembly with a standard iron sight was made to attach to the same mounting surface as an option. Other control and handling characteristics of the Colt ACR candidate had been modified and generally improved from those of the M16A2. A special muzzle brake assembly helped make the weapon more controllable on full automatic or rapid semiautomatic fire.

The final improvement in the Colt ACR, the means to increase its hit probability and terminal effects, was not in the rifle but in a specialized round of ammunition designed for it. A 5.56 mm duplex round was designed so that the Colt ACR had two projectiles leave the barrel for each round it fired. The two projectiles in the final duplex round design were of slightly different weights, thirty-five and thirty-three grains. The leading projectile was the heavier of the two and was intended to fly along the path of aim of the weapon when it was fired. The trailing projectile was designed to disburse randomly along the same flight path as the leading projectile in order to hit anywhere in a 360-degree circle around the main point of impact. The special ammunition gave the Colt ACR candidate twice the hit probability of a standard M16A2 while still retaining much of the terminal effects. But the maximum effective range of the light projectiles in the duplex round was only around 325 meters. That was a factor that would work badly against the Colt ACR candidate weapon.

AAI ACR

The AAI ACR candidate also had a traditional rifle layout, but that was where the resemblance ended. Once more, AAI was championing the concept of the discreet flechette, a single, needle-shaped, fin-stabilized projectile launched at a high velocity. The flechette itself was very much like the earlier versions used by AAI during the SPIW project. The flechette was .062 inch in diameter and slightly over 1.62 inches long, weighing barely over ten grains. The cartridge case used to fire the finned needle was a standard 5.56 × 45 mm one, and it fired the flechette to a muzzle velocity of over 4,500 feet per second. The muzzle velocity was more than fast enough to ensure the hooking effect would take place when the flechette struck flesh.

A drawback with the AAI ACR candidate was that it could chamber a standard 5.56 mm round, but firing regular ball ammunition would badly damage the gas system of the rifle. A modified magazine was made that could not be loaded with a ball round of ammunition. The magazine well of the AAI weapon would only lock the modified magazine in place, preventing a standard magazine from even being inserted. But a single round of ball ammo could have conceivably been loaded into the chamber of the AAI weapon by hand, a serious flaw in the design.

Instead of taking advantage of the very low recoil impulse of the flechette projectile, AAI had their ACR candidate fire mechanically controlled, three-round bursts at 1,800 rounds per minute cyclic rate of fire to help minimize dispersion of the projectiles. The high velocity and light weight of the projectiles gave them a fairly flat trajectory and helped in aiming over distances. There was also a long rib included along the top of the AAI ACR to aid the soldier in conducting quick, instinctive firing without proper aiming.

STEYR-MANNLICHER ACR

The flechette was not uniquely an AAI, or even an American concept. For the Austrian ACR candidate, Steyr also submitted a very advanced weapon that fired a single discrete flechette. The projectile to the Steyr weapon was a 9.85-grain carbon-steel needle ground to a sharp point with four formed fins on its base, the classic antipersonnel flechette. The flechette leaves the barrel of the Steyr weapon at nearly 5,000 feet per second, traveling to its maximum effective range of 600 meters in less than half a second. This speed gives the projectile a flat trajectory, eliminating much of the guesswork a soldier would normally have to do to place his aiming point according to the range to the target. Instead, the flechette simply has to be aimed at the center of mass of a target, and it will strike a critical area of the body from point-blank range out to 600 meters. In addition, the projectile gets out to range so quickly that the effect of movement on the part of the target is minimized; the target just can't duck the shot.

The weapon that Steyr submitted to launch their projectile was obviously based on the extensive experience with the AUG rifle. A compact bullpup design made primarily of polymers, the Steyr ACR is less than a yard long, 25 percent shorter than the control weapon, the M16A2. It was fast and easy to maneuver in confined areas and very quick to bring to the shoulder. One of the noted drawbacks of the bullpup layout in all of the military weapons that use it is the need to take the weapon down from the shoulder to reload it. With the magazine at the back of the stock, it is very difficult for the shooter to simply drop an empty mag and insert a loaded one. Along with the difficulty of a bullpup to be fired in the weak-hand (left) position, it is the slowness of reloading that is pointed at by critics of the design.

The Steyr ACR was designed from the start to be completely ambidextrous. The few controls on the weapon can be easily operated with either hand and from either shoulder. The problem of empty cartridge ejection is taken care of by having the fired casings ejected downward from the underside of the weapon with the ejection port a short distance in front of the magazine.

It is the action of the Steyr ACR that was the most unusual aspect of the weapon when combined with the ammunition. The round was called the synthetic cased flechette (SCF) and was a straight cylinder of plastic with no rim or extractor groove. The primer to the cartridge was formed in a ring around the body of the casing. Using this ignition system allowed the Steyr ACR to utilize a chamber piece that was not an integral part of the barrel. Independently movable, the chamber piece would be below the barrel and in front of the magazine when it was in the loading position. The SCF round would be pushed forward out of the magazine by a rammer mechanism. When a fresh round entered the chamber, the fired casing from the previous cartridge would be pushed forward and ejected out of the weapon. As the action continued to operate, the chamber would be raised into position and locked into place in line with the barrel. The ramming and raising cycle only took place while the weapon was firing. When the trigger hadn't been pulled, the chamber was locked into the lower position. It was essentially an open-bolt system that left the barrel open for cooling but without the accuracy-damaging jar that would normally be caused when an open-bolt weapon is fired.

The gas piston that operated the action of the Steyr ACR was an annular type that surrounded the barrel. A simple mechanical linkage connected it to the chamber piece, and the entire mechanism operated smoothly with no unusual movement noticed by the military testers. It was a sleek, futuristic design with some real possibilities in some of its aspects. But it was not the most advanced weapon in the ACR program.

HECKLER & KOCH ACR

The German submission for the ACR program was the most distinctive of all of the weapons. It effectively utilized a new form of ammunition that had been dreamed about by weapons designers for over one hundred years but never successfully adapted to an effective weapon. The candidate was the H&K G11, a completely enclosed bullpup rifle that fired caseless ammunition.

The caseless cartridge concept, where the round of ammunition consists of little more than the primer, propellant, and projectile, had been one that the Germans had striven to perfect since before the days of World War II.

In the rubble of Hillerslaben Proving Ground and the offices of Polte-Magdeburg in Germany after the war, four rounds of caseless 8 mm rifle ammunition were uncovered. The interrogation of a German Army officer in August turned up information that the Germans had been working on the problem of a caseless cartridge since 1932. In 1969, the caseless problem was tackled once again by German engineers, as it had been in the United States and elsewhere.

The West German military, the Bundeswehr, had issued a requirement for the development of a weapon with a greatly improved hit probability over that of the 7.62 mm NATO rifle they were already equipped with, the G3 rifle. Heckler & Koch decided not to conduct the development of a contemporary rifle but to try to do a quantum leap in firearms technology and develop a whole new concept of weapon and ammunition. And for twenty years, they worked on it.

With the caseless cartridge, there is no fired casing to extract and eject, and these actions are removed from the firing cycle. The propellant that forms the cartridge can be shaped into the most efficient contour for storage and feeding from a magazine. And with the metal cartridge case removed from the equation, a large percentage of the overall weight of the cartridge is removed. As a secondary consideration, with the cartridge case being removed, the amount of critical material demanded by the ammunition manufacture during wartime is also minimized.

The advantages of the caseless round were numerous, and the H&K engineering team assigned to the project developed an innovative approach to the weapon once a basic round had been developed. The problem of fabricating the round itself was given over to Dynamit Nobel, noted experts in the fields of projectile design and propellant composition. The round itself went through a number of different designs as it evolved into what was used in the tests.

An earlier version of the H&K design had been submitted and declined for adoption during the 1978–79 NATO small-caliber trials. The weapon and ammunition had both been improved and modified as a result of those tests. The final result of the development was a weapon that was being scheduled as the next primary small arm of the West German forces to take them well into the twenty-first century. As the G11 was undergoing its final testing in Germany before limited issue began, it was simultaneously submitted in a slightly modified form to the U.S. Army's ACR trials.

The heart of the G11 system is the unique round of ammunition it fires. Known in Germany as the 4.73×33 caseless, the H&K round was referred to as the 4.92×33 in the United States due to a different baseline of measurement. The projectile is fully telescoped into the round; only the plastic-covered nose of the bullet is visible when you look down into the top of the round. The body of the ammunition is a brick red in color, rectangular, with a white plastic cap, and formed into a square cross section. The propellant that the round is made from is a special high-temperature material based on a modified high explosive. It was the temperature issue that affected the development of the round the most after the general operating system had been decided upon.

Without the metallic cartridge case to remove some of the excess heat generated by firing, the caseless round faces the problem of a rapidly heating chamber, one that soon becomes even hotter than when the same number of rounds is fired in a regular weapon. Cook-offs, the uncontrollable ignition of a cartridge from the residual heat in a firing chamber, have long been a problem in automatic weapons. In excessive heating cases in some machine guns, rounds have ignited prior to being locked into the chamber by the bolt. The force of a cartridge rupturing will damage a weapon and the firer operating it from fragments of metal and hot gases. It is the main reason that many automatic weapons designed for sustained fire use the open-bolt principle so that the rounds are not chambered until just before they are to be fired.

These heating problems and the resulting cook-offs were a serious issue with the earlier versions of the G11. Modifications in design of the action and especially that of the propellant helped eliminate much of the overheating problems. During testing, one of the later-generation G11 weapons fired a total of one hundred rounds at a rate of eighty-five rounds per minute. The weapon was then left with a live round in the hot chamber and the barrel pointing downrange. After a full thirty minutes had passed, the weapon had cooled completely with the chambered round never having been fired. The weapon was then picked up, and the round discharged downrange.

To handle the unique rounds of ammunition, Heckler & Koch developed an equally unique action. The round of ammunition is oriented in the magazine in a nose-down position. To feed the shot, a rammer mechanism pushed the round down into a rotating cylindrical disk-shaped breechblock with a square cross-section chamber cut through its center. The round seats in the cylinder, which rotates clockwise a quarter of a turn to both line up the round with the barrel and seal off the chamber. A rotary firing pin at the rear of the chamber strikes the primer of the caseless round, igniting it and continuing the firing cycle.

A small booster pellet of propellant is first ignited by the primer, driving the projectile through the plastic retainer cap and into the barrel, where it seals off the system. The solid propellant making up the remainder of the cartridge case also ignites from the booster pellet and burns to drive the projectile from the barrel.

In the case of a misfire or the need to clear the weapon, the cocking handle on the outside of the casing can be rotated, driving the round remaining in the chamber out of a small port in the bottom of the weapon.

No special seals are used to prevent the escape of propellant gases from the chamber. Instead, the design is dependent on the use of close machining tolerances to maintain a gas-tight seal. These tolerances are made practical by the use of high-tech machining processes in the manufacture of the weapon, processes that were not economically available just a decade or so earlier.

The unusual action of the weapon continues to move during the operating cycle with both rotary and linear motion. A gas cylinder to the side of the barrel

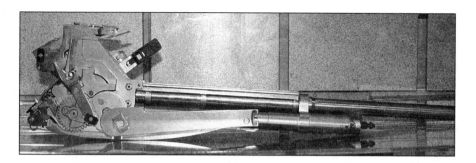

The internal action of the G11 rifle. The barrel is extending out to the right.
Kevin Dockery

operates gearing that rotates the cylinder breech, aligning the chamber with the magazine. There is no extraction and ejection portion of the firing cycle, as the only remains from the caseless round are the bits of a small plastic cap and a bit of copper foil from the primer. None of these materials are able to interfere with the incoming round shoved into place by the rammer.

As the action of the weapon continues through the firing cycle, it is also recoiling along guides built into the body of the G11. As the action recoils in the stock, the long polymer magazine moves with it to maintain the alignment of the feed system. A return spring mechanism drives the action forward and back into the battery position after every shot. The very short, straight feed of the round into the chamber, combined with the removal of the need for extraction and ejection as well as simplification of other portions of the firing cycle, allow the action of the G11 to function at a very high rate of speed.

On normal full-automatic fire, the weapon functions at a relatively sedate 600 rounds per minute maximum cyclic rate as the next round is not fired until the action has moved through its entire length of travel and returned to the forward position. With the selector set at a three-round burst, the mechanism cycles at its maximum mechanical rate of 2,100 to 2,200 rounds per second.

Under normal full-automatic fire, it takes from about 120 to 140 milliseconds for the action of the G11 to reach the full rearward point of its travel, where it bears on the outer casing and the firer feels the recoil of the shot. When set to a three-round burst and fired, it takes the weapon about 55 to 60 milliseconds to cycle through the entire burst. At that rate of fire, the last projectile has left the barrel before the action has reached the end of its travel and the firer can feel the recoil.

Even though the total recoil force of the burst of 4.73 mm projectiles is greater than that of a single 7.62×51 mm round, the effect on the accuracy of the shooter is almost negligible. The salvo fire of three rounds at a very high cyclic rate combined with the delayed effect of recoil on the shooter minimizes dispersion of the projectiles. This gives the shotgunlike pattern to the projectiles fired by the G11, greatly increasing the hit probability for at least one of them striking the target during a high-stress engagement.

In spite of the complex interior mechanism and rapid cycling of the G11 action, it is very dependable. The weapon has a total system malfunction rate of one for every 2,200 rounds fired. Even at that rate, only a third of the malfunctions are directly attributable to the caseless ammunition. This is a comparable rate to many of the accepted conventional-ammunition military weapons of the day.

ACR TEST RESULTS

The advanced combat rifle tests were some of the most grueling range firings that could be conducted on the part of the soldiers. The intention was to come as close as possible to the stress of combat short of actually shooting at the troops as they used the new weapons. The difficulty in reproducing the aiming errors that are experienced in combat had the designers of the tests including task-oriented stresses and well as hard physical exercise included in the workups prior to a range firing. This gave the tests some of the most exacting data available on how the ACR weapons would handle in combat and what the practical hit probabilities might be with them.

None of the experimental weapons produced the 100 percent improvements in hit probability that were desired for a new-issue rifle. One of the reasons for this was that the baseline M16A2 rifles performed particularly well during the tests, which may be due in part to their familiarity with the evaluating troops in the high-stress situations. Though a number of advances in technology had improved the accuracy of the discrete flechette as fired by a rifle, the projectile design still did not come up to the accuracy standard of a conventional projectile. The destructive capacity of the flechette against targets was noted and has been considered as a reason to keep developing them for use in area-effect weapons but not as individual rifle-caliber projectiles.

The caseless system used in the G11 proved very promising, but the weapon was considered to still need a good deal of development and fielding to prove it out further. This would have been provided by the German Army issuing the weapon as was planned to begin in the early 1990s. The conservative opinions of the Army leadership would need much more convincing before a radical change such as abandoning the conventional cartridge case and the vast stockpiles of ammunition already in place could be seriously considered.

The fact that none of the test weapons had managed to meet the 100 percent improvement demand over the performance of the M16A2 was looked at by the U.S. Army Infantry School as more evidence that the conventional rifle had reached the pinnacle of its development. Their opinion was that the only way to greatly improve the hit probability of the basic infantry weapon was to use an exploding warhead. The blast and fragmentation of such a projectile would have an area of effect, a footprint, much larger than could be formed by any solid, kinetic-energy bullet or even a swarm of them. This was part of the justification to begin the development of the Objective Individual Combat Weapon program, the OICW that would be the combination of a point target kinetic energy weapon (rifle) and an area effect explosive projectile weapon. It eventually evolved into the XM29 Integrated Airburst Weapon System. Both it and the OICW are covered in the "Area Weapons" section of this book.

G11K2

The failure of the G11 rifle to surpass all of the other weapons used in the American ACR trials was not the end of the development of the weapon. The weapon continued to be developed in Germany. Fielding tests by the German Bundeswehr in the late 1980s corresponded with the same time frame that the ACR tests were being conducted. The German experiences with the weapon resulted in some suggested changes in the design, mostly on the exterior characteristics of the weapon. Testing had shown that the G11 was easier to use by novice shooters than the issue German G3 rifle. Recruits undergoing marksmanship training averaged 50 percent more hits on the targets when firing the G11 as compared to the much heavier 7.62 × 51 mm G3.

The final pattern of the G11 rifle was the G11K2. It carried three magazines across the top of the receiver, parallel with the barrel. Only the center magazine was feeding into the action while the other two were spares for quick reloading. It was the most convenient way to carry and use the particularly long 4.73 × 33 mm caseless magazines. The magazine capacity had been lessened by five rounds, shortening the feed device by over an inch and a half in length. With three magazines in place, the G11K2 had 135 rounds on the weapon with 45 rounds ready to feed, and it still weighed less than ten pounds.

Modifications to the front end of the G11K2 receiver allowed the weapon to mount a bipod, bayonet, or other accessory. The sight and handle assembly was also modified so that it could be removed by the operator and replaced with a different sighting system such as a thermal or starlight scope. The optical sight in the handle assembly remained the same as earlier versions, a one-to-one-power, well-protected system that allowed the operator to sight on a target while keeping both eyes open. This allowed for a very rapid target acquisition while maintaining full observation of the battlefield. The reticle of the sight was illuminated for easier use at night or in low-light conditions.

An initial lot of approximately 1,000 G11K2 weapons were delivered to the Bundeswehr in 1990 for use by special operations troops. The weapon was being scheduled for general army-wide adoption by the early 1990s. To support the G11 weapon, a light machine gun chambered for the 4.73 × 33 mm caseless round was also being developed. The LMG11 project was intended to result in a weapon that could be easily carried and used by one man. With 300 rounds loaded into the magazine in the buttstock of the LMG11, it would still weigh less than sixteen pounds. The LMG11, along with a select-fire pistol concept chambered for a shorter 4.73 × 25 mm caseless round were never completed.

The reunification of Germany in late 1989 and 1990 changed the political and economic picture for the country. The fall of the Communist East German government and the apparent impending dissolution of the Soviet Union were greatly affecting the possible enemy forces that would have been facing Germany and NATO. There were no funds available for a complete changeover of the military from the 7.62 mm NATO G3 to the 4.73 mm G11 weapon, no matter how promising it looked.

With the development of the weapon being almost complete and the G11K2 ready to go into full production, the project was canceled in 1992. The resulting financial loss from the very expensive development of the G11 concept almost resulted in the destruction of the Heckler & Koch company. It was sold to a series of British firms in the mid-1990s, changing management hands several times in the process. It finally returned to German hands in the early years of the new millennium.

VEC-91

The advanced caseless cartridge concept was not abandoned with the cancellation of the G11 project, although that action effectively ended the military production of such a weapon for years. A civilian firearms firm, the Voere Company of Austria, released a caseless rifle onto the civilian market in 1991. The Voere Electronic Caseless (VEC) Model 91 Lightning rifle has a conventional, traditional sporting layout with a gracefully curved walnut stock in Bavarian style complete with checkering on the wood and hunting-style sling swivels.

The basic action of the VEC-91 appears from the outside to be a standard bolt-action weapon suitable for general hunting within the limitations of its caliber. Internally, the VEC-91 is unlike any civilian rifle ever produced. The bolt of the action locks to seal the barrel through the use of a pair of locking lugs as any standard rifle. What is missing in the bolt is any form of standard firing pin. Instead of a spring-loaded striker, the firing mechanism uses a ceramic pin to ignite the primer, firing the weapon.

The round to the VEC-91 has a body of pressed nitrocellulose propellant, a bolt-action sporting weapon not having the heating and cook-off

Caseless ammunition, from left to right, is an experimental 5.56 mm caseless round made in the USA with a casing of compressed smokeless powder and a binder. In the center is the 4.73×33 mm round of the G11K2; on the right is the 5.56 mm Voere commercial caseless round.
Kevin Dockery

problems of a full automatic military weapon such as the G11. The center core of the caseless round holds a loose booster charge of power above an electrically fired primer. The soft-nosed hunting bullet is seated in the front of the propellant body with about half of the projectile being exposed.

The trigger of the VEC-91 appears as a standard mechanism, but the curved trigger is the bottom part of a spring-loaded electric switch. By adjusting the pressure of the spring on the trigger, the weight of pull required to trip the switch can be adjusted by the user from a very light target trigger to a heavy one that would be suitable for safely hunting while wearing gloves. The trigger switch closes the circuit between the two fifteen-volt camera-type batteries held in the pistol grip cap on the stock to the electrically fired primer of the caseless round in the chamber.

The lack of a standard firing pin and other percussion ignition mechanisms cut back on the lock time of the VEC-91, making the lag between pulling the trigger and the chambered cartridge firing almost instantaneous. In a standard percussion system there is a slight delay, on the order of a fraction of a second, between the trigger being pulled and the weapon firing. Making that delay shorter increases the overall accuracy of the rifle by cutting back on the amount of time that the weapon can vibrate or otherwise move off target while being aimed.

The type of cartridge used by the Voere caseless weapon was developed by an Austrian inventor, Hubert Usel, and has been named the Usel Caseless Cartridge (UCC) in his honor. The commercial sale of the rifle has been limited in spite of a number of different models being produced, including a heavy-barreled Varmint model suitable for target shooting, the VEC-91HB, and a less expensive synthetic stocked filed model weapon, the VEC-91SS. Sales of the weapons in the United States have been limited due to the difficulty in obtaining ammunition in quantity, but if the demand for such a weapon increases, more will be imported, and other caseless designs will be developed all over the world. The production of the innovative rifle series has been a financially risky venture by the Voere Company; however, the weapon and ammunition have remained on the international market since their introduction.

THE SOPMOD KIT AND THE M4/M4A1 CARBINE

With the adoption of the M16A2 rifle, an interest was shown by the military for a new version of the Vietnam-era XM177 weapon to be produced to fire the new M855 cartridge. The new weapon was to be a general-purpose carbine for issue to forces who had a need for a more compact weapon than the issue rifle due to mission constraints or the lack of room in vehicles or other transport. Colt addressed the issue with an examination of the shortcomings of the XM177 series. As had been determined by a number of carbine-type weapons that had been produced for commercial sale, Colt had learned that a slightly longer barrel allowed the gas system of the M16 to operate reliably without a large flash and noise suppressor on the barrel.

A contract for what was to be called the XM4 was issued in June 1985 with the first weapons due early in the following year. The weapon finally developed had a 14.5-inch barrel with a standard flash hider on the end of the muzzle. There was an odd reduced-diameter step in the barrel of the XM4 so that the slightly thicker barrel—for greater heat absorption and strength—could mount the standard M203 grenade launcher. Other improvements in the design had increased the dependability of the shorter weapon as well as lightening it considerably from the parent M16A2 rifle. It was very well-received by the special operations community, who proceeded to make the M4 their standard-issue shoulder weapon.

One of the results of the ACR program that had proved of value was the new sighting systems that could be attached to the flat-top Colt ACR candidate. The further development of the Picatinny rail and its acceptance as military standard 1913 in February 1995 provided a standard means of attaching accessories and sights to weapons. The adoption of the Knight's Armament Company rail interface system (RIS) changed the front handguard system of the M4 carbine to one that was made up of four MIL-STD-1913 mounting rails. This made for a very strong and ridged series of surfaces to attach a number of aiming and handling devices.

The special operations community was able to request the development of a kit made up of off-the-shelf items to be mounted on their M4 carbines in order to increase their value in the unique combat situations often encountered by them. The result of the program was the Special Operations Peculiar Modification Accessory (SOPMOD) kit and the M4A1 carbine. The basic idea for the kit had been under consideration since 1989, while the ACR program was still active. At that time it was known as the Modular Close Combat Carbine Project. By 1993, the official outline of the program had been approved and the SOPMOD kit developed at the Crane Division of the Naval Surface Warfare Center in Indiana.

The M4A1 carbine was the M4 carbine with a full-automatic fire capability and would be the primary base weapon used with the SOPMOD kit. The most notable change in the M4A1 was the removal of the upper carrying handle and sight assembly and its replacement with a flat top made up of a MIL-STD-1913 rail machined into the top of the weapon. A separate carrying handle/sight assembly was produced for the weapon, but with the availability of the SOPMOD kit, the handle sight is rarely used. After the initial production of the M4 carbine had been delivered, all weapons, both the M4 and the M4A1, were built with the flat-top receivers with the MIL-STD-1913 rail machined as an integral part of the assembly.

The SOPMOD kit consists of a selection of sights, aiming devices, illuminators, and grips in addition to a short version of the 40 mm M203 grenade launcher (the M203A1), and Knight's Rail Interface System. The Block I (first issue) kit consisted of the following accessories:

Trijicon Model TA01NSN 4×32 mm Advanced Combat Optical Gun sight (ACOG)

Trijicon Model RX01M4A1 ACOG reflex sight

M203A1 40 mm quick-detachable grenade launcher with a nine-inch barrel

Rail Interface System

Vertical forward handgrip

M203A1 leaf sight assembly

AN/PEQ-2 Infrared target designators

AN/PEQ-5 visible laser

Quick detachable sound suppressor

Visible light illuminator

AN/PVS-14 miniature night vision sight

Backup iron sight (In place of the handle/sight assembly)

Combat sling assembly

Mounts for the various sights

Aimpoint Comp M red dot reflex sight

And additional materials as they became available for issue. The SOPMOD kit does not require any major change in nomenclature or documentation if a new item is deemed valuable for inclusion in the kit. This is a major factor in being able to quickly field new developments in the special operations community.

The SOPMOD kit was improved with input from the users in the field and Block II, III, and more kits had been planned for future use. New developments in weapons technology, particularly the Special Operations Combat Assault Rifle (SCAR) series of weapons, have resulted in the future of the SOPMOD system being put on hold while new requirements are considered.

The basic SOPMOD system had very successfully replaced the duct tape, hose clamps, and other field-expedient methods that special operations troops had used in the past to attach nonissue devices to their primary weapons. By the turn of the millennium and the U.S. entry into combat in Afghanistan and Iraq, the idea of mounting and issuing special sighting devices and accessories had spread out Army-wide. To meet the needs of the troops in the field to securely attach their aiming and illumination aids to their basic weapons, the M16A4 was developed and type classified in July 1997. Otherwise identical to the M16A2, the M16A4 has a removable handle/sight assembly mounted on a MIL-STD-1913 rail-topped upper receiver, like that on the M4A1 carbine. The M5 full-length rail adapter system has also been developed for the weapon that replaces the forearm assembly.

The M16A4 has become the new basis for the M16 Modular Weapon System (MWS), where mission-specific versions of the basic weapon can be assembled from different barreled upper receivers, stocks, under-barrel weapons such as the M203 and XM320 grenade launchers, illumination aids, and sights. When the base weapon is the M4 carbine, the assembly is referred to as the M4 MWS.

G36

With the cancellation of the G11 rifle, and a more conventional 5.56 mm G41 weapon, the German Bundeswehr faced going into the 1990s armed with a weapon that was originally produced in the 1950s, the G3 rifle. The German military wanted a new general-issue service rifle that would be suitable for all of their forces and chambered for the 5.56 mm NATO round. Needing a new moneymaking project since the cancellation of the G11 and other weapons, Heckler & Koch accepted the contract to design and produce a new service rifle, dependent on acceptance after testing by the Bundeswehr. Design work on the new weapon began in 1990 with Ernst Mauch as the head engineer of what was called the HK50 project.

Completely different from all of the previous conventional weapons produced by Heckler & Koch, the action of G36 was not based on the roller-locked, delayed blowback method of operation. Instead, the new design for the HK50 used a conventional short-stroke gas piston arrangement resembling that of the very successful Kalashnikov weapon.

In general, the HK50 project was the development of a conventional, gas-operated, select-fire military weapon. It was the materials that it was to be made of that really made the HK50 stand out. Very advanced manufacturing methods were used to produce the design from the most advanced materials available, primarily carbon-fiber-reinforced polymer plastics. Steel inserts were used where necessary for additional strength and wear. The bolt was a multilugged, rotary design like that used in the M16 weapon, while the bolt carrier was a rectangular block riding between steel plates cast into the walls of the receiver.

The gas operating system of the HK50 kept the interior of the weapon clear of any carbon buildup or even normal fouling. The cleanliness of the action helped make the HK50 design an extremely reliable one. Controls were made fully ambidextrous with them either being duplicated on both sides of the weapon or usable from either side. The cocking handle is underneath the carrying handle on the top of the weapon and swings to either side for use. The folding stock swings to the right of the weapon, locking in place either in the folded

A cutaway illustration of the G36 rifle mechanism.
Heckler & Koch Defense

or extended position. With the stock folded, the ejection port remains clear, and the weapon can be fired comfortably.

To take full advantage of the flexibility of the HK50 design, the barrel was made to be easily removable by a unit armorer. Different-length barrels can be installed for different mission parameters for the weapon. Sights are a carefully considered modular design. The basic sight of the HK50 is a dual sighting system consisting of a 3.5 power optical sight combined with an electronic red-dot reflex sight in the same housing. A simple range finder is included in the reticle of the optical sight, while the reflex sight projects an electronically produced red dot on a glass screen. Both sights are independently adjustable by the user.

The sights are mounted in the rear of a removable carrying handle assembly that can be taken off and an export-model 1.5 power optical sight/carrying handle mounted in its place. Additionally, a carrying handle incorporating iron sights and a MIL-STD-1913 rail can be secured to the top of the receiver.

Extensively tested by the Bundeswehr in 1995, the HK50 design was adopted as the G36 rifle. The G36 weapons system as produced by Heckler & Koch can be assembled as a rifle, carbine, magazine-fed light machine gun, or long-barreled sharpshooter's weapon. The polymer magazines developed for the weapon are extremely strong yet have a translucent body so that the ammunition remaining in the magazine can be seen at a glance. A stud-and-clip arrangement cast into the body of the magazines allows them to be securely locked together in multiples of two or three for a quick reload in a tactical situation.

The overall design of the G36 has resulted in a very flexible weapon that is easily maintained and adjustable to the user's needs and preferences. It was adopted by the Bundeswehr, the Spanish military and other units, as well as seeing good law enforcement sales around the world, including the United States. It is a very successful combination of traditional and new concepts in weapons design and production.

A G36 Carbine with the 40 mm grenade-launcher module attached that evolved into the US XM320.
Kevin Dockery

TAVOR-21

Though it has had mechanical difficulties with its design, the British L85, along with the French FAMAS and Austrian AUG, has shown that the bullpup layout for a military weapon can be both compact and accurate. These were two of the characteristics Israel was looking for in a new weapon when Israel Military Industries undertook the design of a new rifle in the early 1990s. By 1993, IMI, working with the Israeli Defense Force, had begun development of what would be the Tavor rifle.

Internally, the Tavor resembles many of the world's successful assault rifles, the best features of each being used by IMI in the design of the weapon. The gas system of the Tavor uses a long-stroke piston attached to a heavy bolt carrier. The mainspring extends into the hollow stem of the bolt carrier that has the gas piston mounted on the end of it, much like the AK-47 system.

The multilugged bolt is a standard design but has an ejector system that can be mounted for either right- or left-side ejection by the operator. Ejection ports are on either side of the weapon to complete the selectable ejection system. The operating handle is on one side of the weapon but has a matching slot on the opposite side above the forearm of the Tavor. The operating handle can also be switched from one side of the weapon to the other at the choice of the operator. All parts of the weapon are accessible for cleaning through the trapdoor made up of the hinged butt plate assembly.

The receiver and body of the Tavor are made of high-strength polymers, reinforced with steel inserts where necessary. There is no sight installed on the Tavor design; instead, a MIL-STD-1913 rail section was included on the upper part of the receiver. The general-issue sight for the Tavor family is an electronic reflex sight that includes a visible laser aiming module as part of its system.

Barrels are easily changeable in the Tavor, allowing for several variations according to the needs of the mission or operator. The very compact Micro version of the weapon has no forearm as part of the receiver, forcing the use of the large front portion of the pistol grip/trigger guard as a front grip. The weapon uses the M16 magazine design so that feed devices are already well-stocked in the Israeli supply chain.

The Tavor system was tested against other weapons, notably the U.S. M4 carbine, in 2001 and 2002. The weapon also saw field duty with the Givati Brigade during Operation Defensive Shield in April 2002. As the preferred weapon coming out of the tests and receiving high praise from the troops that used it in the field, the Tavor was put into production, with the first Israeli military units receiving the weapon in 2003. India had also shown an interest in obtaining the Tavor for issue to their special operations troops, purchasing a number of the weapons in December 2002 and again in 2003. India has also been considering purchasing a licensing agreement with IMI so that they could

The receiver, barrels, accessories, and tool that make up the Tavor weapons system.
Kevin Dockery

produce the Tavor system in their own country in order to make the weapon general issue to all of their military forces. The high number of M16 and M4 weapons presently in Israeli hands has limited the issue of the Tavor weapons system, though it is in the hands of several of the country's special operations units.

The Tavor weapon has been known by several designations, the most common of which is TAR-21, for Tavor Assault Rifle—21st century. Advanced models of the weapon are already being developed, and it has been selected to be the future primary infantry weapon of the Israeli military.

F2000

The most advanced bullpup weapon presently in production is the Belgian FN F2000 Modular Assault Weapon System. Drawing on their experience in ergonometrics and polymers used in the P90 personal defense weapon, the engineers at FN designed a very futuristic appearance in the F2000. Publicly released in March 2001, the F2000 had been under development since 1995. The action of the system is based on a straightforward gas piston and rotating bolt with the feed being from an M16-style magazine inserted in the well just behind the thumbhole of the pistol grip.

Outside of the general layout of the exterior of the weapon, which makes it much more comfortable to hold and operate than appearances might suggest at first glance, the most unusual aspect of the F2000 is the direction of ejection.

The bolt of the F2000 extracts the fired rounds, and a rocker system kicks the casing up over the barrel of the weapon into an ejection tube that extends forward to the right front side of the receiver. Only after the first three rounds or more are extracted and ejected into the guide tube do empty casings start to eject from the weapon and fall away. Tilting the F2000 forward is all it takes to clear the ejection guide tube of empty brass or an extracted live round that has been cleared from the action.

The combination of the long ejection guide tube with the sealed exterior of the F2000 makes the weapon impervious to most exterior conditions. This helps maintain a high level of reliability in the design. For tactical and mission-oriented flexibility, the smooth lines of the receiver can be broken down into modules and changed for others. The front grip can be removed and replaced with an under-barrel pump-action, single-shot 40 mm grenade launcher that blends smoothly into the lines of the F2000.

The upper sight module of the F2000 can be removed and any other form of sighting device installed on the exposed MIL-STD-1913 rail on the top of the weapon. The front grip module can be replaced with a vertical folding grip assembly with several sections of MIL-STD-1913 rail in the upper part of the assembly. Additional modules that include a less-lethal launcher, twelve-gauge shotgun, and more advanced grenade launchers are also under development to attach to the underside of the F2000.

XM8

Beginning as the kinetic energy weapon portion of the OICW project, the development of the XM8 lightweight modular weapons system was initiated by the Army in 2002 with the awarding of a contract to Alliant Techsystems. The contract was to determine if the kinetic energy weapon from the OICW/XM29 could become an effective stand alone weapon. The kinetic energy portion of the OICW had been developed by Heckler & Koch as a variation on their basic G36 operating system. As such, it was a simple matter for the company to modify the basic receiver to form a common unit that could have various stocks, barrels, handguards, and sights mounted on it along with other components.

The high-strength polymer construction of the XM8 promised to make a very light weapon, one that could be developed as a replacement for the M16 and M4 weapons already in service. As a component of the OICW/XM29, the XM8 weapons system would share a commonality of parts with the original weapon that would simplify the logistics and maintenance needed to support all of the weapons once they were perfected and adopted.

The basic design of the XM8 centered on the common receiver with an easily changed barrel and removable sight system. With the addition of different modules, the weapon could be a baseline carbine, a compact carbine that could act as a personal defense weapon, a designated marksman/automatic rifle variation, or have a 40 mm grenade launcher mounted under the front handguard.

Since the XM8 was internally a G36 rifle, it had a very clean interior operating system. The polymer components of the weapon could be easily cleaned and maintained, much more so than the M16 weapon that was used as a comparison. The design of the controls had also been directly adapted from the G36 and as such were completely ambidextrous in their operation.

An unusual feature of the polymer construction of much of the XM8 system was that the weapon could be offered in a variety of colors, the pigments being added to the polymers prior to the parts being formed. Colors offered included OD green, arctic white, desert tan, urban blue, basic black, and brown. Since they would be a part of the plastic itself, the colors could not fade or chip away, exposing an underlying surface.

In just over a year from the first contract being awarded for its development, thirty prototype XM8 weapons were delivered for testing in November 2003. Some problems with the weapons were noted in troop field testing, notably the overall weight of the design and the overheating of the handguards. The heating problem was addressed with further design. But the weight problem remained as part of the weapons system during its continuing development.

Because there had not been any form of competitive bidding to receive the contract to develop the XM8, a number of weapons companies protested to the Army and the government. Bidding was opened by the Army in November 2004 for what was called the 5.56 mm Modular Weapon System Family. Eight months later, the Army suspended all development of the OICW Increment 1 weapon, which was to have been the Modular Weapon System Family/XM8 in order to add requirements put forward by the other services for the system. On the last day of October 2005, the XM8 program was formally suspended along with the development of the OICW/XM29 and a number of other small arms. Production of the XM8 under any name was over for the foreseeable future. Heckler & Koch and partners have considered offering the weapon as developed so far as the Modular Weapon System Family, but there are no plans that have been announced for its renewed production.

MARK 16 MOD 0 SCAR LIGHT

Avoiding any of the controversy involved in the XM8 or OICW weapons programs, the United States Special Operations Command went forward with their own industry solicitations for a Special Operations Combat Assault Rifle (SCAR) designed for their specific needs. The solicitations for the new weapons were released on October 15, 2003, with the specifications requesting two different basic designs, the light and the heavy.

The SCAR light weapon was to be chambered for the 5.56×45 mm round and use an improved version of the standard-issue M16 magazine. The heavy SCAR was to be a larger weapon, chambered for the 7.62×51 mm round initially but designed to be easily adaptable in the field with minimal tools to different calibers, such as the 7.62×39 mm round. Different lengths of barrels were to be included in the design so that the weapons could be adjusted to better fit mission requirements, particularly those of close-quarters battle. Long barrels and the means to attach different sight systems were also desired for long-range combat. The initial versions of the SCAR weapons were to be the standard model, the close-quarters combat version, and a sniper version.

Working from a completely original pattern, Fabrique Nationale produced the winning design for the SCAR Light and Heavy models as was announced by the Special Operations Command in late 2004. The first weapon to be produced would be the SCAR-L type classified as the Mark 16 Mod 0. Still under development was the SCAR-H, now given the designation Mark 17 Mod 0.

The SCAR weapons are both operated by a short-stroke gas piston working a rotary locking bolt. Both weapons use the same extruded aluminum upper receivers with the only difference between the two being the size of the ejection port. The lower receivers have an extendable side-folding stock that can be adjusted in length to account for the size of the operator or the amount of armor and equipment he is wearing on a mission. Controls are made ambidextrous when practical. The cocking handle can be mounted on either side of the upper receiver according to the desires of the operator. Removable adjustable iron sights are provided for the weapons, and the receivers include a number of integral MIL-STD-1913 rail sections for the mounting of the complete line of SOPMOD accessories as well as other accessories utilizing the same mount interface.

When fully developed, the Mark 17 weapon will be produced in 7.62 × 51 mm NATO using a proprietary twenty-round magazine. For the 7.62 × 39 mm variation, the Mark 17 will be able to accept standard AK-47 magazines, enabling the operators to use captured ammunition and supplies when they are in enemy territory.

Both the Mark 16 and the Mark 17 SCAR designs share 90 percent parts compatibility between the weapons. They are designed with a 90,000-round system service life as well as a 35,000-plus-round barrel life. They are designed for extended use while maintaining a high degree of reliability and low maintenance demands.

THE FUTURE RIFLE

The final version of whatever the future rifle will be has not been determined yet. Designs have been developed that utilize caseless technology, polymer and carbon fiber building materials, and careful attention to being able to fit a wide range of user sizes. It will take a major breakthrough in ballistics to change the dependence on the metal projectile as the means of delivering the kinetic energy of the rifle. Other projectiles such as the discrete flechette show promise, but are too difficult to manufacture economically with the precision necessary to make them more accurate than the pointed, full-jacketed bullet. Small calibers have the advantages of low recoil and controllability, while they give up the penetration and range that are available to the larger calibers.

Whatever the new weapons will be, the soldiers who will carry them will make the best use of them that they can in the most unforgiving of arenas, the combat zone.

▪ Rifle Data ▪

The MKb42(H). *U.S. Army*

NAME—Maschinenkarabiner 42 (Haenel)
COMMON NAMES—MKb42(H)
CALIBER—7.92×33 mm
OVERALL LENGTH—37 inches (94 cm)
BARREL LENGTH—14.38 inches (36.5 cm)
RIFLING (TYPE AND TWIST)—4-groove, right-hand twist
LOAD—Pistolen Patrone 43 mit Eisenkern ("iron-core"—semi–armor piercing)
BULLET DIAMETER—0.323 inch (8.20 mm)
BULLET WEIGHT—126 grains (8.16 g)
MUZZLE VELOCITY—2,100 fps (640 m/s)
MUZZLE ENERGY—1,234 ft./lb. (1673 J)
WEIGHT (EMPTY)—11.06 lbs. (5.02 kg)
WEIGHT (LOADED)—12.94 lbs. (5.87 kg)
SIGHTS—Open, iron, adjustable for range, V-notch/blade, graduated in 100-meter increments from 100 to 800 meters
EFFECTIVE RANGE—400 yards (366 m)
OPERATION—Gas
TYPE OF FIRE—Selective, semi-, and full automatic
RATE OF FIRE—
   40 to 50 rpm—semiautomatic
   100 to 120 rpm—full automatic

CYCLIC RATE OF FIRE—500 to 600 rpm
FEED DEVICE—Removable 30-round steel box magazine
FEED DEVICE WEIGHT (EMPTY)—0.75 lb. (0.34 kg)
FEED DEVICE WEIGHT (LOADED)—1.88 lb. (0.85 kg)
MANUFACTURER—C. G. Haenel Waffen und Fahrradfabrik, Suhl, Germany
SERVICE—Limited quantities produced (about 8,000) for field testing and combat use
STATUS—Obsolete
REFERENCES—Aberdeen Ordnance School, *Submachine Guns*, Volume I, July 1958

The MP43. *U.S. Army*

NAME—Maschinenpistol 43 series/ Sturmgewehr 44

COMMON NAMES—MP43, MP43/1, MP44, StG 44
CALIBER—7.92×33 mm
OVERALL LENGTH—37 inches (94 cm)
BARREL LENGTH—16.5 inches (41.9 cm)
RIFLING (TYPE AND TWIST)—4-groove, right-hand twist
LOAD—Pistolen Patrone 43 mit Eisenkern ("iron-core"—semi–armor piercing)
BULLET DIAMETER—0.323 inch (8.20 mm)
BULLET WEIGHT—126 grains (8.16 g)
MUZZLE VELOCITY—2,247 fps (685 m/s)
MUZZLE ENERGY—1,412 ft./lb. (1915 J)
WEIGHT (EMPTY)—10.06 lbs. (4.56 kg)
WEIGHT (LOADED)—12.07 lbs. (5.47 kg)
SIGHTS—Open, iron, adjustable for range, V-notch/blade, graduated in 100-meter increments from 100 to 800 meters
Optional—Gewehr-Zielfernrohr 4-fach telescopic sight available for post–August 1943 specimens equipped with a scope mounting position
Telescopic sight and mount weight—1.25 lbs. (0.57 kg)
SIGHT POWER—4 power magnification
EFFECTIVE RANGE—400 yards (366 m)
OPERATION—Gas
TYPE OF FIRE—Selective, semi-, and full automatic
RATE OF FIRE—
40 to 50 rpm semiautomatic
100 to 120 rpm full automatic
CYCLIC RATE OF FIRE—540 rpm
FEED DEVICE—Removable 30-round steel box magazine
FEED DEVICE WEIGHT (EMPTY)—0.88 lb. (0.40 kg)
FEED DEVICE WEIGHT (LOADED)—2.01 lbs. (0.91 kg)
MANUFACTURER—C. G. Haenel Waffen und Fahrradfabrik, Suhl, Germany, as well as additional subcontractors
SERVICE—Service with German forces in all theaters, some service with East German and other Warsaw Pact forces after World War II
STATUS—Obsolete
REFERENCES—Aberdeen Ordnance School, *Submachine Guns*, Volume I, July 1958

NAME—Avtomat Kalashnikova obrazets 1947g /Avtomat Kalashnikova skladyvayushchimsa prikladom obrazets 1947g
COMMON NAMES—AK-47/AKS-47
CALIBER—7.62×39 mm
OVERALL LENGTH—
AK-47—34.25 inches (87 cm)
AKS-47—25.4 inches (64.5 cm) with stock folded
AKS-47—34.25 inches (87 cm) with stock open
BARREL LENGTH—16.3 inches (41.4 cm)
RIFLING (TYPE AND TWIST)—4-groove, right-hand twist, 1 turn in 9.25 inches (23.5 cm)
LOAD—M43 ball with copper-washed steel case
BULLET DIAMETER—0.310 inch (7.87 mm)
BULLET WEIGHT—122 grains (7.95 g)
MUZZLE VELOCITY—2,297 fps (700 m/s)
MUZZLE ENERGY—1,429 ft./lb. (1938 J)
WEIGHT (EMPTY)—
AK-47—8.53 lbs. (3.87 kg)
AKS-47—8.65 lbs. (3.92 kg)
WEIGHT (LOADED)—
AK-47—10.56 lbs. (4.79 kg) loaded with 30 rounds in early model magazine
AKS-47—10.68 lbs. (4.84 kg) loaded with 30 rounds in early model magazine
SIGHTS—Open adjustable iron, U-notch, post, adjustable for range 0 to 800 meters in 100-meter increments
SIGHT RADIUS—14.88 inches (37.8 cm)
EFFECTIVE RANGE—328 yards (300 m)
OPERATION—Gas
TYPE OF FIRE—Selective, semi-, and full automatic

RATE OF FIRE—
Semiautomatic—40 rpm
Full automatic—100 rpm
CYCLIC RATE OF FIRE—600 rpm
FEED DEVICE—Removable 30-round box magazine
FEED DEVICE WEIGHT (EMPTY)—
Early steel model—0.95 lb. (0.43 kg)
Late steel model—0.73 lb. (0.33 kg)
FEED DEVICE WEIGHT (LOADED)—
Early steel model—2.03 lbs. (0.92 kg)
Late steel model—1.81 lbs. (0.82 kg)
MANUFACTURER—State factories
SERVICE—Warsaw Pact and various Communist and Communist-supplied organizations around the world
STATUS—Production completed
REFERENCES—*Kalashnikov Arms*, Moscow, 1997; Ezell, Edward, *Kalashnikov: The Arms and the Man*, Collector Grade Publications, 2001; Gander, Terry J., ed., *Jane's Infantry Weapons, 2001–2002*; Dockery, Kevin, *Weapons of the Navy SEALs*, Penguin Putnam, 2004

The AK-47 milled receiver (lightweight). *Smithsonian Institution*

NAME—Lightweight Kalashnikov
COMMON NAMES—AK-47/AKS-47 (milled)
WEIGHT (EMPTY)—
AK-47—7.65 lbs. (3.47 kg)
AKS-47—8.73 lbs. (3.96 kg)
WEIGHT (LOADED)—
AK-47—9.46 lbs. (4.29 kg) loaded with 30 rounds in late-model magazine
AKS-47—10.54 lbs. (4.78 kg) loaded with 30 rounds in late-model magazine
FEED DEVICE WEIGHT (EMPTY)—Late steel model—0.73 lb. (0.33 kg)

FEED DEVICE WEIGHT (LOADED)—Late steel model—1.81 lbs. (0.82 kg)
COMMENTS—This is a modified version of the original AK-47 with a receiver milled from a forging. This lightweight version shared all the same characteristics as the original design, only it was lighter in weight and included a bayonet mount. The magazine had been modified to make it stronger, with ribs formed along the sides, while removing weight. The pilot model of this design was produced in 1951, and it was adopted by the Soviet Army in 1953.

The AKMS-47. *Kevin Dockery*

NAME—Modernizirovanniy avtomat sistemi Kalashnikova obrazets 1947g/Modernizirovanniy avtomat sistemi Kalashnikova skladyvayushchimsa prikladom obrazets 1947g
COMMON NAMES—AKM-47/AKMS-47
CALIBER—7.62×39 mm
OVERALL LENGTH—
AKM-47—34.25 inches (87 cm)
AKMS-47—25.2 inches (64 cm) with stock folded
AKMS-47—34.6 inches (88 cm) with stock open
BARREL LENGTH—16.3 inches (41.4 cm)
RIFLING (TYPE AND TWIST)—4-groove, right-hand twist, 1 turn in 9.25 inches (23.5 cm)
LOAD—M43 ball with copper-washed steel case
BULLET DIAMETER—0.310 inch (7.87 mm)
BULLET WEIGHT—122 grains (7.95 g)
MUZZLE VELOCITY—2,297 fps (700 m/s)
MUZZLE ENERGY—1,429 ft./lb. (1938 J)

WEIGHT (EMPTY)—
AKM-47—6.46 lbs. (2.93 kg)
AKMS-47—6.72 lbs. (3.05 kg)
WEIGHT (LOADED)—
AK-47—8.27 lbs. (3.75 kg) loaded with 30 rounds in steel magazine
AKS-47—8.53 lbs. (3.87 kg) loaded with 30 rounds in steel magazine
SIGHTS—Open adjustable iron, U-notch, post, adjustable for range 0 to 800 meters in 100-meter increments
SIGHT RADIUS—14.88 inches (37.8 cm)
EFFECTIVE RANGE—328 yards (300 m)
OPERATION—Gas
TYPE OF FIRE—Selective, semi-, and full automatic
RATE OF FIRE—
Semiautomatic—40 rpm
Full automatic—100 rpm
CYCLIC RATE OF FIRE—600 rpm
FEED DEVICE—Removable 30-round box magazine
FEED DEVICE WEIGHT (EMPTY)—
Late steel model—0.73 lb. (0.33 kg)
Aluminum magazine—0.37 lb. (0.17 kg)
FEED DEVICE WEIGHT (LOADED)—
Late steel model—1.81 lbs. (0.82 kg)
Aluminum magazine—1.45 lbs. (0.66 kg)
MANUFACTURER—State factories
SERVICE—Warsaw Pact and various Communist and Communist-supplied organizations around the world
STATUS—Production completed

The AKMS-47 with its stock folded. *Kevin Dockery*

REFERENCES—*Kalashnikov Arms*, Moscow, 1997; Ezell, Edward, *Kalashnikov: The Arms*

and the Man, Collector Grade Publications, 2001; Gander, Terry J., ed., *Jane's Infantry Weapons, 2001–2002*; Dockery, Kevin, *Weapons of the Navy SEALs*, Penguin Putnam, 2004

The M-14 rifle. *Smithsonian Institution*

NAME—M14 Rifle
COMMON NAMES—M14
CALIBER—7.62×51 mm NATO
OVERALL LENGTH—44.3 inches (112.5 cm)
BARREL LENGTH—22.0 inches (55.9 cm)
RIFLING (TYPE AND TWIST)—4-groove, right-hand, 1 turn in 12 inches (30.5 cm)
LOAD—M80 ball
BULLET DIAMETER—0.308 inch (7.82 mm)
BULLET WEIGHT—146 grains (9.46 g)
MUZZLE VELOCITY—2,800 fps (853 m/s)
MUZZLE ENERGY—2,541 ft./lb. (3446 J)
WEIGHT (EMPTY)—8.57 lbs. (3.89 kg)
WEIGHT (LOADED)—10.22 lbs. (4.64 kg)
SIGHTS—Adjustable iron aperture/blade, rear sight adjustable from 100 to 1,200 meters with 100-meter interval markings
SIGHT RADIUS—26.75 inches (67.9 cm) with rear sight set at 100 meters
EFFECTIVE RANGE—500 yards (460 m)
OPERATION—Gas
TYPE OF FIRE—Semiautomatic
Selective fire, semi-, and full automatic, when selector switch is installed
RATE OF FIRE—
20 to 30 rpm—semiautomatic
15 rpm—sustained semiautomatic
40 to 60 rpm—full automatic
20 rpm—sustained full automatic
CYCLIC RATE OF FIRE—750 rpm

FEED DEVICE—Removable 20-round box magazine; charger guide on top of receiver for loading installed magazine from 5-round stripper clips

FEED DEVICE WEIGHT (EMPTY)—0.53 lb. (0.24 kg)

FEED DEVICE WEIGHT (LOADED)—1.65 lbs. (0.75 kg)

MANUFACTURER—Springfield Armory, Winchester Repeating Arms, Harrington & Richardson, TRW, various civilian manufacturing concerns

SERVICE—In limited service with U.S. military forces

STATUS—Obsolescent, military production completed

REFERENCES—*Guidebook for Marines*, 9th Edition, 1964; Kuhnhausen, Jerry, *The U.S. .30 Caliber Gas Operated Service Rifles: A Shop Manual*; TM 9-1005-223-12, *Rifles, 7.62 mm M14 and M14A2*, February, 1965; TM 9-500, *Ordnance Corps Equipment Data Sheets*, September, 1962; TM 43-0001-27, *Army Ammunition Data Sheets Small Arms Ammunition*, June 1981

The standard M193 5.56 mm Ball round over an XM645 flechette cartridge. *Kevin Dockery*

NAME—XM70 Special Purpose Individual Weapon

COMMON NAMES—XM70 SPIW, XM70 Simplified Serial Flechette Rifle

CALIBER—5.6 × 57 mmB XM645

OVERALL LENGTH—42 inches (106.7 cm)

BARREL LENGTH—19.8 inches (50.1 cm)

RIFLING (TYPE AND TWIST)—Smoothbore with rifled section

LOAD—XM645 Flechette

BULLET DIAMETER—0.070 inch (1.78 mm)

BULLET WEIGHT—10 grains (0.65 g)

MUZZLE VELOCITY—4,650 fps (1,417 m/s)

MUZZLE ENERGY—480 ft./lb. (651 J)

WEIGHT (EMPTY)—7.4 lbs. (3.36 kg) with reflex sight

WEIGHT (LOADED)—8.5 lbs. (3.86 kg) with 50-round aluminum magazine and reflex sight

SIGHTS—Reflex collimator sight standard w/backup open adjustable iron sights, aperture/post

SIGHT RADIUS (POWER)—1/1

EFFECTIVE RANGE—450 yards (410 m)

OPERATION—Piston-primer

TYPE OF FIRE—Selective, semiautomatic, and 3-round burst

RATE OF FIRE—100 rpm

CYCLIC RATE OF FIRE—2,200 rpm/3-round burst

FEED DEVICE—Removable 50-round aluminum box magazine

FEED DEVICE WEIGHT (EMPTY)—0.27 lb. (0.12 kg)

FEED DEVICE WEIGHT (LOADED)—1.10 lbs. (0.50 kg)

MANUFACTURER—AAI Corp., Cockeysville, Maryland

SERVICE—Prototype only

STATUS—Development concluded

REFERENCES—Archer, Denis, ed., *Jane's Infantry Weapons, 1978*; Stevens and Ezell, *The SPIW: The Deadliest Weapon that Never Was*; company operation and maintenance manual

The M16 rifle (early model). *Smithsonian Institution*

NAME—M16 rifle family
TYPE—Select-fire rifle
CALIBER—5.56 × 45 mm
OVERALL LENGTH—
M16/M16A1—39 inches (99.1 cm)
M16A2/M16A3/M16A4—39.63 inches (101 cm)
BARREL LENGTH—20 inches (50.8 cm), 21 inches (53.3 cm) with flash suppressor
RIFLING (TYPE AND TWIST)—
M16/M16A1—6-groove, right-hand, 1 turn in 12 inches (30.5 cm)
M16A2/M16A3/M16A4—6-groove, right-hand, 1 turn in 7 inches (17.8 cm)
LOAD—
M16/M16A1—M193 ball
M16A2/M16A3/M16A4—M855 ball
BULLET DIAMETER—0.224 inch (5.69 mm)
BULLET WEIGHT—
M193 ball—56 grains (3.63 g)
M855 ball—62 grains (4.02 g)
MUZZLE VELOCITY—
M193 ball—3,250 fps (991 m/s)
M855 ball—3,025 fps (922 m/s)
MUZZLE ENERGY—
M193 ball—1,313 ft./lb. (1780 J)
M855 ball—1,260 ft./lb. (1709 J)
WEIGHT (EMPTY)—
M16—6.35 lbs. (2.88 kg)
M16A1—6.55 lbs. (2.97 kg)
M16A2—7.50 lbs. (3.40 kg)
M16A3—7.50 lbs. (3.40 kg) with rear sight/carrying handle assembly
M16A4—6.92 lbs. (3.13 kg) without rear sight/carrying handle assembly; rear sight/carrying handle assembly weight—0.58 lb. (0.27 kg)

WEIGHT (LOADED)—
M16—7.07 lbs. (3.21 kg) w/20 rounds M193 ball
M16A1—7.27 lbs. (3.30 kg) w/20 rounds M193 ball
M16A2—8.54 lbs. w/30 rounds M855 ball
M16A3/M16A4—8.57 lbs. (3.89 kg) with 30 rounds M855 ball and rear sight/carry handle assembly
SIGHTS—
M16/M16A1—Fixed adjustable rear flip aperture (0 to 300 m/300 to 500 m)/post
M16A2—Adjustable iron target sights, adjustable to 800 meters, aperture/post
M16A3/M16A4—Adjustable iron target sights, adjustable to 800 meters, on rear sight/carrying handle assembly, MIL-STD-1913 (Picatinny) rail machined as integral part of upper receiver
SIGHT RADIUS—
M16/M16A1/M16A2—19.75 inches (50.2 cm)
M16A3/M16A4—19.75 inches (50.2 cm) with rear sight/carrying handle mounted to MIL-STD-1913 rail
EFFECTIVE RANGE—
M16/M16A1—500 yards (460 m)
M16A2/M16A3/M16A4—600 yards (550 m) for point targets
MAXIMUM RANGE—
M16/M16A1—2,900 yards (2,653 m)
M16A2/M16A3/M16A4—3,865 yards (3534 m)
OPERATION—Gas
TYPE OF FIRE—
M16/M16A1/M16A3—Selective fire, semiautomatic, and full automatic
M16A2/M16A4—Selective fire, semiautomatic, and 3-round burst
RATE OF FIRE—
Semiautomatic—45 to 65 rpm
Automatic—150 to 200 rpm
Sustained—12 to 15 rpm indefinitely

CYCLIC RATE OF FIRE—
M16/M16A1—700 to 950 rpm

M16A2/M16A3/M16A4—700 to 900 rpm

FEED DEVICE—Removable 20- or 30-round box magazines

FEED DEVICE WEIGHT (EMPTY)—
20 round—0.20 lb. (0.09 kg)

30 round—0.26 lb. (0.12 kg)

FEED DEVICE WEIGHT (LOADED)—
20 round—0.72 lb. (0.33 kg) w/M193 ball

30 round—

Loaded with M193 ball—1.04 lbs. (0.47 kg)

Loaded with M855 ball—1.07 lbs. (0.49 kg)

MANUFACTURER—Colt Defense, Hartford, Connecticut

SERVICE—In service with all United States military forces and a number of allied forces around the world

STATUS—
M16/M16A1—Obsolescent, some still in reserve inventories

M16A2/M16A4—In production

M16A3—Limited production completed

REFERENCES—TM 9-1005-249-14, *Rifle M16 and M16E1*, Aug. 1, 1966; TM 9-1005-249-20, *Rifle M16A1 and M16*, Sept. 1971; ST 9-159, *Handbook of Ordnance Material*, March 1968; TM 9-1005-319-23&P, *Rifle, 5.56 mm, M16A2, M16A3, M16A4, Carbine, 5.56 mm M4, M4A1*, August 1987; Colt company literature

COMMENTS—The M16A3 is identical to the M16A4 except that the A3 model is capable of full automatic fire

The M16A2 rifle. *Kevin Dockery*

The Colt production M16A4 with rail system. *Kevin Dockery*

The XM177E1. *Kevin Dockery*

NAME—M16 Carbine family

TYPE—Select-fire carbine

CALIBER—5.56×45 mm

OVERALL LENGTH—
XM177/XM177E1—26.77 inches (68 cm) with buttstock telescoped, 30 inches (76.2 cm) buttstock extended

XM177E2—28.27 inches (71.8 cm) with buttstock telescoped, 31.0 inches (78.7 cm) buttstock extended

M4/M4A1—29.75 inches (75.6 cm) with buttstock telescoped, 33 inches (83.8 cm) buttstock extended

BARREL LENGTH—
XM177/XM177E1—10 inches (25.4 cm), 13.5 inches (34.3 cm) with noise and flash suppressor

XM177E2—11.5 inches (29.2 cm), 15 inches (38.1 cm) with noise and flash suppressor

M4/M4A1—14.5 inches (36.8 cm), with flash suppressor

RIFLING (TYPE AND TWIST)—
XM177/XM177E1/XM177E2—6-groove, right-hand, 1 turn in 12 inches (30.5 cm)

M4/M4A1—6-groove, right-hand, 1 turn in 7 inches (17.8 cm)

LOAD—
XM177/XM177E1/XM177E2—M193 ball

M4/M4A1—M855 ball

BULLET DIAMETER—0.224 inch (5.69 mm)
BULLET WEIGHT—
M193 ball—56 grains (3.63 g)
M855 ball—62 grains (4.02 g)
MUZZLE VELOCITY—
M193 ball—
XM177/XM177E1—2,750 fps (838 m/s)
XM177E2—2,825 fps (861 m/s)
M855 ball—2,900 fps (884 m/s)
MUZZLE ENERGY—
M193 ball—
XM177/XM177E1—940 ft./lb. (1274 J)
XM177E2—992 ft./lb. (1345 J)
M855 ball—1,158 ft./lb. (1570 J)
WEIGHT (EMPTY)—
XM177—5.25 lbs. (2.38 kg)
XM177E1—5.45 lbs. (2.47 kg)
XM177E2—5.51 lbs. (2.50 kg)
M4—5.65 lbs. (2.56 kg)
M4A1—5.65 lbs. (2.56 kg) with rear
sight/carrying handle assembly; 5.07 lbs.
(2.30 kg) without rear sight/carrying handle
assembly; rear sight/carrying handle
assembly weight—0.58 lb. (0.27 kg)
WEIGHT (LOADED)—
XM177—5.97 lbs. (2.71 kg) w/20 rounds
M193 ball
XM177E1—6.17 lbs. (2.80 kg) w/20 rounds
M193 ball
XM177E2—6.72 lbs. (2.83 kg) w/20 rounds
M193 ball
M4—6.23 lbs. (3.05 kg) w/30 rounds
M855 ball
M4A1—6.23 lbs. (3.05 kg) with 30 rounds
M855 ball and rear sight/carrying handle
assembly
SIGHTS—
XM177/XM177E1/XM177E2—Fixed
adjustable rear flip aperture (0 to 100 m/100
to 200 m)/post
M4—Adjustable iron target sights,
adjustable to 800 meters, aperture/post
M4A1—Adjustable iron target sights,
adjustable to 800 meters, on rear sight/

carrying handle assembly; MIL-STD-1913
(Picatinny) rail machined as integral part of
upper receiver
SIGHT RADIUS—
XM177/XM177E1/XM177E2—14.75
inches (37.5 cm)
M4/M4A1—14.5 inches (37 cm) with rear
sight/carrying handle mounted to MIL-STD-
1913 rail
EFFECTIVE RANGE—
XM177/XM177E1/XM177E2—300 yards
(275 m)
M4/M4A1—550 yards (500 m) for point
targets
OPERATION—Gas
TYPE OF FIRE—
XM177/XM177E1/XM177E2/M4A1—
Selective fire, semiautomatic, and full
automatic
M4—Selective fire, semiautomatic, and
3-round burst
RATE OF FIRE—
Semiautomatic—45 rpm
Automatic—200 rpm
Burst—90 rpm
CYCLIC RATE OF FIRE—
XM177/XM177E1/XM177E2—650 to
900 rpm
M4/M4A1—700 to 950 rpm
FEED DEVICE—Removable 20- or 30-round
box magazines
FEED DEVICE WEIGHT (EMPTY)—
20 round—0.20 lb. (0.09 kg)
30 round—0.26 lb. (0.12 kg)
FEED DEVICE WEIGHT (LOADED)—
20 round—0.72 lb. (0.33 kg) w/M193 ball
30 round—
Loaded with M193 ball—1.04 lbs.
(0.47 kg)
Loaded with M855 ball—1.07 lbs.
(0.49 kg)
MANUFACTURER—Colt Defense, Hartford,
Connecticut
SERVICE—In service with all United States

military forces and a number of allied forces around the world

STATUS—
XM177/XM177E1/XM177E2—Obsolete, a few still in Air Force reserve inventories
M4/M4A1—In production

REFERENCES—TM 9-1005-249-14, *Rifle M16 and M16E1*, Aug. 1, 1966; TM 9-1005-249-20, *Rifle M16A1 and M16*, Sept. 1971; ST 9-159, *Handbook of Ordnance Material*, March 1968; TM 9-1005-319-23&P, *Rifle, 5.56mm, M16A2, M16A3, M16A4, Carbine, 5.56mm M4, M4A1*, August 1987; Colt company literature and manuals

COMMENTS—The XM177 is identical to the XM177E1 except for the addition of a forward bolt assist on the E1 model. There were several variations of noise and flash suppressors used on the XM177 series; the specifications listed above are all for the last and longest version. The M4/M4A1 models use a standard flash suppressor.

The Colt M4A1 carbine. *Kevin Dockery*

The AUG rifle. *Kevin Dockery*

NAME—Steyr Armee Universal Gewehr
COMMON NAMES—Steyr AUG, Sturmgewehr (StG) 77
CALIBER—5.46 × 45 mm
OVERALL LENGTH—
Commando-25.5 inches (64.8 cm)
Carbine-27.7 inches (70.4 cm)

Rifle—31.7 inches (80.5 cm)
Light Support Weapon 36.2 inches (91.9cm)

BARREL LENGTH—
Commando—13.8 inches (35.0 cm)
Carbine—16.0 inches (40.6 cm)
Rifle—20.0 inches (50.8 cm)
Light Support Weapon—24.5 inches (62.2 cm)

RIFLING (TYPE AND TWIST)—6-groove, right-hand, 1 turn in 7 inches (17.8 cm)

LOAD—M855 ball

BULLET DIAMETER—0.224 inch (5.69 mm)

BULLET WEIGHT—62 grains (4.02 g)

MUZZLE VELOCITY—
Commando—2,893 fps (882 m/s)
Carbine—2,933 fps (894 m/s)
Rifle—3,023 fps (921 m/s)
Light Support Weapon—3,143 fps (958 m/s)

MUZZLE ENERGY—
Commando—1,152 ft./lb. (1562 J)
Carbine—1,184 ft./lb. (1606 J)
Rifle—1,258 ft./lb. (1706 J)
Light Support Weapon—1,360 ft./lb. (1844 J)

WEIGHT (EMPTY)—
Commando—6.69 lbs. (3.03 kg)
Carbine—7.31 lbs. (3.32 kg)
Rifle—7.94 lbs. (3.60 kg)
Light Support Weapon—10.81 lbs. (4.90 kg) with bipod

WEIGHT (LOADED)—
Commando—7.81 lbs. (3.52 kg) with 30 rounds
Carbine—8.43 lbs. (3.82 kg) with 30 rounds
Rifle—9.06 lbs. (4.11 kg) with 30 rounds
Light Support Weapon—12.3 lbs. (5.58 kg) with 42 rounds and bipod

SIGHTS—Standard with optical sight built into handle with fixed notch/blade backup sights built into top of handle

SIGHT POWER—1.5 power magnification

SIGHT RADIUS—7.56 inches (19.2 cm) (backup sights)

OPERATION—Gas

TYPE OF FIRE—Selective, semi-, and full automatic
RATE OF FIRE—200 rpm
CYCLIC RATE OF FIRE—680 rpm
FEED DEVICE—Removable 30- or 42-round translucent polymer box magazine
FEED DEVICE WEIGHT (EMPTY)—
    30-round—0.31 lb. (0.14 kg)
    42-round—0.35 lb. (0.16 kg)
FEED DEVICE WEIGHT (LOADED)—
    30-round—1.12 lbs. (0.51 kg)
    42-round—1.49 lbs. (0.68 kg)
MANUFACTURER—Steyr-Mannlicher GmbH, Austria
SERVICE—Austrian military, also in service with Australia, Ireland, Malaysia, Morocco, New Zealand, Oman, Saudi Arabia, and other military forces
STATUS—In production

The AUG carbine. *Kevin Dockery*

REFERENCES—Hogg, Ian, *The Greenhill Military Small Arms Data Book*; Cutshaw, Charles, *Tactical Small Arms of the 21st Century*; company literature
COMMENTS—First production models off the line in 1978. On the revised A2 model AUG first produced in 1997, a MIL-STD-1913 Picatinny rail attachment was developed that could be installed on existing weapons in place of the optical sight/handle assembly. AUG-A2 weapons are offered with 16-inch (40.7 cm) and 20-inch (50.8 cm) barrel assemblies. Loaded with M193 ball ammunition, the muzzle velocities for the AUG weapons family are:
    Commando—3,050 fps (930 m/s)
    Carbine—3,133 fps (955 m/s)

The AUG Light support weapon. *Kevin Dockery*

    Rifle—3,182 fps (970 m/s)
    Light Support Weapon—3,280 fps (1000 m/s)

The F.A. MAS F1 rifle. *Kevin Dockery*

NAME—F.A. MAS F1
NAME (NATIVE)—Fusil Automatique, Manufacture d'Armes de St-Etienne, *Le Clarion* (The Bugle)
COMMON NAMES—FAMAS
COUNTRY OF ORIGIN—France
CALIBER—5.56×45 mm
OVERALL LENGTH—29.8 inches (75.7 cm)
BARREL LENGTH—19.21 inches (48.8 cm)
RIFLING (TYPE AND TWIST)—3-groove, right-hand, 1 turn in 12 inches (30.5 cm)
LOAD—M193 ball
BULLET DIAMETER—0.224 inch (5.69 mm)
BULLET WEIGHT—56 grains (3.63 g)
MUZZLE VELOCITY—3,150 fps (960 m/s)
MUZZLE ENERGY—1,234 ft./lb. (1673 J)
WEIGHT (EMPTY)—7.96 lbs. (3.61 kg)
WEIGHT (LOADED)—8.95 lbs. (4.06 kg)
WEIGHT (MOUNTED)—9.65 lbs. (4.38 kg) with 25 rounds, bipod, and sling
TYPE OF MOUNT—Folding bipod
WEIGHT OF MOUNT—0.37 lb. (0.17 kg)
SIGHTS—Adjustable open iron aperture/blade
SIGHT RADIUS—13 inches (33 cm)
EFFECTIVE RANGE—322 yards (300 m)
OPERATION—Delayed blowback

TYPE OF FIRE—Selective, semiautomatic, full automatic, and 3-round bursts
CYCLIC RATE OF FIRE—900 to 1,000 rpm
FEED DEVICE—Removable 25-round box magazine
FEED DEVICE WEIGHT (EMPTY)—0.33 lb. (0.15 kg)
FEED DEVICE WEIGHT (LOADED)—0.99 lb. (0.45 kg)
MANUFACTURER—Giat Industries, Division Giat Vecture, Versailles-Satory, France
SERVICE—French Army
STATUS—Production completed
REFERENCES—Dugleby, T. B., *Modern Military Bullpup Rifles*; Gander, Terry J. ed., *Jane's Infantry Weapons: 1997–98*; Giat manual

TYPE OF FIRE—Selective, semi-, and full automatic
CYCLIC RATE OF FIRE—700 to 850 rpm
FEED DEVICE—Removable 20-round box magazine
FEED DEVICE WEIGHT (EMPTY)—0.38 lb. (0.17 kg)
FEED DEVICE WEIGHT (LOADED)—0.89 lb. (0.40 kg)
MANUFACTURER—Royal Small Arms Factory, Enfield, England
SERVICE—Evaluation and tests only
STATUS—Developed into 5.56 mm L85 series
REFERENCES—Archer, Denis, ed., *Jane's Infantry Weapons: 1978*; Dugelby, T. B., *Modern Military Bullpup Rifles*

The British L85A1 rifle. *Kevin Dockery*

NAME—XL64 Individual Weapon
COMMON NAMES—4.85 mm Individual Weapon
CALIBER—4.85×49 mm
OVERALL LENGTH—30.31 inches (77.0 cm)
BARREL LENGTH—20.41 inches (51.85 cm) with flash hider
RIFLING (TYPE AND TWIST)—4-groove, right-hand twist, 1 turn in 4.9 inches (12.5 cm)
LOAD—XL1E1 ball
BULLET DIAMETER—0.197 inch (5.00 mm)
BULLET WEIGHT—56 grains (3.63 g)
MUZZLE VELOCITY—2,953 fps (900 m/s)
MUZZLE ENERGY—1,084 ft./lb. (1470 J)
WEIGHT (EMPTY)—6.88 lbs. (3.12 kg) without sight
WEIGHT (LOADED)—9.09 lbs. (4.12 kg) with SUSAT sight and 20 rounds
SIGHTS—Optical Sight Unit Small Arms Trilux (SUSAT) standard
   SUSAT sight weight 1.32 lbs. (0.60 kg)
SIGHT POWER—4 power magnification
EFFECTIVE RANGE—550 yards (500 m)
OPERATION—Gas

NAME—L85A1 Individual Weapon
COMMON NAMES—L85A1 IW, SA-80
CALIBER—5.56×45 mm
OVERALL LENGTH—30.9 inches (78.5 cm); Carbine—27.9 inches (70.9 cm)
BARREL LENGTH—20.4 inches (51.8 cm); Carbine—17.4 inches (44.2 cm)
RIFLING (TYPE AND TWIST)—6-groove, right-hand, 1 turn in 7 inches (17.8 cm)
LOAD—M855 ball
BULLET DIAMETER—0.224 inch (5.66 mm)
BULLET WEIGHT—62 grains (4.02 g)
MUZZLE VELOCITY—3,084 fps (940 m/s); Carbine—2,690 fps (820 m/s)
MUZZLE ENERGY—1,309 ft./lb. (1775 J); Carbine—996 ft./lb. (1351 J)
WEIGHT (EMPTY)—8.38 lbs. (3.80 kg) with optical sight; Carbine—8.18 lbs. (3.71 kg) with iron sight assembly

WEIGHT (LOADED)—9.73 lbs. (4.41 kg) with optical sight and 30 rounds in SA80 magazine; Carbine—9.53 lbs. (4.32 kg) with iron sights and 30 rounds in SA80 magazine

SIGHTS—Optical Sight Unit Small Arms Trilux (SUSAT) standard; optional rear sight/carrying handle assembly used with removable front sight as adjustable iron sights, aperture/blade

SUSAT sight weight—0.92 lb. (0.42 kg)

Iron sight assembly—0.30 lb. (0.14 kg)

SIGHT POWER—4 power magnification on SUSAT sight

OPERATION—Gas

TYPE OF FIRE—Selective fire, semi-, and full automatic

CYCLIC RATE OF FIRE—610 to 775 rpm

FEED DEVICE—All STANAG 4179–compliant magazines, the HK SA80 steel-bodied, 30-round magazine was designed to improve the system

FEED DEVICE WEIGHT (EMPTY)—0.54 lb. (0.24 kg) (HK SA80)

FEED DEVICE WEIGHT (LOADED)—1.35 lb. (0.61 kg) (HK SA80)

MANUFACTURER—Royal Ordnance

SERVICE—In service with British military and additional forces

STATUS—Production completed, upgrades to A2 configuration under way.

REFERENCES—Gander, Terry J., ed., *Jane's Infantry Weapons: 2001–2002*; Cutshaw, Charles, *Tactical Small Arms of the 21st Century*; Popenker, Maxim, and Williams, Anthony G., *Assault Rifle*; company literature

The AK-74 rifle with fixed wooden stock. *U.S. Army*

NAME—Avtomat Kalashnikova obrazetsa 1974g/Avtomat Kalashnikova skladyvayushchimsya prikladom obrazetsa 1974g

COMMON NAMES—AK-74/AKS-74

CALIBER—5.45×39 mm

OVERALL LENGTH—

AK-74—36.53 inches (92.8 cm)

AKS-74—

27.56 inches (70 cm) with metal stock folded

36.53 inches (92.8 cm) with stock open

BARREL LENGTH—16.34 inches (41.5 cm)

RIFLING (TYPE AND TWIST)—4-groove, right-hand twist, 1 turn in 7.72 inches (19.6 cm)

LOAD—5.54×39 mm Type 7N6 ball

BULLET DIAMETER—0.222 inch (5.64 mm)

BULLET WEIGHT—52.8 grains (3.42 g)

MUZZLE VELOCITY—2,943 fps (897 m/s)

MUZZLE ENERGY—1,015 ft./lb. (1376 J)

WEIGHT (EMPTY)—

AK-74—6.77 lbs. (3.07 kg)

AKS-74—6.55 lbs. (2.97 kg)

WEIGHT (LOADED)—

AK-74—7.89 lbs. (3.58 kg)

AKS-74—7.67 lbs. (3.48 kg)

SIGHTS—Open adjustable iron, U-notch, post, adjustable for range 0 to 800 meters in 100-meter increments

SIGHT RADIUS—14.92 inches (37.9 cm)

EFFECTIVE RANGE—437 yards (400 m)

OPERATION—Gas

TYPE OF FIRE—Selective, semi-, and full automatic

RATE OF FIRE—

Semiautomatic—40 rpm

Full automatic—100 rpm

CYCLIC RATE OF FIRE—650 rpm
FEED DEVICE—Removable 30-round composite plastic/metal box magazine
FEED DEVICE WEIGHT (EMPTY)—0.51 lb. (0.23 kg)
FEED DEVICE WEIGHT (LOADED)—1.12 lbs. (0.55 kg)
MANUFACTURER—IZHMASH, Izhevsk, Russia
SERVICE—In service with Russian military and many ex–Warsaw Pact forces
STATUS—In production as the AKM-74
REFERENCES—Nedelin, Alexei, *Kalashnikov Arms*, Moscow, 1997; Ezell, Edward, *Kalashnikov: The Arms and the Man*, Collector Grade Publications, 2001; Gander, Terry J., ed., *Jane's Infantry Weapons: 2001–2002*

The AKS-74U compact carbine with its stock extended.
Kevin Dockery

NAME—Avtomat Kalashnikova skladnoy ukorochenniy obrazetsa 1974g
COMMON NAMES—AKS-74U, Krinkov—in U.S. only
CALIBER—5.45 × 39 mm
OVERALL LENGTH—
19.29 inches (49 cm) with stock folded
28.74 inches (73 cm) with stock open
BARREL LENGTH—8.27 inches (21 cm)
RIFLING (TYPE AND TWIST)—4-groove, right-hand twist, 1 turn in 7.72 inches (19.6 cm)
LOAD—5.54 × 39 mm Type 7N6 ball
BULLET DIAMETER—0.222 inch (5.64 mm)
BULLET WEIGHT—52.8 grains (3.42 g)
MUZZLE VELOCITY—2,411 fps (735 m/s)

MUZZLE ENERGY—681 ft./lb. (923 J)
WEIGHT (EMPTY)—5.47 lbs. (2.48 kg)
WEIGHT (LOADED)—6.59 lbs. (2.93 kg)
SIGHTS—Open nonadjustable iron, flip-type aperture, post, flip sight adjustable for range 200 or 400 meters
SIGHT RADIUS—9.25 inches (23.5 cm)
OPERATION—Gas
TYPE OF FIRE—Selective, semi-, and full automatic
RATE OF FIRE—
Semiautomatic—40 rpm
Full automatic—100 rpm
CYCLIC RATE OF FIRE—650 to 735 rpm
FEED DEVICE—Removable 30-round composite plastic/metal box magazine
FEED DEVICE WEIGHT (EMPTY)—0.51 lb. (0.23 kg)
FEED DEVICE WEIGHT (LOADED)—1.12 lbs. (0.55 kg)
MANUFACTURER—Tula Arsenal, Russia
SERVICE—In service with Russian military and many ex–Warsaw Pact forces
STATUS—In production

The AKS-74U with its stock folded to the side. *Kevin Dockery*

REFERENCES—Nedelin, Alexei, *Kalashnikov Arms*, Moscow, 1997; Ezell, Edward, *Kalashnikov: The Arms and the Man*, Collector Grade Publications, 2001; Gander, Terry J., ed., *Jane's Infantry Weapons: 2001–2002*

The Colt ACR candidate weapon. *Kevin Dockery*

NAME—Colt Advanced Combat Rifle Candidate

COMMON NAMES—Colt ACR

CALIBER—5.56×45 mm

OVERALL LENGTH—
36.75 inches (93.3 cm) with stock collapsed
40.63 inches (103.2 cm) with stock fully extended
Seven stock position adjustments in 0.5-inch (1.3 cm) increments

BARREL LENGTH—17 inches (43.2 cm) effective barrel length, 20.5 inches (52.1 cm) with Muzzle Brake/Compensator

RIFLING (TYPE AND TWIST)—6-groove, right-hand, 1 turn in 7 inches (17.8 cm)

LOAD—M855 ball or duplex ball

BULLET DIAMETER—0.224 inch (5.69 mm)

BULLET WEIGHT—
M855 ball—62 grains (4.02 g)
Duplex ball—
Lead projectile—35 grains (2.27 g)
Rear projectile—33 grains (2.14 g)

MUZZLE VELOCITY—
M855 ball—3,110 fps (948 m/s)
Duplex ball—2,900 fps (884 m/s)

MUZZLE ENERGY—
M855 ball—1,331 ft./lb. (1805 J)
Duplex ball—
Lead projectile—653 ft./lb. (885 J)
Rear projectile—616 ft./lb. (835 J)

WEIGHT (EMPTY)—7.29 lbs. without sights

WEIGHT (LOADED)—
8.95 lbs. (4.06 kg) with 30 rounds duplex ball and iron sight/carrying handle assembly

9.83 lbs. (4.46 kg) with 30 rounds M855 ball and optical sight assembly

SIGHTS—
Human Engineering Labs (HEL) extended sighting rib mounted above front handguard
Adjustable iron target sights, adjustable from 300 to 600 meters, on rear sight/carrying handle assembly:
Integrated rail machined as integral part of flat-topped upper receiver
Iron sight/carrying handle assembly weight—0.59 lb. (0.27 kg)
Optical sight on adjustable mount interchangeable with iron sight/carrying handle assembly
ELCAN optical sight and adjustable mount assembly weight—1.41 lbs. (0.64 kg)

SIGHT POWER—3.5 fixed power magnification

SIGHT RADIUS—19.75 inches (50.2 cm) with rear sight/carrying handle mounted to upper receiver rail

EFFECTIVE RANGE—
M855 ball—875 yards (800 m)
Duplex round—383 yards (350 m)

OPERATION—Gas

TYPE OF FIRE—Selective, semi-, and full automatic

RATE OF FIRE—
Semiautomatic—45 to 65 rpm
Automatic—150 to 200 rpm
Sustained—12 to 15 rpm indefinitely

CYCLIC RATE OF FIRE—
M855 ball—664 rpm
Duplex ball—624 rpm

FEED DEVICE—All STANAG 4179–compliant magazines, standard removable 30-round aluminum box magazine

FEED DEVICE WEIGHT (EMPTY)—30 round—0.26 lb. (0.12 kg)

FEED DEVICE WEIGHT (LOADED)—
Loaded with M855 ball—1.07 lbs. (0.49 kg)
Loaded with duplex ball—1.13 lbs. (0.51 kg)

MANUFACTURER—Colt Industries, Hartford, Connecticut

SERVICE—Evaluation

STATUS—Development suspended

REFERENCES—Bartocci, Christopher, *Black Rifle II*; *Army Times*, "The Rifle of the Future." May 1, 1989; *International Defense Review*, "Update on the ACR Program," March 1990; *Machine Design*, "Making Rifles More Lethal," August 10, 1989; *Military Technology*, "The Advanced Combat Rifle Programme," October 1989; company literature

COMMENTS—Muzzle Brake/Compensator reduces muzzle blast noise by approximately 15 to 20 decibels

The AAI ACR candidate weapon. *Kevin Dockery*

NAME—AAI Advanced Combat Rifle Candidate

COMMON NAMES—AAI ACR

CALIBER—5.56×45 mm subcaliber flechette

OVERALL LENGTH—40 inches (101.6 cm)

BARREL LENGTH—18.5 inches (47.0 cm) projectile travel

RIFLING (TYPE AND TWIST)—1 turn in 85 inches (216 cm)

LOAD—Flechette

BULLET DIAMETER—0.062 inch (1.57 mm)

BULLET LENGTH—1.63 inches (41.4 mm)

BULLET WEIGHT—10.2 grains (0.66 g)

MUZZLE VELOCITY—4,600 fps (1402 m/s)

MUZZLE ENERGY—479 ft./lb. (650 J)

WEIGHT (EMPTY)—7.78 lbs. (3.53 kg) without sights

WEIGHT (LOADED)—

With iron sight assembly and 30 rounds—8.80 lbs. (3.99 kg)

With optical sight assembly and 30 rounds—9.25 lbs. (4.20 kg)

SIGHTS—

Removable adjustable rear sight assembly:

Rear sight assembly weight—0.135 lb. (0.061 kg)

Optical Trijicon Advanced Combat Optical Gunsight (ACOG)

Optical sight weight—0.59 lb. (0.27 kg)

SIGHT POWER—Fixed 4 power optical sight magnification

EFFECTIVE RANGE—650 yards (600 m)

OPERATION—Gas

TYPE OF FIRE—Selective, semiautomatic, and 3-round burst

RATE OF FIRE—120 rpm

CYCLIC RATE OF FIRE—1,800 rpm

FEED DEVICE—Modified STANAG 4179 removable 30-round aluminum box magazine

FEED DEVICE WEIGHT (EMPTY)—0.32 lb. (0.15 kg)

FEED DEVICE WEIGHT (LOADED)—0.88 lb. (0.40 kg)

MANUFACTURER—AAI Corp. Cockeysville, Maryland

SERVICE—Evaluation

STATUS—Development suspended

REFERENCES—Bartocci, Christopher, *Black Rifle II*; *Army Times*, "The Rifle of the Future," May 1, 1989; *International Defense Review*, "Update on the ACR Program," March 1990; *Machine Design*, "Making Rifles More Lethal," August 10, 1989; *Military Technology*, "The Advanced Combat Rifle Programme," October 1989; company literature

The Steyr ACR candidate weapon. *Kevin Dockery*

NAME—Steyr Mannlicher Advanced Combat Rifle candidate
COMMON NAMES—Steyr ACR
CALIBER—5.56 × 45 mm synthetic cased flechette (SCF)
OVERALL LENGTH—30.12 inches (76.5 cm)
BARREL LENGTH—20.25 inches (51.4 cm)
RIFLING (TYPE AND TWIST)—1 turn in 100 inches (254 cm), fin-stabilized flechette
LOAD—Flechette
BULLET DIAMETER—0.062 inch (1.57 mm)
BULLET LENGTH—1.61 inches (41 mm)
BULLET WEIGHT—9.85 grains (0.64 g)
MUZZLE VELOCITY—4,920 fps (1500 m/s)
MUZZLE ENERGY—529 ft./lb. (717 J)
WEIGHT (EMPTY)—7.12 lbs. (3.23 kg) without sights
WEIGHT (LOADED)—8.49 lbs. (3.85 kg) with 24 rounds and optical sight assembly
SIGHTS—Sight rib with front blade, interchangeable adjustable aperture rear sight assembly, ACR optical sight assembly
   Rear sight assembly weight—0.035 lb. (0.016 kg)
   ACR optical sight assembly weight—0.88 lb. (0.40 kg)
SIGHT POWER—Variable 1.5 to 3.5 magnification power
EFFECTIVE RANGE—650 yards (600 m)
OPERATION—Gas
TYPE OF FIRE—Selective, semiautomatic, and 3-round burst
CYCLIC RATE OF FIRE—1,200 rpm
FEED DEVICE—Removable 24-round translucent polymer box magazine
FEED DEVICE WEIGHT (EMPTY)—0.23 lb. (0.10 kg)

FEED DEVICE WEIGHT (LOADED)—0.49 lb. (0.22 kg)
MANUFACTURER—Steyr-Mannlicher GMbH
SERVICE—Evaluation
STATUS—Development suspended
REFERENCES—Bartocci, Christopher, *Black Rifle II*; *Army Times*, "The Rifle of the Future," May 1, 1989; *International Combat Arms*, "Steyr's Advanced Combat Rifle," November 1989; *International Defense Review*, "Update on the ACR Program," March 1990; *Machine Design*, "Making Rifles More Lethal," August 10, 1989; *Military Technology*, "The Advanced Combat Rifle Programme," October 1989; company literature

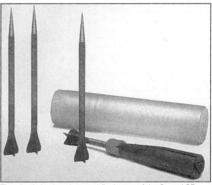

The plastic body, sabot, and flechettes of the Steyr ACR weapon's ammunition. *Steyr Mannlicher*

The Heckler & Koch G11 ACR candidate. *Kevin Dockery*

NAME—G11 Advanced Combat Rifle Candidate
COMMON NAMES—G11 ACR
CALIBER—4.92 × 34 mm Caseless (U.S. designation for German (HK) 4.73 × 33 mm)
OVERALL LENGTH—29.53 inches (75.0 cm)

BARREL LENGTH—21.26 inches (54.0 cm)
RIFLING (TYPE AND TWIST)—Gaine twist
polygonal bore, 1 turn in 6 inches (15.2 cm)
at muzzle
LOAD—DM 11 ball
BULLET DIAMETER—0.194 inch
(4.93 mm)
BULLET WEIGHT—49.2 grains (3.19 g)
MUZZLE VELOCITY—3,050 fps (914 m/s)
MUZZLE ENERGY—1,016 ft./lb. (1378 J)
WEIGHT (EMPTY)—8.44 lbs. (3.83 kg)
WEIGHT (LOADED)—9.2 lbs. (4.17 kg)
SIGHTS—Integral optical sight as part of
carrying handle
SIGHT RADIUS (POWER)—Variable from 1/1
to 3.5 power magnification
EFFECTIVE RANGE—650 yards (600 m)
OPERATION—Gas
TYPE OF FIRE—Selective, semiautomatic,
3-round burst, and full automatic
RATE OF FIRE—85 rpm
CYCLIC RATE OF FIRE—
    Full automatic fire—450 rpm
    3-round burst fire—2,200 rpm
FEED DEVICE—Removable 50-round single-
column box magazine
FEED DEVICE WEIGHT (EMPTY)—0.17 lb.
(0.08 kg)
FEED DEVICE WEIGHT (LOADED)—0.75 lb.
(0.34 kg)
MANUFACTURER—Heckler & Koch GMbH

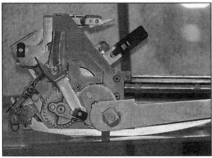

A closeup of the internal action of the G11 weapon. The
linkage is geared to rotate the breechblock mechanism as
the action recoils in the stock assembly. *Kevin Dockery*

SERVICE—Evaluation
STATUS—Development suspended
REFERENCES—Dugelby, T. B., *Modern
Military Bullpup Rifles*; Bartocci, Christopher,
Black Rifle II; *Army Times*, "The Rifle of the
Future," May 1, 1989; *International Defense
Review*, "Update on the ACR Program," March
1990; *Machine Design*, "Making Rifles More
Lethal," August 10, 1989; *Military Technology*,
"The Advanced Combat Rifle Programme,"
October 1989; company literature

The G11K2, the final version of the G11 caseless rifle.
Kevin Dockery

NAME—G11K2
CALIBER—4.73 × 33 mm Ohnehülse
OVERALL LENGTH—29.65 inches
(75.3 cm)
BARREL LENGTH—21.18 inches (53.8 cm)
RIFLING (TYPE AND TWIST)—Gaine twist
polygonal bore, 1 turn in 6.1 inches (15.5 cm)
at muzzle
LOAD—DM 11 ball
BULLET DIAMETER—0.194 inch (4.93 mm)
BULLET WEIGHT—50.2 grains (3.25 g)
MUZZLE VELOCITY—3,051 fps (930 m/s)
MUZZLE ENERGY—1,037 ft./lb. (1406 J)
WEIGHT (EMPTY)—8.05 lbs. (3.65 kg)
WEIGHT (LOADED)—10.09 lbs. (4.58 kg) with
135 rounds in 3 magazines on weapon
SIGHTS—Integral optical sight as part of
carrying handle
SIGHT RADIUS (POWER)—Variable from 1/1
to 3.5 power magnification at 300 m range
EFFECTIVE RANGE—650 yards (600 m)

OPERATION—Gas

TYPE OF FIRE—Selective, semiautomatic, 3-round burst, and full automatic

RATE OF FIRE—85 rpm

CYCLIC RATE OF FIRE—
Full automatic fire—450 rpm
3-round burst fire—2,200 rpm

FEED DEVICE—Removable 45-round single-column box magazine

FEED DEVICE WEIGHT (EMPTY)—0.165 lb. (0.075 kg)

FEED DEVICE WEIGHT (LOADED)—0.681 lb. (0.309 kg)

MANUFACTURER—Heckler & Koch GMbH

SERVICE—Troop trials, 1,000 weapons delivered to Bundeswehr special operations forces before deliveries suspended

STATUS—Development suspended

REFERENCES—Dugelby, T. B., *Modern Military Bullpup Rifles*; Bartocci, Christopher, *Black Rifle II*; Hogg, Ian V., *Jane's Infantry Weapons: 1992–93*; Gangarosa, Gene, Jr., *Heckler and Koch: Armorers of the Free World*; Hogg, Ian, and Weeks, John, *Military Small Arms of the 20th Century*, 7th Edition; company literature

---

NAME—Voere VEC-91 Lightning

TYPE—Bolt-action caseless repeater

COUNTRY OF ORIGIN—Austria

DATE OF MANUFACTURE—1991 to present

CALIBER—5.7×26 mm UCC (Usel Caseless Cartridge)

OVERALL LENGTH—39.1 inches (99.3 cm)

BARREL LENGTH—20.45 inches (51.9 cm)

LOAD—Jacketed soft point

BULLET DIAMETER—0.224 inch (5.69 mm)

BULLET WEIGHT—55 grains (3.6 g)

MUZZLE VELOCITY—3,051 fps (930 m/s)

MUZZLE ENERGY—1,136 ft./lb. (1540 J)

WEIGHT (EMPTY)—6.2 lbs. (2.81 kg)

WEIGHT (LOADED)—6.26 lbs. (2.84 kg)

SIGHTS—Fixed, adjustable V-notch/blade, rear sight set for 200 meters; receiver drilled and tapped for scope mount

EFFECTIVE RANGE—300 yards (274 m)

OPERATION—Manual bolt action

TYPE OF FIRE—Repeating

RATE OF FIRE—15 to 20 rpm

FEED DEVICE—Removable 5-round box magazine

MANUFACTURER—Voere Kufsteiner Gerätebau- und Handelsgesellschaft mbH, Austria

SERVICE—None, commercial sales only

STATUS—Limited production

REFERENCES—Walter, John, *Rifles of the World*, 3rd Edition

The G36 rifle. *Heckler & Koch Defense*

NAME—G36 Weapons System

COMMON NAMES—G36 (originally HK50)
G36 Commando
G36 Carbine (G36K)
G36 Carbine (Export) (G36KE)
G36 Close Quarters Battle (G36CQB)
G36
G36 (Export) (G36E)
G36 Light Support Weapon (G36LSW)
G36 Light Support Weapons (Export) (G36LSWE)

TYPE—Rifle/carbine weapon system

COUNTRY OF ORIGIN—Germany

CALIBER—5.56×45 mm

OVERALL LENGTH—
G36 Commando—
19.69 inches (50 cm) with stock folded
28.27 inches (71.8 cm) with stock open

The G36K carbine variation. *Heckler & Koch Defense*

G36 Carbine/G36 Carbine (Export)
24.21 inches (61.5 cm) with stock folded
33.78 inches (85.8 cm) with stock open
G36 Close Quarters Battle
26.34 inches (66.9 cm) with stock folded
38.79 inches (98.5 cm) with stock open
G36/G36 (Export)/G36 Light Support Weapon/G36 Light Support Weapons (Export)
29.84 inches (75.8 cm) with stock folded
39.29 inches (99.8 cm) with stock open

BARREL LENGTH—
G36 Commando—8.98 inches (22.8 cm)
G36 Carbine/G36 Carbine (Export)—12.52 inches (31.8 cm)
G36 Close Quarters Battle—15.4 inches (39.1 cm)
G36/G36 (Export)/G36 Light Support

The G36K with its stock folded to the side. *Heckler & Koch Defense*

Weapon/G36 Light Support Weapons (Export)—18.90 inches (48 cm)

RIFLING (TYPE AND TWIST)—6-groove, right-hand, 1 turn in 7 inches (17.8 cm)
G36CQB barrel—6-groove, right-hand, 1 turn in 9 inches (22.9 cm)

LOAD—M855 ball

BULLET DIAMETER—0.224 inch (5.69 mm)
BULLET WEIGHT—62 grains (4.02 g)
MUZZLE VELOCITY—
G36 Commando—2,662 fps (809 m/s)
G36 Carbine/G36 Carbine (Export)—2,789 fps (850 m/s)
G36 Close Quarters Battle—2,893 fps (882 m/s)
G36/G36 (Export)/G36 Light Support Weapon/G36 Light Support Weapons (Export)—3,019 fps (920 m/s)

MUZZLE ENERGY—
G36 Commando—975 ft./lb. (1322 J)
G36 Carbine/G36 Carbine (Export)—1,071 ft./lb. (1452 J)
G36 Close Quarters Battle—1152 ft./lb. (1562 J)
G36/G36 (Export)/G36 Light Support Weapon/G36 Light Support Weapons (Export)—1,255 ft./lb. (1702 J)

WEIGHT (EMPTY)—
G36 Commando—6.28 lbs. (2.85 kg)
G36 Carbine (G36K)—7.28 lbs. (3.30 kg)
G36 Carbine (Export) (G36KE)—6.62 lbs. (3.00 kg)
G36 Close Quarters Battle (G36CQB)—7.05 lbs. (3.20 kg)
G36—7.94 lbs. (3.60 kg)
G36 (Export)—7.28 lbs. (3.30 kg)
G36 Light Support Weapon (G36LSW)—8.53 lbs. (3.87 kg) with folding bipod attached
G36 Light Support Weapons (Export) (G36LSWE)—7.87 lbs. (3.57 kg) with folding bipod attached
Bipod weight 0.46 lb. (0.21 kg)

WEIGHT (LOADED)—
G36 Commando—7.37 lbs. (3.34 kg) with 30 rounds
G36 Carbine (G36K)—8.37 lbs. (3.80 kg) with 30 rounds
G36 Carbine (Export) (G36KE)—7.71 lbs. (3.50 kg) with 30 rounds
G36 Close Quarters Battle (G36CQB)—

8.14 lbs. (3.69 kg) with 30 rounds

G36—9.03 lbs. (4.10 kg)

G36 (Export)—8.37 lbs. (3.80 kg) with 30 rounds

G36 Light Support Weapon (G36LSW)—13.22 lbs. (6.00 kg) with 100-round drum and folding bipod

G36 Light Support Weapons (Export) (G36LSWE)—12.56 lbs. (5.70 kg) with 100-round drum and folding bipod

SIGHTS—

Commando—Adjustable iron sights, rear aperture post, mounted on Mil-STD-1913 (Picatinny) rail system.

Standard—Dual-combat sighting system. Optical sight mounted in carrying handle below an electronic red-dot reflex sight. Both sights are independently adjustable for windage and elevation. Optical sight reticle has a 200-, 400-, 600-, and 800-meter range estimation scale as well as 400-, 600-, and 800-meter aiming points. Red-dot sight has dual illumination system with port for ambient light use during daylight periods.

Export—Optical sight as part of carrying rail, backup nonadjustable open square notch/blade iron sight as part of carrying rail

Hensoldt NSA 80 II night vision sight module weight—2.65 lbs. (1.20 kg)

SIGHT POWER—

Commando sight radius—9.84 inches (25 cm)

Standard—3 power magnification

Export—1.5 power magnification

OPERATION—Gas

TYPE OF FIRE—Selective, semi-, and full automatic fire; 2-round controlled burst available as option

CYCLIC RATE OF FIRE—750 rpm

FEED DEVICE—Removable polymer 30-round box magazine, 100-round double-drum

FEED DEVICE WEIGHT (EMPTY)—

30-round polymer box—0.28 lb. (0.13 kg)

100-round drum—1.98 lbs. (0.90 kg)

FEED DEVICE WEIGHT (LOADED)—

30-round polymer box—1.09 lbs. (0.49 kg)

100-round drum—4.69 lbs. (2.13 kg)

MANUFACTURER—Heckler & Koch, GMbH

SERVICE—In service with German Bundeswehr and NATO Rapid Reaction Force (G36), German special operations units (G36 and G36K), and Spanish Armed Forces (G36)

STATUS—In production

REFERENCES—Company literature

COMMENTS—The 30-round polymer magazines developed by H&K are translucent so that the interior ammunition can be seen. In addition, there are mounting lugs, two on each side of the magazine, that allow multiple units to be mounted together, side by side. The NSA 80 night vision sight module attached to the upper part of the carrying handle and to the front of the optical sight, utilizing the reticle zero of the optical sight to mate the night vision capability of the module to the weapon's point of aim.

The G36 Light Support Weapon loaded with a 100-round double-drum magazine. *Heckler & Koch Defense*

The Tavor rifle. *Kevin Dockery*

NAME—Tavor-21 Weapons Family

COMMON NAMES—

Micro Tavor Assault Rifle (MTAR-21)

Commando Tavor Assault Rifle (CTAR-21)

Tavor Carbine (TC-21)

Tavor Assault Rifle (TAR-21)

Sharp Shooting Tavor Assault Rifle (STAR-21)

CALIBER—5.56×45 mm

OVERALL LENGTH—

Micro Tavor Assault Rifle (MTAR-21)—18.90 inches (48.0 cm)

Commando Tavor Assault Rifle (CTAR-21)—25.2 inches (64.0 cm)

Tavor Carbine (TC-21)—26.3 inches (66.9 cm)

Tavor Assault Rifle (TAR-21)—28.3 inches (72.0 cm)

Sharp Shooting Tavor Assault Rifle (STAR-21)—28.3 inches (72.0 cm)

BARREL LENGTH—

Micro Tavor Assault Rifle (MTAR-21)—9.84 inches (25.0 cm)

Commando Tavor Assault Rifle (CTAR-21)—15.0 inches (38.0 cm)

Tavor Carbine (TC-21)—16.1 inches (40.9 cm)

Tavor Assault Rifle (TAR-21)—18.1 inches (46.0 cm)

Sharp Shooting Tavor Assault Rifle (STAR-21)—18.1 inches (46.0 cm)

RIFLING (TYPE AND TWIST)—6-groove, right-hand, 1 turn in 7 inches (17.8 cm)

LOAD—M855 ball

BULLET DIAMETER—0.224 inch (5.66 mm)

BULLET WEIGHT—62 grains (4.02 g)

MUZZLE VELOCITY—

Micro Tavor Assault Rifle (MTAR-21)—2,526 fps (770 m/s)

Commando Tavor Assault Rifle (CTAR-21)—2,854 fps (870 m/s)

Tavor Carbine (TC-21)—2,904 fps (885 m/s)

Tavor Assault Rifle (TAR-21)—2,953 fps (900 m/s)

Sharp Shooting Tavor Assault Rifle (STAR-21)—2,953 fps (900 m/s)

MUZZLE ENERGY—

Micro Tavor Assault Rifle (MTAR-21)—878 ft./lb. (1191 J)

Commando Tavor Assault Rifle (CTAR-21)—1121 ft./lb. (1520 J)

Tavor Carbine (TC-21)—1,161 ft./lb. (1574 J)

Tavor Assault Rifle (TAR-21)—1,200 ft./lb. (1627 J)

Sharp Shooting Tavor Assault Rifle (STAR-21)—1,200 ft./lb. (1627 J)

WEIGHT (EMPTY)—

Micro Tavor Assault Rifle (MTAR-21)—5.29 lbs. (2.40 kg)

Commando Tavor Assault Rifle (CTAR-21)—5.95 lbs. (2.70 kg)

Tavor Carbine (TC-21)—6.06 lbs. (2.75 kg)

Tavor Assault Rifle (TAR-21)—6.17 lbs. (2.80 kg)

Sharp Shooting Tavor Assault Rifle (STAR-21)—7.50 lbs. (3.40 kg)

WEIGHT (LOADED)—

Micro Tavor Assault Rifle (MTAR-21)—7.05 lbs. (3.20 kg) with 30 rounds, sling, and Falcon sight with laser

Commando Tavor Assault Rifle (CTAR-21)—7.72 lbs. (3.50 kg) with 30 rounds, sling, and Falcon sight with laser

Tavor carbine (TC-21)—7.83 lbs. (3.55 kg) with 30 rounds, sling, and Falcon sight with laser

Tavor Assault Rifle (TAR-21)—8.02 lbs. (3.64 kg) with 30 rounds, sling, and Falcon sight with laser

Sharp Shooting Tavor Assault Rifle (STAR-21)—9.37 lbs. (4.25 kg) with 30 rounds, sling, folding bipod, and ACOG sight on mount

SIGHTS—Elbit Falcon optical red-dot reflex sight with integral laser designator mounted directly to barrel assembly; Sharp Shooting Tavor Assault Rifle (STAR-21)—Optical Trijicon Advanced Combat Optical Gunsight (ACOG); optical sight weight—0.59 lb. (0.27 kg)

SIGHT POWER—1/1 power reflex sight; Sharp Shooting Tavor Assault Rifle (STAR-21)

with ACOG—Fixed 4 power optical sight magnification

OPERATION—Gas

TYPE OF FIRE—Selective fire, full, and semiautomatic; Tavor Carbine (TC-21)— semiautomatic fire only

CYCLIC RATE OF FIRE—750 to 900 rpm

FEED DEVICE—STANAG 4179–compliant magazines

FEED DEVICE WEIGHT (EMPTY)—0.26 lb. (0.12 kg) 30-round aluminum magazine

FEED DEVICE WEIGHT (LOADED)—1.07 lbs. (0.49 kg) loaded with 30 rounds M855 ball

MANUFACTURER—Israel Military Industries Limited, Ramat Hasharon, Israel

SERVICE—Evaluation by Israeli and Croatian military forces

STATUS—Ready for production

The Tavor Commander's rifle (carbine). *Kevin Dockery*

REFERENCES—Gander, Terry J., ed., *Jane's Infantry Weapons, 2001–2002*; Cutshaw, Charles, *Tactical Small Arms of the 21st Century*; company literature

The F2000 standard version with sight module. *FN USA, LLC*

NAME—F2000

COMMON NAMES—FN2000

CALIBER—5.56×45 mm NATO

OVERALL LENGTH—27.32 inches (69.4 cm)

BARREL LENGTH—15.75 inches (40.0 cm)

LOAD—M855 ball

BULLET DIAMETER—0.224 inch (5.69 mm)

BULLET WEIGHT—62 grains (4.02 g)

MUZZLE VELOCITY—2,953 fps (900 m/s)

MUZZLE ENERGY—1,200 ft./lb. (1627 J)

WEIGHT (EMPTY)—7.95 lbs. (3.61 kg)

WEIGHT (LOADED)—9.02 lbs. (4.09 kg) with 30 rounds in aluminum magazine

SIGHTS—Optical sight in molded housing on top of receiver secured to MIL-STD-1913 Picatinny rail; fixed, nonadjustable notch/post backup sights normally covered by optical sight housing

SIGHT POWER—1.6 power magnification

OPERATION—Gas

TYPE OF FIRE—Selective, semi-, and full automatic

CYCLIC RATE OF FIRE—850 rpm

FEED DEVICE—All STANAG 4179–compliant magazines

FEED DEVICE WEIGHT (EMPTY)—0.26 lb. (0.12 kg) 30-round aluminum magazine

FEED DEVICE WEIGHT (LOADED)—1.07 lbs. (0.49 kg) loaded with 30 rounds M855 ball

MANUFACTURER—FN Herstal, Belgium

SERVICE—Evaluation

STATUS—Ready for production

REFERENCES—Cutshaw, Charles, *Tactical Small Arms of the 21st Century*; company literature

The F2000 with MIL-STD-1913 rail upper receiver exposed. *FN USA, LLC*

The XM8/MSWF Compact Carbine above the Baseline
Carbine variation. *Kevin Dockery*

NAME—Modular Weapon System Family
(MSWF)

COMMON NAMES—XM8 Lightweight
Modular Weapon System

TYPE—Rifle/carbine weapon system

CALIBER—5.56×45 mm

OVERALL LENGTH—

Compact carbine w/o stock (butt cap)—
21.1 inches (53.6 cm)

Compact carbine—w/MP-7 style
retracting stock

22.4 inches (56.9 cm) with stock
retracted

30 inches (76.2 cm) with stock fully
extended

Carbine—

30.3 inches (77 cm) with stock
collapsed

33.3 inches (84.6 cm) with stock fully
open

Sharpshooter (Designated Marksman)/
Automatic Rifle

37.3 inches (94.7 cm) with stock
collapsed

40.2 inches (102.1 cm) with stock fully
open

BARREL LENGTH—

Compact carbine—9 inches (22.9 cm)

Carbine—12.5 inches (63.5 cm)

Sharpshooter (Designated Marksman)/
Automatic Rifle—20 inches (50.8 cm)

RIFLING (TYPE AND TWIST)—6-groove,
right-hand, 1 turn in 7 inches (17.8 cm)

LOAD—M855 ball

BULLET DIAMETER—0.224 inch (5.69 mm)

BULLET WEIGHT—62 grains (4.02 g)

MUZZLE VELOCITY—

Compact carbine/carbine—2,425 fps
(739 m/s)

Carbine—2,695 fps (821 m/s)

Sharpshooter (Designated Marksman)/
automatic rifle—3,005 fps (916 m/s)

MUZZLE ENERGY—

Compact carbine/carbine—809 ft./lb.
(1097 J)

Carbine—1,000 ft./lb. (1356 J)

Sharpshooter (Designated Marksman)/
automatic rifle—1,243 ft./lb. (1686 J)

WEIGHT (EMPTY)—

Compact carbine—7.10 lbs. (3.22 kg)

Carbine—7.51 lbs. (3.41 kg)

Sharpshooter (Designated Marksman)—
10.18 lbs. (4.62 kg)

Automatic Rifle—10.18 lbs. (4.62 kg)

WEIGHT (LOADED)—Compact carbine w/o
stock (butt cap)

Compact carbine—8.21 lbs. (3.72 kg)

Carbine—8.62 lbs. (3.91 kg)

Sharpshooter (Designated Marksman)—
11.29 lbs. (5.12 kg)

Automatic Rifle—15.09 lbs. (6.84 kg)
w/100-round drum

SIGHTS—

Standard—Electronic and optical
Integrated Sight Module (ISM) with red-dot
reflex reticle, adjustable for windage and
elevation, integral infrared laser illuminator
and pointer; folding backup iron sights

Sharpshooter (Designated Marksman)/
Automatic Rifle—Electronic and optical
Advanced Magnified Optics (AMO) with
adjustable red-dot reflex reticle, etched
ranging reticle sight with integral infrared
illuminator/pointer, adjustable for windage
and elevation; backup folding iron sights

SIGHT RADIUS (POWER)—
ISM—1/1 power
AMO—4 power
OPERATION—Gas
TYPE OF FIRE—Selective, semi-, and full automatic
RATE OF FIRE—85 rpm for 210 rounds (90 seconds)
CYCLIC RATE OF FIRE—825 rpm
FEED DEVICE—Removable polymer 30-round box magazine, 100-round double-drum
FEED DEVICE WEIGHT (EMPTY)—
30-round polymer box—0.30 lb. (0.14 kg)
100-round drum—2.20 lbs. (1 kg)
FEED DEVICE WEIGHT (LOADED)—
30-round polymer box—1.11 lbs. (0.50 kg)
100-round drum—4.91 lbs. (2.23 kg)
MANUFACTURER—HK Defense, Sterling, Virginia
SERVICE—None
STATUS—Developmental
REFERENCES—Company literature

An early version of the MK 16 Mod 0 SCAR—Light weapon with a proposed enhanced grenade launcher model attached under the barrel. *Kevin Dockery*

NAME—Mark 16 Mod 0 Special Operations Forces Combat Assault Rifle—Light
COMMON NAMES—MK 16, SCAR-l
CALIBER—5.56×45 mm
OVERALL LENGTH—
24.09 inches (61.2 cm) with stock folded
31.02 inches (79.8 cm) with stock collapsed
33.0 inches (83.8 cm) with stock fully extended
BARREL LENGTH—13.78 inches (35.0 cm); Close Quarters Combat barrel—9.96 inches (25.3 cm)
RIFLING (TYPE AND TWIST)—6-groove, right-hand twist, 1 turn in 7 inches (17.8 cm)
LOAD—M855 ball or Mk 262 Mod 0 or 1 ball
BULLET DIAMETER—0.224 inch (5.69 mm)
BULLET WEIGHT—
M855 ball—62 grains (4.02 g)
Mk 262 Mod 0 and 1 ball—77 grains (4.99 g)
MUZZLE VELOCITY—
M855 ball—2,870 fps (875 m/s)
MK 262 ball—2,630 fps (802 m/s)
MUZZLE ENERGY—
M855 ball—1,134 ft./lb. (1538 J)
Mk 262 Mod 0 and 1 ball—1,182 ft./lb. (1603 J)
WEIGHT (EMPTY)—7.24 lbs. (3.28 kg) with iron sights
WEIGHT (LOADED)—8.65 lbs. (3.92 kg) loaded with 30 rounds Mk 262 ball and steel magazine
SIGHTS—MIL-STD-1913 Picatinny rail along full length of receiver top; rail sections along sides and bottom of fore end; backup

The author holding the XM8 Compact Carbine with the butt cap installed. This is the shortest variation of the weapon system and is the closest to the version that was mounted on the OICW weapon. *Kevin Dockery*

adjustable iron sights, fixed hooded front post, folding rear aperture

SIGHT RADIUS—Variable

EFFECTIVE RANGE—875 yards (800 m) w/Mk 262 ball

OPERATION—Gas

TYPE OF FIRE—Selective, semi-, and full automatic

CYCLIC RATE OF FIRE—550 rpm

FEED DEVICE—All STANAG 4179–compliant magazines, steel-bodied, 30-round magazine developed with weapon

FEED DEVICE WEIGHT (EMPTY)—0.54 lb. (0.24 kg)

FEED DEVICE WEIGHT (LOADED)—
M855 ball—1.35 lbs. (0.61 kg)
Mk 262 Mod 0 or 1 ball—1.41 lbs. (0.64 kg)

MANUFACTURER—FNH USA, LLC, McLean, Virginia

SERVICE—In limited service with U.S. Special Operations forces

STATUS—In production

REFERENCES—Cutshaw, Charles, *Tactical Small Arms of the 21st Century*, company literature

An early version of the 7.62×51 mm Mark 17 Mod 0 SCAR—Heavy rifle. *Kevin Dockery*

NAME—Mark 17 Mod 0 Special Operations Forces Combat Assault Rifle—Heavy

COMMON NAMES—MK 17, SCAR-H

CALIBER—7.62×51 mm NATO

OVERALL LENGTH—
31.4 inches (79.8 cm) with stock folded

38.7 inches (98.3 cm) with stock collapsed
40.2 inches (102.1 cm) with stock fully extended

BARREL LENGTH—19.7 inches (50.0 cm)

RIFLING (TYPE AND TWIST)—6-groove, right-hand twist, 1 turn in 7 inches (17.8 cm)

LOAD—M80 ball

BULLET DIAMETER—0.308 inch (7.62 mm)

BULLET WEIGHT—146 grains

MUZZLE VELOCITY—2,342 fps (104 m/s)

MUZZLE ENERGY—1,778 ft./lb. (2411 J)

WEIGHT (EMPTY)—7.74 lbs. (3.51 kg) with iron sights

WEIGHT (LOADED)—9.39 lbs. (4.26 kg) with iron sights and 20 rounds M80 ball

SIGHTS—MIL-STD-1913 Picatinny rail along full length of receiver top; rail sections along sides and bottom of fore end; backup adjustable iron sights, fixed hooded front post, folding rear aperture

SIGHT RADIUS—Variable

OPERATION—Gas

TYPE OF FIRE—Selective, semi-, and full automatic

CYCLIC RATE OF FIRE—550 rpm

FEED DEVICE—Removable steel 20-round box magazine

FEED DEVICE WEIGHT (EMPTY)—0.53 lb. (0.24 kg)

FEED DEVICE WEIGHT (LOADED)—1.65 lbs. (0.75 kg)

MANUFACTURER—FNH USA, LLC, McLean, Virginia

SERVICE—Evaluation and testing by U.S. Special Operations Forces

STATUS—Under development

REFERENCES—Cutshaw, Charles, *Tactical Small Arms of the 21st Century*; company literature

■ Magazines ■

In order to allow the North Atlantic Treaty Organization (NATO) to more easily interoperate with all the member organizations, the standardization agreement (STANAG) system was developed and put into place. STANAG 4179 is the standard for 5.56×45 mm ammunition feed devices and the corresponding feed device interfaces and controls (magazine catch, bolt stop, etc.) so that all of the weapons that can feed from a STANAG 4179 device can do so with magazines made by any country meeting the mechanical standard. This standard is based on the original removable box magazine first designed for the M16 weapon family used by the American armed forces. Any feed device, whether a small box magazine or a large-capacity drum, meeting STANAG 4179 will be able to fit and function in any of the M16 family of weapons from any era. The feed devices will also be able to operate correctly in any other weapon with a magazine well and controls also built to meet the standard.

For the M16 family of weapons, and those built to STANAG 4179 specifications, there are three basic sizes of feed devices normally encountered, with some variations based on the material the device is made from. The original M16 and M16A1 magazines had a twenty-round base capacity.

Many users would only load the magazines with eighteen rounds to maintain a safety factor by keeping the strain on the magazine spring to a minimum and leaving some flexibility in the ammunition column to allow for easier seating and locking into the weapon. The most common STANAG 4179 magazine encountered today is the aluminum-bodied thirty-round magazine with a slightly curved body. Optionally, the thirty-round magazine is also made of polymer, as are a number of other STANAG 4179 magazines. Working for the British and their L85 (SA80) and L86 weapons, Heckler & Koch designed a STANAG 4179 magazine that holds thirty rounds and is constructed of steel. Precision-made on computer-controlled machinery, the steel SA80 magazine is very dependable and functions well in all environments. This is due in part to the advanced alloys and finish materials that the magazine is made from. The most common large-capacity 5.56 mm feed device that meets the STANAG requirements is the one hundred-round double-drum system known as the Beta C-Mag. The C-Mag has an interchangeable tower system that can be changed to interface with other 5.56×45–caliber weapons that do not meet the general STANAG 4179 requirements.

STANDARD

Magazine	30-round	30-round	H&K SA80
Material	Aluminum	Nylon	Steel
Weight (empty)	0.258 lb. (0.117 kg)	0.249 lb. (0.113 kg)	0.54 lb. (0.24 kg)
Weight (loaded)	30-rds	30-rds	30-rds
w/M193 ball	1.038 lbs. (0.471 kg)	—	—
w/M855 ball	1.071 lbs. (0.486 kg)	1.063 lbs. (0.482 kg)	1.353 lbs. (0.61 kg)

Magazine	20-round	100-round drum
Material	Aluminum	Polymers
Weight (empty)	0.201 lb. (0.091 kg)	2.20 lbs. (1.00 kg)
Weight (Loaded)	20-rds	100-rds
w/M193 ball	0.721 lb. (0.327 kg)	—
w/M855 ball	—	4.91 lbs. (2.23 kg)

5.56 × 45 MM U.S. MILITARY AMMUNITION

	Cartridge Weight	Projectile Weight	Muzzle Velocity*	Rifling twist rate for Stability
M193 ball	182 grains	56 grains	3,250 fps	1 turn in 12 inches
(30.5 cm)	(11.79 g)	(3.63 g)	(991 m/s)	
M855 ball	190 grains	62 grains	3,025 fps	1 turn in 7 inches
(17.8 cm)	(12.31 g)	(4.02 g)	(922 m/s)	

* Mv for 20-inch (50.8 cm) length rifle barrels

Rifle rounds (from right to left) The 7.93 x 33 mm Kurz ball round with a steel case, the 7.26 x 51 mm ball round, the 7.26 x 39 mm ball round in a copper-washed steel case, the M193 5.56 x 45 mm ball round, the 5.45 x 39 mm tracer round with a steel case.
Kevin Dockery

PISTOLS

SIDEARM

The light coloring the far edges of the mountains behind them told Maxwell that dawn was not very far away as the transport helicopter flew across the desert plateau. The special operations unit that had inserted would be well into their mission before the pair of transport birds would be back over friendly soil.

The dark-painted Blackhawk helicopter was flying nape-of-the-earth, a roller coaster ride of a flight as the bird stayed down low to avoid detection. The rocky peaks of the upper Zagros Mountains shot past at hundreds of miles an hour. Sometimes the mountain peaks seemed to actually be above the pair of helicopters as the two craft stayed below the horizon and out of the range of most radar.

"Turkish border in three-zero mikes," the voice of the pilot, Captain Ed Armand, came over the headset. "Say good-bye to beautiful northern Persia."

"At least until extraction," Lieutenant Steve Jackson, the copilot of Iron Knight Two Zero, said over the intercom.

Iron Knight Two Zero was the identifier for the Blackhawk special operations craft that Sergeant Dave Maxwell was a crew member of. The other bird in their flight was Iron Knight Two One. Only a short while earlier they had both dropped off a special operations team deep into Iranian territory. Maxwell hadn't been briefed on the whole of the mission, just his part of it as the door gunner on the port side of Iron Knight Two Zero. The dark-faced, serious men they had been flying with for hours had spoken little and communicated less. He didn't know that the mission was to locate and seize a possible Islamic bomb from the hands of extremists. The weapon had been brought down from Azerbaijan after being obtained on the Russian black market. The Iranians hadn't yet been able to make a nuclear weapon for themselves, but they had managed to buy one.

What Maxwell knew as he leaned over his 7.62 mm minigun and peered out at the mountains flashing past was that they were inside a foreign country, a far from friendly one, and had some time to go before they would be safe. What he didn't know was just how long that time was going to be.

From one of the ridgelines to the south, there was a sudden flash and a smoke trail appeared heading up to the two helicopters. The first trail was followed by a second and then a third.

"Missiles, missiles, from the left side!" Maxwell shouted into the boom mike on his helmet.

"Missiles on the right," came from Master Sergeant Brian Saxon on the other side of the bird. As the crew chief, Saxon was the ranking noncommissioned officer in the bird and was manning the right-side minigun.

There was no word from either of the men in the seats on the flight deck as they put the helicopter into a series of violent maneuvers to try to lose the deadly heat-seeking missiles. There was nothing that could be done for Iron Knight Two One as it was suddenly enveloped in a huge ball of flame as several of the missiles struck the bird almost simultaneously. The roar of the blast bounced off the surrounding mountains even as the sounds of the destroyed bird's rotor blades were still echoing though the rocks. The shock wave that smacked into Maxell's bird went unnoticed among the gyrations and forces that were already acting on the desperately dodging aircraft. The burning flares that had been popping out from dispensers on both helicopters did nothing to distract the missiles. They burned in to their targets within a few seconds of launch.

A shock wave struck Maxwell on the back of the head and body that made him feel as if he had slammed up against the rear bulkhead of the bird rather than being securely strapped down in his armored seat. The shoulder harness he had pulled in tightly as the craft started her struggles held him in place, but it didn't feel like it. There had been an explosion from the right side of the helicopter that told Maxwell that they were hit and hit bad. The shuddering helicopter made it over the mountain line right in front of them, missing the rocks by only feet. Captain Armand was fighting the wounded bird for every foot of distance he could put between themselves and the people who had shot them down. As the floor of the valley in front of them grew closer, control started slipping away fast. The sounds of grinding metal and crushing gears were drowning out all of the other noises except for a shouted "Brace for im—" Then there was a thundering noise and blackness.

When Maxwell recovered enough of his senses to realize he was still alive, he wasn't sure for how much longer that situation would remain. The helicopter had smashed in on its right side. He could look over to where Saxon had been, and there was nothing but rocks and torn metal. The smell of leaking fuel, hydraulics, and burning plastic was thick in the air, and there was a horrible taste in his mouth combined of the burned plastics, explosive fumes, and the coppery tang of his own blood.

Maxwell was unhurt for the most part, though banged up and very dizzy for the moment. He had bitten his lip, and blood was pouring down off his chin, but that was nothing at all. The helmet he was wearing had been smashed up against the padding around the armor of his seat and was knocked askew, but there wasn't a sound coming over the headphones any longer, and he just pulled it off. As he pulled at the buckles of the harness that had saved his life, Maxwell looked around to see if there was any other movement in the compartment. Through the smoke and haze he saw nothing more than a few sparks in the darkness.

"Anyone else make it?" he said loudly. At every word, he sprayed out bright red blood from his bitten lip.

"In here," came a weak voice from the flight deck.

It would have been more accurate to say where the flight deck had been when Maxwell looked in to where the pilot and copilot had controlled the helicopter. The right side of the bird was smashed up badly. It looked as if captain Armand had tried to put the bird in on her side to keep the rotor blades from collapsing in and slashing through the compartments. Whatever the reason, it had cost him everything, as his body hung limply in the harness that held him to his seat. His head was no longer shaped the way it had been, it couldn't be with the huge dent in the side of his flight helmet crushed in the way it was. But Lieutenant Jackson was still alive, though injured.

Working as carefully as he could in the dark—dawn was still a few minutes away at least—Maxwell managed to get his injured officer up and out of the helicopter without the man screaming. Jackson's legs were bent where there weren't any joints, so it was obvious that both of them were broken. But the officer gutted out being pulled from the wreckage and moved a short distance away. In the cover of the rocks, Maxwell performed what first aid he could do to keep the lieutenant from bleeding to death and to try to secure his broken limbs. One thing was for sure, they weren't going to be walking out of there.

"Max," Jackson said weakly as shock started to set in, "I got a transmission out before we went in. The PJs will be on their way."

The idea of the Air Force Pararescuemen knowing that they were down and what their general location would be gave Maxwell some hope, but not much for the moment. The only weapons available to the two men were the Beretta M9A1 pistols they both had strapped to their survival vests. That gave Maxwell two guns and ninety rounds of ammunition in six magazines. Not a hell of a lot to make a stand with. The minigun he had been manning was still back in the wreckage of the helicopter. The 4,000 rounds a minute it could put out would have been a comfort in their situation. But the powered weapon couldn't be dismounted and used, and it would have been too heavy for him to handle anyway, even if he could have pulled the gun, ammunition, and a battery from the downed bird.

Nope, it was going to be sidearms against—what? If the enemy had any heavy weapons, then the survivors of the crash were done. Whoever had brought them down could just sit on the mountainsides and pound the area around the crash site into even finer rubble with just a few mortars. If the opposition was armed with just small arms, then Maxwell and his lieutenant had a chance, a vanishingly small one, but a chance. He grabbed at that small hope and held it tightly as his mind cleared and he examined the surrounding geography of the valley.

There were some lights in the mountains around them, small pinpricks of brightness in the growing glow of the approaching dawn. As he watched, he could now see the heads of men bobbing up and down as they clambered among the rocks; the closest of them were just a couple of hundred meters away, then two hundred, then one hundred.

It was roughly clothed men carrying small arms, AK-47s by the looks of the distinctive curved magazines. One thing was certain; Maxwell didn't think they were there to be helpful. Bandits, smugglers, terrorists, or Iranian militia, it didn't matter to him. The one thing they had going for them at that moment was the fact that the approaching men didn't know where Maxwell and Jackson were, and he wasn't going to let them find out.

He had always liked shooting, had been a competition shooter for years. He had even taken prizes while on the base pistol team down at Hurlburt Field. Maxwell may have only had a pair of handguns to his name just then; he hadn't been able to quickly find any of the other shoulder arms that should have been somewhere in the downed helicopter. The only reason he even had the sidearms was that they had been strapped into the holsters he and the lieutenant had been wearing.

But if all he had were two handguns, at least he was good with them—very, very good. And he had a little edge to the situation. The Beretta that Jackson had been carrying was equipped with a suppressor. The lieutenant had slipped into unconsciousness, but not before he had pulled the long black cylinder from a pocket of his vest and handed it to Maxwell. The pain from his broken legs had to be almost unbearable, but the officer never made a sound. With his ashen face visible even in the dim, dawning light, he didn't have to say anything. Unconsciousness was a blessing. As the sergeant locked the suppressor to the barrel of the Beretta, he carefully chose his targets. The man lying next to him could not defend himself; Maxwell would fight for both of them as he leveled the gun for his first shot.

There was a dull thud from the suppressed pistol, the sound lost among the rocks scattered around the valley floor. Nearly seventy-five meters away, one of the approaching armed men threw up his hands and pitched over backward. The bullet had torn through the center of his chest, stopping his heart instantly. As his AK-47 flew up into the air, the dead man's partners opened fire blindly into the dark, aiming generally toward the wreckage of the downed helicopter, the only possible source of fire that they could see around.

With the fire of the assault rifles covering his own noise, Maxwell fired three quick rounds in succession. The hissing thuds of the suppressed pistol went unheard, but not the impact of the bullets it had launched. Three shots, three hits. One man went down and remained still, the other two screamed in pain and jumped back under cover.

The lethal marksmanship of Sergeant Maxwell proved enough to hold the approaching men at bay for over two hours. With the valley in full daylight, Maxwell had to be very careful not to expose himself, but the armed men all around him had also learned that lesson. No one was within a hundred meters of the downed helicopter, at least not anyone who was willing to expose themselves.

Lieutenant Jackson had been on the survival radio before he had passed out, trying to raise someone on the emergency frequency. His efforts had not been in vain when he contacted an electronic warfare aircraft circling high overhead and miles away. The AWACs plane had been vectoring in a group of rescue helicopters full of armed PJs coming to pick up the downed men. That last act had taken up what remained of his strength and was one of the reasons he had passed out.

The pistols-against-AKs firefight had gone on for an unknown length of time. Maxwell fired and fired. The suppressor on his pistol was so heated that he could smell the hot metal over the powder smoke. Reloading without active thought, Maxwell ejected the empty magazine and slapped in a fresh one from his dwindling supply as he hit the slide release and the metal clacked home on a new round.

The sound of approaching salvation almost cost Maxwell his life. Jackson, who was now only semiconscious, tried to shout a warning as a pair of AK-carrying locals appeared and opened fire. They had been sneaking in among the rocks while Maxwell had been keeping their fellows at bay.

As Maxwell rolled over from where he lay in the rocks and pulled up into a sitting position, he knew he wouldn't be fast enough. Both guns came up in his hands, the slides jerking back as he fired them. Slugs went out the muzzles, but not before other rounds were fired back at him.

The 9 mm bullets Maxwell sent out struck their targets, but the fanatics' rounds found their target as well; 7.62 mm rifle slugs smashed into Maxwell's chest and right leg. He went down, knocked over backward by the impact. The tearing pain in his chest told him he was still alive, but the breath was knocked out of him. The hammer blow he took to his right leg was the bad one. It didn't hurt, or at least it didn't hurt yet. At least one 7.62 mm slug had ripped into his outer right thigh, tearing open the skin and muscle to momentarily lay bare the bone below. The wound quickly filled with blood, obscuring the view of the damage, but the blood was a heavy flow, not the spurting fountain that would have indicated a major severed vessel.

In spite of his injuries, he had held onto his pistols. Maxwell was still in the fight. When the other fanatics started to come ahead, they were met with withering fire from just a brace of pistols.

Standing up on his one good leg, blood streaming down the torn uniform covering his right leg, Maxwell dumped round after round from both his weapons out toward the men who had tried to kill him and his lieutenant. The recoil popped the pistols up into the air, and he pulled them back down into line. It was the best shooting he would ever do in his life, and something deep inside the man knew it. His body was broken, but it listened to the commands of his indomitable will. As AKs were lifted to the sky to fire on the approaching threat, the 9 mm projectiles from the wounded man cut through the others like a scythe. Whatever shoulder-fired missiles had been available to the men, they must have used them all in that first opening barrage, as no smoking trails rose up to meet the incoming black-painted helicopters.

Miniguns on the rescue helicopters roared, and the ground was plowed by steel-jacketed bullets. The heavily armed PJs jumped from the hovering birds and ran to where they could see their downed comrades.

"That others may live" is the creed of the Pararescuemen, and they were there to get the others out. As he turned and saw his salvation coming in to him in the form of heavily laden, camouflaged, merciless angels, whatever strength had been sustaining the man drained from him like water. Maxwell collapsed, falling down across his lieutenant as the PJs came up to where he and Jackson lay. But even as he collapsed, he never let the pistols out of his hands. Not even the PJs could pry the weapons from the man's hands, and they stopped trying as they could see that both of the slides were locked back on empty magazines. Scattered around on the ground were dozens of spent brass casings and the long metal shapes of empty magazines.

The survivors of Iron Knight Two Zero were picked up and put on board the rescue birds along with the covered bodies of their crewmates. As the rescue birds lifted off, the hull of the downed helicopter burned from the intense heat of the incendiary grenades the PJs had used to destroy all of the classified equipment they hadn't been able to recover. The brilliant actinic white light of the burning metal was a funeral pyre for the men who had died in that isolated spot among the uncaring rocks and sand.

PISTOLS

There is probably no less-used firearm in combat, or a more desired one, than a handgun. In a variety of forms, the pistol has been around since almost the beginning of gunpowder weapons. It was only a few decades after the creation of the cannon in Europe that experimentation was being done with making smaller weapons that an individual could handle. These experiments resulted in single-shot miniature cannons that were usually mounted on the end of a staff or pole and fired with a hot ember, wire, or length of burning cord. As they evolved, one branch of these "hand-gonnes" became shoulder arms, the long gun of the infantry. Moving in the other direction, some of these weapons became smaller and lighter until they could be fired when held with only one hand.

The capability of being fired while held in one hand is the classic definition of the pistol. This flexible means of use made the weapon class very popular with the mounted cavalry. While a horseman was controlling his mount with one hand, he would be able to draw and fire a handgun with the other. This tactic didn't come about until the invention of a positive means of ignition with the wheel lock in the middle 1500s. And even then, the wheel lock, with its spring-driven wheel knocking sparks into a powder pan, was prohibitively expensive.

Only officers and the elite cavalry of more affluent monarchs were able to afford sufficient of the costly weapons to arm themselves with what was considered the most technologically advanced weapon of their day.

Pistols were carried on horseback in long pouches that fit to either side of the saddle, usually in front of the horseman. With the gunner on foot, the pistol was most often carried slipped into the belt. All of these weapons shared several characteristics that were not to change for centuries: they were single-shot muzzle-loaders, of generally large bore, and tended to be a smoothbore weapon well after rifling had been invented.

Repeating handguns were never very successful, except for the limited models that utilized a separate barrel for each shot. Some of this style of weapon used a group of barrels formed into a cylinder to allow for repeated firings of as many as six or more shots before reloading. But the multibarreled pepperbox design was a mechanically simple but also heavy and expensive one for its caliber and size. It wasn't until the invention of the percussion revolver by Samuel Colt in the 1830s that a truly effective repeating handgun became available.

First patented in 1835, the Colt design was for a revolving cylinder that was mechanically lined up with a single barrel by the internal mechanism of the weapon. The cylinder held a number of separate chambers, usually six, which each held a charge of powder, projectile (ball), with a percussion cap on the outside rear. The cap-and-ball revolvers proved very successful. In 1847, an improved revolver was produced by Colt, the six-round Walker model. One thousand of these massive revolvers were purchased by the Army for use during the Mexican War (1846–47). That was the first United States military use of the revolver and the beginning of the military use of the weapon for the next century.

It was during the American Civil War that both sides of the conflict used large numbers of handguns for both their mounted and unmounted troops. When they couldn't come up with an issue weapon or a battlefield pickup, both officers and enlisted men would purchase their own weapons.

The pistol started to become a very valuable weapon to keep at hand when the vast majority of shoulder arms were single-shot weapons. Having a pistol at his belt gave a man the assurance that he could come up with a fast five or six rounds when the fighting got close. When at rest or on horseback, a pistol in a belt or holster could be brought into action much faster than a long gun could be, especially at night when your opponent was often at almost arm's reach before he was even recognized as an enemy.

For the nearly one million men under arms in the Union Army, the Ordnance Department obtained about 400,000 revolvers. In addition to these numbers were the thousands of privately purchased weapons. The Confederate Army, always smaller than the Union in terms of men and weapons, had obtained nearly 25,000 revolvers officially, with the nearly quarter million active combat troops augmenting their official issues with battlefield pickups.

During the Civil War, the Union Ordnance Department (including the Navy Department for these numbers) purchased over 171,000 Colt pistols of different models, 128,000 Remington weapons, and 47,000 Starr revolvers. The majority of these weapons were of .44 caliber with most of the rest being .36 caliber, especially those of the Navy. Shortly before the outbreak of hostilities, the Smith & Wesson Company had developed and patented a revolver that fired a metallic cased round, the original .22-caliber Short rimfire round. In spite of the weakness of this round as a defensive cartridge, the gun saw brisk sales during the Civil War as a personal weapon that could be carried in a pocket. When the patent ran out on the Smith & Wesson weapon in 1869, Colt was already preparing to offer a new pistol design to both the military and civilian population.

In 1872, one of the new Colt revolvers was offered chambered for a round developed at Colt's Firearms. The round was a long, brass-cased, rimmed cartridge loaded with 40 grains of black powder and topped with a 255-grain, round-nosed lead bullet. This was the soon-to-be-famous .45 Long Colt round, and the weapon chambered for it was a big, single-action weapon that required the hammer to be manually cocked for each round.

Offered to the U.S. Army, the weapon was adopted in 1873 as the New Model Army Metallic Cartridge Revolving Pistol; to the rest of the world it would soon be known as the Colt Peacemaker. From 1873 to 1891, about 37,000 of the Colt pistols were purchased for use by the U.S. Army. Almost every cavalryman in the Army was issued a seven-and-a-half-inch barreled Colt to carry with his single-shot carbine. The simple, classic weapon was slipped into a holster at the side of almost every U.S. soldier at one time or another during the last quarter of the 1800s. With his holster on his belt, the soldier always had a dependable sidearm available to him. The heavy lead slug of the Colt was only moving at about 810 feet per second when it was fired, but it transferred its energy very well and would put a target down fairly quickly.

By 1897, the Colt single-action Army revolver had been withdrawn from front line service, replaced with a new Colt revolver, the Model 1892. Chambered for the .38 Long Colt round, the Model 1892 was a double-action gun, one where the hammer could be cocked manually or the trigger pulled back over a longer travel and the hammer lifted and dropped to fire the gun. This double-action mechanism made the Model 1892 Colt easier to use and faster to shoot. In addition, the six-round cylinder of the Model 1892 could be hinged open, swinging out to the right side of the weapon and allowing all the empty cartridges to be ejected at one time. This weapon was the first of the accepted standard for revolvers that extends to modern days.

What proved the undoing of the Colt Model 1892 was the relatively weak .38 Long Colt cartridge it was chambered in. Employed for the fighting in Cuba during the Spanish-American War, the 148-grain lead bullet was pushed by its 15.4-grain charge of black powder to a muzzle velocity of 750 feet per second. The round was found to be very lacking in stopping power. It would take nearly a cylinder full of ammunition to drop a man, and even that wasn't enough when the United States saw combat against the Moros in the Philippines.

One of the results of the Spanish-American War was the U.S. purchase of the Philippines from Spain. The Filipinos had already been fighting for their independence from Spain and, in 1899, turned against the United States Army forces now on the islands. Among the fiercest fighters in the Philippines were the Muslim Filipinos, commonly called the Moros. The Moros wanted their own independence from both the Philippines and the United States. After the war in the Philippines was declared officially over in 1902, the Moro Rebellion continued the fighting well past that year.

As Islamic warriors, the Moros had their own version of a jihad against the United States forces. Taking an oath to kill as many of the infidels as possible before they would themselves die, the Moro suicide attackers were known to go juramentado, a variation of the Spanish term for oath-taking. When amok, another term for their suicidal fighting style, the Moros would attack with their kris swords, a distinctive wavy-edged blade, killing and slashing even while being shot themselves.

It was soon learned by the United States troops that the .38 Long Colt round could not easily put down a Moro warrior who had gone juramentado. Captain John J. "Blackjack" Pershing had issued an urgent request for a more powerful sidearm for issue to his troops. When swinging their lethal kris, the Moro fighters would be in too close for effective use of a rifle. The U.S. bolt-action repeating Krag rifles were little more than clubs or short spears at close-combat ranges. An effective pistol was needed, and the old 1873 Colt Army revolver was pulled out of storage and reissued. The heavy .45 caliber lead slug from the Model 1873 Colt would more effectively dispatch an amok Moro warrior, though it still had to be aimed at a lethal spot and fired by a cool hand. An additional 5,000 double-action Colt revolvers, chambered in .45 Long Colt, were purchased by the Army for use in the Philippines. By 1913, the Moro Rebellion was mostly over, though there are Muslim guerilla groups still fighting in the Philippines to this day.

One result of the urgent call for .45-caliber revolvers in the Philippines was the suspension of any further purchases of the Model 1892 Colt. A new weapon was desired, and a new caliber was needed for it. The Ordnance Department began exhaustive tests to determine just what the new caliber should be, and the movement was on for the new pistol to be a semiautomatic design,

The semiautomatic pistol used some form of energy from the firing of a cartridge—recoil, gas, or other—to operate the action to extract the empty cartridge, feed a fresh round into the chamber, and lock the round safely in place after recocking the action. All the operator had to do was to pull the trigger for each shot; the weapon would conduct the rest of the cycle, functioning by itself. The day of the revolver as a front-line combat weapon in the United States military was close to being over.

The United States Ordnance Department had been interested in adopting a semiautomatic pistol since before the turn of the century. In 1901, the Ordnance Department purchased 1,000 German-manufactured Model 1900 Luger pistols for evaluation and field testing. The Luger weapons were chambered for the high-velocity 7.65 mm (.30 caliber) Luger cartridge, which put out a ninety-three-grain, full-jacketed bullet at 1,220 feet per second. The weapons were tested by the U.S. Cavalry for a number of years, but the caliber was considered inadequate, especially in light of the experiences in using the .38 Long Colt round in the Philippines.

The Ordnance Department, headed by Brigadier General William Crozier as its chief, had decided in 1901 that the revolver was going to be replaced with a semiautomatic pistol. It was the caliber of the new weapon that had yet to be decided. Crozier assigned two officers, Infantry Captain John T. Thompson and Major Louis Anatole LaGarde of the Medical Corps, to conduct a series of tests to determine what caliber and weight of projectile should be used for the new weapon. What has become known as the Thompson-LaGarde study involved shooting a variety of calibers from different weapons into live cattle and human medical cadavers to see just what it took to make up an effective handgun round.

At stockyards near Chicago, the officers oversaw the discharge of dozens of rounds into live cattle weighing an average of 1,200 pounds. At first, it was how long it took a live animal to die after being shot in a selected target area. Of the eight head of cattle shot, half of them were finally killed with a hammer blow to the skull—considered a humane method of slaughter and far faster than killing these large creatures with handgun bullets to the body. Unsatisfied with the results, the next day the tests were continued, only the cattle were quickly shot with up to ten rounds unless they died first. Two of these animals were also finally dispatched with a hammer.

The concentration on bullet strike effects on such large animals as beef cattle did not happen just because of simple availability. One of the effects of the ammunition desired by the Army was for the bullet to be able to quickly drop a horse or dispatch a wounded one. It had been noted by Army officers that it could take several close-range shots from the .38 Long Colt revolvers to dispatch a horse, even when hitting it in the head. The thought was that a proposed cavalry pistol should quickly put a horse or a man out of the fight, but particularly the horse.

The final series of test shots involved striking human cadavers at various ranges up to seventy-five yards with rounds ranging from the 7.65 mm Luger to the .45 Long Colt and a massive British round, the .476 Eley. The final results of the cadaver shootings was a listing of the rounds by a subjective measurement of effectiveness; that is, the observers gave an arbitrary rank of the projectiles on a scale of one hundred, according to how much they made the suspended bodies sway. The lowest ranking was fifty for the .38 Long Colt and one hundred for the .476 Eley. The .45 Long Colt rated an eighty-five with hollow point ammunition and an eighty with the normal lead bullet. The 9 mm Luger, a new round at the time, also was given an eighty rating, while the standard 7.65 mm Luger was rated a sixty.

The 9 mm Luger round had been developed from the 7.65 mm Luger round by blowing out the bottleneck of the smaller caliber, resulting in a straight-walled case nineteen millimeters long that would accept a 9 mm projectile. This was the beginning of the 9×19 mm round as it is known today.

The result of the Thompson-LaGarde study was a recommendation that the minimum caliber for a future U.S. service pistol should be not less than .45 inches. In addition, they stated that soldiers should be trained and drilled on the range for accuracy with their weapons. The two officers added that their studies had shown them that hitting a human being anywhere but a vital spot gave "no hope of stopping an adversary by shock or other immediate results when hit." A rule that has been repeated in various ways by thousands of firearms instructors up to the present day. No amount of power delivered by a standard handgun projectile could replace poor accuracy. There was no miracle bullet, no consistent one-shot stop that could be guaranteed by a handgun projectile. But a powerful projectile, a large, heavy, relatively slow-moving one, did transfer its energy to the target well, and that did increase the margin of error in hitting a target to the shooter's favor.

For their submissions to the military automatic pistol market, Colt had already secured the services of the eminent firearms designer, John M. Browning. Having failed to interest Winchester Repeating Arms, who was manufacturing his rifle designs, in producing his handguns, Browning had turned to Colt in the mid-1890s to see if they would be interested in his smaller weapons.

Seizing the opportunity that presented itself, Colt entered into a production and development agreement with Browning to make and market his semiautomatic pistols in the United States. The ammunition for the weapons would also be designed by Browning, and his agreement with Colt resulted in a number of cartridges being identified by the letters ACP, for Automatic Colt Pistol, in their designations.

John Browning's first completed large-caliber pistol design was the Model 1900, a .38 caliber weapon. This design was later modified in 1902 and given the designation Model 1902 Military when Colt put it into production. Chambered for the .38 ACP round, the Model 1902 remained in production primarily for the commercial market until 1929. In spite of the designation, the Model 1902 saw no significant quantities of military sales, though a number were purchased by the U.S. Army for extensive testing.

Having begun design work on a .45 caliber version of the M1902 pistol in 1904, Colt was in a good position to submit a developed handgun and ammunition for army trials. The cartridge case used by Browning was originally that of the .45 Long Colt round, the rim removed and an extractor groove cut in place. That proved an excessively long cartridge for functioning of the pistol, and the case was shortened significantly. The new cartridge launched a 200-grain .45 caliber bullet at a muzzle velocity of 850 feet per second. The improved pistol to fire the new ammunition was also ready for use in 1905.

As the Ordnance Department people examined the new Colt/Browning round, they expanded and improved upon it, thickening the metal jacket on the projectile and modifying the case dimensions, particularly those around the head and extractor groove. Just prior to the end of 1906, a new list of pistol requirements was issued by the Ordnance Department and endorsed by the secretary of war. These requirements included the minimum caliber of .45 inches, a magazine capacity of at least six rounds, and a bullet weight of 230 grains.

Eleven weapons were submitted for testing, including three revolvers, which were soon rejected. Eight more companies had considered submitting weapons, but their pistols were either never completed, didn't work well enough, or were too expensive to produce. Only three weapons were considered worth modification and development prior to further testing. Of the final test weapon designs, the .45 caliber Luger was withdrawn for a number of technical reasons, one of which was that the close tolerances built into the gun made it sensitive to dirt and jamming. The Colt/Browning design and that of the Savage Arms Company were recommended for further examination and field trials in the hands of troops.

Modifications to the designs continued with feedback from the testing, and the weapons were improved over several years of trials. A grip safety had been added to the Browning design to give the weapon an automatic safety feature. There were difficulties with the field trials of the Colt weapons. Improper heat treatment of some of the parts caused them to break while in use. One particularly exciting malfunction that resulted from this parts breakage was the gun firing uncontrollably on full automatic—a stunning experience for the shooter, as the gun would empty itself in under a second with most of the rounds going straight up into the air.

The Colt/Browning weapon evolved into the Model 1909 version, and finally the Model 1910. In March 1910, there was a final endurance test firing of both the Colt and the Savage weapons. After 6,000 rounds had been fired, during the process of which the weapons had been covered in sand and mud, only the Colt completed the test without a single malfunction or parts breakage.

It turned out that the greatest opponents of the new pistol were among the cavalry officer corps. They thought that a self-loading pistol would be too dangerous for a trooper on horseback to handle. There was also the problem that it took two hands to load the weapon, pulling back the slide and releasing it to chamber the first round. And there was the standard argument that a semiautomatic weapon was too easy to fire and would only result in wasted ammunition. On the other hand, slipping in a new magazine and releasing the slide was a much, much faster means of reloading while on horseback, or on foot for that matter, rather than fumbling with loose rounds and stuffing them individually into the chambers of a cylinder.

The final examination of the modified Colt and Savage designs took place on March 3, 1911. The Colt weapon was recommended for adoption by the U.S. Army Infantry and Cavalry troops. On March 28, 1911, the adoption of the Browning-designed and Colt-produced weapon was approved by the secretary of war as the U.S. Pistol, Automatic, Caliber .45, Model 1911.

COLT M1911

By December 14, 1912, over 16,000 of the new Model 1911 pistols had been delivered to the Army, including 500 weapons going to the Navy in February 1912. By May 1913, this number had almost doubled to over 31,000 guns.

When the United States finally declared war on Germany and entered into World War I on April 6, 1917, it was badly short of all of the tools of war, including pistols. The intent of the United States was to have 1.25 million soldiers under arms by 1918, and 60 percent of them would have pistols, preferably the M1911. Colt was the largest single firearms company in the United States in 1917, and they were turning out 450 pistols a day. By January 1918, Colt was cranking out over 2,200 pistols a day. To make up the numbers, contracts were let out to a number of other firearms manufacturers, but only Remington-UMC turned out any real numbers of M1911 pistols. Three million M1911 pistols were on order by the U.S. government when the war finally ended on November 11, 1918.

To make up the shortages in available handguns, the Army adopted two revolvers, modifications of Colt and Smith & Wesson weapons that were already tooled up and in production. These weapons were identified as the Model 1917 Colt or Smith & Wesson revolvers, both being chambered for the .45 M1911 round carried in sheet-metal clips to allow the rimless round to properly function in a revolver.

The high percentage of handguns available to the American troops in France made their use much more common than in any other forces fighting during the war. This was a greater percentage of handguns issued than had been used during the American Civil War. The M1911 was extremely well-received by the troops who carried them on the front lines. The Colt and Smith & Wesson revolvers were primarily for issue to troops who were not directly involved in the fighting.

The big bullet and heavy striking power of the M1911 was something that was quickly feared by the German troops who faced it. Even in the mud and horrible conditions of trench warfare, the Browning design gave sterling service. It had been made with the only really close tolerances being those directly involved with supporting the barrel and cartridge at the moment of firing. Other than that, the design was loose enough to absorb a tremendous amount of dirt, mud, sand, and abuse and still keep operating. The fine mechanism of the hammer and trigger system were mostly sealed from outside materials being able to get into them. In the final analysis, Browning's soon to become most famous pistol design worked every time and any time it was called on to do so.

The legend of the big, flat-sided American pistol and the soldiers who carried it kept growing as the combat continued. In the close quarters of trench combat, the big pistol proved itself a man-stopper and more flexible in fighting than even the rifles and machine guns that were otherwise dominating the battle-field. By the end of the war and the year following it, 268,000 Model 1917 revolvers had been manufactured from both Colt and Smith & Wesson. By the end of production in 1919 and including the prewar years, over 723,000 M1911 pistols had been produced by all manufacturers. Production still continued after World War I but on a much smaller scale. Changes suggested by the wartime experiences with the weapon were soon incorporated into the design.

Modifications that included changing the spur on the back of the hammer, enlarging the top of the grip safety, installing an arched mainspring housing at the bottom of the pistol grip, shortening the trigger, and making the sights easier to see, as well as enlarging and lowering the ejection port, were completed on five sample weapons in September 1923. Primarily, these were ergonomic changes intended to make the pistol easier to use by a wider range of personnel rather than anything that directly changed the operation of the gun. The basic design of the M1911 had proven itself in combat during the Great War, and there was little reason to change the interior workings. On May 20, 1924, the modified pistol was adopted by the U.S. Army and shortly given the nomenclature M1911A1. The weapon was manufactured to the same standard for the military until the end of World War II, but regardless of the exact model, it remained simply the "45" to the soldiers who carried it.

When the United States actively entered into World War II in December 1941, the M1911A1 was still the primary handgun of all of the U.S. forces, and it served well throughout the war. The M1911A1 saw duty in every environment on earth short of the Antarctic, from frozen Alaska to the North African deserts, from the steaming jungles of the Pacific islands to the mud of Europe. It was not the most effective implement of war available to the American fighting man, but it was among the most desired ones.

Prior to World War II, the opinion of the military weapons experts was that the pistol and revolver were outmoded weapons of war, replaced by the variety of shoulder arms available to the soldier. The low priority given to pistol manufacture at the beginning of the war reflected that expert opinion. As far as the men in the field went, they wanted the dependable power of the pistol, a defensive weapon that could be kept immediately at hand. The relatively small size of the M1911A1 also made it the weapon of choice to be constantly carried in the close quarters of vehicles and tanks, the things that became commonplace in the new style of combat during World War II.

There was no question that it was a great comfort to a soldier in the field to have a pistol close at hand. If his assignment didn't entitle a man to be issued a pistol, many troops came up with their own means of obtaining one. Men serving in vehicles, on artillery pieces, machine guns, mortars, and other such hardware were issued an M1911A1. So were many noncommissioned officers and most officers. Even clerks and other support personnel could find themselves with a .45 hanging at their hip.

The popularity of the big pistol wasn't that it would be used in combat as much as a soldier's rifle would be. But when a combat soldier wanted a pistol during a fight, he wanted it badly and immediately. Having an M1911A1 hanging from a belt on a holster, strapped to the chest in a shoulder rig, or simply slipped inside of a uniform jacket became a common situation in a combat zone. The Ordnance Department people recognized the demand for the M1911A1, and they increased the priority for having the weapons made.

When U.S. government production of the M1911A1 ended in the fall of 1945, over 1.9 million weapons had been produced. When these numbers were combined with the production of the M1911 in the prewar and World War I years, the total number purchased by the government from 1911 to 1945 was around 2.5 million pieces. Those numbers do not include the hundreds of thousands of .45 automatics manufactured for commercial sale or produced by other governments under license. The .45 was produced in greater numbers than any other U.S. military handgun. It was one of the most common handguns in the world. The only pistol that was produced in greater numbers was the German P08 Luger and its variations.

When there were considerations put forward to replace the M1911A1 in the postwar military with a lighter, smaller-caliber weapon, the vast numbers of finished pistols and available spare parts caused that idea to be quickly dropped. The M1911A1 served with distinction in the U.S.

The Beretta M9 pistol above the weapon it replaced, the venerable M1911A1 "45."
Kevin Dockery

military through the Korean War in the early 1950s, Vietnam in the 1960s and early 1970s, and a large number of conflicts in between.

STECHKIN APS
In the bulk of the world's military organizations, the issue of a pistol as a secondary weapon is considered of significantly less tactical importance than is placed on it in the United States. For many military organizations, the issue of a pistol is more of a badge of rank for officers and other leaders rather than a practical weapon. The relative rarity of handguns in some armies make the men who carry them stand out. The wearing of a pistol is taught to snipers to be a means of picking out the officer in a group of soldiers.

In the Soviet Union, the pistol had been of only slight tactical importance during World War II, what they call the Great Patriotic War. During the tremendous buildup and modernization of the Soviet military in the post–World War II world, the tactical use of the pistol was carefully considered. During World War II, the Soviet military had made massive use of the submachine gun as a tactical weapon. Whole units were armed with nothing more than drum-fed submachine guns and hand grenades. So the effect of a large volume of fire in overwhelming an infantry objective was not lost on the Soviets.

In 1945, a competition was announced in the Soviet Union for the development of a new pistol. One of these weapons would be used as a standard sidearm, a compact defensive weapon for use by officers and other forces, including undercover use by state security organizations. The other weapon would be an offensive handgun, one that could be used to fight with during an attack. A new round of ammunition was designed along with the new weapons, a short 9×18 millimeter cartridge of less power than the standard 9×19 millimeter Luger round that had been used in large numbers by the Germans during World War II. The lower power of the new round meant that it could be used in a weapon with a simpler operating system, a straight blowback system where the slide is held shut against the pressure of a firing round only by the inertia of its weight and the strength of the recoil spring that drives it.

The general pistol that resulted from the competition was the Makarov, adopted in 1951 as the PM (Pistolet Makarova). It is a compact handgun of simple lines and bears a more than passing resemblance to the German Walther PP series of handguns. The 9×18 millimeter round for the pistol became known as the 9 mm Makarov. The other handgun that came out of the competition also made use of the blowback system for operating the action of the weapon. The limited power of the 9×18 mm round also allowed for a very unusual characteristic to be added to the new Soviet handgun. It was capable of full-automatic fire.

Known as the Stechkin, officially the APS, the pistol was a large-frame weapon, slightly larger than the M1911A1, which was considered a big handgun. The magazine of the Stechkin holds twenty rounds of ammunition, enough to make automatic fire with the weapon somewhat more practical. By pushing the safety/ selector lever on the slide forward, the gun can fire at what would normally be an uncontrollable rate of fire. But a reducer was added to the trigger mechanism to retard the rate of fire considerably. Instead of firing at an excessive rate due to the light

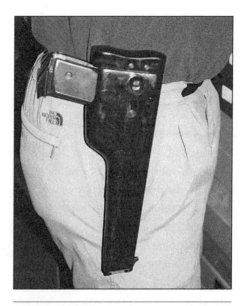

A Stechkin pistol secured in its stock and clipped to a belt, the stock acting as the holster.
Kevin Dockery

weight and short length of travel of the slide, the Stechkin fires slowly enough that controllable bursts can be put out by an experienced shooter.

As a handgun, the Stechkin would still require a great deal of training to be able to be fired accurately and effectively while just being handheld, even if held in both hands. To make the weapon more controllable, it was issued with a holster that could also be attached to the butt of the pistol and act as a stock. In effect, the shoulder stock made the Stechkin a short, compact submachine gun.

The tactical experiment that was the Stechkin did not prove a complete success. It was the last full-automatic handgun to be issued in numbers to any major army. The fact that the weapon came with five magazines, giving one hundred rounds ready for use by the operator, shows that it was to be used as an offensive rather than simple defensive weapon. The weapon was particularly heavy to be carried on a simple belt. It could be torn free and lost easily in the exertions that have to be conducted by a soldier on a battlefield. It remained in use by Internal Security forces long after it had been removed from general military issue. In the 1970s, the weapon was resurrected as a suppressed pistol with a new-style shoulder stock for use by Soviet special operations troops (the Spetsnaz). Those weapons were modified with extended barrels and had easily attachable suppressors issued for them. The new-style shoulder stock was a simple folded wire design. The use of a suppressed fully automatic handgun would have tremendous psychological effect when used as part of an ambush, especially at night. It is an aspect of the selective fire pistol that has yet to be fully explored in any military organization.

GYROJET ROCKET GUN

What was probably the most futuristic firearm developed so far was the promising Gyrojet family of weapons produced in the United States during the 1960s. The inventors of the weapon, Dr. Robert Mainhardt and Dr. Arthur T. Biehl, do not claim to have originated the idea of a rocket-firing personal weapon, only to have brought it into the future age. The rocket gun was one of the earliest hand weapons, considering that the Chinese had handheld bamboo tubes that launched crude rockets, little more than fireworks. But a number of other inventors over the centuries had much the same idea. Though only experimental in nature, there are several musketlike flintlock rocket launchers in the Tower of London armory dating from the 1810–1820 time period that launched a small war rocket from the shoulder. A considerably more sophisticated application of the rocket was the Danish Voss rocket cartridge that was a complete projectile launched from a shoulder weapon. The Voss rocket ball would be fired as a normal round of ammunition, the internal rocket of the projectile being ignited by the hot gases of the propelling charge fired by the musket. Later versions of the Voss rocket were completely self-contained with their own percussion ignition system. Patented in 1834, the Voss rocket was primarily used as a signaling device by the Danish Army and was examined by a number of other European nations.

Additional self-contained cartridges were developed over the decades that were close in appearance to a rocket but were not truly self-contained projectiles. Usually these were projectiles that contained the propellant in a hollow base. As percussion priming compounds became more common, some of these base-charged projectiles also held their own ignition system, becoming a caseless cartridge more than a rocket. As the metallic cartridge case became more developed, these unusual rounds lost much of their appeal, and their development stopped.

During World War II in Germany, the Walther firm developed a true self-contained rocket intended for small arms, specifically a pistol for the development work. Very little is known of the project outside of a few rare rounds in extensive cartridge collections. The Walther rocket was nominally a nine-millimeter-diameter projectile with a thirty-millimeter overall length. The threaded-in base of the rocket held six straight exhaust nozzles surrounding a standard-style percussion primer on a central extension. A thin metal disk was held in place on the inside of the projectile by the nozzle body. It was also pierced by six holes surrounding a central ignition opening. The entire round was made of machined steel and held a charge of solid propellant. Other data list the manufacturer of the rocket rounds as a DWM-Lubeck project, possibly an experiment to develop a caseless round that would have conserved scarce brass during wartime. There has been no information released on just what the launcher for the 9×30 millimeter rocket would have been, but the project held some promise as a small arms round. Interest was strong enough to cause the U.S. Navy to copy the 9×30 mm rocket round exactly for post–World War II experimentation.

Beginning in 1960, the MBA Company (Mainhardt and Biehl Associates) began investigations to prove that rockets less than one inch in diameter could be made both effectively and economically. The basic idea was to produce a light handgun that had no recoil, was cheap, and was very easy to use. The means by which the men intended reaching their goal was to make roughly half-inch-diameter rockets that were completely self-contained with a simple ignition system and spin stabilization. The ignition system was a standard percussion cap, the spin stabilization produced by canted exhaust ports surrounding the central primer cap, and the final length only a little more than one and a quarter inches on a half-inch-diameter rocket.

The projectile was named the Gyrojet for its rocket propulsion and spinning gyroscopic stability system. Originally, the developmental rockets were .49 caliber, 12 mm. During testing, the diameter was increased to 13 mm (.51 caliber) for convenience during experimentation. This was to later prove a costly mistake on the part of MBA, which could not have been foreseen by anyone involved with the project.

The commercial result of the Gyrojet project was the Mark I, a six-shot rocket-launching handgun. Because the launcher saw almost no internal stresses when fired, the bulk of the weapon was made from Zamac, a 7 percent silicone/

The Gyrojet rounds (left to right): the 13 mm "Wadcutter" target round, a second 13 mm target round with the steel body cleanly showing the copper wash to prevent corrosion, a 13 mm ball round with a rolled seal holding the base, the 12 mm ball round with a roll-crimped base, the 13 mm rocket flare as issued to the military.
Kevin Dockery

The Gyrojet pistol with the loading gate in the open position. The thumb of the hand is pressing down on the hammer, the V-shaped nose of which can be seen just inside the breech end of the barrel.
Kevin Dockery

aluminum alloy. Certain internal parts and springs were made from steel as required, but the alloy construction gave the Gyrojet pistol a very light empty weight. The barrel is very noticeably ported for its entire length. This is because the barrel of the weapon consists of four guide rails spaced a few thousandths of an inch wider than the diameter of the rocket. There is no internal pressure within the gun itself, and the ports are there to guide the exhaust gases from the rocket to the outside air.

The ignition system is a standard percussion primer initiated by a firing pin. But the firing pin does not strike the cartridge as much as the Gyrojet rocket is driven down onto the firing pin. There is no chamber in the Gyrojet as there would be for a round in a normal-cartridge handgun. Instead, the Gyrojet round sits at the top of the magazine where it is struck on the nose by a forward-cocked hammer. Being stuck by the hammer drives the Gyrojet round back against a fixed firing pin at the rear of the "chamber." Ignited by the primer, the single large fuel grain inside the Gyrojet round exhausts out the angled ports, driving the projectile forward, where it pushes the hammer back down into the cocked position before continuing up the guide rails.

When fired, the Gyrojet pistol makes a slight whooshing sound, not like any other firearm. There is a sonic crack sound some fifty feet in front of the point of firing where the projectile breaks the sound barrier at the point of fuel burnout. It is in part this constant acceleration and distant burnout point that contribute to one of the most severe drawbacks of the Gyrojet system: its poor accuracy.

In order for a production lot of .45 ACP M1911 ball ammunition to be accepted for issue, it must be tested for accuracy. The fired test rounds must make a group no larger than four inches in diameter at a distance of fifty yards to pass inspection. In terms of mils, this means the group cannot have a spread of more than 2.2 mils at fifty yards. During some of the first testing of Gyrojet rounds and handguns by an outside agency in 1963, the group size was very poor: seventy-two inches at fifty yards. A second series of tests later that same year showed a marked improvement in accuracy, but group size was still nearly forty-four inches at fifty yards. Some lots of ammunition in some launchers showed excellent accuracy as the system was developed, but they never approached that of a conventional-style handgun.

Improvements in the ammunition increased the basic accuracy of the system, but there was still the underlying difficulty of the Gyrojet pistol launching a projectile that was still accelerating long after it had left the barrel of the weapon. Generally, the propellant charge burned for a hundred milliseconds, long enough for the round to spin up to its maximum rpm for stabilization. This burning time also meant that the round was speeding up long after it left the barrel. The penetration of the steel-bodied rocket was excellent after it had reached maximum velocity. The Gyrojet rocket had punched through steel plate, thick boards, and other obstacles that would stop the standard M1911 .45 ball round. But close to the launcher, the round was moving relatively slowly and had no real power to it. If a sheet of heavy cardboard was placed over the muzzle of the pistol when it was fired, the Gyrojet rocket wouldn't even penetrate it, simply stick up against it and spin.

In spite of the drawbacks, the Gyrojet pistol was placed on the commercial market in the middle 1960s. The weapon was sold almost as a novelty and priced far more than its construction should have drawn. Ammunition was expensive to produce and correspondingly very costly to buy. Then the legal situation changed. In the Gun Control Act of 1968, a definition of a new kind of weapon, a *destructive device*, was coined. A destructive device could be anything that fired an explosive-filled projectile with the charge weight being over a very small minimum. Among other restrictions intended to limit the private ownership of such things as small modern cannons and such, any weapon that fired a projectile over half an inch in diameter and had no recognized sporting purpose was considered a destructive device. This required special licensing and a tax to be paid before an individual who was not a government entity could possess the weapon. A short amnesty period was allowed in the law so that individuals who wanted to obey the obscure requirements of the legislation could submit their paperwork and pay the proper fees.

This legal machination affected the commercial sales of the Gyrojet drastically as the thirteen-millimeter model being sold was a .51 caliber weapon and as such was classified as a destructive device. The onerous registration situation was eventually changed, but not until a number of years had passed. Suddenly, the MBA Company's most popular product had been outlawed because

The base ends of various Gyrojet rocket rounds. The central percussion primer ignited the fuel and the exhaust exited through the nozzles. The round second from the right has slit-cut nozzles, an economy measure, and the flare round at the far right has only two canted rocket ports.

Kevin Dockery

of ten-thousandths of an inch. To bypass the restriction and stay within the letter and intent of the law, MBA went back to the twelve-millimeter Gyrojet, a .49 caliber weapon.

Changing the caliber did nothing to improve the basic accuracy of the weapon system. An attempt to mass-produce the ammunition to make it cheaper to purchase added other factors into the system that caused even more inaccuracy to be created in some versions of the ammunition. Commercially, the Gyrojet was a failure, the ammo was expensive, the pistol inaccurate, and the promised carbine and other versions were hardly available, so the weapon was removed from the market long before it could reach its potential.

There was a great deal of promise in the Gyrojet concept. The weapon was effectively recoilless. When fired, the forces of the hammer driving back the cartridge onto the firing pin were almost balanced by the ignition of the rocket and its recocking the hammer. In most cases, the weapon just seemed to rock in the hand a little rather than kick back hard as any other conventional handgun of its caliber would be expected to do.

Being a self-contained rocket, the Gyrojet could be fired in the air, underwater, even in a hard vacuum. There was an underwater version of the weapon produced, the Lancejet, which launched a long spear powered by a Gyrojet rocket motor. That weapon was examined by the U.S. Navy for possible use by the Navy SEALs or underwater demolition teams but was not adopted. A recoilless Gyrojet-powered signal flare, launched from a small pen gun, was the closest the system came to reaching a major military market as a large number of the devices were purchased for inclusion in military survival kits. Given new methods of manufacture and more development, the Gyrojet concept could return in the future, given a specific enough demand for it. It was truly a weapon ahead of its time.

COLT SCAMP

With the end of the 1960s approaching, it looked to a number of firearms industry professionals and military personnel that the M1911A1 pistol was reaching the end of its practical service life. It was not unnoticed by the leadership at

Colt that the standard sidearm of the U.S. Army had been a Colt product for well over one hundred years. The Colt people had a strong interest in maintaining that situation for as long as possible. The best way to do that would be to offer the Army a new sidearm that would fulfill many of their needs for a general handgun.

Colt engineers, notably Mr. Henry A. Into, were interested in developing a whole new kind of pistol, one that was not common at all in the United States. One of the problems with any standard type of handgun was the difficulty in accurately shooting it. No matter how the weapon was built, it took time to master the intricacies of firing a weapon held only in the hands. To reach the necessary skill level took up a great deal of the limited training time available to a soldier. The weapon also had to be lightweight so that carrying it would appeal more to the already overloaded soldier, and effective; the factor that everyone agreed stood most in the M1911A1's favor was the big .45 caliber bullet it fired. To meet these needs, the Colt engineers looked to developing a new caliber of ammunition as well as a completely new style of handgun. The concept they came up with was for a specialized machine pistol, a weapon capable of full automatic fire.

What Colt was developing was a new concept in firearms, the personal defense weapon (PDW). This was an improved pistol capable of a greater volume of fire than a standard semiautomatic handgun, and it would fire a round with greater effective range and penetration than the usual pistol round. This would be a weapon that could help an evading soldier hold off an enemy force while awaiting rescue and give a radio operator, support personnel, or heavy weapons crewman the ability to fight a suddenly appearing enemy. The idea of a personal defense weapon would give a vehicle operator, whether the driver of a tank or a truck, something that he could fight with for at least a short time if he had to bail out of his vehicle after it was damaged or destroyed. The PDW idea was not completely a new one, but the application of the concept as Colt envisaged it was novel, gathering thoughts from a variety of weapons.

In their researches, the Colt personnel looked at a large number of existing weapons designs, including submachine guns such as the Uzi, intermediate weapons like the Vz 61 Skorpion, and true machine pistols such as the Stechkin APS, as well as converted weapons such as the 9 mm Browning Hi-Power pistol converted to fire on full automatic. None of these weapons, or others like them, combined the requirements of compact size, light weight, controllability, accuracy, and effectiveness.

What the engineers determined was in order for a full automatic weapon to employ the most common pistol-caliber cartridge in NATO, the 9×19 mm round, it would have to weigh at least 5.5 to 6 pounds in order for it to be controllable on full automatic fire. A true machine pistol in 9×19 mm would be far too light to be fired accurately by anyone not extensively trained in its use. Adding a shoulder stock to the weapon would make it easier to fire but detracted from the idea of a small, light weapon that could be slipped into a holster to carry. The easiest way to eliminate the weight and cut down on the controllability problem would be to come up with a high-velocity, small-caliber round with an effective projectile but a low-recoil impulse, the same situation that made the M16A1 rifle with its 5.56 mm high-speed projectile a controllable automatic rifle.

With the development of the new round being the first priority, the Colt engineers looked to the experience they had at hand with their years of working on the M16A1 rifle family. A .22-caliber projectile had proven itself an effective combat round, given a high enough velocity. The use of the common .22 caliber rimfire rounds, even the Magnum loading, was examined and abandoned. The power of the rounds was limited; they could not be loaded to a higher pressure due to their method of priming. Additionally, the prominent rims of all of the rimfire rounds made feeding them rapidly from a standard magazine a difficult proposition.

In the civilian shooting fraternity, there were a number of production center fire cartridges and even more custom-made wildcat rounds (a *wildcat* is a modified version of an existing cartridge case) that were close to fulfilling the needs of the Colt people. Commercial ammunition such as the .221 Remington Fireball and .22 Hornet were both on the market and fired projectiles that came close to matching the parameters developed by Colt. What the engineers wanted was a forty-grain, .22-caliber jacketed projectile fired at 2,100 feet per second from a pistol-length barrel. The .221 Remington Fireball had already been tested in another Colt project at the time, and the designers were familiar with it. It was the nearly two-inch overall length of the .221 Fireball that made it difficult to use in a handgun magazine without making the grip too big for comfortable use by most of the military population. By using a cut-down version of the .22 Hornet, blown out to a straight-sided case with a sharp shoulder and removing the rim while cutting an extractor groove, the Colt designers had a round that would match their needs and could fit in a reasonably sized pistol magazine. Since the .22 Hornet was a solid-base center fire round, there was no difficulty in cutting off the rim as well as cutting an extractor groove to make the rimmed round into a rimless one.

The effectiveness of a bullet doesn't matter if it can't hit the target. Most handguns are far more accurate than their shooters can make use of. It is this basic difficulty of firing a handgun that made the Colt engineers turn to an automatic weapon. Putting out a short, controlled burst of low-recoil impulse rounds greatly

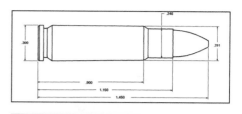

A line drawing of the Colt SCAMP round.
Colt Manufacturing

increases the hit probability for every "shot" fired. By making the weapon have a large magazine capacity (twenty-seven rounds), a shooter could still fire nine times, putting out a three-round burst every time he pulled the trigger. With a higher level of shooter skill, or tactical demands of the situation, putting the weapon on semiautomatic would give it a greater volume of fire between reloading of any handgun in existence at the time.

The new weapon was named the Small Caliber Machine Pistol, or SCAMP for short. As a handgun, the SCAMP was only slightly longer and heavier than the M1911A1 pistol. But the volume of fire that could be put out of the compact weapon was out of proportion to its size, a characteristic of machine pistols. The difference with the SCAMP was that it was completely controllable on full automatic fire. At the front of the barrel was a compensator that helped redirect the muzzle blast of firing to help hold the pistol down during a burst. The layout of the weapon kept the line of the barrel and recoil low in the hand so that it also minimized climb, where the barrel goes up and off target during automatic fire. The cyclic rate of fire was made very high, 1,500 rounds per minute. With the extremely high cyclic rate, no shooter could operate the trigger fast enough to only fire a short burst no matter what his skill level. Additionally, during the stress of sudden violent combat, it would be extremely easy to just hold the trigger back and empty the weapon in a single burst. So the mechanism of the SCAMP had a mechanical limiter that held the length of burst down to three rounds only. On semiautomatic fire, the SCAMP could be fired as quickly as the shooter could pull the trigger. On full automatic, only a three-round burst would be fired before the trigger had to be pulled again. This controlled burst and rapid cyclic rate gave the SCAMP a high hit probability as the projectiles would move downrange in a fairly tight group.

To make the weapon lightweight and easy to maintain, stainless steel was used to fabricate the metal parts. The receiver of the weapon was formed from glass-fiber-reinforced plastic. The box magazine was a standard-layout

The author shoulder-firing a VP-70 with the stock attached. A round has just left the barrel, the expended case spinning away in the upper right corner and smoke still visible around the ejection port.
Kevin Dockery

double-column design that made for an easy grip that could be held by the majority of users, and the power of the .22 SCAMP round gave it an effective range of over one hundred meters.

The construction of the single SCAMP prototype proved out the design when it was tested in 1972. But the release of the interesting weapon concept was badly timed as the United States was reaching the end of its involvement in active combat in Southeast Asia. There was little funding available for a new handgun, especially one that utilized a round of ammunition unique to it, and the weapon did not go past the prototype stage.

VP70

Being developed at roughly the same time as the Colt SCAMP was a German idea for a handgun that met many of the requirements put forward for a personal defense weapon. The Heckler & Koch Company looked at producing a handgun chambered for the NATO standard 9 × 19 mm round but also possessing a limited full automatic capability. Their design was the VP70, the Volkspistole (people's pistol) 1970 (for the year it was first developed). The VP70 is a huge handgun but an extremely light one for all of its size. The light weight comes in part from the simple action of the weapon. The VP70 uses a straightforward blowback system of operation where the pressure inside the cartridge case presses it back against the slide. The weight of the slide and the large spring around the barrel of the weapon hold the breech shut until the bullet has left the barrel and pressures have dropped to safe levels. When the inertia of the slide and pressure of the mainspring have been overcome, the residual pressure in the barrel acts on the cartridge case as a piston, driving it backward and operating the action.

The straight blowback action is not normally seen in a handgun firing the 9 × 19 mm round; the heavy slide adds too much weight for the weapon to be acceptable. The system works in the VP70 and the pistol retains a relatively light weight because of the very simple operating mechanism being held in a polymer receiver. Released for sale in 1972, the VP70 in both the military and civilian versions was the first commercially produced handgun with a plastic receiver. The slide moved along metal parts cast into the plastic of the receiver and helped give the weapon an expected service life of over 30,000 rounds. The support for the fixed barrel is also cast into place in the plastic frame.

The double-column magazine for the VP70 is a large-capacity model that holds eighteen rounds. The magazine catch is in the usual place for European handguns, underneath the rear of the pistol grip. To remove the magazine, the spring-loaded catch is pushed in with the thumb, and the magazine ejects into the waiting hand. The European-style catch slows the reloading of the pistol, but with the large magazine capacity, that was not considered a major drawback for most shooting. With no major parts in the pistol grip except for the magazine catch and the magazine itself, the grip kept a reasonably slim profile so that it is comfortable to hold for a majority of shooters.

Care was taken by the Heckler & Koch engineers to keep the parts of the weapon to a minimum. The firing pin is carried on a spring-loaded striker and is not cocked until a moment before it is released. To cock the striker and fire the weapon, the large trigger of the VP70 is a double-action-only system with a very long travel under a consistent level of spring pressure until the striker is fully cocked and released. After a shot has been fired, the striker remains uncocked until the trigger is again pulled through its entire length of travel. The long trigger pull and striker cocking system were considered enough to maintain the safety of the weapon during normal handling, so no external mechanical safety was normally included as a part of the action. A push-button safety could be installed and was designed to go on the receiver just behind the bottom of the trigger where a magazine catch would usually be located.

The long double-action-only trigger pull was considered a drawback for a semiautomatic pistol by many shooters of the VP70. The heavy pull combined with the long trigger travel helped make the system safe from accidental firing, but it soon tired the average trigger finger. But the design of the VP70 was not intended for it to be used primarily as a standard layout pistol.

The most unusual feature of the VP70 comes when it is attached to a removable holster/stock. Also cast from a lightweight, strong polymer, the hollow stock of the VP70 can act as a holster. Opening up the hinged back portion of the stock exposes the internal cavity of the holster/stock, and the pistol can be slid into place. A simple stud arrangement on a belt loop allows the holster to be hung from a belt or other load-bearing web gear and still be quickly removed. Clips on the upper and lower extensions of the holster/stock can be slipped into place on the back of the pistol, into slots at the top of the receiver and bottom of the pistol grip.

Three rounds travel downrange as this shooter has just fired a burst of tracers through a VP70. The three spots of light from the tracers form a round triangle inside the circle in the upper right corner.
Kevin Dockery

With the stock attached, a selector lever on the left side of the upper stock extension can be switched to the position marked by the numeral "3." When the trigger is pulled with the selector set, the VP70 fires a controlled, three-round burst at a cyclic rate of 2,200 rounds per minute. The three rounds are out of the weapon before the firer can have the muzzle rise under recoil and greatly increase the overall hit probability of the system.

With the selector switch set at the numeral "1" the weapon fires as a normal autoloading pistol, even with the stock attached. The use of the stock makes the VP70 act as a small carbine but with the increased capability of firing three-round bursts. Without the stock attached, the weapon can still be used as a normal pistol. A civilian version of the VP70 was released for sale (the VP70Z) that had no mounting provisions for the stock and only fired as a semiautomatic weapon. The military version of the weapon, the VP70M, saw limited international sales. It was the first handgun to make use of a polymer receiver, a design characteristic that became very popular in the handgun industry within a few decades of the development of the VP70.

GLOCK

Introduced in 1982, the Glock model pistol has grown into one of the most commercially successful handguns on the world market. By 2001, it was estimated that approximately half a million Glock pistols were being carried as law enforcement service weapons in the United States alone. Available in an almost bewildering variety of models and calibers, the Glock has seen only limited military service but established a market for a type of semiautomatic pistol that was unknown as late as the 1960s. Today, most major pistol manufacturers offer models of their products that share several characteristics in common with the Glock.

The name of the first Glock pistol design was the 9×19 mm Model 17. The weapon was named after its designer and owner of the company, Gaston Glock, and the number of rounds it held in its magazine. The most noticeable characteristic of the Glock, and the one that gave it the most notoriety and bad press, is the

A field-stripped Glock 17 showing the major parts. Only the receiver in the center and the magazine at the bottom are made of significant amounts of polymer plastic. All of the other components shown are steel.
Kevin Dockery

fact that it is made with a polymer receiver. Though the Glock was not the first handgun to be produced with what was effectively a plastic receiver, it received the most press because of that fact. In spite of the large amount of steel in the slide, barrel, and other parts in the design, and that there are some metal parts cast into the polymer of the receiver, the public got the idea that the Glock was a "plastic" gun and could pass through airport X-rays.

The notoriety of the "plastic" gun almost eliminated there being any chance of Glock handgun sales in the United States. This was due to an erroneous newspaper article that was published in 1985 claiming that Muammar Qaddafi of Libya was purchasing one hundred of the plastic pistols from Austria, where the GLOCK company was originally based, and that the pistols were particularly easy to slip past airport security. According to the GLOCK company, the story was a fabrication, and no sales were being planned for Libya or any terrorist organization. And it was flatly denied that the pistol could be slipped through any competent airport security. It was pointed out that the lightweight Glock Model 17 pistol, the available model at that time, had more steel in it than a number of handguns that were already out on the market. It was a matter of a newspaper story being written for shock value and sales, not facts. The only real value of the story would be in the fact that unscrupulous readers might use the information and obtain a Glock pistol specifically to use it to try to get a weapon through security. The fact that the Glock could be easily detected by the standard means available at the time would simply get those people caught.

Developed specifically to meet the needs of the Austrian military, the Glock Model 17 pistol had a plastic frame with rails cast into the material to act as guide points for the steel slide. Additional steel components are also cast into the frame. Operationally, the Glock functions as a standard handgun, using the force of recoil to move the slide to the rear, unlock the barrel, and otherwise work the action. The double-column magazine of the weapon is also made primarily of polymer, giving the design a very light overall weight.

The other very noticeable characteristic of the Glock is the lack of a mechanical safety. The weapon is striker fired, and the double-action design only has the striker cocked into the firing position after an intentional pull on the double-action trigger. As the trigger is pulled, a firing pin lock is released before the weapon can be fully cocked to fire. Before the trigger can even be pulled, there is a trigger safety, a small lever on the front of the trigger itself that is released only when the operator's finger is actually in position to fire. Lastly, there is a drop safety that prevents the firing pin from moving forward if the loaded weapon is dropped or struck.

Tested extensively by the Austrian military, the Glock Model 17 surpassed all other weapons in the trials. The light weight and ease of use of the Glock were also greatly appealing factors. The weapon was adopted by Austria as their P80 pistol in 1982. Within a few years, both Norway and Sweden also adopted the Glock as a military sidearm. Military sales were the initial push behind the Glock series, but it was also purchased by various governmental and law enforcement agencies all around the world. In 1985, the GLOCK company opened a U.S. manufacturing facility to meet the developing demand for the weapon in this country. Over several decades, the basic design of the Glock has remained the same with the primary changes being made to accept new calibers or to change the size of the weapon for greater concealability or other market demands. Expanding from the original design, there are now more than two dozen different Glock models available in half a dozen calibers.

GLOCK 18/18C

There is one model of Glock pistol that has never been offered for sale to the general public. Designed at a specific request of the Austrian antiterrorist Cobra Unit in 1986, the Glock Model 18 is a true machine pistol, a variation of the Model 17 that includes a selector switch and the capability for full automatic fire.

The Cobra unit wanted a very concealable submachine gun, a weapon that could saturate an area with

A cloud of brass falls around the author's hands as he fired a full-automatic 9mm Glock pistol.
Kevin Dockery

fire if necessary. The Glock Model 18 can do that easily with its cyclic rate of automatic fire being 1,100 to 1,200 rounds per minute. In more practical terms, that's a rate of fire of 18 to 20 rounds per second. The standard 17-round magazine is emptied in under a second at that cyclic rate. The long, extended 33-round magazine specifically made for the Glock 18 is still less than two seconds of automatic fire, though a trained operator can fire several bursts before that long magazine would be emptied.

The selector switch of the Glock 18 is mounted on the left rear side of the slide, in the position that a safety switch might be found on other designs. Pushing the switch up so that the lever points to a single dot embossed into the metal sets the Glock 18 on semiautomatic fire. In the semiautomatic setting, the Glock 18 operates like any other model in the line. Set to point to the lower two dots on the slide, and the selector lever is set to full automatic. The Glock does not fire mechanically controlled bursts. Any limitation of fire at full automatic is a matter of operator control.

In spite of the polymer frame of the Glock, the design of the weapon keeps the heat from the barrel from damaging the frame, even during extended periods of firing. The recoil of the 9 mm round in the Glock 18 forces the barrel up into the air in spite of the ergonomic design of the weapon. It is a difficult job to hold the weapon down on full automatic, adding to the training time that an operator must be willing to dedicate to the weapon. An additional model of the Glock 18, the 18C, aids the shooter in holding the muzzle down during firing.

The *C* in the designation of the Glock 18C indicates that the weapon has a compensated barrel. In a compensated Glock, there are normally two slotted ports on either side of the slide, to the rear of the front sight. With the slide closed in the forward position for firing, the ports in the slide are lined up with ports in the upper part of the barrel of the weapon. When the weapon is fired, propellant gas escapes from these ports and is directed upward and to the sides of the slide. The high-speed gases help hold the front of the weapon down during firing, compensating in part for the force of recoil. Any of the Glock models with a *C* in the designation have compensated barrels, though the use of the system is most noticeable when used with the 18C and firing on full automatic.

BERETTA 93R

Another European manufacturer of handguns released a version of a popular weapon, modified to be capable of full automatic fire. The Italian Beretta company did an extensive rework of their Model 92 weapon to create the 93R, *R* standing for the Italian *raffica* (burst). The receiver of the Model 92 was extensively reworked, the most noticeable change being the extended trigger guard. In front of the trigger guard is a folding handle that can be pushed up against the frame to streamline the gun in order to carry it in a holster. For use, the forward handle is pulled down to where it locks it into an approximately forty-five-degree angle to the weapon. The nonfiring hand of the operator can grasp the front handle, slipping the thumb of that hand through the extended trigger guard, and hold the weapon down against the climb of an automatic burst.

One reason the front handle is so important on the 93R is the folding shoulder stock that can be attached to the butt of the pistol. A stud on the folding stock slides into a lug at the bottom of the pistol grip, behind the magazine well. The stock can be extended out from behind the pistol and the butt end placed against the shoulder. This arrangement makes for a steadier means of holding the weapon, but it also gives an added mechanical advantage to the force of recoil pushing back on the slide and forcing the muzzle of the weapon up. It is by holding down on the folding front grip that this bad muzzle climb can be partially negated.

To also help in holding down the front of the 93R during automatic fire, the extended barrel has a number of slots cut into it just be-

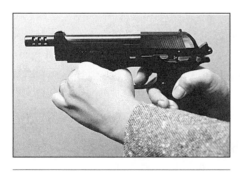

The holding position for the Beretta 93R pistol with the front handle down.
Kevin Dockery

hind the muzzle. These slots guide the propellant gases up and aid in compensating for the force of recoil.

The slide of the 93R is also made slightly heavier than that found on the standard pistol to cut back on the cyclic rate of fire of the weapon. In spite of the heavier slide, the 93R can fire 3-round mechanically controlled bursts at a cyclic rate of about 1,100 rounds per minute. The selector switch of the 93R, on the frame above the rear of the pistol grip, can be pushed up to the single dot that signifies semiautomatic fire or pressed down to where it points forward to the three dots that indicate a 3-round burst.

Even without the use of the stock, the Beretta 93R can be fired effectively through the use of the forward grip and a two-handed hold. An extended twenty-round magazine was developed for the weapon, but the 93R can also use the standard fifteen-round magazines from the Beretta 92 series. The long, twenty-round magazine extends out several inches from the bottom of the pistol, making concealment more difficult. The 93R is an interesting approach to the personal defense weapon variation of a standard pistol.

XM9/XM10 TRIALS

In August 1977, the Air Force initiated a search for a possible replacement for both the M1911A1 pistol and a number of the revolvers that were still in use. In part because of their compact size and ease of use, the Air Force had retained the use of revolvers long after the rest of the service had relegated them to secondary use at most. One of the reasons the revolver, specifically the Smith & Wesson Model 15, remained in use for so long was that the weapon could be operated with no more action to prepare it to fire other than pulling the trigger. The appeal of this simple operation was the concern that air crew and pilot, the individuals who were most often issued a revolver as a survival/personal defense weapon, would have a great chance of being injured if they were involved in a crash. The revolver could be drawn and fired with either hand.

In the post–World War II Army, there had been an investigation of a possible replacement for the M1911A1 both to give a smaller and lighter weapon as well as to examine the use of the 9 × 19 mm round to bring the U.S. military into a more common ammunition usage with NATO. The tests were conducted in 1955 and resulted in no new weapon for the military; the existing stocks of the M1911A1 were considered satisfactory for the foreseeable future. What did result from the tests were several new handguns that were released on the civilian market. As a smaller and lighter M1911A1, the Colt Firearms Company produced the Commander, a slightly shortened version of the government-model pistol with a variation chambered for 9×19 mm. Smith & Wesson developed the Model 39, a 9 mm semiautomatic pistol with a double-action trigger mechanism. That weapon was later adopted by the U.S. Navy SEALs as their 9 mm handgun in the 1960s. A suppressed version of the Model 39 was also produced for the SEALs in 1968, the Mark 22 Mod 0, commonly called the Hush Puppy.

Tests had established that the 9 mm cartridge could be as effective as the .45 ACP, if not more so as an effect of its higher velocity. The examination of both rounds had shown that there was very little difference between the two when they were placed side by side during lethality tests. No appreciable difference could be seen between the .45 ACP and the 9×19 mm in terms of the damage they did to the human body. The primary means of stopping power from a handgun round was based on shot placement; the more accurately the round hit the target in a lethal spot, the quicker the target went down. There was no true knock-down power in the .45 that made it superior to the 9 mm that could be found in the tests. There was little argument that the 9 mm was an easier round to learn to shoot, and as such, that made it more accurate. Additionally, it was easier to carry a large number of 9 mm rounds in a magazine and still have a reasonably sized pistol grip as compared to the .45 ACP.

By the end of the 1970s, the Army could see that the supply of M1911A1 pistols on hand was no longer sufficient to meet the needs of the service. Under the Joint Services Small Arms Program, the Air Force was given the task of selecting a new sidearm. The Air Force trials examined eight different handgun designs, gradually eliminating them one by one through the testing procedure. The tests were extensive and included firing thousands of rounds in a hot room range at a temperature of 125 degrees Fahrenheit, conducting the same series of shooting tests in a cold room range facility held at a temperature of −60 degrees Fahrenheit—a test that eliminated a number of the contenders—a mud test where the weapon and magazine were placed in a cement mixer with a mud slurry and then fired (minor manual assistance was allowed to get the pistol functioning during the mud test), and range shooting tests with a variety of personnel of both sexes and all the services acting as the firers. During the final reliability tests, the weapons had to fire 5,000 rounds with a maximum number of eight major malfunctions being allowed before a weapon would be eliminated.

The final result of these grueling tests was the Air Force recommendation that the Beretta Model 92S-1 be adopted as the new sidearm to replace all revolvers and M1911A1 pistols in Air Force use. The new Army XM9 Service Pistol Trials (XM9-SPT) tests were as comprehensive as any pistol test could be. A number of people considered the tests too extensive and almost impossible to match, a point brought out by several of the manufacturers whose weapons failed to meet the Army requirements. Many of the weapons tested were modified versions of the same handguns supplied for the Air Force testing. The final result was very close to the same as that found by the Air Force; the weapon chosen was the Beretta 92SB-F.

The M9 Beretta pistol above the SIG P226.
Kevin Dockery

In April 1985, a five-year contract was awarded to the Beretta U.S.A. Corporation to supply over 300,000 weapons, spare parts, and magazines. The new sidearm was adopted as the Beretta M9 pistol. The M1911A1 had been the primary service sidearm for the U.S. military for nearly three-quarters of a century, and it had now been replaced by a foreign design, which did not sit well with a number of people, no matter how good the Beretta had proven to be.

There were a number of protests raised about the fairness of the XM9 tests by some of the manufacturers who had not made the cut with their designs. A third set of trials for a follow-on contract were demanded by the politicians prodded by manufacturers familiar with using the political system. The original contract with Beretta would stand, and they would be supplying hundreds of thousands of sidearms to the U.S. military. The XM10 trials were for an add-on contract for an additional 142,292 weapons. The Pentagon announced on May 24, 1989, that the Beretta M9 had also won the XM10 trials and would be supplying those weapons as well. To manufacture the weapons, parts, and magazine, as well as to meet the requirements of their contract, Beretta established a new company in the United States, Beretta USA, and built a manufacturing plant in Accokeek, Maryland.

SIG P220

The runner up to Beretta in the M9 trials was the SIG-Sauer P226 pistol, made specifically to meet the requirements of the tests. The SIG (Swiss Industrie Gesellschaft—Swiss Industrial Company) company of Switzerland had absorbed several other gun companies in the 1970s, notably Hammerli of Switzerland and JP Sauer & Sohn of Germany. Through the Sauer Company,

SIG was able to bypass the very restrictive Swiss export laws and release their weapons onto the world market.

Designed for the military market, the SIG-Sauer P220 is an updated version of the Swiss P210, considered one of the most accurate military pistols in the world and also one of the most expensive. The P220 design retained the dependability and much of the accuracy of the earlier model in a simpler package. One feature introduced on the P220 is the side-mounted decocking lever.

The SIG decocking lever takes the place of a manually operated safety on the outside of the pistol. It is located on the upper front of the left-side grip where it can be easily operated by the thumb of the firing hand. After a round has been chambered and the slide is forward, pressing down on the decocking lever releases the hammer while keeping the firing pin locked and immobile. Letting the decocking lever up lowers the hammer, where it rests while still being held clear of the firing pin. Pulling the trigger through a long double-action pull raises and cocks the hammer while only unlocking the firing pin just as the hammer is released. The firing pin lock solidly prevents any accidental discharge of the weapon from any outside force other than an intentional pull of the trigger, whether the hammer is locked back in single action or forward for double-action operation. This safety and decocking action makes the SIG series of handguns, starting with the P220, extremely fast and easy to use.

In comparison to the original P210 weapon, the P220 was designed from the outset to make maximum use of metal stampings in place of machine parts. Even the slide is formed from a metal stamping, shaped and then set around a steel breechblock and welded in place. Many of the steel parts of the weapon that cannot be formed from stampings are made of investment castings as another cost-saving measure while still maintaining the high quality that SIG handguns had been long known for. The receiver of the pistol is made from aluminum to reduce weight, and the whole weapon is considered one of the better military pistols on the world market adopted by the Swiss as the 9 mm Pistole 75, by the Japanese Self-Defense Force (army) as their standard sidearm, and a number of special operations units and law enforcement groups around the world. Military, civilian, and law enforcement sales of the P220 have topped 150,000 in service worldwide

SIG P225

At a request from the West German Police, SIG reengineered their P220 pistol to a reduced size for the German police pistol trials in the mid-1970s. The result was a handgun that extended the appeal of the military and law enforcement pistol line. Mechanically almost identical to the P220, the SIG P225 has one less round of magazine capacity in 9×19 mm and is slightly smaller overall than the earlier weapon. Adopted by both Swiss and German police forces, the P225 is identified in Germany as the P6.

SIG P226

While the SIG P225 was proving to be an effective and popular seller for SIG as a law enforcement weapon, its limited magazine capacity did not allow it to meet the upcoming demands of military organizations. What the P225 also did was help prove out the SIG pistol concept and give a base for further development of the design. Looking at the upcoming United States XM9 pistol trials, the SIG corporation engineers used the P225 as the basis for a pistol designed to meet the XM9 requirements.

The primary modification to the P225 to meet the XM9 demands was for the magazine capacity to be nearly doubled. By going from a single column of ammunition to a double column, where the rounds lay nestled with each other in staggered rows, a fifteen-round magazine was developed that was of the same height as the original eight-round design. The only major change to the mechanism of the pistol was a widening of the frame. In spite of the large magazine capacity, the pistol grip was not too wide for easy handling by most shooters. The very flat textured grip panels and small part of the operating mechanism at the rear of the grip aided in keeping the design reasonably slim.

The other major modification to the basic SIG design was placing the magazine catch behind the trigger guard, rather than in the common European location of the bottom rear of the pistol grip. To make the weapon more completely ambidextrous, the new magazine catch was designed so that it could be easily switched from left-side operation to right-side. Being able to flip the magazine catch over made the weapon easily used by left-handed operators.

Out of all of the handguns in the XM9, and later XM10 pistol trials, the SIG P226 either matched or actually bested the Beretta M92 model. The final factor that determined which pistol won the competition and was the recipient of the military contract was a financial one. Beretta offered their design at a unit price of $178.50 U.S. The SIG P226 was offered at the slightly lower unit price of $176.33 U.S. But the overall cost was not just the pistols themselves but was to include spare parts and additional materials. The Beretta offer was around $3,000,000 U.S., less than the SIG offer. So it was not the cost of the pistols that made the Beretta the overall winner of the competition but the package price of everything that the military wanted included in the way of support. The SIG P226 was in no way the lesser handgun, just not the most economical one.

The SIG Corporation had been looking forward to the huge order that would have come with being the winner of the U.S. competition. Orders did come in for the SIG P226, including a 1,500-unit purchase by the American FBI in 1988. The only modification of the basic weapon desired by the FBI was a change of the sights to the SIG-Lite version that included tritium inserts. The tritium, a mild beta-emitting nuclear material, glows in the dark sufficiently to make the sights stand out in low-light conditions. With the tritium inserts, the shooter sees three green-glowing dots in the darkness and simply puts them in line to aim his weapon.

Additional law enforcement agencies and military organizations examined the SIG P226, and a number of them adopted it. Among these organizations were parts of the British Army, the Royal Canadian Mounted Police, the New Zealand Forces, and the Japanese Self-Defense Forces. The P226 has also been adopted by a number of special forces organizations, including the French GIGN, the Japanese Special Assault Team, both the British and Australian SAS, and the U.S. Navy SEALs.

The Navy SEAL switch to the SIG P226 was a direct result of a failure of the Beretta. In September 1987, a member of SEAL Team Six was injured when the slide of his Beretta pistol cracked into two pieces at the rear of the cuts where the locking block secured the barrel against the pressure of firing. The slide cracking took place during one of the range shooting sessions that were conducted extensively at the SEAL counterterrorist unit as part of their normal training. The rear of the slide came off the weapon and struck the shooter in the face. Within six months, the same accident happened, once in January and once in February 1988, where the slides cracked and the rear struck the shooter in the face during a Team Six range session. Of the injuries, one needed dental work, while two required stitches. Army testing of the M9 Beretta showed several weapons with incipient cracking, and these were tested to destruction.

In all, there were fourteen Beretta pistols that cracked and suffered slide separation. Only the weapons on the SEAL Team Six range resulted in any injuries, as the rest all took place in the testing laboratories. Examination of the problem showed a metallurgical difficulty that was addressed and eliminated when the Beretta factory in Accokeek was able to begin production in April 1988. But the damage was done to the Beretta reputation as far as SEAL Team Six and the Naval Special Warfare community as a whole were concerned. They abandoned the Beretta M9 and purchased the SIG P226 as a replacement.

SIG P228

The only market drawback to the SIG P226 as far as sales went centered on the size of the weapon. The P226 was very satisfactory as a combat weapon to all of its users, but the size was considered large for the average person to carry the weapon concealed. As they had done with the P220, reducing it in size to make the P225, SIG engineers shortened the slide, barrel, and grip of the P226 to come up with the SIG P228.

Still using the double-column design, the P228 had a magazine capacity of thirteen rounds of 9×19 mm ammunition. With the only change in the magazine being that the body was shorter than the P226, the P228 can lock in place and feed from the longer fifteen-round magazines of the earlier weapon. Reasonably small and light, the P228 was available on the market in 1989 and saw good sales. The big boost to the P228 came when the U.S. Army adopted it as the standard-issue 9 mm automatic for plainclothes investigators and other personnel who had need of a concealed sidearm. In 1993, the SIG P228 was adopted by the U.S. military as the "Pistol, Compact, 9 mm M11" and issued to such agencies as the Army Criminal Investigation Division (CID). The Naval Criminal Investigation Services (NCIS) also issues the M11 pistol as do the special operations groups when they have need for a concealable weapon for covert work.

HECKLER & KOCH MARK 23

In spite of the almost universal military use of the 9×19 mm round, there were still some reservations in the United States military, particularly from the Special Operations community. For the bulk of the military anywhere in the world, the use of a sidearm is primarily defensive. The primary weapon of the fighting man is his shoulder arm. If he is assigned to operate a crew-served or heavy weapon, that is his primary weapon. The pistol is a secondary weapon at most, an important one for certain, but not the type of firearm a soldier would normally be expected to fight with.

In the Special Operations community, the situation is different. The pistol can be a primary weapon given the proper circumstances. And it is often used as an offensive weapon rather than just a defensive one. The 9 mm handgun is satisfactory for most Special Operations uses; it can be quickly drawn in a close-combat situation where a shoulder weapon may have malfunctioned or simply run out of ammunition. The pistol keeps the man in the fight as long as it has to in order for him to keep the enemy engaged until they are defeated or he has the opportunity to clear or reload his primary weapon.

The other use of a handgun in Special Operations is when the combat is in a very tight area, and the use of a shoulder arm, carbine, or submachine gun is either too clumsy or the weapon isn't available for other reasons, such as a covert infiltration. In these situations, the handgun is used as an offensive weapon; the trooper goes into the fight intending to use his sidearm to engage the enemy directly. For that purpose, the Special Operations fighter would want the most powerful projectile that he could practically use in order to put the enemy down in a decisive manner. Additionally, the covert, surreptitious needs in conducting a covert infiltration of an objective could easily require the use of a suppressor to cut down on the possibility of detection. And the utmost in accuracy would be needed for these operations where the chance for a second shot might never come.

These were the ideas behind the United States Special Operations Command (USSOCOM) search for a pistol system to fulfill their unique needs when they put out their request for submissions to the firearms industry in 1991. The contract parameters for the Offensive Handgun Weapon System (OHWS) were for a .45-caliber pistol with a minimum magazine capacity of 10 rounds. The weapon was to be double-action, have a decocking lever, have adjustable sights, be supplied with a removable suppressor, and be able to mount a laser aiming module or LAM that was able to illuminate a target with white light (flashlight), infrared light, a visible laser, and an infrared laser. Additionally, the weapon had to be able to function for 10,000 rounds without a failure and 2,000 rounds without a stoppage. The pistols had to operate effectively with both the standard-issue 230-grain, 850-feet-per-second M1911 ball round and a special high-pressure 185-grain jacketed hollow point round with a muzzle velocity of over 1,100 feet per second.

The use of subsonic 9 mm ammunition had been common for years with the Special Operations community. To eliminate the supersonic crack of the normal 9 mm NATO loading, special heavy bullet, subsonic loads were developed and issued, beginning with the Mark 144 round developed for the Navy SEALs during the Vietnam War. The additional logistical load of issuing a special round of ammunition for an efficient suppressed pistol had been a difficulty for years. During the evolution of the counterterrorism mission, it was found that the normal subsonic 9 mm loads had poor terminal effects on the target. It was simply too small and slow to do significant damage without absolutely precise bullet placement on the part of the firer.

It had been decided by the legal councils of the military (judge advocate general's office) that using hollow point ammunition for counterterrorist work was not against the Geneva Convention as that agreement was for conventional warfare. There already was a 9×19 millimeter hollow point round being issued for special operations use as well as military law enforcement use, especially by agencies such as CID or NCIS. Additionally, a subsonic hollow point 9 mm round had been developed for suppressed use, but this was still a limited-power projectile. The use of a .45-caliber projectile was considered to be the best means of delivering a maximum projectile impact, the same as it had when the round was first being considered in 1905. The OHWS would be the first military-issue .45-caliber handgun intended for high-performance ammunition, and the impact of such a round on a target would leave little room for technical arguments about stopping power.

Recognizing the physical limits of what they were asking for, USSOCOM allowed for a fully loaded and equipped (suppressor and LAM) weight of the final weapon to be up to 5.5 pounds. Other accepted limitations centered on the suppressor. Being supersonic and having a ballistic crack sound as a result, the high-pressure hollow point ammunition was not considered for practical use with the suppressor, which was otherwise required to lower the sound signature of firing by thirty decibels.

Both Colt Firearms and Heckler & Koch submitted new handgun designs for the special operations offensive handgun. Extensive testing was done on both submissions. Built with a polymer frame and machined steel slide, the Heckler & Koch candidate weapon passed all requirements: environmental, functional, and accuracy. It was in the accuracy department that the H&K OHWS candidate showed startling capabilities. The weapon was designed to pass the stringent requirements that included exposure to mud, water, dust, sand, and ice while maintaining consistent functioning, and yet it also maintained match-quality accuracy. Out of 450 accuracy firings, there were more than sixty that had five-round groups under an inch in diameter. Four of the groups were a half-inch in diameter. That's five rounds of .45-caliber ammunition practically going through the same hole at twenty-five meters.

Adopted as the Mark 23 Mod 0, the first of the production Heckler & Koch pistols were delivered to USSOCOM on May 1, 1996. It had proved a successful offensive handgun with a new, much smaller laser aiming module than had originally been developed for the system, as well as an efficient, easily attached sound suppressor. With the normally subsonic M1911 ball ammunition, the Mk 23 could put out a muffled, very quiet shot delivering a heavy punch to the target.

FIVE-SEVEN

A very unusual handgun has been recently developed that goes to the other extreme from the .45 caliber to meet its applications. NATO had put out a request for a possible replacement for the 9×19 mm round for submachine guns, personal defense weapons, and handguns, and this fit in well to plans already under way at FN. To develop a new round of ammunition Fabrique Nationale of Herstal, Belgium, looked at the volumes of information that had been developed over the decades on small-caliber, high-velocity rounds. In August 1986, FN began practical experiments with high-velocity .22 caliber projectiles fired from small casings. Some of these experiments involved using discarded plastic sabots to fit a .22 caliber projectile into a short .30 caliber casing. Others had the new plastic-cored SS90 projectile designed by FN loaded in .22 Hornet casings, much as Colt had done during the SCAMP development. The final result of FN's development was the diminutive 5.7×28 mm round, a slim, bottlenecked round with a sharply pointed projectile.

The 5.7×28 mm ball loading (SS190) puts out a thirty-one-grain composite projectile with a full metal jacket surrounding a steel penetrator tip and aluminum filler developed by FN in 1994. From a pistol-length barrel, the projectile leaves the muzzle at a velocity of over 2,100 feet per second. The high velocity of the round gives it a very flat trajectory. For the average user, the point of aim at ten meters is the same one that would be used at a hundred meters, making aiming over range a very simple proposition.

The damage done by the projectile is significant. The composition of the bullet allows it to quickly lose stability when it strikes tissue, dumping all of its energy into a target rather than simply penetrating and continuing downrange. Range is also a significant factor if the target is missed with the 5.7×28 mm round. With a 9×19 mm projectile, the bullet is still very dangerous at over 800 meters' range. For the 5.7 mm rounds, the projectile has lost much of its energy by the time it reaches 400 meters' range, lowering the chance of collateral damage to targets outside of the immediate combat zone.

The limited range of the

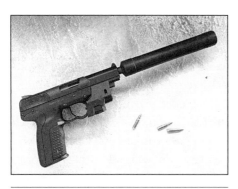

The Five-seveN pistol with suppressor and laser-aiming module. A special subsonic loading of the 5.7×28 mm round was made for use with suppressors.
FN USA, LLC

5.7 × 28 mm round is not considered a drawback for the weapons it is intended for, the P90 submachine gun, and the FN Five-seveN pistol. The limited range comes from the light weight of the projectile and that the slight mass cannot carry a large amount of kinetic energy along with it. What the sharp-pointed composite projectile can do is penetrate soft body armor and, to a limited extent, hard body armor.

Testing by FN showed that the SS190 5.7 mm ball round could penetrate a PASGT (U.S. Kevlar) military-issue armored vest or helmet at ranges over 150 meters. The NATO CRISAT future body armor test target, made up of a 1.6 mm thick titanium plate and twenty-two layers of Kevlar, could be penetrated by the SS190 at ranges greater than 100 meters. When projectiles were fired through Kevlar armor panels and into ballistic gelatin blocks, there was almost no difference in the tremendous amount of damage done to the simulated tissue whether or not the projectile had passed through the armor. This gave not only the soldier who would probably face a body armor–wearing opponent a sidearm that could bring him down, it gave the same capability to a police officer who might face a criminal wearing body armor, a still rare but increasingly more common situation. On the positive side, the projectile, though it can penetrate soft body armor, still had a limited effective range and much shorter danger area than most of the handgun cartridges on the market.

To fire the new round, FN developed the P90 and the companion weapon, the Five-seveN pistol. The pistol is an extremely lightweight weapon for the amount of power that it can deliver to the target. What is more astonishing to most shooters is the lack of recoil in the weapon. Firing the 5.7 × 28 mm Five-seveN has been compared to shooting a target-weight .22 automatic pistol. Recoil is very light, about two-thirds that of a comparable 9 × 19 mm pistol.

The problem is that there are no 9 × 19 mm pistols that can be reasonably compared to the Five-seveN weapon. The receiver of the pistol consists of a polymer frame with very few controls on it. Outside of the trigger, magazine catch, and takedown lever, there are no other controls on the Five-seveN. The pistol has a double-action trigger system that only releases the firing pin and the firing pin lock after an intentional trigger pull. The firing pin spring is not compressed after the weapon is fired, and the trigger must be pulled through its full length of travel to cock the firing pin, release the firing pin safety, and fire the weapon.

The high-pressure cartridge is safely controlled during the firing cycle by a delayed blowback system. The slide cannot open until the pressure on the fired cartridge has overcome a mechanical disadvantage. Then the residual pressure in the round can open the slide and operate the system. The slide is made from several steel stampings formed to a breechblock and the entire assembly coated with polymer. The plastic coating keeps the internal metal parts protected from corrosion and maintains a dull exterior finish to cut down on light reflection.

To feed the weapon, the small size of the 5.7 × 28 mm ammunition allows the Five-seveN to have a twenty-round removable box magazine in the grip while still maintaining a reasonable grip size. The overall construction of the Five-seveN and the size of the ammunition give the weapon such a light over-all weight that the loaded pistol and two full spare magazines (sixty rounds in total) weigh less than a loaded steel-framed 9 mm handgun with no spare magazines. In spite of the light weight, the low recoil of the round and flat trajectory of the projectile give the Five-seveN an accurate range of about 125 meters in competent hands.

USP TACTICAL 45

The basis for the USSOCOM Mark 23 handgun as developed by Heckler & Koch was their commercial USP (universal self-loading pistol) series. Characteristics and modifications learned during the extensive testing of the Mark 23 prior to adoption were incorporated in the USP weapons, increasing their market value. The Mark 23 was well liked as a suppressed pistol by many of the users who carried it except for one aspect of the weapon: it's big. The size of the Mark 23 with the suppressor and LAM in place puts it in the class of a small submachine gun. For many of the commercial and military users who might want the capabilities of the Mark 23 but in a smaller package, H&K developed the USP Tactical 45.

The USP Tactical 45 uses the same extended barrel and muzzle O-ring alignment system that gives the Mark 23 its excellent accuracy. The thin polymer O-ring centers the front of the barrel in the slide shot after shot, giving the USP Tactical 45 a near-match pistol accuracy while also having an expected service life of 20,000 rounds before requiring a simple operator replacement of the part. High-profile adjustable target sights also give the USP Tactical 45 a precise adjustment to align the sights to a particular operator's preferences. The over-sized trigger guard, match-grade trigger, and corrosion-resistant finish give the USP Tactical 45 easy handling and aid in shooting while wearing gloves.

For specific uses, the long-threaded barrel of the USP Tactical can also be mounted with an efficient sound suppressor. The design of the mounting system of the suppressor allows it to be screwed onto the barrel and adjusted so there is no difference in the point of impact for the weapon from when it was fired without the suppressor. The tall target sights give a good, clear sight picture in spite of the bulk of the suppressor attached to the end of the barrel. The suppressor available from Heckler & Koch for the USP Tactical is a wet technology suppressor. A small amount of water or other liquid poured into the suppressor, a few teaspoonfuls, is enough to lower the sound signature of the weapon considerably.

The USP Tactical 45 has proven popular with those U.S. Special Operations units that did not adopt the use of the Mark 23 when it became available. Several organizations maintained the use of the M1911A1 pistol, though in a somewhat customized version where the pistols were fitted with new barrels, triggers, and other modifications. For these units, the USP Tactical 45 provides a suppressed pistol capability and more modern handgun in a much smaller package than the Mark 23

USP9SD

The concept of the Mark 23 and USP Tactical 45 meets the needs of a number of other military and security organizations, except for the use of the .45 ACP caliber. To make a more universally usable suppressed weapon, Heckler & Koch produced the USP9SD *(Schalldämpfer)*, essentially a smaller version of the Mark 23 but in a 9×19 mm version. The weapon has all of the characteristics that proved the Mark 23 and USP Tactical 45 popular with United States special operations organizations and other security units, but the weapon has the much more common 9 mm NATO chambering. In addition, the H&K USP9SD uses a Brügger & Thomet (B&T) Impuls IIA stainless steel suppressor that is not manufactured in the United States. Not having been produced in the U.S. eliminates the U.S. State Department restrictions of the exporting of suppressors. The B&K suppressor is also a wet-type suppressor that operates at peak efficiency with a small amount of water in the system. The only drawback with the use of the 9×19 mm round in the USP9SD is the need to fire a subsonic loading of the 9 mm round for maximum suppression. The sound of firing even with normal supersonic ammunition would not be detectable as a gunshot when the weapon is used with a suppressor. But the supersonic crack of the projectile could be heard and recognized as a shot, even though the firer could not be located.

USP45CT

To meet a demand for an even smaller, more compact, suppressed pistol for covert special operations use, Heckler & Koch shortened and further modified their USP design. The modified weapon is designed for concealed, covert use of a suppressed handgun, particularly for counterterrorist operations. The intended target gave the pistol its designation, USP45CT (counterterrorist). No external safety is provided on the USP45CT to ease use and minimize any protrusions that could get caught on clothing when being drawn. There is a contoured slide stop on the left side of the weapon as well as the standard ambidextrous USP magazine release. The sights are fixed and nonadjustable but raised up to clear the sight picture above the suppressor when it is attached. A straightforward, double-action trigger mechanism makes getting the USP45CT into action a simple draw-and-fire proposition. Mounting rails are provided under the front of the polymer frame for the attachment of a laser aiming module.

For the general soldier serving in Iraq as part of Operation Iraqi Freedom, his choice of a sidearm is limited to the single general-issue weapon, the Beretta M9 pistol. Overall, the soldier's opinion of the weapon is high; it is easily maintained, and the large magazine capacity is considered a real plus. Some problems with the design have greatly weakened the trust the soldiers have in their weapon, and a suggested correction for a specific problem eliminates one of the weaknesses of the design.

In spite of passing the strenuous dust and sand exposure tests during the XM9 and XM10 pistol trials, there have been a number of problems with M9 pistols feeding from the magazine. The double-stack magazine design gets jammed up from the very fine dust and sand that is common in Iraq and fails to raise the rounds into position as the weapon is fired. One of the causes of this problem was traced to magazines that were purchased by the military from another manufacturer other than Beretta. While new magazines are procured from Beretta, it has been suggested to the soldiers in the field that they frequently clean the magazines to their M9 pistols and only load eight rounds.

Another complaint by the soldiers serving in Iraq has been the same one heard for decades from the American fighting man: there aren't enough pistols being issued for everyone. It was pointed out by the men in the field that a handgun would make it easier to search personnel, something done by almost all soldiers in Iraq at one time or another, while still remaining armed. The issue rifle and carbine are just too long to hold while also searching a prisoner or just a detainee on the street. Pistols were also considered a necessity for soldiers who had to clear confined spaces, like tunnels, house attics, crawl spaces, and sewers. Drivers wanted a handgun in order to return fire in hostile situations while still operating their vehicle. And every soldier wanted a sidearm to be able to use as an immediate backup if their primary weapon ran out of ammunition or jammed during a fight. Even the lower accuracy of a handgun was considered a much better alternative than trying to clear a jam while in the middle of a firefight.

The answer to the soldier's desire for more sidearms was a simple one: make a pistol standard issue for every soldier in a combat zone.

The use of a laser sight for the M9 was also desired by a number of soldiers. The use of such a sight was not as much for increased accuracy as it was for the psychological effect it had on a belligerent civilian. Soldiers who had privately purchased laser sights and installed them on their M9 pistols noticed that when a civilian saw the red dot of a laser on his chest, he tended to calm down and stop committing whatever action he had been doing that caused the weapon to be aimed at him in the first place.

The recommendation to meet this request and others that centered on attaching a white light illuminator to the M9 was to speed up the issue of the new M9A1 with the integral Picatinny rail and also add a laser aiming module to the weapon package.

The last problem soldiers stated they had with the M9 pistol is the hardest one to address. There is a noted lack of confidence in the lethality and apparent stopping power of the standard-issue M882 9 mm ball round. What soldiers wanted was the power of the old .45 ACP or even one of the new commercial rounds popular with police use, the .40 Smith & Wesson round. Some of this lack of confidence rose from a perception of weakness in the round on the part of the soldiers. Others who had used the M9 and the M882 ball round in combat had seen dedicated Muslim combatants coming toward them and not going down when they were hit, even when shot multiple times with the M9. It was a repeat of the situation in the Philippines almost exactly a century earlier with the juramentado Moro fighters. The recommendation to solve this problem was far from a simple one.

JOINT COMBAT PISTOL SYSTEM

The combat use of the 9×19 mm ball round in both Iraq and Afghanistan was restricted to full-jacketed ball ammunition for most soldiers in the field. Only under very special circumstances, ones that the average soldier would never see, could a hollow point be used in combat by the military. The fanaticism of the Muslim warrior, whether an insurgent or terrorist, made them difficult to put down with just a pistol shot when all they wanted to do was kill as many infidels as they could before being killed themselves.

The leadership at the Special Operations Command had recognized this situation and had started to address it in 2005. USSOCOM had issued a request for submissions for their Special Operations Forces Combat Pistol. It would be a high-capacity handgun, chambered for the .45 ACP round, and fitted with a removable suppressor. For a short while, the Army Future Handgun System was combined with the USSOCOM acquisition program, resulting in the solicitation being released to the industry for the Joint Combat Pistol System.

The Joint Combat Pistol System proposal was enough to have the handgun industry salivating at the thought of receiving the contract. In general, the new handgun was to be chambered for the .45 ACP round, have an integrated MIL-STD-1913 rail, self-illuminated sights for day/night use, and a detachable suppressor. Other specifications for the weapon were that it would have a standard magazine capacity of not less than eight rounds, and a high-capacity magazine holding not less than ten and preferably fifteen rounds. The weapon was to be produced in two models, one with an external safety and one without. There should be a decocking lever on the mechanism, and the firing system should be capable of both double- and single-action operation. Weapons were to be supplied complete with a manual and cleaning kit, two standard-capacity magazines, four high-capacity magazines, a holster, and a magazine holder. It was the quantities being suggested in the JCPS proposal that were staggering. The estimated maximum quantity of materials that would be ordered included:

45,000 pistols with no external safety (for USSOCOM use)

600,000 weapons with an external safety

649,000 holsters

96,050 standard magazines

192,099 high-capacity magazines

667,000 magazine holders

132,037 suppressor kits

Considering the numbers of magazines listed are less than the number of handguns possibly being ordered, it is logical to assume that they are in addition to the two standard and four large-capacity magazines that were to come with each weapon. The proposal also does not mention the quantities and types of spare parts that would be ordered, since that would depend on the specific weapon that won the contract.

The most unusual aspect of the weapon that was desired was for an ammunition counter to be included in the system. The counter was to be an electronic device within the weapon itself that would keep track of the number of rounds that had been fired by a specific pistol. The information would be downloadable to a computer so that maintenance could be allocated to a weapon depending on its actual use rather than a standard time schedule as is normally done in the military. Such a counting system was desired but not mandatory in the new weapon.

The Joint Combat Pistol System proposal was posted on August 26, 2005. On March 10, 2006, a modification to the proposal was issued. Now, the name of the proposal was for the Combat Pistol, and it was only to be obtained for USSOCOM use. The general characteristics of the desired weapon hadn't changed; it was the maximum quantities that would be covered by the contract that were considerably different. Now, the contract would be for a maximum of:

50,000 Combat Pistol systems, which included the pistol, two standard-capacity magazines, operator's manual, and cleaning kit

200,000 standard magazines

360,000 high-capacity magazines

50,000 magazine holders

15,000 suppressor kits

Only two general-issue handguns had been adopted by the U.S. military in the last hundred years. One was the venerable M1911 and M1911A1. The other was the Beretta M9 and now the M9A1. For whatever reason, the Army was not yet ready to go back to the .45 ACP as their standard pistol round, and what changes are in the future for the program are yet to be seen.

TASER

Not quite a true handgun, or even a firearm by legal definition, the Taser X26 is a very well-known and effective example of the new class of devices known as nonlethal weapons. Defined by the U.S. Department of Defense as "weapons

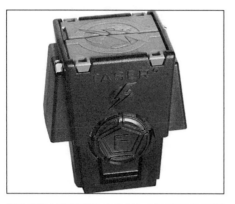

The 25-foot Taser cartridge, identified by the color-coded plastic cover over the "muzzle" of the cartridge.
Taser International

systems that are explicitly designed and primarily employed so as to incapacitate personnel or matériel, while minimizing fatalities, permanent injury to personnel, and undesired damage to property and the environment . . ." nonlethal weapons are intended to give the soldier or law enforcement officer a means of controlling a situation without resorting to lethal force.

The earliest versions of these weapons involved firing a projectile that was not intended to penetrate a target but to strike it a blow, knocking it down and rendering it helpless. Judging the power and point of impact of such devices has caused them to be called "less lethal," because they have caused deaths. The electronic form of nonlethal force can be much more precisely controlled and was developed into the Taser device by Jack Cover in 1969. Cover was the individual who coined the name Taser, an acronym based on a fiction series and standing for Tom A. Swift's Electric Rifle.

Instead of being a directed-energy weapon, such as a laser or electron beam, the Taser system is a conducted-energy electronic control device. The electric current travels to the target along a pair of wires. In the X26 and other Taser devices, the wires follow a pair of probes launched by compressed nitrogen, the probes, wire, and nitrogen propellant being held inside of a replaceable cartridge that snaps into the front of the Taser launcher. The tips of the probes hold small barbed points, 0.375 inches (9.5 mm) long in the standard cartridges, 0.525 inches (13.3 mm) long in the XP model, which penetrate through the outer clothing of the target and can stick into the flesh. The thin, insulated wires connected to the probes carry the very high voltage but extremely low current pulse of electricity into the target.

Electronic circuitry inside the Taser launcher develops what the company calls a Shaped Pulse, which can penetrate the skin even if the probes have not already done so. The active pulse of electricity is at 50,000 volts but has a current of just 2.1 milliamps, a minuscule amount of current that is not considered enough to do any form of permanent harm to the human body. The rate of pulsing is at nineteen per second with the device normally set to deliver current for up to five seconds.

Though the electric current from the Taser system is not enough to do lasting damage, the effect on the body is startling. The current overrides the normal functioning of nerves and muscles, causing pain and skeletal muscle tetany (lockup). The contraction of the muscles of the body normally causes the target to drop to the ground and be incapacitated for the time that the pulsed current is active. While the subject is incapacitated during the five seconds of the current discharge, it is physiologically impossible for them to voluntarily control their muscles. Recovery is almost immediate following cutoff of the current, though the subject may not be able to easily move due to a feeling of muscular exhaustion.

In spite of the pain and contractions caused by the electrical pulse of a Taser system, there is no damage to the heart, nerves, or muscle tissue of a subject struck with the darts. During training, law enforcement officers and others are exposed to the current of a Taser device, proving to them the efficiency of the system. In spite of the research that has gone into the device, which shows that it has no effect on pacemakers or other electronic devices, there have been fatalities connected with the use of a Taser. The deaths have been attributed to other causes than the use of the Taser, most often from excessive use of drugs and excited delirium, but the public still attaches a stigma to the use of the device in some areas. Careful training in the use of the Taser system as well as only conscientious applications of the device when other force options are more injurious, are going to prove the value of Taser technology as a nonlethal device that helps prevent deaths, limits the need for lethal force being applied to a situation, and reduces injuries to officers and suspects.

The military has looked into the Taser systems and has issued the Advanced Taser M26 and Taser X26 to combat troops to give them a nonlethal option. The Taser X26 has a mounting device available for it that allows the unit to be placed underneath the barrel of an M16-series weapon. Additional aspects of the Taser system include an electronic record of every time the device is fired. The Taser X26 has a data port that allows the internal record of the date and time of every discharge of the device to be downloaded into a computer record. This record helps track employers of the Taser X26 to provide accountable use of the system and corroborate a user's report.

To further maintain a record of Taser X26 employment, a Taser Cam audio/video device has been developed that inserts into the grip of the Taser X26 in place of the normal power supply. The Taser Cam can record up to 1.5 hours of video in MPEG-4 format (black and white) that can later be downloaded into a computer for observation and analysis. An infrared illumination

The Taser X26 with the Taser Cam module installed in the grip.
Taser International

system in the Taser Cam also allows it to continue recording in complete darkness. The power cells that are part of the Taser Cam device are enough to power both the video and audio recorder as well as power the Taser X26 itself through a normal cycle of functioning. In the base of the Taser Cam is a space where a spare cartridge can be inserted, as it can in the normal power supply module.

THE FUTURE

A large number of experts have consistently predicted the end of the sidearm as a military-issue weapon. These individuals list the limited tactical application of the weapon and say that the time of the handgun is over. The opinion is that a sidearm is not something that a soldier would fight with, and it is just too time-consuming to train users to any real degree of skill, let alone mastery of the weapon.

That relatively small group of fighting men whose lives have been saved by having a dependable sidearm immediately to hand would argue for the continued use of such a weapon. For the very large group of soldiers who have taken comfort in the weight of a pistol at their hip, chest, or hand, there is no question of the value of such a weapon, even if it is never fired in combat.

The practical question is more one of just what form a future handgun may take. Past and recent experiences have suggested that the caliber of an effective handgun should be around 10 or 11 millimeters (the .45 is 11.46 mm) to ensure a good transfer of energy to the target without a great deal of overpenetration. Magazine capacity needs to be as large as practical, but at least ten rounds or more if possible while still keeping the grip down to a manageable size for the general military population. Sights would have to have a low-light capability, luminous inserts of some type, and laser indicators would likely become an integral part of the system. Sound suppressors would have to be an available item for special operations and covert uses.

Receivers, if not the bulk of the weapon, would be formed from polymers or possibly ceramics for the high-wear parts, in order to keep the weight down.

This factor becomes increasingly more important as the caliber of the weapon is increased, as is the normal fighting load of the soldier. Experiences with some designs suggest that a full-automatic or mechanically limited burst fire capability would be a possibility as it greatly increases hit probability, especially during a sudden encounter situation. Without an effective recoil mitigation system, the automatic fire capability, even in limited form, would be improbable for use with the heavier-caliber handguns.

Small, high-velocity rounds have also established a place for themselves in handgun design since they have been successfully fielded to a limited extent. An example of how far this concept can go is shown in the Heckler & Koch G11 PDW project. A NATO document produced in 1989 suggested the need for a personal-defense weapon to be made available for the year 2000 and beyond. As part of their G11 rifle project, H&K looked at producing a caseless handgun firing the 4.73×25 mm round, developed specifically for such a weapon. The cartridge would have allowed a forty-two-grain projectile to be launched at a muzzle velocity of more than 1,900 feet per second from a handheld weapon capable of semi- or full-automatic fire. The handgun-sized weapon would have held twenty rounds in its magazine, with an available optional forty-round magazine. The end of the G11 project prevented the G11 PDW from ever moving much past the conception stage, but it does show one possible future weapon that has yet to reach maturity.

Electronic weapons utilizing projected energy will have to wait for a number of major scientific breakthroughs before they can be much more than an idea. The closest thing to the much-desired electronic stun-beam weapon will have to remain the Taser and such devices for the foreseeable future.

■ Pistol Data ■

The M1911A1 has a rubber pad installed on the bottom of the magazine. *Kevin Dockery*

NAME—M1911A1

COMMON NAMES—.45

CALIBER—.45 Automatic Colt Pistol (ACP) (11.43×23 mm)

OVERALL LENGTH—8.63 inches (21.9 cm)

BARREL LENGTH—5 inches (12.7 cm)

RIFLING (TYPE AND TWIST)—6-groove, right-hand twist, 1 turn in 16 inches (40.6 cm)

LOAD—M1911 ball

BULLET DIAMETER—0.452 inch (11.48 mm)

BULLET WEIGHT—230 grains (14.90 g)

MUZZLE VELOCITY—830 fps (253 m/s)

MUZZLE ENERGY—352 ft./lb. (477 J)

WEIGHT (EMPTY)—2.31 lbs. (1.05 kg)

WEIGHT (LOADED)—2.79 lbs.

SIGHTS—Fixed, nonadjustable, iron, notch/blade

SIGHT RADIUS—6.48 inches (16.5 cm)

EFFECTIVE RANGE—50 yards (45 m)

OPERATION—Short recoil

TYPE OF FIRE—Semiautomatic

TYPE OF TRIGGER ACTION—Single action

FEED DEVICE—Removable 7-round box magazine (commercial versions are 8 rounds and more)

FEED DEVICE WEIGHT (EMPTY)—0.16 lb. (0.7 kg)

FEED DEVICE WEIGHT (LOADED)—0.48 lb. (0.22 kg)

MANUFACTURER—Various military contracts during wartime, Colt Firearms primary contractor

SERVICE—In service with special operations units

STATUS—In commercial production

REFERENCES—TM 9-500, *Ordnance Corps Equipment Data Sheets*, Sept. 1962; government technical drawings

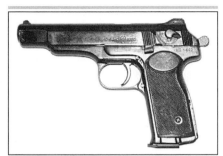

The Stechkin pistol. *Kevin Dockery*

NAME—Avtomaticheskiy pistolet Stechkina
COMMON NAMES—Stechkin APS
CALIBER—9×18 mm
OVERALL LENGTH—
  Pistol—8.86 inches (22.5 cm)
  Stock—12.04 inches (30.6 cm)
  Pistol mounted on stock—20.64 inches
(52.4 cm)
BARREL LENGTH—5.5 inches (14 cm)
RIFLING (TYPE AND TWIST)—4-groove,
right-hand twist
LOAD—57-N-181S "PM" ball
BULLET DIAMETER—0.364 inch (9.24 mm)
BULLET WEIGHT—91 grains (5.9 g)
MUZZLE VELOCITY—1,115 fps (340 m/s)
MUZZLE ENERGY—251 ft./lb. (340 J)
WEIGHT (EMPTY)—
  Pistol—2.15 lbs. (0.98 kg)
  Stock weight—1.23 lbs. (0.56 kg)
WEIGHT (LOADED)—
  Pistol—2.70 lbs. (1.22 kg) with 20 rounds
  Pistol mounted on stock—3.93 lbs.
(1.78 kg) with 20 rounds
SIGHTS—Open, adjustable, iron,
U-notch/blade, settings for 25, 50, 100, and
200 meters
SIGHT RADIUS—7.25 inches (18.4 cm)
EFFECTIVE RANGE—109 yards (100 m) with
stock
OPERATION—Blowback
TYPE OF FIRE—Selective fire, semi-, and full
automatic
RATE OF FIRE—40 rpm

CYCLIC RATE OF FIRE—750 rpm
TYPE OF TRIGGER ACTION—Single or
double action
FEED DEVICE—Removable 20-round box
magazine
FEED DEVICE WEIGHT (EMPTY)—0.11 lb.
(0.05 kg)
FEED DEVICE WEIGHT (LOADED)—0.55 lb.
(0.25 kg)
MANUFACTURER—Soviet state arsenals
SERVICE—Obsolete, some specimens still in
use with security (border guards), special
operations, and other Russian forces
STATUS—Production completed

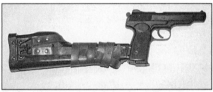

The Stechkin mounted on its holster/stock. The leather
carrying straps assembly is wrapped around the body of the
stock. *Kevin Dockery*

REFERENCES—Datig, Fred, *Soviet Russian
Postwar Military Pistols and Cartridges 1945–
1986*; Nelson, Thomas, and Musgrave,
Daniel D., *The World's Machine Pistols and
Submachine Guns*; Cutshaw, Charles, *The
New World of Russian Small Arms and
Ammo*; Bolotin, D. N., *Soviet Small Arms and
Ammunition*

The Gyrojet rocket pistol as it was commercially sold. The
long slot on the front of the grip panel is an opening to see
at a glance how many rocket-rounds are in the magazine.
Kevin Dockery

NAME—Gyrojet Mark I, Model B; Gyrojet
Mark II, Model C

COMMON NAMES—Gyrojet rocket pistol
CALIBER—13 mm Rocket (13×36 mm)
    Mk II Mod C—12 mm Rocket (12×36 mm)
OVERALL LENGTH—10.88 inches (27.6 cm)
BARREL LENGTH—5 inches (12.7 cm)
RIFLING (TYPE AND TWIST)—Smoothbore
LOAD—Standard ball
BULLET DIAMETER—0.510 inch (12.95 mm)
    Mk II Mod C—0.495 inch (12.57 mm)
BULLET WEIGHT—188 grains (12.18 g)
    Mk II Mod C—166 grains (10.76 g)
MUZZLE VELOCITY—About 100 to 125 fps
(30 to 38 m/s)
MAXIMUM VELOCITY—1,250 fps (381 m/s)
at 16 yards (15m)
MUZZLE ENERGY—4.2 to 6.5 ft./lb. (5.7 to
8.8 J)
    Mk II Mod C—3.7 to 5.8 ft./lb. (5.0 to 7.9 J)
MAXIMUM ENERGY—652 ft./lb. (884 J)
    Mk II Mod C—576 ft./lb. (781 J)
WEIGHT (EMPTY)—0.88 lb. (0.40 kg)
WEIGHT (LOADED)—1.08 lbs. (0.490 kg)
    Mk II Mod C—1.07 lbs. (0.485 kg)
SIGHTS—Fixed nonadjustable iron,
V-notch/blade
SIGHT RADIUS—8.5 inches (21.6 cm)
EFFECTIVE RANGE—55 yards (50 m)
OPERATION—Blow-forward
TYPE OF FIRE—Semiautomatic
RATE OF FIRE—20 rpm
TYPE OF TRIGGER ACTION—Single-action
FEED DEVICE—Fixed 6-round internal box
magazine
FEED DEVICE WEIGHT (LOADED)—0.20 lb.
(0.091 kg) 6 rounds
    Mk II Mod C—0.19 lb. (0.086 kg)
MANUFACTURER—MB Associates, San
Ramon, California
SERVICE—No official service, commercial
sales
STATUS—Out of production
REFERENCES—Archer, Denis, ed., *Jane's
Infantry Weapons 1978*; Mainhardt, Robert,
Gyrojet Rocket Small Arms Technology

COMMENTS—The second model of Gyrojet
Pistol, the Mark II version, was virtually
identical to the first except for a caliber
change to 12 mm (0.49 caliber). This was
necessary in 1968 when the federal Gun
Control Act put additional restrictions on any
weapon with a caliber greater than 0.50 inch.

Actual test firings of the weapon produced
large groups, averaging 11.2 inches at 10
yards (24.4 cm at 9.1 m). Penetration near the
muzzle, when the projectile had burned only
about 10 percent of its propellant, was so
poor that the round reportedly couldn't
penetrate a single sheet of cotton cloth with a
corrugated cardboard backing. At full velocity,
the projectile could easily punch through a
steel plate that would stop a .45 ACP bullet
with only a severe dent.

The 13 mm (left) and 12 mm (right) Gyrojet rocket rounds.
Kevin Dockery

The company drawing of the Colt SCAMP machine pistol.
Colt Manufacturing

NAME—Colt Small Caliber Machine Pistol
COMMON NAMES—Colt SCAMP

CALIBER—.22 SCAMP (5.56×29 mm)
OVERALL LENGTH—11.6 inches (29.5 cm)
BARREL LENGTH—7 inches (17.8 cm)
LOAD—Ball
BULLET DIAMETER—0.224 inch (5.69 mm)
BULLET WEIGHT—40 grains (2.59 g)
MUZZLE VELOCITY—2,100 fps (640 m/s)
MUZZLE ENERGY—392 ft./lb. (532 J)
WEIGHT (LOADED)—3.62 lbs. (1.64 kg) with
27 rounds
SIGHTS—Open adjustable iron
EFFECTIVE RANGE—100 yards (91 m)
OPERATION—Gas
TYPE OF FIRE—Selective, semiautomatic,
and 3-round burst
CYCLIC RATE OF FIRE—1,200 to 1,500 rpm
TYPE OF TRIGGER ACTION—Single-action
FEED DEVICE—Removable 27-round box
magazine
MANUFACTURER—Colt Industries Operating
Corp, Weapons Group
SERVICE—Evaluation
STATUS—Prototype only
REFERENCES—Company literature,
Proposal No. 850-2144, November 1971
COMMENTS—The ammunition for this
experimental weapon was developed from a
wildcat round, the .22 K-Hornet, a cartridge
developed from the .22 Hornet by Lysle
Kilborne in 1940. The K-Hornet has the sides
of the casing blown out to parallel with each
other and a sharp shoulder added.
Modifications to the K-Hornet to develop the
SCAMP round involved shortening the
casing for an overall round length of 1.45
inches (36.8 mm), removing the rim to rimless
configuration and cutting an extractor groove
in the resulting casing.

The VP70 pistol underneath the shoulder stock assembly that can also act as a holster. The slot in the side of the holster/stock is to lock on to a stud in a belt loop for carrying the weapon. *Kevin Dockery*

NAME—Volkspistole 70 Militär
COMMON NAMES—VP70M
CALIBER—9×91 mm
OVERALL LENGTH—
    Pistol—8.01 inches (20.4 cm)
    Pistol mounted on stock—21.4 inches
(54.5 cm)
BARREL LENGTH—4.55 inches (11.6 cm)
RIFLING (TYPE AND TWIST)—Standard-
profile, 6-groove, right-hand twist
LOAD—M882 NATO ball
BULLET DIAMETER—0.355 inch (9.02 mm)
BULLET WEIGHT—124 grains (8.04 g)
MUZZLE VELOCITY—1,180 fps (360 m/s)
MUZZLE ENERGY—383 ft./lb. (519 J)
WEIGHT (EMPTY)—
    Pistol—1.80 lbs. (0.82 kg)
    Stock—1.01 lbs. (0.46 kg)
WEIGHT (LOADED)—
    Pistol—2.51 lbs. (1.14 kg) with 18 rounds
    3.52 lbs. (1.60 kg) mounted on stock with
18 rounds
SIGHTS—Fixed, open iron sights, notch/
"shadow" front bar
SIGHT RADIUS—6.90 inches (17.5 cm)
EFFECTIVE RANGE—
    Pistol—55 yards (50 m)
    Stocked pistol—164 yards (150 m)

OPERATION—Blowback

TYPE OF FIRE—Semiautomatic; selective fire, semiautomatic, and 3-round burst when mounted to stock

RATE OF FIRE—

Semiautomatic—40 rpm

3-round bursts—100 rpm

CYCLIC RATE OF FIRE—2,200 rpm

TYPE OF TRIGGER ACTION—Double-action only

FEED DEVICE—Removable 18-round box magazine

FEED DEVICE WEIGHT (EMPTY)—0.22 lb. (0.10 kg)

FEED DEVICE WEIGHT (LOADED)—0.71 lb. (0.32 kg)

MANUFACTURER—Heckler & Koch, Oberndorf, Germany

SERVICE—Limited military and civil use in South America, commercial sales

STATUS—Production completed

REFERENCES—Archer, Denis, ed., *Jane's Infantry Weapons 1978*; company literature

COMMENTS—The VP70Z (*zivil*—civilian) is the semiautomatic-only version of this weapon intended for commercial sales. The VP70Z has no provision for the attachment of the shoulder stock.

The VP70 mounted for firing. The selector switch is the small lever on the upper "arm" of the shoulder stock where it is attached to the receiver of the pistol. *Kevin Dockery*

The Glock Model 17 pistol, the first and most common of all of the Glock models. *Kevin Dockery*

NAME—Glock pistols

COMMON NAMES—

Glock 17

Glock 20

Glock 21

Glock 22

CALIBER—

Glock 17—9×19 mm

Glock 20—10 mm auto

Glock 21—.45 ACP (11.48×23 mm)

Glock 22—.40 Smith & Wesson (10×22 mm)

OVERALL LENGTH—

Glock 17—7.21 inches (18.3 cm)

Glock 20—8.27 inches (21 cm)

Glock 21—8.27 inches (21 cm)

Glock 22—7.40 inches (18.8 cm)

BARREL LENGTH—

Glock 17—4.49 inches (11.4 cm)

Glock 20—4.60 inches (11.7 cm)

Glock 21—4.60 inches (11.7 cm)

Glock 22—4.49 inches (11.4 cm)

RIFLING (TYPE AND TWIST)—

Glock 17—Hexagonal, 6-sided profile, 1 turn in 9.84 inches (25 cm)

Glock 20—Hexagonal, 6-sided profile, 1 turn in 15.75 inches (40 cm)

Glock 21—Octagonal, 8-sided profile, 1 turn in 15.75 inches (40 cm)

Glock 22—Hexagonal, 6-sided profile, 1 turn in 15.75 inches (40 cm)

LOAD—
Glock 17—M882 NATO ball
Glock 20—.40 S&W Winchester JHP
Glock 21—Winchester Silvertip
Glock 22—10 mm Auto Winchester
Silvertip
BULLET DIAMETER—
Glock 17—0.355 inch (9.02 mm)
Glock 20—0.400 inch (10.16 mm)
Glock 21—0.452 inch (11.48 mm)
Glock 22—0.400 inch (10.16 mm)
BULLET WEIGHT—
Glock 17—124 grains (8.04 g)
Glock 20—180 grains (11.66 g)
Glock 21—180 grains (11.66 g)
Glock 22—175 grains (11.34 g)
MUZZLE VELOCITY—
Glock 17—1,230 fps (375 m/s)
Glock 20—990 fps (302 m/s)
Glock 21—1,000 fps (305 m/s)
Glock 22—1,290 fps (393 m/s)
MUZZLE ENERGY—
Glock 17—416 ft./lb. (564 J)
Glock 20—392 ft./lb. (532 J)
Glock 21—400 ft./lb. (542 J)
Glock 22—647 ft./lb. (877 J)
WEIGHT (EMPTY)—
Glock 17—1.37 lbs. (0.62 kg)
Glock 20—1.65 lbs. (0.75 kg)
Glock 21—1.58 lbs. (0.72 kg)
Glock 22—1.40 lbs. (0.64 kg)
WEIGHT (LOADED)—
Glock 17—1.96 lbs. (0.89 kg) with 17
rounds M882 ball
Glock 20—2.40 lbs. (1.09 kg) with 15
rounds Winchester 175-grain Silvertip
Glock 21—2.20 lbs. (1.00 kg) with 13
rounds Winchester 180-grain Silvertip
Glock 22—2.07 lbs. (0.94 kg) with 5 rounds
Winchester jacketed hollow point
SIGHTS—Open fixed, adjustable for
windage, square notch/blade;
optional fully adjustable target sights
available

SIGHT RADIUS—
Glock 17—6.50 inches (16.5 cm)
Glock 20—6.77 inches (17.2 cm)
Glock 21—6.77 inches (17.2 cm)
Glock 22—6.50 inches (16.5 cm)
OPERATION—Short recoil
TYPE OF FIRE—Semiautomatic
TYPE OF TRIGGER ACTION—Double-action
only
FEED DEVICE—Removable polymer box
magazine, capacity depending on caliber
and model
Glock 17—17 rounds
Glock 20—15 rounds
Glock 21—13 rounds
Glock 22—15 rounds
FEED DEVICE WEIGHT (EMPTY)—
Glock 17—0.13 lb. (0.059 kg)
Glock 20—0.13 lb. (0.059 kg)
Glock 21—0.12 lb. (0.054 kg)
Glock 22—0.12 lb. (0.054 kg)
FEED DEVICE WEIGHT (LOADED)—
Glock 17—0.59 lb. (0.27 kg)
Glock 20—0.75 lb. (0.34 kg)
Glock 21—0.62 lb. (0.28 kg)
Glock 22—0.67 lb. (0.30 kg)
MANUFACTURER—Glock, Inc., Smyrna,
Georgia
SERVICE—Model 17 in service with the
Austrian, Norwegian, and Swedish military,
extensive commercial sales of all models
STATUS—In production
REFERENCES—Company literature

NAME—Glock Model 18 Machine Pistol
COMMON NAMES—Glock 18
CALIBER—9 × 19 mm
OVERALL LENGTH—7.32 inches (18.6 cm)
BARREL LENGTH—4.49 inches (11.4 cm)
RIFLING (TYPE AND TWIST)—Hexagonal,
6-sided profile, 1 turn in 9.84 inches (25 cm)
LOAD—M882 NATO ball
BULLET DIAMETER—0.355 inch (9.02 mm)
BULLET WEIGHT—124 grains (8.04 g)

MUZZLE VELOCITY—1,230 fps (375 m/s)
MUZZLE ENERGY—416 ft./lb. (564 J)
WEIGHT (EMPTY)—1.29 lbs. (0.59 kg)
  IGP Model tactical GL shoulder stock
weight—1.43 lbs. (0.65 kg)
WEIGHT (LOADED)—2.42 lbs. (1.10 kg) with
33 rounds
  3.85 lbs. (1.75 kg) with 33 rounds and
mounted on shoulder stock
SIGHTS—Open fixed, adjustable for
windage, square notch/blade; optional fully
adjustable target sights available
SIGHT RADIUS—6.5 inches (16.5 cm)
OPERATION—Short recoil
TYPE OF FIRE—Selective, semi-, and full
automatic
CYCLIC RATE OF FIRE—1,100 rpm
TYPE OF TRIGGER ACTION—Double-action
only
FEED DEVICE—Removable 17-, 19-, and
33-round polymer box magazine
FEED DEVICE WEIGHT (EMPTY)—
  17-round—0.13 lb. (0.059 kg)
  19-round—0.18 lb. (0.082 kg)
  33-round—0.23 lb. (0.10 kg)
FEED DEVICE WEIGHT (LOADED)—
  17-round—0.59 lb. (0.27 kg)
  19-round—0.70 lb. (0.32 kg)
  33-round—1.13 lb. (0.51 kg)
MANUFACTURER—Glock, Inc., Smyrna,
Georgia
SERVICE—Commercial sales
STATUS—In production
REFERENCES—Heyman, Charles, *Jane's
Police and Security Equipment: 1999–2000*;
company literature
COMMENTS—The Glock 18C model is
identical to the Model 18 except that it has a
compensated barrel and slide system. The
top of the slide is open, exposing the forward
half of the barrel. The barrel has four ports
cut into it, allowing propellant gases to
escape upward and aid in controlling the
weapon on full automatic fire.

The IGB (Impulse Gun Barrels) Model
Tactical GL stock will securely fit all full-sized
models of the Glock pistol series without
modification to the host weapon. The stock
locks in place on the grip of the pistol and
rear of the frame. There are two slots
underneath the rear of the stock that accept
two spare magazines. The 8.125-inch (20.6-
cm) long 33-round magazine developed for
the Glock 18 will fit in the rear magazine
pockets of the stock but are too long to be
secured with the attached Velcro strips.

The Beretta Model 93R pistol mounted on its detachable
folding stock with the forward handgrip on the pistol folded
down for use. *Kevin Dockery*

NAME—Beretta Modello 93 Raffica
COMMON NAMES—Beretta 93R
CALIBER—9 × 19 mm
OVERALL LENGTH—
  Pistol—9.45 inches (24 cm)
  Pistol with stock folded—17.13 inches
(42.5 cm)
  Pistol with stock extended—23.94 inches
(60.8 cm)
  Stock only, folded—7.68 inches (19.5 cm)
  Stock only, opened—14.49 inches
(36.8 cm)
BARREL LENGTH—6.14 inches (15.6 cm)
with flash hider/muzzle break
RIFLING (TYPE AND TWIST)—6-groove,
right-hand twist, 1 turn in 9.84 inches (25 cm)
LOAD—M882 ball
BULLET DIAMETER—0.355 inch (9.02 mm)
BULLET WEIGHT—124 grains (8.04 g)
MUZZLE VELOCITY—1,230 fps (375 m/s)
MUZZLE ENERGY—416 ft./lb. (564 J)
WEIGHT (EMPTY)—2.24 lbs. (1.02 kg)
  Stock—0.60 lb. (0.27 kg)

WEIGHT (LOADED)—3.12 lbs. (1.42 kg) with 20 rounds

3.72 lbs. (1.69 kg) with 20 rounds and mounted on shoulder stock

SIGHTS—Open, fixed, nonadjustable iron, V-notch/blade

SIGHT RADIUS—6.30 inches (16 cm)

OPERATION—Short recoil

TYPE OF FIRE—Selective, semiautomatic, and 3-round bursts

RATE OF FIRE—Bursts—110 rpm

CYCLIC RATE OF FIRE—1,100 rpm

TYPE OF TRIGGER ACTION—Double-action

FEED DEVICE—Removable 15- or 20-round box magazine

FEED DEVICE WEIGHT (EMPTY)—
15-round—0.23 lb. (0.11 kg)
20-round—0.34 lb. (0.15 kg)

FEED DEVICE WEIGHT (LOADED)—
15-round—0.64 lb. (0.29 kg)
20-round—0.88 lb. (0.40 kg)

MANUFACTURER—Armi Beretta, Italy

SERVICE—Military use by Italian Special Forces, commercial sales

STATUS—In production

REFERENCES—Heyman, Charles, *Jane's Police and Security Equipment: 1999–2000*; Dockery, Kevin, *Compendium of Modern Weapons*; company literature

The Beretta M9 pistol. *Kevin Dockery*

NAME—M9 Pistol

COMMON NAMES—Beretta M9

CALIBER—9 × 19 mm

OVERALL LENGTH—8.56 inches (21.7 cm)

BARREL LENGTH—4.94 inches (12.5 cm)

RIFLING (TYPE AND TWIST)—6-groove, right-hand twist, 1 turn in 9.84 inches (25 cm)

LOAD—M882 NATO ball

BULLET DIAMETER—0.355 inch (9.02 mm)

BULLET WEIGHT—124 grain (8.04 g)

MUZZLE VELOCITY—1,280 fps (390 m/s)

MUZZLE ENERGY—451 ft./lb. (612 J)

WEIGHT (EMPTY)—1.89 lbs. (0.86 kg)

WEIGHT (LOADED)—2.53 lbs. (1.15 kg)

SIGHTS—Open, fixed, nonadjustable, square-notch/blade

SIGHT RADIUS—6.09 inches (15.5 cm)

EFFECTIVE RANGE—50 yards (45.7 m)

OPERATION—Short recoil

TYPE OF FIRE—Semiautomatic

RATE OF FIRE—45 rpm

TYPE OF TRIGGER ACTION—Double-action

FEED DEVICE—Removable 15-round box magazine

FEED DEVICE WEIGHT (EMPTY)—0.23 lb. (0.11 kg)

FEED DEVICE WEIGHT (LOADED)—0.64 lb. (0.29 kg)

MANUFACTURER—Beretta USA, Accokeek, Maryland

SERVICE—In service with all U.S. military forces

STATUS—In production

REFERENCES—Dockery, Kevin, *Weapons of the Navy SEALs*; company literature

COMMENTS—A new version of this weapon is presently being produced, the Beretta M9A1. Specific differences in the M9A1 from the M9 include a reversible magazine catch button for better use by left-handed shooters, a flared magazine well for easier reloads, a corrosion-resistant finish (PVD) for the magazine, and most noticeably, an MIL-SPEC-1913 (Picatinny) rail has been added to the frame directly forward of the trigger guard for the mounting of tactical lights, laser aiming devices, and other accessories. Specifications for the M9A1 are

identical to those of the original M9 except
for the empty weight (without magazine)
being slightly greater at 1.95 lbs. (0.88 kg).

The SIG P226. *Kevin Dockery*

NAME—SIG P220 and P226
CALIBER—
  P220—.45 ACP (11.48×23 mm)
  P226—9×19 mm
OVERALL LENGTH—7.72 inches (19.6 cm)
BARREL LENGTH—4.41 inches (11.2 cm)
RIFLING (TYPE AND TWIST)—
  P220—6-groove, right-hand twist, 1 turn
  in 15.75 inches (40 cm)
  P226—6-groove, right-hand twist, 1 turn
  in 9.84 inches (25 cm)
LOAD—
  P220—M1911 ball
  P226—M882 ball
BULLET DIAMETER—
  P220—0.452 inch (11.48 mm)
  P226—0.355 inch (9.02 mm)
BULLET WEIGHT—
  P220—230 grains (14.90 g)
  P226—124 grains (8.04 g)
MUZZLE VELOCITY—
  P220—804 fps (245 m/s)
  P226—1,132 fps (345 m/s)
MUZZLE ENERGY—
  P220—330 ft./lb. (448 J)
  P226—353 ft./lb. (479 J)
WEIGHT (EMPTY)—
  P220—1.61 lbs. (0.73 kg)
  P226—1.66 lbs. (0.75 kg)

WEIGHT (LOADED)—
  P220—2.08 lbs. (0.94 kg)
  P226—2.28 lbs. (1.03 kg) with 15 rounds
SIGHTS—Open fixed nonadjustable iron,
square-notch/blade; adjustable for zero by
moving front sight and exchanging rear sight
for ones of different heights; optional
adjustable target sights available
SIGHT RADIUS—6.30 inches (16 cm)
OPERATION—Short recoil
TYPE OF FIRE—Semiautomatic
TYPE OF TRIGGER ACTION—Double-action
FEED DEVICE—Removable box magazine,
capacity depending on caliber
  P220—7 rounds
  P226—15 rounds
FEED DEVICE WEIGHT (EMPTY)—
  P220—0.15 lb. (0.07 kg)
  P226—0.21 lb. (0.10 kg)
FEED DEVICE WEIGHT (LOADED)—
  P220—0.47 lb. (0.21 kg)
  P226 15-round—0.62 lb. (0.28 kg)
MANUFACTURER—SIG Arms, Switzerland;
SIGARMS Inc., Exeter, New Hampshire
SERVICE—P226 in service with U.S. Navy
SEALs and other special operations forces
around the world. Both weapons see
extensive law enforcement and commercial
sales.
STATUS—In production
REFERENCES—Company literature

NAME—SIG Sauer P228
COMMON NAMES—SIG P228, M11
CALIBER—9×19 mm
OVERALL LENGTH—7.09 inches (18 cm)
BARREL LENGTH—3.86 inches (9.8 cm)
RIFLING (TYPE AND TWIST)—6-groove,
right-hand twist, 1 turn in 9.84 inches (25 cm)
LOAD—M882 ball
BULLET DIAMETER—0.355 inch (9.02 mm)
BULLET WEIGHT—124 grains (8.04 g)
MUZZLE VELOCITY—1,130 fps (344 m/s)

MUZZLE ENERGY—352 ft./lb. (477 J)
WEIGHT (EMPTY)—1.63 lbs. (0.74 kg)
WEIGHT (LOADED)—2.17 lbs. (0.98 kg) with 13 rounds
SIGHTS—Open fixed nonadjustable iron, square-notch/blade; adjustable for zero by moving front sight and exchanging rear sight for ones of different heights; optional adjustable target sights available
SIGHT RADIUS—6.30 inches (16 cm)
OPERATION—Short recoil
TYPE OF FIRE—Semiautomatic
TYPE OF TRIGGER ACTION—Double-action
FEED DEVICE—Removable 13-round box magazine
FEED DEVICE WEIGHT (EMPTY)—0.19 lb. (0.086 kg)
FEED DEVICE WEIGHT (LOADED)—0.54 lb. (0.24 kg)
MANUFACTURER—SIG Arms, Switzerland; SIGARMS Inc., Exeter, New Hampshire
SERVICE—U.S. military service as M11, extensive law enforcement and commercial sales around the world
STATUS—In production
REFERENCES—Gander, Terry J., *Jane's Infantry Weapons: 2001–2002*, company literature

The H&K Mark 23. *Heckler & Koch Defense*

NAME—Heckler & Koch Offensive Handgun weapon system Mark 23 Mod 0
COMMON NAMES—H&K Mk 23 Mod 0
CALIBER—.45 ACP (11.43×23 mm)

OVERALL LENGTH—9.65 inches (24.5 cm); 16.72 inches (42.5 cm) with suppressor mounted; suppressor length—7.62 inches (19.4 cm)
BARREL LENGTH—5.87 inches (14.9 cm)
RIFLING (TYPE AND TWIST)—Polygonal bore, right-hand twist, 1 turn in 15.98 inches (40.6 cm)
LOAD—M1911 ball
BULLET DIAMETER—0.452 inch (11.48 mm)
BULLET WEIGHT—230 grains (14.90 g)
MUZZLE VELOCITY—886 fps (270 m/s)
MUZZLE ENERGY—400 ft./lb. (544 J)
WEIGHT (EMPTY)—2.42 lbs. (1.10 kg)
Suppressor weight—1 lb. (0.45 kg)
LAM module weight—0.46 lb. (0.21 kg) with 2 AA batteries
WEIGHT (LOADED)—3.21 lbs. (1.46 kg) with 12 rounds
3.67 lbs. (1.66 kg) with 12 rounds and laser aiming module attached
4.67 lbs. (2.12 kg) with 12 rounds, LAM model, and suppressor
SIGHTS—Open, fixed, iron, adjustable for windage only, square-notch/blade; visible and infrared laser and while light illuminator aiming module attachable underneath frame forward of trigger guard
SIGHT RADIUS—7.76 inches (19.7 cm)
EFFECTIVE RANGE—55 yards (50 m)
OPERATION—Short recoil
TYPE OF FIRE—Semiautomatic
TYPE OF TRIGGER ACTION—Double-action
FEED DEVICE—Removable 12-round box magazine
FEED DEVICE WEIGHT (EMPTY)—0.24 lb. (0.11 kg)
FEED DEVICE WEIGHT (LOADED)—0.79 lb. (0.36 kg)
MANUFACTURER—Heckler & Koch, Inc., Sterling, Virginia
SERVICE—In service with U.S. special operations forces
STATUS—In production

REFERENCES—Dockery, Kevin, *Weapons of the Navy SEALs*; Gander, Terry J., *Jane's Infantry Weapons: 2001–2002*; company literature

COMMENTS—Suppressor reduces the overall sound signature of the weapon by 30 decibels, taking a peak 169 db sound signature to 139 db or less

The Mk23 with Knight Armaments (issue) suppressor in place on the muzzle. *Heckler & Koch Defense*

The Five-seveN pistol. *FN USA, LLC*

NAME—Five-seveN
CALIBER—5.7×28 mm
OVERALL LENGTH—8.2 inches (20.8 cm)
BARREL LENGTH—4.82 inches (12.25 cm)
RIFLING (TYPE AND TWIST)—8-groove, right-hand twist, 1 turn in 9 inches (23.1 cm)
LOAD—SS190 ball
BULLET DIAMETER—0.220 inch (5.59 mm)
BULLET WEIGHT—31 grains (2.01 g)
MUZZLE VELOCITY—2,133 fps (650 m/s)
MUZZLE ENERGY—313 ft./lb. (424 J)
WEIGHT (EMPTY)—1.21 lbs. (0.55 kg)
WEIGHT (LOADED)—1.63 lbs. (0.74 kg)
SIGHTS—Open fixed, nonadjustable notch/blade

EFFECTIVE RANGE—55 yards (50 m)
OPERATION—Delayed blowback
TYPE OF FIRE—Semiautomatic
TYPE OF TRIGGER ACTION—Double-action only; single-action trigger available in the Five-seveN Tactical SA model
FEED DEVICE—Removable 20-round box magazine
FEED DEVICE WEIGHT (EMPTY)—0.15 lb. (0.070 kg)
FEED DEVICE WEIGHT (LOADED)—0.42 lb. (0.19 kg)
MANUFACTURER—Fabrique Nationale Nouvelle, Herstal, Belgium
SERVICE—Commercial sales
STATUS—In production
REFERENCES—Company literature; Heyman, Charles, *Jane's Police and Security Equipment: 1999–2000*

NAME—Heckler & Koch Universal Selbstladepistole 45 Taktisch
COMMON NAMES—HK USP Tactical 45
CALIBER—.45 ACP (11.48×23 mm)
OVERALL LENGTH—8.64 inches (21.9 cm); 15.71 inches (39.9 cm) with suppressor mounted; suppressor length—7.62 inches (19.4 cm)
BARREL LENGTH—5.09 inches (12.9 cm)
RIFLING (TYPE AND TWIST)—Polygonal, 1 turn in 15.98 inches (40.6 cm)
LOAD—M1911 ball
BULLET DIAMETER—0.452 inch (11.48 mm)
BULLET WEIGHT—230 grains (14.90 g)
MUZZLE VELOCITY—830 fps (253 m/s)
MUZZLE ENERGY—352 ft./lb. (477 J)
WEIGHT (EMPTY)—1.90 lbs. (0.86 kg); 2.90 lbs. (1.32 kg) with suppressor mounted; suppressor weight—1 lb. (0.45 kg)
WEIGHT (LOADED)—2.68 lbs. (1.22 kg) with 12 rounds; 3.68 lbs. (1.67 kg) with 12 rounds and suppressor mounted

SIGHTS—Open, adjustable, high target type iron, square notch/blade
SIGHT RADIUS—6.34 inches (16.1 cm)
OPERATION—Short recoil
TYPE OF FIRE—Semiautomatic
TYPE OF TRIGGER ACTION—Double-action
FEED DEVICE—Removable 12-round box magazine
FEED DEVICE WEIGHT (EMPTY)—0.23 lb. (0.105 kg)
FEED DEVICE WEIGHT (LOADED)—0.78 lb. (0.355 kg)
MANUFACTURER—Heckler & Koch, Oberndorf, Germany
SERVICE—Commercial sales
STATUS—In production
REFERENCES—Company literature

The USP-9 suppressed pistol. *Kevin Dockery*

NAME—Heckler & Koch Universal Selbstladepistole 9 Schalldämpfer
COMMON NAMES—HK USP9SD
CALIBER—9 × 19 mm
OVERALL LENGTH—8.40 inches (21.3 cm); pistol with suppressor mounted—15.65 inches (39.8 cm); suppressor length—7.80 inches (19.8 cm)
BARREL LENGTH—4.70 inches (11.9 cm)
RIFLING (TYPE AND TWIST)—Polygonal, 6-groove
LOAD—M882 ball
BULLET DIAMETER—0.355 inch (9.02 mm)
BULLET WEIGHT—124 grains (8.04 g)
MUZZLE VELOCITY—1,247 ft./lb. (380 m/s)
MUZZLE ENERGY—428 ft./lb. (580 J)
WEIGHT (EMPTY)—1.65 lbs. (0.75 kg); 2.65 lbs. (1.20 kg) with suppressor mounted;

Brügger & Thomet Impuls IIA suppressor weight—1 lb. (0.45 kg)
WEIGHT (LOADED)—2.16 lbs. (0.98 kg) with 15 rounds; 3.16 lbs. (1.43 kg) with 15 rounds and B&T suppressor in place
SIGHTS—Open, adjustable, high target type iron, square notch/blade
SIGHT RADIUS—6.22 inches (15.8 cm)
OPERATION—Short recoil
TYPE OF FIRE—Semiautomatic
TYPE OF TRIGGER ACTION—Double-action
FEED DEVICE—Removable 15-round box magazine
FEED DEVICE WEIGHT (EMPTY)—0.10 lb. (0.06 kg)
FEED DEVICE WEIGHT (LOADED)—0.51 lb. (0.23 kg)
MANUFACTURER—Heckler & Koch, Oberndorf, Germany
SERVICE—Commercial sales
STATUS—In production
REFERENCES—Gander, Terry J., ed., *Jane's Infantry Weapons: 2001–2002*; company literature

NAME—Heckler & Koch Universal Selbstladepistole 45 Gegenterrorist
COMMON NAMES—HK USP45CT (counterterrorist)
CALIBER—.45 ACP (11.48 × 23 mm)
OVERALL LENGTH—7.72 inches (19.6 cm); 13.19 inches (33.5 cm) with suppressor mounted; suppressor length—5.83 inches (14.8 cm)
BARREL LENGTH—4.46 inches (11.3 cm)
RIFLING (TYPE AND TWIST)—Polygonal, 1 turn in 15.98 inches (40.6 cm)
LOAD—M1911 ball
BULLET DIAMETER—0.452 inch (11.48 mm)
BULLET WEIGHT—230 grains (14.90 g)
MUZZLE VELOCITY—828 fps (252 m/s)
MUZZLE ENERGY—350 ft./lb. (475 J)
WEIGHT (EMPTY)—1.54 lbs. (0.70 kg)

WEIGHT (LOADED)—2.12 lbs. (0.96 kg) with 8 rounds

SIGHTS—Fixed open raised iron adjustable for windage, square notch/blade

SIGHT RADIUS—5.83 inches (14.8 cm)

OPERATION—Short recoil

TYPE OF FIRE—Semiautomatic

TYPE OF TRIGGER ACTION—Double-action

FEED DEVICE—Removable 8-round box magazine

FEED DEVICE WEIGHT (EMPTY)—0.21 lb. (0.095 kg)

FEED DEVICE WEIGHT (LOADED)—0.58 lb. (0.263 kg)

MANUFACTURER—Heckler & Koch, Oberndorf, Germany

SERVICE—U.S. special operations, commercial sales

STATUS—In production

REFERENCES—Company literature

The Taser X26 pistol with a cartridge module in place on the muzzle. *Taser International*

NAME—Taser X26

OVERALL LENGTH—6.0 inches (15.2 cm) without cartridge; 7.25 inches (18.4 cm) with cartridge

LOAD—Taser Cartridge 25 XP

ENERGY OUTPUT—5-second pulsed output from 15 to 20 pulses per second depending on batteries, each pulse output of 5,000 volts at 2.1 milliamps

WEIGHT (EMPTY)—0.41 lb. (0.19 kg) without cartridge or power module

WEIGHT (LOADED)—0.52 lb. (0.024 kg) with XDPM power module; 0.67 lb. (0.30 kg) with XDPM and 25 XP cartridge; 0.82 lb. (0.37 kg) with XDPM, 25 XP cartridge, and spare 25 XP Cartridge attached to bottom of XDPM

SIGHTS—Fixed, nonadjustable, open iron, square-notch/blade; primary sighting mechanism, integrated 650nm visible laser

SIGHT RADIUS—2.75 inches (7.0 cm)

EFFECTIVE RANGE—Dependent on wire length in cartridge; 25 XP Cartridge—25 feet (7.6 m) range

OPERATION—Muzzle-loaded

TYPE OF FIRE—Single-shot, double projectile

TYPE OF TRIGGER ACTION—Single-action

FEED DEVICE—Single Taser cartridge module containing 2 darts, wire, and compressed propellant gas; XDPM—Extended digital power module—at 195 five-second discharges (rechargeable)

FEED DEVICE WEIGHT (LOADED)—0.15 lb. (0.068 kg); 1 25 X P cartridge; XDPM—0.11 lb. (0.05 kg)

MANUFACTURER—TASER International, Inc., Scottsdale, Arizona

SERVICE—Commercial sales

STATUS—In production

REFERENCES—Company literature

The Taser X26 in place on a mounting rail that allows it to be placed underneath the front grip of any weapon with a proper mounting rail forearm. This gives the shooter an immediate lethal and nonlethal option at his fingertips. *Taser International*

SUBMACHINE GUNS
AND PERSONAL
DEFENSE WEAPONS

FIREPOWER

Moving through the tight confines of the tunnels would have been a claustrophobic nightmare for most people. But the team of special operations troopers who were moving down it was not "most people." They were trained to endure the worst situations for extended times during the conduct of a mission. In spite of their abilities, several of the men would have sworn that they could actually feel the oppressive weight of the thousands of tons of rock and stone hanging over their heads. Training couldn't always get rid of the last vestiges of a fear of enclosed places, but it could help men at least be fully functional in such a situation.

Part of the reason several of the men felt the way that they did was because they were not fully dependent on themselves to get through their present situation. They were following a local asset, someone whose loyalty belonged to no one but himself, no matter what the intelligence weenies had said was really the case.

Well inside northern Iran, the team had inserted during the dark hours prior to dawn. Normal human sleep rhythms made most guards lax and inattentive during those hours just before dawn. It was the perfect time to slip in and land a few kilometers away from where they were now but with the thickness of a mountain between where they had met their local asset and where they presently found themselves. It had been a harrowing ride in a pair of specially equipped helicopters that had flown bare meters above the sandy soil of the valleys and rocky peaks of mountain ridges. Now, with their weapons in their hands, the men felt that the ride in had probably been the easiest part of the mission.

The tunnel system they were in led through the mountain and supposedly out the other side. *Supposedly* was the word as they followed Mahmoud, or at least that's what the asset said to call him. He was supposed to have been a geologist who had worked in setting up the facility they were approaching. That's why he had known about the long series of narrow caves they had been following. Why he had turned against the leadership of Iran, none of the special operations troopers knew or cared. They all just knew that if a man turns his coat once, it isn't very hard for him to do it again.

They didn't speak much at all while in the cave; it wasn't just a matter of operational security; the oppression coming from the rocks overhead, the dry, dusty smell of the place, and the fact that they had to move along in a crouch at best, on their hands and knees a couple of times, was setting everyone on edge.

Then there was the really weird way everything looked. They couldn't afford the danger of using white light to illuminate their way through the caves. In the absolute darkness, the glow of even a small flashlight could give away their position to a guard who was so far away that they couldn't see him. But he might see their light. So the six special operations soldiers and their guide were seeing with the help of night vision goggles and small infrared lights.

The goggles gave everything a two-dimensional look, like you were watching a very badly adjusted television screen. Only on this TV things weren't black and white, they were green and shades of green fading into kind of a sparkling black. Strange things seemed to almost glow as they reflected the infrared light. Then there was the illumination coming from the infrared light on the LT's pistol. It flashed off things in the dark. Once a bunch of brightly glowing spots turned out to be nothing but the multiple eyes of a big cave spider. Sergeant Thatcher had crushed the pale arachnid under his boot as the column moved along.

Lieutenant Spencer Martin was up front, right behind their guide. In his hands was a Mark 23 pistol. The huge .45-caliber handgun was made to look even larger because of the laser aiming module and light that were secured underneath the frame of the weapon. The long, dark cylinder of the sound suppressor attached to the end of the barrel looked ominous, even in the green view through the night vision goggles.

The pistol was big, lethal, and quiet. The muzzle never moved any real distance from being centered on the back of Mahmoud. He had given all of the proper countersigns when he had met the team on their insertion. The men from the second helicopter had moved off on their own mission and had never seen the contact. They were to cross the mountain in the dark and set up a laser designator on the opposite slope from the side where the team had inserted. If they received a signal from the powerful beacon Lieutenant Martin had in his pack, they would shine their laser on the spot.

From high above the mountains, there would appear a black shape, dropping from the clouds. It would be a BLU-113 bunker buster bomb. The 4,400-pound weapon was capable of penetrating more than twenty feet of concrete before detonating its load of 630 pounds of high explosive. If Martin and his team couldn't locate and recover the bomb they had been sent here to get, or if they felt that designating the target was their only option, then the stealth bombers would unload dozens of the heavy bunker busters. If they couldn't get the bomb, no one would be able to have it—if it existed at all.

Deep in the mountain, Mahmoud suddenly stopped. Raising his closed fist in the air, Lieutenant Martin brought the patrol to an immediate stop. Without having to be told, the men turned their submachine guns outward, back along the tunnel they had been traveling down and forward into the unknown. The long suppressors on the MP5-N model guns would cut down on the noise of their firing, even in the enclosed environment of the cave walls magnifying every sound. The ammunition in the weapons were 9 mm frangible slugs, in case they had to fire anywhere near a nuclear bomb or the machinery used to make one.

"What is it?" Martin whispered practically into Mahmoud's ear.

Leaning back, Mahmoud said in an equally quiet whisper, "We are here."

With further hand signals Lieutenant Martin sent Staff Sergeant Malcolm Rogers and Master Sergeant Dick Williams forward. The two men were the best scouts and point men that he had. If there was something up ahead, they would be able to see it long before anyone else did.

In a sudden glare of light, everyone's night vision goggles bloomed for an instant. For that short moment, the entire team was blind. Then the light was gone.

For long moments, everyone just waited in the dark. Then the light bloom showed once more. It was only because of the iron discipline that each man had instilled in himself to make it to the elite special operations team that kept anyone from accidentally pulling a trigger and shooting into the light. No matter what may have been coming at them, fire discipline was absolute.

Then the two NCOs came back, crawling along in the darkness.

"LT," Williams's whisper came out of the dark.

"Here," Martin said as he waved the muzzle of his Mk 23, moving the infrared light across the cave floor.

From around a corner came Williams and Rogers. Williams quickly slipped up to where the lieutenant sat crouching on the floor of the cave.

"This is it," Williams whispered, "but it looks like we missed the party. There're only a handful of tangos in the cave up ahead. The place is lit up like New Year's on the Strip in Vegas and we could see just about everything. There's a heavy cloth hanging down along the walls, keeps the dust down, I guess. You can push it out of the way and see right down into the cave on the other side."

"I counted five guys with AKs and one wearing a pistol," Rogers joined in with a whisper. "No one looked to be very concerned, more like they were waiting for transport or something."

"There were two dozen men in there not more than a few hours ago," Mahmoud said as he inserted his whisper into the conversation. "They were to have had the bomb with them."

"Like I said, LT, nothing," Williams finished.

"We take them down and search the place," Martin said as he made his decision. "Remember, we want prisoners on this one, that guy with the pistol if it's at all possible. Williams, Rogers, take point, Mahmoud, you're with me. Thatcher, Graves, take right and left flanks. Powell, on overwatch."

Each of the men had practiced their maneuvers a hundred times in the past. Then they had practiced doing everyone else's part in the upcoming ambush. The only thing that was going to make this operation different was that the targets could shoot back, and the stakes were a hell of a lot higher than anyone would like.

Each of the men moved ahead silently, removing the night vision goggles before they slipped through the overlapping edges of the cloth across the opening to the cave. The light seemed much brighter than it was, and they crawled along the rocks and scree along the floor of the larger cave. The broken cover hid them from the eyes of the men close to the center of the big cave. They were gathered around a pair of tables and seemed to be just waiting for something. Most of the weapons in sight were either hanging from shoulders on slings or lying across the tables. The one tall man with a full black beard could be seen with a large holster on his hip. Out of all of the targets in the cave, he was the most likely one to be an officer. Martin wanted him alive.

All of the special operations troops were experts at stealthy movement. What it might have been that warned the terrorists in the middle of the cave,

Martin would never know. But one of the men with an AK hanging from his shoulder looked up and squarely into the eyes of Martin.

With a strangled shout, the terrorist tried to unsling the weapon from his shoulder. They weren't thirty feet away from Martin and his men and never had a chance. There was no reason at all for the special operations troops to give them one.

Short stuttering bursts of fire came from the muzzles of five suppressed submachine guns. Frangible 9 mm projectiles meant that they wouldn't penetrate cooling pipes or ricochet into something that shouldn't have holes poked in it. As far as the terrorists went, the bullets smashed into their bodies and ripped through their internals.

Fast, controlled bursts of two rounds each thudded into the targets, six terrorists in the room, and five bodies hit the floor within seconds of the shooting starting. Not one AK-47 discharged a round. The submachine guns delivered a stunning, violent swarm of lethal projectiles in just a few seconds. The fight was over almost before it seemed to have started. All except for one small part of it.

Big Beard, the leader type, stood stunned for a moment. Then he tried to grab at the holster on his hip. Martin wanted this guy alive and undamaged enough to answer some questions. The last thing he wanted to do was shoot him, with his suppressed pistol at least. In his left hand, Martin had drawn a strange-looking handgun from a skeleton holster on his left hip. He had practiced the maneuver on the range so much that he could make the shot with his eyes closed. But he held them open as he pointed the square-muzzled weapon and pulled the trigger. With a pop, two short, barbed darts trailing thin wires sped across the twenty-foot distance between Lieutenant Martin and the man trying to pull his weapon from a covered holster. When the darts impacted, they stuck deeply into the man's flesh. Then the electrical charge hit him from the circuits in the Taser.

Instantly, Big Beard doubled up as his muscles contracted and froze him in place. The current from the Taser ran for an eternity, or the normal five second cycle, depending on which end of the wires you were using. Big Beard collapsed as the current cut. When he tried to struggle to his feet, another pull of the trigger sent the circuits cycling again. The bearded man couldn't even scream as his muscles locked up.

"Mahmoud," Martin said, "ask this guy where the bomb is or I'll let him feel the juice again."

As Mahmoud talked in rapid Farsi, Martin looked at Sergeant Thatcher standing attentively nearby. Thatcher was listening carefully to every word being said.

Almost sobbing, Big Beard babbled at Mahmoud, and the conversation became a quick one between the two men.

"Okay, what?" Martin asked.

"Under the table," Mahmoud said.

"You have got to be kidding me," Martin exclaimed as he looked over at Thatcher. He saw the sergeant nod slightly. There was no reason to let Mahmoud know that Thatcher spoke fluent Farsi along with three other languages.

"Lord love a duck," Master Sergeant Williams said in as close to a curse as anyone remembered ever hearing him say. He had reached under the table and pulled out a heavy, square metal box. Waving a small device he had pulled from his pocket over the box, everyone in the room could hear the rapid, faint clicks.

"Whatever it is, it's hot LT," Williams said.

"Isotopes," Mahmoud said flatly. "It wasn't an atomic bomb they were building. It was a dirty bomb. And they were going to make it with isotopes they bought off the Russian black market. These fools were waiting for the smugglers to come in to take the material on the next leg of its trip. They are due here an hour from now."

"Fine," Martin said. "Bind and gag this little darling. He's coming back with us. Williams, you found it, you get to carry it. See if you can find a stick or something and maybe two of you can carry it between you."

As he spoke, Martin was pulling a pack from his back and setting it on the floor.

"I'm setting the timer on the beacon for twenty mikes," he said. "We had damned well better be on the other side of that mountain when those bombs come punching through the ceiling here. Let's allow the men who want this stuff to spend a little time trying to dig this crap out from under a mountain of rock."

SUBMACHINE GUNS

As a class of weapon, the submachine gun has yet to see its hundredth birthday. Like so many other modern weapon concepts, the submachine gun traces its beginnings back to the crowded, nightmare close combat of the trenches of World War I. The idea of a handheld, one-man, automatic weapon came about in the attempt to give a single soldier the ability to saturate an area with fire, keeping the heads of the enemy down while the rest of his unit approached. Additionally, the small automatic weapon would allow a man to more easily hit a target seen only fleetingly as the combatants moved about in the crowded trenches full of obstacles, bodies, and mud.

Originally, the Germans attempted to give their personnel a close-combat weapon, something used primarily to arm the crews of heavier weapons such as machine guns and artillery pieces. The first such guns were semiautomatic pistols, the long-barreled Artillery Model 1908 Luger. The eight-inch barreled handgun was issued with a removable shoulder stock. When attached, the stock turned the weapon into a short, fast-firing carbine. To increase the volume of fire available to the gunner, a thirty-two-round "snail" or drum magazine was developed in 1916. The Trommelmagazin 1908 was issued beginning in 1917 and made the Artillery Luger a potent piece of firepower. But the weapon was still a semiautomatic pistol, and the close tolerances and design of the Luger made it susceptible to jamming in the dirt and mud of the trenches.

The first pistol-caliber automatic weapon was the Italian 9 mm Villar Perosa designed in 1915. But the Villar Perosa was never employed as a submachine gun would be. During World War I, the Italian weapon was only seen either mounted or braced on the ground with a bipod attached to the muzzles of the twin barrels of the weapon. A curiosity, the Villar Perosa was in effect two automatic weapons attached to each other, side by side, and operated with a pair of spade grips at the rear of the weapon. It was much more of a miniature machine gun than a true submachine gun.

The first true handheld submachine gun was the carbinelike Bergmann Muskete, officially the MP 18, designed by Hugo Schmeisser. The very simple weapon used a straight blowback action where the heavy bolt was driven back by the pressure of the fired cartridge. Only the inertia of the bolt combined with its driving spring held the breech shut until the bullet had left the barrel and the pressure had dropped to safe levels. Additionally, the MP 18 was an open-bolt weapon. The heavy breech bolt was drawn back until it was held in the open position by the sear. Pulling the trigger released the bolt to move forward, strip a round from the—in this case—side-mounted magazine, chamber, and fire it. Then the bolt would be blown back and, if the trigger was still held back, go through the firing cycle again and again until the trigger was released or the ammunition ran out.

The Bergmann MP 18 was heavy for a weapon that only fired the 9 × 19 mm round. The blowback system of operation prevents most powerful calibers of ammunition to be used with it, so most blowback weapons are limited to pistol-caliber cartridges. The overly complex Luger snail-drum magazine was also used to feed the ammunition into the Bergmann MP 18. But the MP 18 fired, and it fired a lot. The German troops who knew it called the MP 18 the *Kuglespritz* (bullet squirter). The gun impressed a large number of the soldiers who used it and those who survived facing it.

The MP18 submachine gun with 32-round Luger "Snail drum" magazine in place.
Kevin Dockery

The United States never fielded a submachine gun during World War I. The closest the American Expeditionary Forces in Europe came to having such a weapon was the very secret Pedersen device. By replacing the bolt in a slightly modified Springfield M1903 rifle, the Pedersen device allowed the weapon to fire a .30-caliber pistol-sized cartridge semiautomatically from a forty-round magazine. Thousands of the Pedersen devices were made, but the war ended before they were ever used, and they were scrapped some years later.

The Pedersen device was not the only U.S. recognition of the need for a higher volume of close-range fire in the trenches; General John T. Thompson independently came up with the idea of a lightweight automatic weapon that could be handled by a single trooper assaulting an enemy trench. Again, too late to see combat in World War I, the weapon that became the Thompson submachine gun soon made its name famous in the world, both as a military weapon and as a favored weapon of the movie-style gangster of the Roaring Twenties and Prohibition.

The classic submachine gun had been established as a short, carbinelike shoulder weapon that could be held in the hands and fired. The weapon would fire automatically at a minimum, and a large number of weapons could fire semiautomatically as well. And the true submachine gun was chambered for a pistol-caliber cartridge, a factor that separated it from the rifle-caliber automatic weapons. The general characteristics of submachine guns is that they can put out a heavy volume of fire at relatively short ranges (less than 200 meters, normally) and are loaded from large-capacity magazines. Magazines could range in size from the twenty-round box magazines that held two staggered rows of cartridges to complex drum magazines that held fifty, seventy, or more rounds of ammunition in spiral feed guides.

In the years between World Wars I and II, the development of the submachine gun continued, but on a low priority basis in most countries. In nations where the possibilities and tactical use of the submachine gun had been recognized, such as Nazi Germany, the design and manufacture of new weapons continued under a restrictive blanket of secrecy. In the United States, only a handful of the Thompson submachine guns were in military hands. The bulk of these weapons were being used by the U.S. Marine Corps, particularly in Central America.

In England during the 1920s and '30s, there was no serious military interest in submachine guns at all. Outside of a few specimens in museums and government collections for examination, there were effectively no submachine guns in the country outside of some in criminal hands, most notably in Ireland. The English position was that the submachine gun was a gangster weapon and had no place in civilized modern warfare.

This was the era of what is referred to as first-generation submachine guns, or machine pistols as they were referred to in Europe. The characteristics of a first-generation type weapon included almost exclusively open-bolt operation, machined receivers and parts, usually of a high finish and precision, wooden stocks and grips (furniture), and a general carbine layout. With these aspects in the design, first-generation submachine guns tend to be heavy, complex, and both time consuming as well as expensive to manufacture.

World War I was the time that gave rise to the concept of the submachine gun, but it was World War II that was the true genesis of the weapon and time of its greatest popularity. In 1930s Germany, the country was rearming under the leadership of Adolf Hitler and the Nazi Party. The rising military force of the country was concentrating on automatic weapons as a major part of the firepower base of the squad. One of the weapons they used to provide this base of fire was the submachine gun. The relatively large, heavy, and unnecessarily complex designs that characterized the submachine guns of World War I and the 1920s were abandoned. Instead, the German ordnance engineers developed what is considered the first successful model of the second generation of submachine guns, the MP38. Intended for use by armored and airborne troops, the MP38 was a compact design to fit in with the German concept of rapid, mobile warfare and overwhelming fire. Much more easily manufactured than first-generation designs, the MP38 was made up of steel tubing and metal stampings with machined parts being held to a minimum. The wooden stock was gone; in its place was a folding stock that could be extended for firing the weapon from the shoulder or bracing it under the arm for quick hip-shooting. Or the stock could be folded up underneath the weapon, locking in place against the plastic furniture and giving the weapon a much more compact size. With the stock folded, the MP38 and its successors could still be held in the hands and fired effectively.

Further improvements in the MP38 design as the war continued came from both suggestions rising from its combat use as well as attempts to even further simplify its manufacture. These modifications resulted in the MP38/40 and finally the MP40, probably one of the most recognized submachine guns of World War II. Over a million MP40s alone were produced by Germany before the end of the war. Occasional specimens are still cropping up around the world in guerrilla and criminal hands more than fifty years after the end of the war.

The military setbacks of 1939 and 1940 changed the British mind-set about the submachine gun as a military weapon. They wanted as many of the guns as they could get. The United States had gone into heavy production of the Thompson M1928A1 model, but it was still a first-generation submachine gun design and was time consuming to make. The British started manufacturing what was effectively a copy of the slightly improved MP18, the post–World War I German MP28. This was still a big, ungainly weapon, far too carefully made for wartime production demands. The Sten series of submachine guns were designed and put into production in a matter of months following the British evacuation of her army at Dunkirk. The Sten is a true example of a second-generation submachine gun. Stripped to its barest essentials, the Mark II model from the Sten series was built from little more than pipe and welded parts. It was made by the millions and was even turned out in makeshift underground workshops in occupied countries in Europe.

In the United States, the M3 submachine gun was developed and adopted to replace the Thompson submachine guns. Even in the simplified versions of the M1 and M1A1 Thompson weapons, they still took a large amount of machine time to produce. The M3 submachine gun was made from stampings, a skill that was adopted from the automotive industry. In the time it took to make a handful of Thompsons, dozens of complete M3 submachine guns could be produced. It was also a solid example of the second generation of submachine gun, characterized by the extensive use of stampings, welds, and tubing in the weapons manufacture, the elimination of the fixed wooden buttstock, and its common replacement with a folding metal stock design and plastic furniture. Second-generation guns have a simplified action and usually fire from an unlocked open bolt.

In the post–World War II years, the glut of small arms on the world market cut back on submachine gun design and production for a number of years. Some of the smaller countries maintained their design groups and developed new patterns of weapons, but in general, the assault rifle was making inroads on what used to be the tactical territory of the submachine gun. By the 1950s, new submachine guns were being produced in those countries that needed the quick and easily manufactured firepower of that class of weapon. New patterns of weapon were produced that became the third generation of submachine guns.

Third-generation submachine guns are generally made from stampings, though some include tubing or extrusions as the basis for their receivers. One very useful characteristic of the third-generation submachine gun is that the magazine is located in the center pistol grip of the weapon. The pistol grip location of the magazine aids in reloading the weapon, as it is a very natural movement for one hand to find the other in the dark. This means an empty magazine can be removed and another slipped into place with the operator barely having to even look at his weapon. An additional characteristic considered distinctive of the third-generation guns is the telescoping bolt. A telescoping bolt is still generally a blowback-operated weapon, but the necessary mass of the bolt is not concentrated in the area behind the barrel of the weapon. Instead, the telescoping bolt partly surrounds the barrel, extending up and over it like a cup slipped over a rod. The actual bolt face where the extractor and firing pin are located, is not at the front of the bolt but in the middle of the part or even toward the rear. This technique allows the third-generation gun to still use the simple blowback system of operation while having a much shorter overall length to the receiver than earlier designs. Some telescoping bolt weapons are extremely short, little more than machine pistols, while others have a very compact size while still possessing a relatively long barrel for efficient ballistic employment of the ammunition.

The creation of the compact version of the assault rifle in the 1960s made further inroads into the tactical arena of the submachine gun, supplying a compact source of individual automatic fire, and has confused the definition of specifically just what a submachine gun is. Fourth-generation submachine guns were being developed in this same time period, which helped maintain the importance of the submachine gun as a separate class of weapon. The specific characteristics of just what makes a fourth-generation submachine gun are still debated. In general, they are a lighter, more accurate type of submachine gun, no longer married to the blowback, open-bolt system of operation.

The fourth-generation submachine gun in general fires from a closed bolt for greater accuracy. When the trigger is pulled on a closed-bolt design, a striker is released or a hammer strikes a firing pin to fire the chambered round rather than the entire mass of the bolt moving forward several inches. The lack of a moving mass aids the operator in maintaining his sight picture and weapon alignment with the target. The closed-bolt system of a fourth-generation submachine gun can be operated by simple blowback or utilize a locked breech and more complex systems of operation such as recoil or gas. Some weapons that could be identified as fourth-generation submachine guns are effectively pistol-caliber conversions of existing assault rifle designs. It is their conversion to firing pistol-caliber ammunition, usually but not limited to 9 × 19 mm, that makes the weapon a submachine gun rather than an assault rifle.

Rather than just being made from simple stampings, the fourth generation of submachine gun can also be made of metal forgings, usually aluminum or other alloys to maintain light weight. There are also very light submachine guns with polymer receivers and magazines. These weapons are distinct from the assault rifle due to their caliber, which is also why they fill a certain tactical niche. The lower power of the pistol projectile gives it less of a chance of overpenetrating a target in close-quarters situations. This is a particular concern in hostage situations or terrorist incidents where a bullet could go through a terrorist to strike an innocent hostage on the far side of the target. The compact submachine gun, especially the closed-bolt patterns with their greater inherent accuracy, can be more easily maneuvered in the close confines of an aircraft, office, or apartment room than the longer assault rifles. Also, the pistol-caliber weapon can be easily fitted with a more efficient suppressor than the more powerful assault rifle, even in the compact carbine version.

The newest form of submachine gun is the most confusing. That is the personal defense weapon. The concept has been around for decades in the form of very small submachine guns and true machine pistols. But it has become of more importance in recent years with the increase of specialized personnel involved in operations other than direct combat. The fluid nature of the modern combat arena makes the concept of the front lines a somewhat outmoded one. An ambush can strike at a convoy far away from any areas of active combat, forcing the drivers to quickly defend themselves while still operating their vehicles. Communications center technicians, heavy weapons and missile emplacement operators, even pilots who may be shot down over hostile territory need a more effective weapon to defend themselves with than a standard sidearm, but it has to be one that takes a minimum of training to employ. The way to limit the necessary training needed to hit a target with a specific weapon is to make the weapon easier to employ, to increase its hit probability through specialized sights or putting out a salvo of projectiles for every trigger pull. Mechanically limiting the burst length of such a weapon on automatic fire would aid the shooter in keeping his rounds on target without having to spend long hours on the range developing the proper trigger feel in order to control the number of rounds he would fire, a feel that would likely instantly disappear in a high-stress, sudden combat situation.

The personal defense weapon can be short-range, a positive characteristic if the fight is taking place in a crowded rear area, but must be light and compact so that the operator would always have it with him. It does no good to have the most effective hand weapon in the world if the man who needs it had to take it off in order to conduct his job. Or that the weapon is so long that the driver of a vehicle can't keep it strapped to his person and still bail through a hatch in case of an emergency. It is to fulfill this need of a compact weapon with good firepower, a high hit probability, low weight, and a large ammunition capacity that may keep the submachine gun in the military inventory for a number of years to come.

UZI

Probably the most popular example of a third-generation submachine gun, certainly a very successful one, is the Israeli-designed Uzi. After the cease-fire of the 1947 Arab-Israeli War, the fledgling country found itself without any major arms industry and dependent on munitions and weapons from abroad being imported for its defense. Development began immediately following the cease-fire on a submachine gun that could be produced with a minimum of machinery by the company that would become Israel Military Industries.

Making a study of the available submachine gun designs in the world, Lieutenant Uziel Gal of the Israeli Army concentrated on the weapons produced in Czechoslovakia as his primary inspirations. The ZK 476 may have been the first submachine gun made that fed from a magazine inserted through the grip. It had been developed during the German occupation of Czechoslovakia but never really put into production. It also utilized the telescoping bolt that overhung the barrel, allowing the system to have a short overall length while retaining a long barrel. The receiver had a square cross section and a top-mounted cocking knob with a large U-shaped slot cut in the center of it so that it didn't block the sight line for the shooter. Significantly, the ZK 476 also had a safety on the back of the pistol grip. The grip safety would lock the bolt either in the open (cocked) or closed (fired) position. It was only after the operator had firmly grasped the pistol grip that the cocking knob could be drawn back to prepare the weapon for firing, or the trigger release the bolt.

Two additional Czech weapons, the Model 23 and 25 submachine guns, also influenced Uziel Gal. While the ZK 476 was an obscure weapon that was probably only produced in prototype form, the Model 23 and 25 submachine guns were made in large numbers. These two guns were almost identical, the only difference being a fixed wooden stock on the Model 23 and a side-folding metal stock on the 25. Both weapons used the same pistol-grip magazine well. They also utilize the telescoping bolt, which allows the Model 25 to have an overall length of 17.5 inches with its stock folded, but still have an 11.2-inch barrel.

With the ideas from these weapons at his disposal, Uziel Gal developed the Uzi submachine gun, which was originally issued with an easily removable wood stock. Like the Czech Model 23 and 25 guns, the Uzi could have its wooden stock removed and a folding metal model installed in its place with a minimum of fuss. The manual safety and selector switch for the weapon is on the upper left side of the pistol grip, in a good position for it to be operated by the firer's thumb without him having to change his grip on the weapon.

Also on the left side of the pistol grip but down at the bottom is the magazine catch, set so that it can be pressed in with the thumb of the weak hand as it holds the magazine. An empty magazine can be quickly pulled out of the weapon, abandoned, and a loaded one shoved into place within seconds. Then the weak hand slaps down across the top of the receiver and draws the cocking knob to the rear. In addition to the bolt-locking grip safety at the rear of the pistol grip, and the manual safety on the grip, there is a special ratcheting safety that runs along the top of the weapon, inside the top cover mechanism. The top cover ratchet would prevent the bolt of the Uzi from going forward and accidentally firing the weapon if the operator's hand slipped off the cocking knob before the bolt was pulled back far enough to be caught by the sear.

The square cross-sectioned bolt of the Uzi is the telescoped model with the bolt face in the rear third of the bolt. To aid in using a lighter bolt, the Uzi operates with the advanced primer ignition system. In that system, the cartridge being chambered by the bolt is actually fired in the last few hundred-thousandths of an inch of the bolt travel, right before it slaps up against the breech end of the barrel. In this system, the blowback action of the fired cartridge has to overcome the forward inertia of the bolt before it can start to move the bolt to the rear.

The action of advanced primer ignition can be likened to an individual trying to push a car without the engine running. Shoving hard on the front of a car sitting on a level roadway, the average person can get the car rolling backward fairly easily. If the car was rolling forward at a very slow speed, just a few miles an hour, toward the person and without the engine running, a single person would find it almost impossible to stop the car and push it in the other direction before he had been shoved backward with his feet dragging on the ground for a good distance. It is that same kind of inertia that has to be overcome by the cartridge in order to work the action of the weapon.

The use of the advanced primer ignition system is far from being unique to the Uzi, but the weapon has made great use of the technique. The stamped-metal receiver of the Uzi has long, raised ribs along the side of it. The ribs give the receiver additional rigidity and strength while also making grooves along the interior of the action. The grooves give accumulated dirt, sand, and dust someplace to go inside the receiver of the Uzi, a serious consideration in the dusty, sandy environment of much of the Mideast.

The Uzi saw action within months of it going into production in Israel in 1951. It quickly developed a reputation for accuracy and, most of all, dependability. The open-bolt system used in the Uzi leaves the action open between bursts and allows air to circulate through the receiver and barrel, cooling the weapon down from the heat of firing. The weapon became a symbol of the Israeli military and was recognized across the world. It has become commonplace for almost any submachine gun to be called an Uzi by people who have only heard the name and never seen the compact little Israeli weapon in use. It has remained in production and use by a number of military organizations around the world as well as serving law enforcement and security forces.

VZ-61 SKORPION

In the Warsaw Pact countries, the Soviet equivalent of NATO, the submachine gun was quickly supplanted as a major weapon by the introduction in volume of the AK-47 assault rifle. It was the compact size offered by the submachine gun class of weapon that brought forward a number of new designs in countries outside of Russia itself. In countries such as Czechoslovakia the submachine gun was still being produced in large numbers in the 1950s. Among the smallest of these weapons was the Czech Vz-61, commonly called the Skorpion.

In the late 1950s, the Czechoslovakian arms control agency, Om-

The author shoulder-firing the Skorpion submachine gun. The very small size of the weapon and short length of the folding stock make this position a difficult one in which to shoot the weapon, especially for a large person.
Kevin Dockery

nipol, was pushing hard to have new military small arms go into production. The Skorpion was produced not only as a Czech military-issue weapon but also as a commercial product. The appeal of the gun was much along the lines of the Stechkin; it was effectively a full-automatic machine pistol as much as it was a submachine gun, in spite of the fact that it came equipped with a folding stock.

Originally, the Skorpion may have been conceived of as a commercial product that would appeal to law enforcement or security force use. As a military weapon, it is a very low-powered firearm whose compact size would have allowed it to be issued as a sidearm rather than a primary weapon.

In this mission, the Skorpion is very much an early form of personal defense weapon. The short weapon fits easily into either a hip or shoulder holster, being issued with a ten-round magazine primarily for concealment purposes. To supply a decent amount of firepower, the Skorpion is also issued with four additional twenty-round magazines in two pouches. The magazine well of the Skorpion is located in front of the trigger guard, the classic location for a submachine gun magazine. One of the most unusual aspects of the Skorpion centers on what is carried in that ammunition magazine. The Vz-61 Skorpion is chambered for the .32 ACP, known in Europe as the 7.65 mm pistol round. The very weak power of the .32 ACP in the Skorpion is compensated for by the weapon being able to fire controllably on full automatic.

One of the reasons the Skorpion can be fired on full automatic while still being held in the hands has to do with its relatively slow cyclic rate of fire. The cyclic rate of fire for the short travel of the light bolt in the Skorpion would be excessively high if it wasn't for the rate-reducing mechanism contained in the pistol grip of the weapon. The rate reducer is a pair of hooks that grab the bolt at the rear of its travel and hold it while a weight moves up and down in the pistol grip. Once the weight reaches the top of its travel, it forces the hooks to release the bolt, and it again moves forward.

Other than its very small size and light caliber, the Skorpion is a standard blowback-operated, open-bolt submachine gun. The very short wire stock that folds over the top of the weapon can be extended and braced against the shoulder, but it is almost as effective a hold just to grasp the weapon in both hands. To further extend the appeal of the Skorpion for covert use, it can be supplied with a removable suppressor. The design of the suppressor is unsophisticated, but it is still somewhat effective in disguising the sound of firing. The very concealable size, the capacity for automatic fire, and the availability of a suppressor have also made the Skorpion a favorite of a number of terrorist groups of the

1970s and 1980s, notably the Red Brigades of Italy, who used the outline of the Skorpion as one of their identifying symbols.

PM-63

A native design of Poland, the Pistolet Maszynowy (PM-63) is also known as the Wz-63, Wz standing for *Wzor*, which can be loosely translated as the Polish word for "model." The concept of the PM-63 follows that of the Czech Vz-61 and the Soviet Stechkin, a small automatic weapon that can be carried as a sidearm.

Though thin, the shoulder stock of the PM-63 makes it fairly easy to shoot accurately. The front grip aids in stabilizing the weapon but the operator has to keep his head back from the rear of the pistol, out of the way of the slide shown here in its fully rearward "cocked" position.
Kevin Dockery

Equipped with a slender folding stock, the PM-63 qualifies as a submachine gun rather than a true machine pistol, though the weapon is commonly carried in a holster.

Tactically, the PM-63 was designed to be a compact secondary weapon for combat leaders, airborne troops, and vehicle crews. The concept of the weapon comes closer to matching the present outline of a personal defense weapon rather than the diminutive Skorpion Vz-61. One of the factors that make the PM-63 a more effective weapon than the Vz-61 is that the Polish submachine gun is chambered for the standard Warsaw Pact pistol round, the 9 × 18 mm Makarov.

Rather than simply being a large handgun with a full-automatic-fire capability, like the much less successful Soviet Stechkin, the PM-63 has a number of ingenious characteristics that make it a much more controllable and convenient weapon.

The action of the PM-63 is a straight blowback design, but it does not use a conventional bolt. Being built much more along the lines of a pistol than a submachine gun, the PM-63 utilizes an upper slide assembly in place of a bolt. In effect, the top half of the weapon reciprocates during firing while the barrel remains locked to the lower frame. At the front of the slide is a long, troughlike compensator made up of the bottom curved portion of the slide extending well out past the muzzle of the barrel. This compensator is forward only when the slide is in the fired position and is fully closed. Since the long trough is below the muzzle when a chambered round would be fired, it acts as a compensator to the front of the weapon rising during firing. The expanding muzzle blast would press down on the compensator, holding down the front of the weapon against at least some of the forces of firing.

Since the PM-63 fires from what is an open-bolt system, the slide is locked to the fully rearward position when the weapon is ready to fire. The shooter can either grasp the slide by the two serrated sections on the rear and pull the slide back to cock the weapon for firing, or the front of the weapon can be pushed down on something hard and that will also drive the slide to the rear, where it will be held in the cocked position by the sear.

Underneath the weapon and in front of the trigger guard is a folding plastic grip that can be pulled down and locked into the vertical position. In the down position, the grip helps give the firer a solid hold for his weak hand, stabilizing the weapon during full automatic firing. Locked up into the horizontal folded position, the front grip is streamlined against the lower receiver, allowing the PM-63 to be easily holstered. There is a thin collapsing stock that has struts extending along both sides of the receiver with a folding butt plate that can be flipped up and locked in against the receiver section extending back behind the pistol grip.

Overall, the PM-63 demonstrates some sophisticated engineering to make such a compact weapon controllable on full automatic. Operation of the weapon is also simplified by the selector mechanism. The PM-63 has what is known as a progressive trigger. Instead of there being a selector switch in the mechanism, the trigger is pulled back to release the slide and fire the weapon. Pulling the trigger back further against spring pressure allows the slide to keep on reciprocating, continuing to fire the weapon automatically.

To lower what would otherwise be an uncontrollable cyclic rate in such a short, light weapon, the PM-63 includes a rate reducer mechanism in the back of the slide. When the slide reaches the full recoil position, it is caught and held by a latch. A sliding weight is released when the slide stops and continues to move backward, compressing a small spring. When the weight has reached the end of its travel, the spring pushes it forward, where it releases the latch, and the slide continues with the firing cycle or is stopped by the sear if the trigger has not been fully pulled back.

The compact PM-63 is issued with a hip holster and four magazines, one fifteen-round and three twenty-five-round, giving the operator ninety rounds of ready ammunition. The fifteen-round magazine sits flush against the bottom of the pistol grip, allowing the weapon to be more conveniently carried and holstered. The three twenty-five-round magazines fit in a canvas and leather pouch assembly that counterbalances the weight of the PM-63 when it is carried in the belt holster. The one drawback with the design of the PM-63 that would make it a more useful PDW-style weapon is that the long compensator on the front of the slide prevents the attachment of a suppressor to the muzzle of the barrel.

INGRAM M10/M11

In the 1960s, there was considerably more experimentation and development of weapons such as submachine guns than goes on today. This was the time before the Gun Control Act of 1968 made it more difficult for an entrepreneur to design and develop a weapon to either put on the market or sell to the military without a major outlay of capital to purchase the proper licenses. One such engineer was Gordon Ingram, a World War II veteran who had designed and manufactured several submachine guns in the 1950s and into the 1960s. Some of his weapons received a reasonable amount of success on the international market, his Ingram Model 6 submachine gun having several military sales overseas and his Model 9 being built in Thailand. Far more than any of his other designs, Ingram is known for a compact series of submachine guns that are inseparably connected with his name.

The Ingram Model 10 is an extremely compact submachine gun manufactured primarily of stamped metal parts. The first few M10 prototypes were made in 9×19mm caliber. In 1966, the second prototype weapon produced was sold to the U.S. Army for testing. Several other specimens had been made,

The Ingram M10 submachine gun with its stock extended.
Kevin Dockery

including one chambered for the .45 ACP round and fitted with a removable suppressor. Improvements suggested by the Army testing were incorporated into the design, but no further sales went to the Army at that time.

Mitchell L. Werbell III, an entrepreneur with a reputation for interesting products, met with Gordon Ingram and obtained both a 9 mm and a .45 ACP suppressed model M10 for a demonstration in Southeast Asia. On his return, Ingram made a deal for production of his gun by Werbell as well as a new design of his, the M11.

Knowing that one of the major appeals of his weapon was its compact size, Ingram had produced an even smaller version, the M11 chambered for the .380 ACP round. All of the weapons were equipped with a threaded barrel for the attachment of a suppressor produced by Werbell's company, Sionics. The suppressed version of the Ingram M10 and M11 weapons impressed a number of personnel who saw them. The small guns, particularly the M11, could be carried in a hip or shoulder holster. With an open bottom, a holster could even carry an M10 with the suppressor screwed into place.

The basic design of the Ingram M10 and M11 guns was that of a square cross-section receiver containing a telescoping bolt. The upper part of the receiver fitted down into the bottom half of the weapon, cradled in a channel of the lower receiver with high walls and a square socket at the rear. The magazine was inserted into a central pistol grip, and there was no front handgrip at all on the early models of the weapon. At a suggestion from the Army, Ingram added a front strap to the gun that hung down from a bracket near the muzzle. Though extremely simple, the bracket allowed a second hand to hold the front of the weapon down during full-automatic fire.

All of the Ingram M10 and M11 submachine guns fired from the open-bolt position. There were a number of closed-bolt semiautomatic weapons produced as commercial handguns for the open market. A large number of these weapons were later converted for full-automatic fire by suppliers of weapons to the entertainment industries. With the relatively short travel of the light bolt, all of the Ingram M10 and M11 weapons operated at a high cyclic rate of fire. This was not considered a major drawback even for such a compact weapon, as it could be used to saturate an area with fire, giving the operator a chance to leave or get to a more effective combat weapon.

Given that an empty M10 was only slightly larger and heavier than an M1911A1 pistol, there was serious hope by a group of investors that there could be major sales to the U.S. military. By the early 1970s, the Ingram M10 and M11 series were in full production along with their suppressors. The legal restriction on the exporting of suppressors put in place by the State Department in the 1970s caused a number of overseas sales of the Ingram weapons to be canceled. One of the big appeals of the little submachine guns was how well they operated in the suppressed mode. Without the suppressors, there simply wasn't enough appeal for the Ingram weapons to keep them selling.

By the middle of the 1970s, poor management on the part of a group of investors in producing the Ingram series helped lead the Military Armament Company (MAC), formed in 1970, to produce the Ingram and its supporting materials, into bankruptcy. A number of companies purchased the assets of the MAC organization and kept the Ingram M10 and M11 in limited production for a number of years. The final 1986 legal restrictions on the production of automatic weapons for private ownership caused the production of the Ingram to come to an almost complete halt. The popularity of the compact Ingram weapons makes them a consistently seen gun on television and in the movies. The common sight of an Ingram submachine gun in the hands of criminal forces in popular entertainment has given the weapons a notoriety that was never desired by the designer. Only a small handful of Ingram M10 submachine guns were used by the U.S. military, some of these in the hands of the Navy Special Warfare units (SEALs), but they were replaced after a few years by other weapons.

MP5 SERIES

Very possibly the most commercially successful submachine gun of all time is the Heckler & Koch MP5 series from Germany. The weapon sees duty every day all over the world in the hands of military and law enforcement alike. It is a particular favorite of special operations units, especially those with counterterrorist duties. Additionally, it is constantly seen in the hands of police SWAT teams

MP5N with suppressor in place.
Kevin Dockery

all over the United States as well as other countries. Arguably, it is the first and best-known of the fourth-generation submachine guns.

A complex weapon for a submachine gun, one of the reasons it qualifies as a fourth-generation weapon, the MP5 was developed in Germany beginning in 1964. Internally, the weapon was a reduced-size version of the G3 rifle, also a Heckler & Koch product. The heart of the HK weapons system centered on the use of a roller-locked breech mechanism operating on the delayed or retarded blowback principle.

Developed in World War II Germany near the end of 1945, the roller-locked system was used in the Mauser Sturmgewehr 45 rifle. The StG.45(M) was intended as a simplified, easier-to-produce replacement for the MP44/StG44 series of assault rifles, which already had a minimum of machine parts in their design. The war ended before more than a handful of specimens were completed, and the system was later perfected in Spain in the 1950s before returning to Germany.

The roller-locked system is not as firmly locked a bolt system as is found in most other locked-bolt weapons. When the bolt closes on the breech in a roller-locked system, a flat, rectangular locking piece with two angular sides is pushed up into the bolt, where it drives two hardened steel rollers out into recesses built into the barrel extension. When the chambered round is fired, the bolt head is driven back by the pressure on the fired round, pushing back against the rollers that are bearing on slight angles cut into the back of their recesses in the barrel extension. Working at a mechanical disadvantage, the rollers have to squeeze the locking piece between them, moving it to the rear, before they can be driven back into their recesses in the bolt head. Once the rollers are back inside of the bolt head, the pressure in the barrel has dropped to safe levels, and the breech starts to open. The bolt is driven back by the residual pressure from the propellant gases acting on the cartridge case, and it moves to the rear to complete the firing cycle.

The operating power available to the bolt for functioning can be varied by a different locking piece with different angles acting on the locking rollers. This flexibility in the system allowed an action designed for the powerful, high-pressure 7.62×51 mm NATO round to be easily adapted to the much lower power and pressures of the 9×19 mm cartridge. The action of the roller-locking system in retarding the blowback of the bolt softens the recoil of the weapon, spreading out the time of the recoil impulse felt by the operator.

This spreading out of the recoil impulse over a short interval of time makes the action of the system feel much smoother and lighter to the operator than other operating actions using the same ammunition. It also makes for a very violent extraction of the cartridge case; so much so that the chamber of roller-locked weapons have flutes cut into their front half. The flutes allow propellant gases to flow back over part of the cartridge case, raising it away from the chamber walls and easing extraction. Fired cartridge casings from Heckler & Koch weapons using the fluted chamber have a distinctive series of longitudinal lines on the outside of the case from the gases flowing along the flutes. The ejection of the fired casings is also noticeably powerful.

The roller-locked delayed blowback operating system of the MP5 combined with its closed-bolt, hammer-fired action give the weapon some of the best first-round accuracy of any submachine gun made. Once the MP5 entered production in 1966, it was immediately adopted by the German Bundesgrenschütz (Border Police), the federal police force of Germany. Soon after it became available, the MP5 was also adopted by Swiss police agencies as well as additional law enforcement organizations in Germany.

The original layout of the MP5 submachine gun was as a fixed-stock weapon. The first major modification to the design was the addition of a very strong collapsible stock. The stock was built on two rails that extended along the sides of the receiver. A latch mechanism at the rear of the receiver, between the two stock rails, could be moved by the operator's thumb to unlock the stock for extension. Modifications and improvements on the basic weapon continued to enhance the functioning, handling, and accuracy of the MP5.

The trigger group of all of the Heckler & Koch G3-based weapons can be removed and exchanged for other versions that have different mechanical and operational characteristics. The traditional trigger group has a single safety selector switch on the left side of the weapon where it can be reached with the thumb of the firing hand. The selector can be moved from safe to semiautomatic fire to full automatic fire usually without the operator having to release his grip on the weapon. Other types of trigger groups can fire semiautomatically only, or combinations of semiautomatic, controlled bursts (two or three shots), and full automatic. Setting identification for many of the more recent trigger groups is in the form of pictograms.

In the pictogram system, the outline of a single projectile inside a closed box with an X over it, the lines of the whole symbol filled with white, is the marking for safe. A closed box surrounding a projectile outline with the lines filled with red is semiautomatic. Multiple projectile outlines in a closed box, also filled with red is the marking used to indicate a multiple-round burst, the number of projectiles in the box being equal to the shots fired in the burst.

Finally, an open-ended box outlining as many as seven projectiles, the symbol colored in red, is the indicator for full-automatic fire.

To identify the various options on the MP5 weapons that could be obtained from Heckler & Koch, a code system was used that has been extended unofficially by users of the system. The standard weapon is identified as the MP5, followed by an *A* and a number. The number indicates whether the weapon has a simple cap over the rear of the receiver and no buttstock (A1), a fixed stock (A2), or collapsing stock (A3). Further numbers, A4, A5, A6, indicate what kind of stock was on the weapon when it came from the factory as well as the original trigger group that was mounted on the weapon. The easy changing of stocks and trigger groups by the operators make the identification system changeable according to just what has been assembled by the user.

The MP5 developed a reputation for accuracy and dependability, with Heckler & Koch continuing to improve and modify the system to fit customers' needs. The first real public notice was made of the weapon during the Iranian embassy siege in London from April 30 to May 5, 1980.

A group of terrorists who were part of the Democratic Revolutionary Front for the Liberation of Arabistan took over the embassy and seized twenty-six hostages. When negotiations broke down and hostages were shot, the British Special Air Service (SAS) counterterrorist unit was ordered into action. What was called Operation Nimrod took place under the eye of the camera, and the public all over the world watched the SAS takedown of the Iranian embassy. The black-clothed, gas-masked figures of the SAS troopers slid down ropes, blew open doors and windows, and charged into the building. In the hands of these extremely competent fighting men were MP5 submachine guns.

It was the first-round accuracy and dependability of the MP5 that made it hold such appeal to the various counterterrorist organizations around the world who quickly adopted the weapon after they saw its effectiveness in action. Police agencies picked the gun up for the same reason. The basic MP5 series has been sold by the hundreds of thousands all over the free world to the military of over forty countries, law enforcement, and security organizations.

MP5SD SERIES

In 1974, the most unusual version of the MP5 series was produced, the *Schalldämpfer* (muffler or sound dampener) integrally silenced series. Identified by the SD in their designation, the MP5SD series is difficult to miss with the long, thick suppressor body and round handguard installed in place of the much shorter standard barrel and forearm. The apparent length of the barrel is deceptive. The actual barrel of the MP5SD is 5.73 inches long, a little over three inches shorter than the standard barrel, with a series of thirty 2.5 mm holes drilled into the bore less than an inch from the front of the chamber. The holes act as gas ports for the propellant gases of the cartridge. By bleeding the gases off close to the chamber of the weapon, the muzzle velocity of the projectile can be lowered considerably. In the MP5SD, the average lowering of the muzzle velocity is on the order of about 200 feet per second. For most 9 × 19 mm ammunition, particularly the NATO standard ball loading, this is enough velocity loss to put the muzzle velocity below the speed of sound (about 1,080 feet per second at sea level).

The complex barrel porting system allows the MP5SD series to have maximum sound suppression without resorting to specialized ammunition. The drawback is that the ammunition is slightly less effective due to the lower projectile velocity. Surrounding the short barrel is a twelve-inch-long sealed aluminum suppressor that screws onto a threaded area just behind the ported area of the barrel. At the threads is a small rubber O-ring that seals off the back end of the suppressor.

Inside the body of the suppressor is a square cross-section aluminum insert with a series of four angular baffle sets bent in toward the center of the suppressor and pointing back to the breech of the weapon. The baffles are cut from the sides of the square aluminum tubing that makes up the internal part of the suppressor. A notch is cut in the center of each baffle side so that when they are bent in toward the bore and welded in place, there is a central passage for the projectile. The eight individual baffles deflect the propellant gases, slowing and cooling them before they exit at the hole on the domed end cap of the suppressor body. The aluminum construction of the suppressor helps keep the weight of the system down as well as acting as a heat sink for the propellant gases, the aluminum being an excellent conductor of heat. The suppressor itself does not require major cleaning, and the unit is sealed at the factory. The gas portholes on the barrel of the MP5SD can get clogged with carbon buildup and do require periodic maintenance with a special scrubbing brush.

Overall, the sound suppressor characteristics of the MP5SD system work very well. The weapon fires dependably with a variety of ammunition and reduces the muzzle velocity effectively and consistently. The sound of firing the MP5SD is something of a series of rapid stuttering thuds overlaid with a hiss, unrecognizable as gunfire on an average day at a distance of fifteen meters. An additional action of the suppressor is to eliminate the muzzle flash of the weapon firing almost completely. Besides being useful for concealment purposes, this

Firing the MP5SD3 from the shoulder.
Kevin Dockery

flash suppression has another value to law enforcement. When tactical teams have to enter an area where there is an illicit drug lab operating, the atmosphere can often be very inflammable. The use of a sound suppressor not only makes the weapon easier on the officer firing it by not flooding him with the sound of indoor firing, it cuts back considerably on the chances of the weapon firing setting off a gas explosion.

The model codes identifying the MP5SD weapons use the same suffix as that of the standard series. This includes codes such as MP5SD1 (no buttstock), MP5SD2 (fixed buttstock), MP5SD3 (collapsible buttstock), MP5SD4 (no buttstock and three-round burst trigger group), and so on.

Later models of the standard MP5 series, originally produced at a request of the U.S. Navy SEALs, have a slightly extended barrel at the muzzle of the weapon. This model MP5, identified as the Navy variant and having the letter *N* in the designator, has the extended length of barrel threaded for the attachment of a muzzle sound suppressor. Without the suppressor in place, the threads are normally covered with a small knurled sleeve. This modification increases the flexibility of the MP5 for suppressed use. For maximum noise suppression, special subsonic ammunition must be used with the MP5-N weapons.

MP5 KURZ SERIES

At the request of a sales representative in South America, the very concealable Kurz (short) variation of the MP5 submachine gun was produced beginning in 1976. Both the receiver and the barrel of the K model MP5 were reduced in length, though the basic operating system was not modified. The shorter length of travel for the bolt raised the cyclic rate of fire for the K model guns to around 900 rounds per minute. The new pressure curve of firing the 9 mm round in a shorter barrel required changing the angles on the locking piece as well as other slight modifications to the action. Even the trigger group cannot interchange with the other MP5 weapons since it was also shortened to reduce the size of the Kurz model.

The final result of the design modifications was a full-power submachine gun not much larger than a big pistol. There was no provision for the standard MP5 sliding stock to be fitted on the K models. The rear of the K action was sealed off with a flat receiver cap, held in place with two smaller locking pins rather than the single large locking pin of the full-sized MP5 models. To aid in controlling the stockless MP5K weapon, a large vertical front grip was added to the gun. Just below the muzzle of the MP5K, the front grip assembly has a large downward-curved hook. The hook is there to help prevent a shooter's fingers from accidentally slipping in front of the muzzle of the weapon while it is firing.

At the center of the large butt cap on the MP5K is a pivoting sling swivel. By attaching a sling assembly to the swivel, the little gun can be carried under the arm fairly easily. Grasping the weapon by both grips and pushing it out against the tension of the sling makes the MP5K series much more controllable to shoot than if it was just handheld.

To reduce the outline of the weapon still further, The KA1 and KA5 were produced without the adjustable sights found on all of the other versions of the MP5. Instead of the taller sights, the KA1 and KA5 (with burst control trigger group) have a very low-profile set of fixed sights, little more than a front blade and a square rear notch. When loaded into the MP5K, the short fifteen-round magazine does not extend out the bottom of the weapon past the pistol grip, making for a very compact outline.

The small size of the MP5K series resulted in a number of concealable carry options being developed specifically for the weapon. The most unusual of these are the two carrying cases, one a hard-sided briefcase, the other a soft-sided satchel. The MP5K model gun with a thirty-round magazine in place fits inside either case, locking into a bracket just below the handle. In the briefcase, there is an opening in the side for the fired projectile and a trigger on the underside of the case handle. The MP5K can be fired while completely concealed within the briefcase. In the satchel, there is an opening on one end of the bag for the projectile to pass and a

The MP5K submachine gun locked in place in the hard briefcase carrying system. The curved trigger underneath the handle of the briefcase can fire the weapon while the lid of the case is shut.
Heckler & Koch Defense

second, much larger opening on the opposite end. The operator simply slips his hand inside the case and grasps the pistol grip to fire the weapon. Neither case is a particularly accurate way to fire a submachine gun, but with the MP5K series, they are among the best in concealment for VIP protection and other security duties.

The MP5K-N variation is a model also built to the specifications of the U.S. Navy SEALs. The weapon has a semiautomatic and full automatic trigger group, but what is called the Navy group also has an ambidextrous selector switch with the control lever being found on both sides of the trigger group. The MP5-N has a full-sized set of H&K sights installed on the upper side of the receiver as well as the extended barrel with the threaded section at the tip. Navy barrels also have a special three-lug locking point on the muzzle, behind the threaded section, for the attachment of accessories such as a flash hider, blank adapter, grenade launcher, or other specialized muzzle device.

MP5K-PDW

No matter how expert the shooter, the MP5K series of weapons are not as accurate to fire as the weapon allows. This is due to the lack of a bracing shoulder stock on the short guns. In 1991, The U.S. offices of Heckler & Koch Incorporated turned to an American manufacturer to make a shoulder stock to fit the MP5K series of weapons without any modification to the gun. The Choate Machine & Tool company was chosen to develop and manufacture the stock, which was made of synthetic materials, something the company was well known for. The final product was a strong, single-strut stock that could fold to lie along the right side of the weapon.

With the stock folded, the MP5K series guns could still be fired, the ejected brass just clearing over the top of the stock. By pressing against the stock with the thumb of the forward hand, the latch would be overcome, and a spring would help swing it out and to the rear, where it would snap firmly into position.

Though the folding stock would fit any of the MP5K weapons, it was particularly intended for use with the MP5K-N model weapon. When mounted on the Navy weapon, the configuration is referred to as the MP5K-PDW, a personal defense weapon. The stock eliminated the final argument against the K models, their lack of accuracy when fired. With the stock extended, individual targets can easily be engaged by a competent shooter out to 200 meters' range.

To take advantage of the concealment potential of the MP5K-PDW, a nylon carrying rig was made to transport the weapon as if in a shoulder holster. A quick movement of the hand on a restraining strap, and the weapon is released for use, the stock unfolding in the same movement as the weapon is drawn. On the opposite side of the shoulder rig is also the means to secure a pair of thirty-round magazines for the weapon, giving the operator up to ninety rounds of ready ammunition with a single magazine in the weapon and the two spares. The shoulder rig is also ambidextrous so that it can be set up to carry the weapon on either side according to the operator's preferences.

A thigh-holster rig is also available for the MP5K-PDW. Additionally, there is also available a five-cell magazine pouch made of the same ballistic nylon material as the thigh holster. The sizing of the individual magazine pockets on the pouch are such that a standard Heckler & Koch muzzle suppressor can be carried in one of the pockets. The pouch assembly can be strapped around the lower leg of the operator below the thigh holster of the MP5K-PDW if desired.

MP5PT

The popularity of the MP5 series of weapons had proven large enough to support the production of a specialized training version of the weapon in 1984. The MP5PT is a special adaptation of the MP5 design to allow the weapon to function when firing 9×91 mm plastic training ammunition. The plastic ammunition has been developed by Dynamit Nobel to allow military weapons to be live-fired on limited-distance ranges. The 9×19 mm plastic round has a blue plastic body with a solid light plastic projectile formed as part of the round. The base of the cartridge is an aluminum head with an extractor groove and central primer pocket.

When fired, the plastic training ammunition has a dangerous downrange distance of about 125 meters. This compares very well with the normal 1,500-meter danger area for a standard 9 mm ball round. The accuracy of the plastic bulleted training ammunition is comparable to the ball round with a maximum training range of 8 to 15 meters, placing all of the rounds fired from an MP5PT inside of a 10-centimeter group at a range of 8 meters. Inside of that range, the plastic projectiles can still be dangerous, even lethal if carefully placed, and would have some application in situations where the distance is short and the danger from overpenetration very high, such as aboard a hijacked aircraft.

To operate the action of the MP5 dependably with the low-recoil plastic ammunition, the breech end of the barrel has been modified with a movable chamber and no locking rollers in the bolt head. The weapon operates as a gas-boosted straight blowback system. The front of the movable floating chamber is pushed back by some of the propellant gases when the weapon is fired. This shove from the floating chamber aids the light blowback of the plastic cartridge in pushing back the bolt and carrier assembly with enough force to completely operate the action. Because of the floating chamber and lack of locking rollers, none of the PT models of the MP5 can be fired with regular ball ammunition. Though the weapon can fire the round, and it would be safe to the operator, the weapon would be badly damaged by the error.

The MP5PT models come as any of the standard MP5 weapons, but with the PT added to the model nomenclature. The MP5PTA2 would be a standard fixed stock with a semiautomatic and full automatic trigger group. The MP5PTA5 would be a retractable stock and a semiautomatic, three-round burst, and full automatic trigger group in place.

COLT 9 MM

Part of the popularity of the MP5 series of submachine guns being due to the accuracy of the weapon was not lost on a number of weapons manufacturers. The close-bolt action used by the German submachine gun was recognized as one of the major factors in the system having a very good first-round accuracy, something the usual open-bolt submachine guns didn't share. The other aspect of the submachine guns that gave them appeal for the counterterrorist and law enforcement role was the lower penetration and power of the pistol cartridge as compared to any of the standard assault rifle rounds.

Rather than design a completely new weapon for the submachine gun market, several arms manufacturers did conversions of their existing rifle-caliber weapons to a compact pistol ammunition version. An added benefit of this approach to the design of a submachine gun was the sales appeal of the weapon to any user already employing the original base assault rifle. With the constant concern of available training time, using a submachine gun version of a standard rifle would mean the operator would already be familiar with the placement and operation of the controls and general functioning of the weapon, no matter what its caliber.

Colt's Manufacturing Company, LLC (the new name for Colt Firearms) recognized the market niche of the 9 mm submachine gun and began their answer to filling it in the mid-1980s. The very general outline of the Colt 9 mm variation of the M16 rifle family is based on the XM177 carbine of the Vietnam era. Internally, the Colt 9 mm weapon was much different from the M16 design. Since the operating pressure of a 9 mm pistol round is much less than that of the 5.56×45 mm cartridge, the internal mechanism of the Colt 9 mm weapons could be made much simpler, easier, and less expensive than the original model.

The direct-action gas system of the M16 was removed and the 9 mm variation operates on straight blowback while firing from the closed-bolt position for accuracy. Without any need for the gas system, the bolt carrier was simplified from the 5.56 mm version; the separate rotating bolt and its supporting components were removed completely for the 9 mm conversion. The magazine well was fitted with an adapter block that was pinned in place and allowed the 9 mm weapon to originally operate with converted Uzi submachine gun magazines. Later, Colt improved on the magazine design and produced their own version for use with the 9 mm series of guns.

The result of the conversion was a compact 9 mm weapon that handled and operated much like an M16 rifle. The fact that many law enforcement and security personnel are ex-military meant that the training these men had received in the military would give them an immediate level of familiarity with the Colt weapons. While making the conversion to the 9 mm system, Colt took some pains to retain some of the operational characteristics of the original 5.56 mm weapon. A noticeable retention in the 9 mm weapon is the bolt catch device. When the last round in the magazine is fired, the bolt locks to the rear in the open position. This tells the operator to reload immediately. Inserting a fresh magazine and pushing in the top of the bolt catch releases the bolt to go forward and chamber a new round for firing. This last-round hold-open device is a relative rarity in submachine guns. The first indication that the weapon is empty to most operators is when the bolt slams forward on an empty chamber or they just hear the click of the hammer falling.

As in the M16 rifle series, the straight-line layout of the 9 mm submachine gun keeps the muzzle of the weapon down during automatic firing. The stock can be locked into four different positions to vary its length according to the operator's preference. This allows the 9 mm submachine gun to still be easily shouldered, even when the operator is wearing heavy body armor or load-bearing equipment. Or the stock can be fully extended and used by uniformed security personnel who are wearing little more than a shirt.

COLT NINE MILLIMETER DOE MODEL

With the Colt 9 mm design using blowback to operate the action, there was little restriction on cutting the barrel back to an even shorter length outside of ballistic considerations. The Colt Model RO633 and Model RO633HB were the shortest versions of the Colt 9 mm submachine guns. Both weapons had a seven-inch barrel on the standard-length receiver equipped with a sliding stock. With the stock closed, the overall length of the weapon was short enough for it to fit in a large briefcase or satchel without drawing a second look, a situation that gave the weapon the nickname, "the briefcase gun."

The Model RO633 used the standard-model mechanical buffer in the buttstock of the weapon, leaving it with a relatively high cyclic rate of fire. Reportedly made to the specifications of the Department of Energy, the Model RO633HB utilized a hydraulic buffer as part of its operating system. The hydraulic buffer lowered the cyclic rate of fire by about 200 rounds per minute, making the short weapon more controllable on full automatic fire. The extremely short handguard of the 633 models would have been dangerous to the operator, as there was no extending muzzle of the weapon. The barrel ended just a fraction of an inch in front of the handguard and the forward, non-firing hand could easily slip under recoil and accidentally pass in front of the muzzle as the weapon was firing. To prevent this accident from happening, the Colt engineers placed a large plate on the front of the handguard, the bottom lip of which extended down past the bottom level of the handguard. The size of the plate did not detract from the compact layout of the weapon but did prevent a hand from slipping off the front of the handguard. The front plate was also a support for the folding front sight of the compact weapon as well as providing a location for a front sling swivel to be attached.

On the right side of the weapon, just at the rear of the ejection port, is the gas block/cartridge case deflector that was added to the production models of the Colt 9 mm submachine guns. The block deflects ejected cartridge cases, allowing easier left-handed operation of the weapon. In addition, the large block kept unburned powder and propellant gases away from the firer's face. This was especially important in the very compact versions of the Colt 9 mm, as they tended to have even more unburned powder due to the cartridge firing in a shorter barrel.

STEYR AUG NINE MILLIMETER PARA

In Europe, the appeal of the 9 mm round for certain tactical considerations was also noticed by rifle manufacturers. Following the Colt example, the Steyr-Daimler-Puch company of Austria developed a 9 mm conversion of their AUG rifle, making it available to the market in 1987. As Steyr was already producing two third-generation submachine guns, the MPi 69 and MPi 81, the company adopted a good deal of the technology from those weapons to their conversion of the AUG. The overall construction of the AUG is modular, and the final conversion of the weapon from 5.56×45 to 9×19 mm was a simple exchange of parts.

By field-stripping the weapon as would be done for cleaning, the 5.56 mm bolt assembly would be replaced with a 9 mm bolt. Locking the 9 mm barrel in place and inserting an adapter in the magazine well made the AUG bullpup rifle the first bullpup submachine gun. The new system operated on straight blowback with the weapon firing on closed bolt for accuracy. The magazine well adapter allowed the use of the Steyr 9 mm magazines that were already in use for the MPi 69 and 81 submachine guns. The adapter had its own type of magazine catch to retain the 9 mm magazine and was retained in place by the catch used for the 5.56 mm magazines.

The conversion was simple, reliable, and accurate. As a bullpup layout, the AUG 9 mm Para could not have any form of collapsing or folding stock, but the compact size of the weapon kept that from being much of a drawback. The advantage of the bullpup design gave the AUG 9 mm version the longest barrel of any submachine gun on the market while still being shorter than most existing carbines would be when they had their stocks extended. The integral optical sight also aided the accuracy of the 9 mm conversion of the AUG, though the sights did have to be readjusted to the different point of impact for the 9 mm projectiles.

MINI UZI

In the latter part of the twentieth century, submachine guns continued to be redesigned to extend their usefulness and increase their share of the firearms market. Particular concentration was being spent on what was called the domestic market, meeting the needs of law enforcement and security forces in addition to the requirements of the military. One of the aspects of the submachine gun that gave it an advantage over many other military weapons was its ability to be carried in a concealed manner. This was a factor dependent on the basic size of the weapon, and a number of new models were developed that were just shortened versions of the existing pattern.

A well-known early version of a reduced-size submachine gun was the Mini Uzi produced by Israeli Military Industries in 1980. Known as the Mini Uzi, the weapon was a shortened version of the famous military weapon. The basic action of the Mini Uzi had not changed from the original system. It was also a very dependable firearm that could keep functioning in some of the worst environments. The receiver of the standard Mini Uzi had the same general outline as the Uzi but was shortened at both the front and rear. The folding stock had been changed to a single-strut metal stock that folded to the right side of the weapon. In the folded position, the butt plate of the stock could be used as a vertical front grip.

Internally, the action of the standard Mini Uzi had not been changed; only the length of travel for the bolt was much shorter, raising the cyclic rate of fire from the 600 rounds per minute of the full-sized Uzi to 950 rpm in the Mini version. A second model of Mini Uzi was produced that supplied the greater accuracy demanded of security and law enforcement over that of the standard model. The closed-bolt Mini Uzi shared all of the characteristics of the standard Mini Uzi except that it fired with the bolt in the forward position.

The closed-bolt firing position made the Mini Uzi more prone to overheating and the type of malfunction known as a cook-off, where the residual heat of the barrel is enough to fire a chambered round without the trigger being pulled. But the additional accuracy on both full and semiautomatic fire was considered desirable enough to accept the slightly lesser tolerance for extended firing. Most encounters where the Mini Uzi would be involved would usually be short, savage firefights where only a few magazines would be discharged, and the gunfight would be over in seconds.

One additional variation of the Mini Uzi was marketed for a short time; the heavy-bolt model. By adding inserts of heavy metal to the bolt, the cyclic rate of fire was reduced, making this version of the Mini Uzi the most controllable. The weapon fired from the open-bolt position, but the cyclic rate had been reduced to 750 rounds per minute.

All of the Mini Uzi models were compact enough to fit in a briefcase along with several spare magazines. A strong person could fire the weapon one-handed like a pistol, but the preferred method of firing was to extend the stock and brace it against the shoulder while holding the weapon with both hands. A simplified shoulder rig was produced for carrying the Mini Uzi in a concealed manner. Instead of the weapon being slipped into a holster, straps were attached to the rear receiver of the weapon and hung down underneath the operator's firing arm. Just by grasping the pistol grip and pulling the gun up, the Mini Uzi could be immediately put into operation.

MICRO UZI

The last and shortest model of the Uzi submachine gun family was the Micro Uzi produced first in 1986. The Micro Uzi was little more than the Uzi pistol, a semiautomatic-only weapon made for civilian sales, with a shoulder stock added to it and the action converted to be able to fire on full automatic. The entire weapon is several inches less than a foot long with the stock folded and is considered very concealable. The same style of folding stock that is used on the Mini Uzi is mounted on the Micro version, and the butt plate may also be used as a front grip, particularly since there is no other way to hold the front end of the weapon.

The action of the Micro Uzi is designed to fire from the closed-bolt position. The very short bolt travel gives the Micro Uzi the very high cyclic rate of fire of 1,200 rounds per minute, even with heavy tungsten metal inserts in the bolt. This rate of fire is useful only to saturate an area quickly, the rounds coming out of the weapon so fast that the individual shots blur into one roar of sound. There is also a version of the Micro Uzi that has been produced with the weapon chambered for .45 ACP. One particular drawback in using the larger round is that the converted magazines can only hold 16 rounds of ammunition. On the reduced cyclic rate of the .45 Micro Uzi (1,100 rounds per minute) a 16-round magazine gives less than one full second of fire on full automatic.

HK53

Since it is chambered for the 5.56 × 45 mm rifle round rather than a true pistol-caliber cartridge, the Heckler & Koch HK53 is not an actual submachine gun. It is instead one of the compact carbines that are starting to blur the distinction of what is and is not a submachine gun to a confusing level. Introduced in 1975, the HK53 is the shortest version of the Heckler & Koch HK33 assault rifle family. It has the same style of collapsing stock as is used on the MP5 submachine guns. A fixed stock can be fitted to the HK53, though that does not really fit in with the philosophy and application of a compact carbine.

The operating system of the HK53 is the same roller-locked, delayed-blowback mechanism that is used on the bulk of the Heckler & Koch weapons. A semi- and full automatic fire trigger group is available for the HK53 as is a semi-three-round burst and full automatic fire trigger group. To cut back on the tremendous ball of fire that blooms at the front of the weapon when the full-power 5.56 mm round is fired in the very short barrel, a long, four-prong flash hider is attached to the muzzle of the barrel in the latest production models. The sound signature of such a short-barreled rifle is also as distinctive as the muzzle flash. The booming roar of the HK53 can be heard from a considerable distance and sounds like few other weapons can.

The short barrel of the HK53 robs the 5.56 mm projectile of a lot of its power. Ballistically, the 5.56 × 45 mm round is used in a very inefficient manner in the HK53, though it still has nearly double the muzzle energy of the 9 × 19 mm round. But the pointed 5.56 mm projectile at the lower velocities it is fired at in the HK53 does not transfer its energy to the target very well. It is considered to be lacking in stopping power, though this is as much a matter of bullet placement as physics. The HK53 could be used in all of the same applications where the MP5 would fit, except those where the problem of overpenetration would be considered too great a risk, such as on an aircraft or in a high-density technological area such as a power station or other such facility.

HK54A1

To develop a submachine gun intended for special operations use into the next century, the Joint Services Small Arms Program (JSSAP) started the JSSAP 6.2 Submachine Gun Project in the early 1980s to research just what would be needed in such a weapon if it were to be an improvement over the use of a compact rifle-caliber carbine or other weapon. The improvements desired in a submachine gun included greater accuracy, easier handling, lighter weight, and positive sound suppression as needed. Heckler & Koch were issued the contract in April 1983 to develop the new weapon for testing. Their first design was a highly modified variation of the basic MP5. Known as the HK54A1, the new submachine gun had a number of unique features added to it to make it a far more versatile weapon than the MP5. The weapon was fed from a fifty-round drum magazine to increase the unit of fire available from a single gun before reloading.

Overall, the HK54A1 was highly streamlined, even the sliding buttstock blending in to the overall outline of the weapon. The most noteworthy features of the HK54A1 centered on the use of a suppressor and the means of eliminating the need for special subsonic ammunition. Like the MP5SD series of guns, the HK54A1 has a porting system near the breech of the barrel to lower the muzzle velocity of standard ammunition to below the speed of sound. Unlike the MP5SD series, or any other submachine gun for that matter, the porting system on the HK54A1 could be turned on or off as the operator desired.

Underneath the forearm, just in front of the magazine well, is a lever-type switch that is connected to the porting mechanism. With the switch turned to the on position, sufficient propellant gases are tapped off from the barrel to take the muzzle velocity of the projectile below the speed of sound, eliminating any sonic crack. The long suppressor slipped over the barrel, down into the handguard, where it screwed down onto a threaded section at the base of the barrel. The trigger group was also modified to aid in reducing the sound signature of the HK54A1 when it was fired.

The HK54A1 trigger group has four positions that the selector switch can be set to: 0 (zero) for safe, 1 for semiautomatic fire, 3 for a three-round controlled burst, 50 for full automatic, and an arrow pointing to a line that indicates locked breech. In the locked breech position, the weapon will not open the action when it is fired. Instead, a single round is discharged, and the action has to be manually operated to load a fresh round. This made the internal system of the HK54A1 very complex but also made the weapon one of the quietest suppressed submachine guns available.

With the gas port selector lever set to closed, all of the propellant gases would remain in the barrel, giving the projectile its maximum muzzle velocity. The long suppressor can be removed, reducing the overall length of the weapon by nearly a third of its suppressed length. Without the suppressor in place, the HK54A1 is a very handy, light weapon that can be easily used with one hand if necessary. The weapon utilized the standard roller-locked, retarded blowback system as well as the raised sights of the parent weapon, the MP5. An addition to the system was a last-round bolt hold-open device, the release button being the large square button above and in front of the trigger on the left side of the weapon. The magazine catch is on the right side of the HK54A1, in the same location as the bolt release but marked with a large engraved M on the face of the control.

Though the HK54A1 operated reasonably well for a new weapon design, there was room for considerable improvement in terms of reliability. It proved that one weapon could combine a large number of desired characteristics in a single design, but the weapon was also considered unnecessarily complex and expensive. Further development of a new submachine gun would be continued by JSSAP.

JSSAP 6.3A SMG

The HK54A1 was considered the completion of the JSSAP 6.2 submachine gun project, but the weapon was not considered sufficiently advanced to be recommended for adoption. The JSSAP 6.3A submachine gun project was the follow-on to the project that resulted in the HK54A1. The new 6.3A project was funded with the final intention being the development of a submachine gun design that could be adopted by the U.S. military as a standard service weapon by the mid-1990s.

Taking the HK54A1 as a starting point, Heckler & Koch were awarded the 6.3A contract as they obviously had the most experience with the results of the first design. The final weapon that was developed by H&K has been referred to as the SMG I or the more complicated HK SMG 94054. Both designations refer to the same weapon, a very compact, light, streamlined weapon that had quick handling characteristics and was able to be satisfactorily suppressed.

The JSSAP submachine gun.
U.S. Navy

The extensive use of polymers in the construction of the SMG I aided in keeping the overall weight of the weapon down. The lower receiver, including the trigger group, magazine well, and pistol grip, were formed from a reinforced polymer plastic. The fifty-round drum of the HK54A1 had been abandoned and a new magazine developed for the SMG I based on the standard MP5 magazine. The new magazine was a thirty-round box design, curved to feed more effectively, and made from a tough polymer plastic. This was one of the first such magazines developed by H&K, and it proved popular with the weapon.

The internal mechanism of the SMG I had been simplified a great deal from all of the other H&K 9 mm weapons. The roller-locking system was gone; in its place was a closed-bolt system that operated from simple blowback. The closed bolt had an integral safety lock that kept the firing pin from being released before the bolt was within a few millimeters of the breech. Once the pin was unlocked, the hammer could be released by the trigger mechanism, firing the weapon.

The simplified operating system worked very well with a variety of ammunition. Accuracy was tested by having a number of shooters try the weapon both in the suppressed and unsuppressed modes at a range of twenty-five meters. Group size had an average maximum spread of 3.7 inches when firing unsuppressed ammunition and 5.2 inches when firing suppressed (subsonic) ammunition. This is not only a good indicator of the general accuracy of the weapon, it also shows how the weapon handled and what effect the suppressor had on the operators. When the same test was conducted with the SMG I secured in a firing cradle with no human error in the firing procedure, the gun made unsuppressed groups of 2.7 inches and suppressed subsonic groups of 2.0 inches.

One concern with the closed-bolt system was the effect of residual chamber heat cooking off a chambered round. One suppressed specimen of the SMG I was fired with 500 rounds going downrange in a few seconds less than five minutes. There were three stoppages during that firing test, two of them attributed to a defective part. The weapon was secured in a cradle and allowed to cool to room temperature with a round chambered and a loaded magazine in place. The weapon cooled without a cook-off of the chambered round.

For a second cook-off test, a suppressed SMG I fired 900 rounds in four minutes, fifteen seconds, again with three stoppages, two of them charged to a malfunctioning magazine. The weapon was so hot that part of the front grip assembly softened and melted off the weapon. About two inches of the breech end of the barrel was glowing red hot. Five rounds cooked off as the weapon cooled to room temperature while secured in a cradle. Outside of the melted plastic on the front grip, there was no other damage to the weapon.

The trigger group of the SMG I included the magazine well for the weapon. The mechanism itself had been simplified, being capable of semiautomatic and full automatic fire only. The three-round burst capability could be added to the system if desired. The porting system had also been removed but was still offered as an option to the design. The complex sights were made so that the rear sight could be zeroed for use with either supersonic or subsonic ammunition and changed by the operator at will. There is also a set of raised sights that are intended to be used when the operator is wearing a gas mask.

The compact suppressor designed for the SMG I is easily removed or attached by the operator, and the system is more efficient than the suppressor used with the HK54A1. The bolt latch device was retained with the square button control being duplicated on both sides of the lower receiver. The magazine release is also duplicated on both sides of the lower receiver, the control being located underneath the bolt latch.

One unusual device is mounted on the right side of the rectangular cross-sectioned metal upper receiver. A long forward bolt assist is secured well behind the ejection port. The forward bolt assist can help force the bolt closed in a dirty environment, an action not recommended except in the direst situation as it could make a bad jam much worse. Additionally, the forward bolt assist can be used to close the bolt quietly after it has been eased forward to chamber a round.

The SMG I project was completed to the satisfaction of JSSAP with the specifications and engineering instructions for manufacture being supplied to the government as part of the contract. The SMG I was considered an excellent weapon but not a necessary one. Many of the features best liked by the operators, the removable suppressor, ambidextrous safety/selector lever, and simplified trigger group were incorporated into the Navy version of the MP5 a few years after completion of the JSSAP 6.3A submachine gun project.

MP5/10 AND MP5/40

A request from the Federal Bureau of Investigation for a more powerful version of the MP5 submachine gun resulted in a slightly larger model being made that also incorporated some of the improvements developed during the JSSAP contracts. For the FBI, Heckler & Koch made a version of the MP5 that could chamber the 10 mm Auto cartridge that was also used in some of the agency's handguns.

Internally, there are a few differences in the MP5/10 and the 9 mm versions. There is a bolt hold-open device added to the mechanism that locks the bolt to the rear on an empty magazine. Insertion of a fresh magazine and depressing the catch releases the bolt to go forward and chamber a fresh round. The addition of the bolt hold-open device and its controls keeps the MP5/10 from being able to use the standard trigger groups. Trigger groups unique to the MP5/10 have been made that supply semiautomatic, three-round burst, and full automatic fire with the selector lever duplicated on both sides of the weapon.

The roller-locked, delayed blowback operating system is used with the MP5/10, but the weapon is more ammunition-sensitive than the 9 mm versions. When firing a high-intensity 10 mm Auto load, the MP5/10 has to be used with the number 25 locking piece. With the lighter standard 10 mm Auto load in use by the FBI, the number 24 locking piece should be used. Not using the correct locking piece can either increase the wear on the weapon (using a number 24 with high-intensity loads) or cause failure to eject or feed (using a number 25 with lighter loads).

The muzzle of the MP5/10 has the threaded section first seen on the MP5-Navy guns. This threaded section allows the mounting of a muzzle suppressor on the weapon. One very noticeable feature of the MP5/10 is the straight, plastic magazines made for the weapon. The original magazines were made of a translucent plastic so that an operator could tell at a glance how much ammunition he had available. The later production magazines were more opaque, and the internal ammunition columns could not be seen. Stud and socket arrangements on the outside of the translucent magazines allowed several magazines to be attached together in a single stack. Such stacks allowed for a very quick reload when one of the magazines became empty.

Soon after the MP5/10 appeared on the market, Heckler & Koch released the MP5/40. This was an almost identical weapon to the MP5/10 but chambered for the .40-caliber Smith & Wesson round (the .40 S&W). Both weapons were released some months apart in 1991 but saw limited sales. Their production has ceased.

UMP45

Experience developed in the making of the G36 rifle series as well as the JSSAP submachine gun projects were brought together in the Heckler & Koch universal machine pistol (UMP) design. Made primarily for the American market, the original UMP model is chambered for the .45 ACP round to give a traditionally hard-hitting projectile in a modern package. Throughout the 1990s, Heckler & Koch was examining the possibilities of a replacement weapon for the MP5 series; in 1999, the UMP45 was released to be the first of those possible replacements.

As the first new submachine gun to be chambered for the .45 ACP in well over a decade, the UMP45 drew a lot of attention, not only for its design and characteristics but also for its simple existence. For Heckler & Koch to release a totally new submachine gun on the market, especially following the success of their MP5 series, demonstrated that the company thought that the concept of the submachine gun for military and law enforcement use was far from having ended.

The UMP package is a completely new design for a submachine gun. A large number of major components are made from reinforced polymer plastic. The plastic parts include the magazine, trigger group/lower receiver, upper receiver, and buttstock. Instead of the sliding-style collapsing buttstock, the UMP has a very strong folding stock that lies across the

The UMP submachine gun with its stock folded.
Kevin Dockery

right side of the weapon when folded. Flipping open the stock is a matter of pressing out on the front of the stock, the entire assembly unlatching, swinging back, and snapping into place automatically. The stock locks up to give a very solid shoulder brace for firing the weapon and making maximum use of the accuracy inherent in the design.

The accuracy of the UMP design is enhanced by the use of the closed-bolt firing system and simple blowback method of operation. The same style of firing pin safety developed for the JSSAP guns are included in the UMP bolt design, preventing the possible accidental firing of a weapon even if it were dropped onto a hard surface with a round chambered. Only pulling the trigger would release the hammer to fire the weapon. Instead of a forward bolt closure device, a small notch is cut in the right side of the bolt, accessible through the ejection port. By using the thumb, the bolt can be pressed closed in case of a slight jam. It is a simple and fairly elegant solution to a very controversial problem, the idea of forcing a bolt closed on a possible jam.

The barrel, one of the few major metal parts in the design, is hammer-forged over a mandrel to form the rifling. There is a flared cone near the muzzle of the barrel for the quick attachment of a sound suppressor. Instead of the suppressor being threaded onto the barrel, the UMP model has the suppressor snap over the muzzle cone, allowing for a quick connection to be made and the suppressor mounted in place in less than a second.

The use of the .45 ACP round allows for the standard subsonic M1911 ball loading to be used, allowing the UMP a maximum sound suppression without requiring an adjustment to the weapon or special ammunition. The design of the UMP also allows the use of much more powerful loadings of the M1911 round. Civilian-developed, high-performance ammunition, including high-pressure hollow point rounds, can be fired through the UMP without difficulty or undue strain on the weapon.

The polymer magazine is opaque and a dark gray in color, as is the rest of the weapon. There is a translucent viewing strip cast into the side of the magazine body to allow the internal ammunition columns to be seen at a glance. The bottom of the magazine well is flared to have a wide mouth, making inserting a magazine easier and faster than was practical with the MP5 series. A bolt catch is part of the system, locking the bolt to the rear automatically after the last round in the magazine is fired. The latch can be hit with the fingers of the hand loading the new magazine in place, releasing the bolt to automatically chamber a fresh round and also speeding up the reloading process. Two sizes of magazine are produced for the UMP45, a long twenty-five-round and a short ten-round magazine to help hide the weapon underneath a coat or other form of concealment.

Hard points are cast into the receiver of the UMP in a variety of locations to allow the attachment of MIL-STD-1913 rail sections so that a variety of accessories can be mounted, such as optical or electro-optical sights on top of the receiver, a vertical front handgrip underneath the front of the receiver, or laser aim-

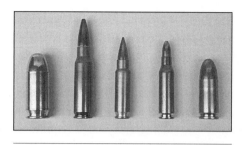

Submachine gun ammunition (left to right): the .45 ACP, the 6×30 mm Knight PDW round, the 5.7×28 mm FN PDW round, the 4.6×30 mm H&K PDW round, and the 9×19 mm ball round. *Kevin Dockery*

ing devices or tactical lights on either side of the front of the weapon. The controls for the UMP are either fully ambidextrous, such as the selector lever, or placed in such a position that they can be operated with either hand, such as the magazine catch or cocking lever.

The requirements of the human body to hold and fire a weapon effectively were paid close attention to in the layout of the UMP. The ergonomics of the design make it a fast and easy-to-handle weapon, with or without the stock being folded. The excellent layout and handling of the UMP allow for an entire twenty-five-round magazine to be fired by an experienced operator in one long burst with all of the rounds impacting on the target. With the suppressor snapped into place, the sound of the heavy slugs can be heard thudding into a target a few dozen meters away while the UMP rips through a magazine.

UMP9 AND UMP40

The success of the UMP45 suggested the development of additional versions of the weapon to extend sales. A 9×19 mm model of the UMP was designed, the UMP9, to have worldwide sales appeal. For the bulk of the United Sates law enforcement agencies that did not use the .45 ACP round, the UMP40 was designed. Chambered for the .40 S&W round, the blowback action of the UMP design allows it to utilize a range of different ammunition loads. All other aspects of the UMP9 and UMP40 are the same as the slightly larger UMP45. All the accessories that will fit on the UMP45 will also mount on the UMP9 and UMP40.

PERSONAL DEFENSE WEAPONS

The future of the submachine gun as a military weapon may very well depend on the development of the idea of a personal defense weapon. The aid of automatic fire in hitting a target seen for only a second or two greatly increases the individual's chance of hitting the target. The pistol has been the standard weapon for individuals to defend themselves, at least until they fight their way to something more effective. But the question of practice firing the handgun, the only way to really build skill with the weapon, is a hard one to find the time and facilities for. The increasingly technical nature of warfare means that the time a soldier spends on the range is not the time he is spending learning to operate a complex piece of hardware, or conducting maintenance, or simply keeping up with new developments. As the individual's rank goes up, the increasing responsibilities of their position takes even more time away.

Controllable automatic fire has been a way to increase hit probability for nearly a century. That will not be a fact that will change in the reasonable future. What will have to change is the amount of skill it takes to handle a pistol-caliber automatic weapon, the classic submachine gun. New weapons will have to be easier to use, faster to get into operation, light, strong, and simple to operate and maintain. And they will also need to be easy to hit a target with and put that target down.

Nearly two-thirds of the force of a modern army is not combat troops. These are the soldiers who drive the supply trucks, man the artillery, the radar, the radios, and the mortars. Their jobs are technical in nature and take a lot of concentration and training to accomplish well. It is for these forces that the PDW is intended, but for a well-designed weapon, the mission applications will grow with the imagination of the users.

On April 16, 1989, NATO published Document D/289 in which stated the need for a personal defense weapon for the army of the future and that such a weapon should be available by the year 2000. More specifications were put forward for the new class of weapon in the NATO Document AC/255-D/1177. In those specifications it was suggested that the new weapon should be able to defeat the CRISAT body armor target at ranges of up to 200 meters. The breakup of the Soviet Union and the dropping of the Iron Curtain had resulted in a great deal of ex-Soviet equipment going on the black market all over Europe and elsewhere. Among this equipment was the issue body armor of the Soviet Army, and a lot of it was ending up in criminal and terrorist hands. This was the armor that the CRISAT target was designed to duplicate and what NATO wanted defeated.

According to NATO, the PDW was to be a "weapon of desperation," something a soldier would turn to when he had nothing heavier to fight with. It was to be light in weight, low in recoil, and easy to operate. This was to be the personal defense weapon, arguably not a submachine gun, certainly not a rifle, and more than a pistol.

GG-95 PDW

Though a fairly large weapon, the GG-95 is almost qualified to be a true machine pistol rather than a submachine gun or personal defense weapon. Originally developed as the Jati-Matic submachine gun of Finland, the new incarnation of the design is the GG-95, produced by a Finnish company that has acquired the manufacturing rights to the design. Designed by Jali Timari and first introduced in 1982, the Jati-Matic bears little resemblance to a traditional submachine gun. There is no provision for the attachment of a buttstock, the weapon being intended for handheld fire. The overall action and layout of the weapon does work well, and the Jati-Matic is a quick-acting and controllable full-automatic weapon. To aid in the controllability of the design, the bolt travel of the weapon takes an unconventional path.

Looking at the weapon from the side, it appears that the barrel is at an angle to the rest of the weapon. It is actually the bolt that travels at an upward angle away from the bore line of the barrel. Firing from an open bolt position, the Jati-Matic makes very effective use of the telescoping bolt principle to shorten the overall length of the weapon. When driven backward from the force of blowback acting on the cartridge case, the bolt moves upward along an inclined plane in the very deep rear section of the receiver. This patented feature of the weapon reportedly pushes the receiver down during the firing cycle, cutting back on muzzle climb.

Having the bolt move at an upward angle from the barrel also allows the layout of the Jati-Matic to have the rear pistol grip in an unusually high position in relation to the bore line of the barrel. Having a high rear grip also helps maintain controllability of the weapon on automatic fire, and the force of recoil is in more of a straight line to the supporting hand and does not help force the muzzle up as in a more conventional layout.

The operation of the weapon was designed to make maximum use

Firing the Jati submachine gun with one hand. The bolt is moving to the rear as a round has just been fired and the casing is not yet ejected.
Kevin Dockery

of the telescoping bolt principle. With the bolt in the forward position, the ejection port on the right side of the weapon is blocked by the rear section of the bolt body. With the bolt cocked fully to the rear, the ejection port is once again blocked, this time by the front section of the bolt. The difference between the two positions of the bolt is obvious to an observer as the front part of the bolt has deeply cut into it block letters spelling out the word *Fire* inside a box with a point indicating the muzzle of the weapon. On a number of the weapons, the background of the box is filled with red paint. Only when the bolt is actually traveling either forward to fire or to the rear under blowback is the ejection port exposed and open at the position it would have to be to clear an ejected round. This design of the bolt helps keep the interior of the weapon sealed from outside dirt, mud, and snow.

Underneath the front end of the weapon is a multifunction folding front grip. When folded up against the bottom of the receiver, the front grip is held firmly in place by a spring-loaded detent. With the grip folded up, the weapon has a streamlined position and can be easily carried or drawn from a large hip holster. In the folded position, the grip securely locks the bolt in either the cocked or uncocked position, preventing any bolt travel, no matter what the position of the receiver or if the trigger is pressed or not. With the front grip unfolded, it is the cocking handle for the bolt. Drawing the grip to the rear moves the bolt against the mainspring until it is held in place by the sear.

With the front grip held firmly in the nonfiring hand, the Jati-Matic fires from a pull of the two-stage progressive trigger. Pulling the trigger through to the first stage fires the weapon semiautomatically. Pulling the trigger all the way to the rear of its travel, against a noticeably heavier spring pressure, moves the sear completely out of the way of the bolt and allows the weapon to fire on full automatic.

Even though it was a very progressive and unique design, the Jati-Matic was not a commercial success, and less than five hundred specimens were produced by the original company between 1983 and 1986. The Oy Golden Gun Ltd. Company put the weapon back into limited production in 1995 as the GG-95. Overall, the design of the weapon is very concealable in spite of its size, and it is very controllable on full-automatic fire. The limited effectiveness of the simple iron sights can be greatly improved by the addition of a laser designator or other electro-optical sight mounted on the smooth top of the receiver.

P90

Developed from the start as a practical personal defense weapon, the P90 is considered by some to be a very compact assault rifle rather than a true submachine

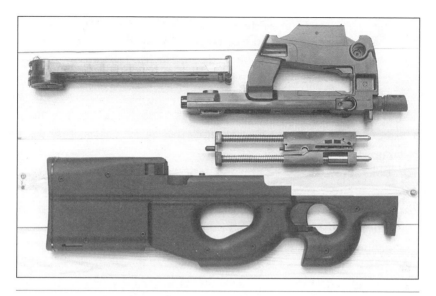

The P90 stripped down into its major components for cleaning.
FN USA, LLC

gun. This is due to the very small 5.7×29 mm bottlenecked cartridge that the P90 was designed to fire. Since the only other weapon presently marketed that uses the 5.7×38 mm is a pistol, the Five-seveN from the same manufacturer as the P90, half the weapons chambering the round are handguns. It is reasonable enough to state that the 5.7×28 mm round can be declared a pistol cartridge and the P90 classified as a submachine gun.

Besides the ammunition it fires, the P90 has a number of very unusual and unique features that make it stand out in the field of firearms. The bullpup layout of the weapon makes the P90 the most compact fixed-stock submachine gun made. Overall, the weapon is less than twenty inches long while still retaining a 9.8-inch barrel length. The overall compact appearance of the polymer-framed bullpup submachine gun is enhanced by its use of a horizontal magazine lying along the top of the weapon.

Fifty rounds of ammunition lies in two rows in a traditional double column feed form inside the translucent polymer magazine. At the end of the magazine there is a turntable design that rotates the rounds ninety degrees, orienting them to feed into the chamber of the barrel near the rear of the weapon. The action of the P90 is a straight blowback type, the bolt riding on a removable rail assembly in the rear third of the receiver. The action conducts the firing cycle of the weapon; the rotation of the round for feeding is conducted entirely by the magazine. The lack of a protruding magazine adds greatly to the outline of the P90 and its capacity for easy carry. For loading, the magazine is first inserted forward under the raised sight platform. The rear round feed turntable of the magazine is then pressed down into the receiver of the P90, where it locks into place. The magazine catch is on either side of the rear of the magazine well, where it can be pressed back by the thumb of the hand. Like all of the other controls of the P90, the magazine catch is duplicated on both sides of the weapon and is completely ambidextrous.

The bolt is drawn to the rear by cocking levers riding in rails on the front of the weapon at either side of the receiver, above the unusual-appearing front handgrip. When fired rounds are extracted and ejected, the empty cases come out the bottom of the receiver behind the pistol grip. Bottom ejection prevents the ejecting brass from interfering with the weapon being fired from either side but does present a slight problem if the operator is lying prone. From the prone position, the operator must make certain that the ejection port remains clear of the ground for the fired brass to fall free from the weapon.

To complete the ambidextrous design of the weapon, the safety and selector switch is located in the bottom of the trigger guard, where it can be operated with the trigger finger. The safety and selector switch is a partially rotating disk underneath the trigger. Turning the selector disk to the side takes the weapon off safe and either sets it to semi- or full automatic fire capability. To fire the weapon on full automatic with the selector disk set on A, the trigger is pulled all of the way back the length of its travel. Pulling the trigger back only halfway fires a single shot. Setting the selector disk on 1 puts the weapon on semiautomatic fire only, no matter how far or hard the trigger is pulled.

The physical layout of the P90 is very unusual the first time an operator sees it. The grips underneath the weapon are oddly curved with elongated holes above them to allow the fingers to wrap over the grip. Once the weapon is picked up, the style of holding the weapon dictated by the layout of the grips becomes automatic. The rear firing hand wraps the fingers underneath the grip with the thumb over the top. The front hand has the thumb go in through the elongated trigger guard, and the hand grasps the small, curved handle. The short stock seats naturally against the shoulder, and the weapon is surprisingly fast to shoulder and handle.

The most appealing feature of the P90 is felt when the operator fires one for the first time. The recoil of the weapon is very light, and there is almost no muzzle climb, even when firing a long burst. The recoil impulse of the 5.7×28 mm round is about one-third that of a standard 9×91 mm NATO loading and nearly two-thirds less than the recoil of a full-sized 5.56×45 mm

round. This light recoil makes the
weapon very easy to hold on target.
To aid in aiming the P90, several
systems are offered by the manufacturer. The original system was a reflex sight built into the top of the
raised sight platform. The optical
sight does not magnify the image
and is constructed as almost a solid
unit. A white ring reticle with a center dot is used with the sight during
the day, while for night use there is
a set of red crosshairs illuminated

The proper method of holding the unusual grip of the P90.
FN USA, LLC

by a tritium (beta) light source. The crosshairs can be easily seen through any
night vision goggles the operator may be wearing.

There is also a visible laser available for the P90 that is part of the lower
front handgrip. The laser fits inside the flat, forward-facing section of the
downward-turned finger guard at the very front of the weapon. A triple rail version of the P90 is available where there is no optical sight on the upper side of
the sight platform. Instead of the sight, there are three sections of MIL-STD-
1913 rail on the top and both sides of the sight platform. The rails allow the
mounting of a wide variety of sights, illumination aids, and laser designators to
meet the operator's preferences or mission needs.

Firing from the closed breech position makes the P90 a particularly accurate weapon when combined with the very low recoil of the fired round. The
polymer layout of the P90 keeps weight very low, but the weapon has been
tested extensively and has an expected operation life of over 20,000 rounds. The
overall length of the weapon was kept to a size that allows it to be carried
strapped diagonally across a vehicle operator's chest and still be out of the way
so that the man can continue his assigned job without interference from his
weapon. Additionally, the weapon would not get in the way of a man moving
through the hatch of an armored vehicle. The P90 also goes easily across the
back of an operator who may be riding a motorcycle or operating a heavy
weapon or other piece of equipment.

The power and range of the P90 have made it a weapon to be considered
by security forces and counterterrorist units. The weapon has excellent terminal ballistics within its effective range envelope, even after the projectile has
passed through body armor. Both a subsonic round of ammunition and effective

suppressor design have been designed and adapted for the P90. Along with its companion handgun, the FN Five-seveN, the P90 makes a complete weapon system for both shoulder and hand-fired applications.

MP7 PDW

To meet the NATO suggestions for a personal defense weapon, the engineers at Heckler & Koch first turned to developing a round to defeat the target. Penetration of the CRISAT-armored target was considered a minimum requirement for the new round. Heckler & Koch wanted the ammunition to be able to do much more. Research had shown that the best way to defeat such a target and to minimize the forces acting on the weapon and the firer was with a high-speed, small-caliber projectile. A nondeforming bullet of small caliber and careful design would penetrate between the weave of the Kevlar material that made up the armor with little loss of velocity. The same projectile could then punch through the titanium plate and strike at the target on the other side.

Turning to their experience with a prior experimental rifle produced in the 1960s and '70s, the HK36, a short, lightweight weapon with a large magazine capacity and chambered for a small-bore round, the 4.6×36 mm. Eventually, the HK36 (not to be confused with the G36, a completely different weapon) project was abandoned to concentrate research and development efforts on the G11, but not before some interesting designs for the ammunition, specifically the projectile, were developed.

To increase the terminal effects of the forty-two grain, .18-caliber, lead-cored jacketed projectiles that had a muzzle velocity of 2,756 feet per second, the very tip of the bullet jacket had a small curved scoop or trough cut into it. Referred to as the *löffelspitz* (spoon tip), the modification of the projectile was said to cause it to yaw and move off axis, tumbling very soon after it struck tissue. The projectile was said not to breach the Geneva Convention against excessively destructive small arms projectiles, but the weapon was never adopted, and the question of legality became moot.

To meet the NATO requirements for the effectiveness of a PDW, Heckler & Koch developed a very small, high-velocity family of ammunition identified as the 4.6×30 mm round through their partners at BAE Systems at Radway Green in England. The tiny bottlenecked .18-caliber cartridge has a variety of loads made for it, the Combat Steel (ball) round, identified by a black bullet tip, and having a steel-cored 26.2-grain projectile with a standard muzzle velocity of 2,379 feet per second. There is also a training round with a solid-copper projectile weighing 26.2 grains and having the standard muzzle velocity for the weapon. Besides the almost now-standard tracer, blank, drill (dummy), and frangible training rounds, there is one more combat round, based on the G36 ammunition, the 24.7-grain solid-copper Spoon Nose projectile. It will require the fielding and combat use of such ammunition to determine its final effectiveness, but Heckler & Koch guarantees a penetration of at least 15 centimeters into tissue after the projectile has penetrated clothing or the CRISAT vest with the steel ball round at 100 meters' range. The projectile has proven itself capable of defeating the CRISAT-armored target at 200 meters' range with good terminal ballistic effects after penetration.

Once the cartridge had been developed in 1995, the engineers turned to producing a weapon to fire it. The high operating pressures of the 4.6 × 30 mm cartridge, over 46,000 pounds per square inch mean pressure, required a locked bolt to properly secure the breech. Utilizing the gas pistol and bolt system from the G36 rifle series, Heckler & Koch produced their first prototype of the proposed PDW later in 1995. By the year 2000, the final configurations had been produced in five prototype weapons.

The MP7 has a central pistol grip surrounding the magazine well. The standard twenty-round box magazine fits flush with the bottom of the grip with an extended forty-round magazine available when concealment characteristics are not important. Controls are duplicated on both sides of the receiver, just above the pistol grip where they can easily be reached with the thumb of the firing hand. An ambidextrous magazine catch is located at the bottom rear of the trigger guard, where it can be operated with the trigger finger or thumb. The T-handle of the cocking lever is on the back of the receiver, above the shoulder stock, where it can be grasped from either side and drawn to the rear. The sliding shoulder stock is made up of a large butt pad and two rails that slide on either side of the receiver.

To aid in the mounting of various sighting devices, a short section of MIL-STD-1913 rail is on the back half of the upper receiver. A fixed front blade and rear notch set of sights are also on the top of the receiver to act as backup sights. Finally, there is a folding vertical handgrip in front of the trigger guard. A hooked front plate underneath the muzzle of the weapon helps prevent the firer's fingers from accidentally slipping in front of the weapon when shooting.

To cut down on overall weight, the bulk of the weapon is made from carbon-fiber-reinforced polymers. The entire receiver is made from the reinforced polymer with metal parts cast into place as needed. The short-stroke gas pistol operates the bolt assembly with the rotary locking bolt head as taken from the G36. Firing from the closed bolt position helps give the MP7 good accuracy for such a small weapon, the firing pin being struck by a hammer released by the trigger mechanism with settings for semiautomatic or full automatic fire. The overall accuracy of the MP7 is considered excellent by all of the users who have tried it. Reports have the weapon producing two-inch ten-round semiautomatic groups at forty-five meters. Overall, the weapon handles much like a pistol or submachine gun but allows targets to be engaged as if the shooter were armed with a rifle, according to the manufacturer.

The MP7 was adopted by the German Army Kommando Spezialkräfte (KSK) in 2002. The German KSK is a 1,000-man special operations unit formed in 1997 and tasked with conducting all forms of military operations outside the borders of Germany. They have found the MP7 an excellent choice of weapon for dignitary and VIP protection as well as a personal defense weapon. A variety of shoulder, hip, and thigh holsters have been developed by Heckler & Koch to aid in the carry and concealment of the MP7.

Minor additions to the MP7 design resulted in the MP7A1 designation. These changes include the addition of MIL-STD-1913 rails to both sides of the front end of the weapon as well as extending the top rail to run the entire length of the receiver. The butt pad of the sliding stock was made thicker and reshaped with a serrated butt plate area. The front grip was given a latch to help hold it in the closed position, and the fixed iron sights were taken off and replaced with a removable set of folding iron sights.

The primary German sighting device designed for the MP7 and MP7A1 is a quickly detachable reflex sight designed by Hensoldt SystemtechNik GmbH. The reflex sight has a day or night capability, the reticle being illuminated by an ambient light collector, a tritium (beta) source for night work, or an optional battery. The threaded muzzle of the MP7 can accept the detachable flash hider, muzzle extension, blank firing adaptor, or sound suppressor that have been designed for it.

Andre Dalla'u kneeling and firing the Knight PDW.
Andre Dalla'u

KNIGHT'S PDW

Some of the new PDWs being developed follow the general outline of a short rifle, resembling more of a carbine-class weapon rather than a submachine gun, though their caliber puts them in the submachine gun class. The Knight's Armament Company followed the general lines of the M16 weapon series when they laid out their close quarters battle PDW project, tentatively named the CQB PDW. The magazine well, magazine catch, trigger, safety/selector lever, and cocking handle are all adapted directly from the M16 family, with the exception that the selector lever is duplicated on both the right and left side of the weapon to make it ambidextrous. Using the control layout of the M16 weapon makes the CQB PDW immediately familiar to troops already trained on the M16 rifle or M4 carbine.

Outside of portions of the trigger mechanism, the internal arrangements of the Knight's PDW are completely original from those of the M16. The dual gas system that operates the action is a modification of a traditional gas-operated piston, preventing the direct impingement of propellant gas into the action of the weapon. This keeps the internal action of the weapon cleaner while also simplifying routine maintenance. Duplicating the gas system gives the action of the weapon greater operating power to aid in reliability.

Between the twin gas piston systems runs the mainspring of the action. With the mainspring on top of the receiver, the rear of the weapon is free to have a folding stock installed. The side-folding stock is a very solid design, resembling those triangular stocks found on members of the AK-74 family.

The stamped aluminum magazines are heavily ribbed for strength and are fully curved for reliable feeding. The barrel has a noticeable appearance resulting from Knight's patented dimpling process that results in rows of circular depressions spaced out along its length. The dimples lighten the weight of the barrel as well as increase the surface area for additional cooling. The barrel is free-floating for accuracy, meaning that it does not contact the forearm of the upper receiver.

The upper receiver of the CQB PDW is made from a single piece of alloy with MIL-STD-1913 rail sections machined into the receiver as integral parts. A rail section runs the full length of the upper receiver and holds a pair of operator-removable folding sights. Additional rail sections run along the sides and bottom of the firearm. A vertical grip is available for attachment to the lower rail sections, making the CQB PDW a very quick-handling weapon.

The cartridge the CQB PDW is chambered for is the 6×30 mm round that is unique to the weapon. Putting out a 6 mm projectile at over 2,400 feet per second gives the CQB PDW an effective range of 300 meters, where the sixty-five-grain bullet will still penetrate body armor. Recoil of the round is slight and has been further mitigated by the "controlled motion" operating group of the action. This results in a very controllable weapon on full automatic fire when either handheld or shoulder-fired.

To make an even more compact weapon, an eight-inch barrel is available for the CQB PDW. A Knight's-designed suppressor is available for the CQB PDW that significantly reduces the sound signature of the weapon for more covert use.

18.5 MM ROCKET SUBMACHINE GUN

The most unusual submachine gun ever produced was not a true submachine gun—it did not fire a pistol cartridge—but that was the designation placed on the weapon by the developers. The weapon is much more of a very exotic shotgun, launching multiple subprojectiles for each round fired. Sponsored by the Defense Advanced Research Projects Agency in the early 1970s, the effort was to develop two basic gun-launched, rocket-assisted (GLRA) small arms weapons systems. One system was to be a complete weapon and ammunition. The other was to be a round of rocket-assisted ammunition for the 40 mm low-velocity grenade launcher (M79 and M203). The company receiving the contract was the AAI Company, and the project was monitored by the U.S. Army. The end result of the program was the design, manufacture, and testing of an 18.5 mm submachine gun and ammunition. The final design of the weapon was functional, and the manufacturers thought it could also be converted to a conventional ballistic system instead of a rocket-powered one.

To eliminate the possibility of injury to an unprotected gunner firing the weapon, the round was designed to be launched ballistically through a rifled barrel, coast for twenty feet, and then the rocket motor would fire and boost the projectile to maximum velocity and range. The use of the ballistic launch and rocket boost system allowed a much heavier than normal projectile (623 grains) to be fired than could otherwise normally be done in a handheld or shoulder-fired weapon.

The round fired by the 18.5 mm submachine gun is effectively a caseless rocket cartridge, as the entire round is projected from the barrel when the weapon is fired, and there is no cartridge case remaining to be extracted or ejected. The propellant train is initiated by a standard percussion primer, which ignites the launching charge that drives the entire round as the projectile through the barrel. The firing of the launching charge also initiates a pyrotechnic delay element to the rocket motor. Two small driving bands near the base of the aluminum body of the round engage the rifling in the barrel, in order to stabilize the projectile for the first part of its flight.

The initial muzzle velocity of the projectile from the force of the launching charge is 436 feet per second. The burn time for the delay element to the rocket

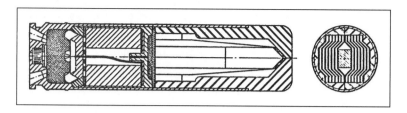

A cutaway drawing of the 18.5 mm Multi-Scimitar rocket round.
AAI Inc

propellant is forty-eight milliseconds. That delay is enough time for the projectile to travel about 20 feet from the muzzle of the weapon before the rocket propellant ignites.

The rocket motor boosts the velocity of the projectile an additional 500 feet per second before it reaches the burnout point. The canted exhaust ports in the base of the projectile maintain and increase the spin rate for further stabilization in flight. The rocket propellant burns for eighteen milliseconds to drive the projectile and ignite the pyrotechnic train to the separation charge. At the rocket motor burnout point, the projectile has traveled about 45 feet from the muzzle of the weapon, when the separation charge fires.

The firing of the separation charge ejects the four-piece plastic sabot assembly from the aluminum body of the cartridge. Air pressure and rotational forces split the sabot assembly apart, releasing the payload of fourteen scimitar subprojectiles. The two stacks of aerodynamic scimitars spread out from the force of rotation given to them from the projectile body as they fly on to impact with the target.

The scimitar subprojectile is a flat, 12.5-grain, fin-stabilized dart formed from stamped sheet metal. The leading edges of the nose of the scimitar are sharpened to a more aerodynamic shape. Additionally, the front portion of the body behind the nose is thicker than the rest of the scimitar, giving it a front-heavy center of gravity. The combination of the fins' shape, angles of the stamping, and heavy nose make the scimitar a very stable projectile in flight. The pattern of the scimitar stacks forms a roughly two-foot-wide group at fifty feet from the point of separation. At one hundred feet from the point of separation, eight of the fourteen scimitar payloads remain in a roughly sixteen-inch-wide pattern.

The velocity of the scimitar projectiles combines with the sharp nose and wide fins of their construction to cause large wound tracks in tissue as well as deep penetration. The destructive characteristics of the scimitars evolved

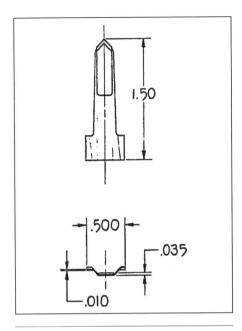

1.50

.500

.035

.010

A dimensioned drawing of a single Scimitar projectile.
AAI Inc

from the experiences AAI had with the development of the flechettes used in their submissions to the SPIW rifle project. Unlike flechettes fired in a normal shotgun shell, the scimitar projectiles maintain a point-first stability from the time of firing to impact. Most flechettes fired at shotgun velocities do not regain a point-first orientation until they have traveled twenty to thirty yards from the muzzle of the weapon.

To fire the exotic round of ammunition, AAI designed a closed-bolt firing submachine gun with an aluminum receiver for light weight. The relatively low operating pressures of the system allowed the designers to keep the overall weight of the weapon low in spite of its rather large size. The entire round of 18.5 mm scimitar rocket ammunition is about the size of a twelve-gauge three-inch Magnum shell without the rim. The size of the 18.5 mm cartridge limited the size of the initial magazine to twenty rounds to keep the overall length to a manageable size.

The 18.5 mm submachine gun feasibility model operated as a delayed blowback weapon. A retarding wedge held the bolt of the weapon closed until the pressures within the barrel fell to a low level. This retarding action was also necessary to control the amount of operating energy transmitted to the bolt and slide so that their velocity of travel during functioning would not damage the light receiver. A shoulder stock was not included in the overall design of the feasibility model, though provision for adding a folding or fixed stock can easily be added to the weapon.

The 18.5 mm submachine gun could fire in either the semiautomatic or full automatic mode and remain much more controllable than any other weapon of a similar caliber. To increase the capabilities of the weapon, a second round of ammunition was proposed and designed that did not use the rocket-powered aspect of the scimitar round. The new round was to be a high-explosive fragmentation grenade to give the weapon an area-fire effect.

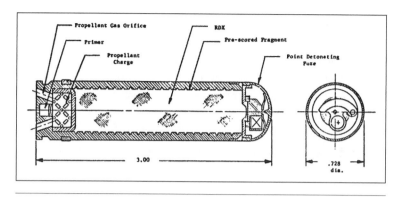

The high-explosive fragmentation projectile proposed for the 18.5 mm rocket submachine gun.
AAI Inc

This would allow the 18.5 mm submachine gun system to engage point targets such as individual soldiers with the scimitar ammunition, resulting in a very high hit probability due to the multiple subprojectiles directed to a target. The explosive fragmentation round would be used for area targets such as groups of men, the interior of a room or bunker engaged through an opening, or targets obscured or concealed behind cover.

To give the high-explosive round a maximum lethal area, it was planned to employ 2.0-grain preformed fragments in the body of the projectile. The steel wall of the projectile was internally scored for it to break up from the force of the explosive filler into 0.1-inch cubical fragments weighing about 2.1 grains each. The size of the high-explosive projectile body resulted in about 415 fragments, each one moving at an initial velocity of about 3,800 feet per second from the power of the RDX explosive filler.

The overall design of the high-explosive cartridge followed that of the scimitar rocket round without the inclusion of the rocket motor itself. The ports in the bottom of the high-explosive round were not canted, and the round was stabilized from the rifling of the barrel engaging the rifle band near the bottom of the cartridge. The propellant charge was initiated by a standard percussion primer and gave the projectile a muzzle velocity of 250 feet per second. The 1,470-grain projectile had an effective range of about 500 meters, a 25 percent improvement over the 40 mm low-velocity ammunition in use in the M79 and M203 grenade launchers of the time. A simple point-initiation impact fuse with a safety delay system was in the nose of the explosive grenade.

The 18.5 mm submachine gun was probably the ultimate weapon of its class. With the ammunition intended for it, the weapon could have easily engaged a very wide range of targets with the operator only having to load the proper magazine into the weapon. The drawback of the rocket-powered ammunition was that it required further development, and extremely tight manufacturing tolerances needed for the production of a number of its components made each round an expensive proposition. The post–Vietnam War reduction of the U.S. military forces in the 1970s, when the weapon was first developed, resulted in the funding for such an exotic piece of hardware being cut after the initial contract was fulfilled, and the project was shelved.

Submachine Gun Data

The standard Uzi submachine gun with a folding metal stock. *Kevin Dockery*

NAME—Uzi submachine gun
CALIBER—
9×19mm
.45 ACP
OVERALL LENGTH—
18.5 inches (47 cm) with metal stock folded
25.59 inches (65 cm) with wooden or extended metal stock
BARREL LENGTH—10.24 inches (26 cm)
RIFLING (TYPE AND TWIST)—
4-groove, right-hand twist, 1 turn in 10 inches (25.4 cm)
6-groove left-hand twist, 1 turn in 16 inches (40.6 cm)
LOAD—
M882 NATO ball
.45 ACP—M1911 ball
BULLET DIAMETER—
0.355 inch (9.02 mm)
.45 ACP—0.452 inch (11.48 mm)

BULLET WEIGHT—
124 grains (8.04 g)
.45 ACP—230 grains (14.90 g)
MUZZLE VELOCITY—
1,273 fps (388 m/s)
.45 ACP—925 fps (282 m/s)
MUZZLE ENERGY—
446 ft./lb. (605 J)
.45 ACP—322 ft./lb. (437 J)
WEIGHT (EMPTY)—
7.94 lbs. (3.60 kg) with wooden stock
7.72 lbs. (3.50 kg) with metal folding stock
WEIGHT (LOADED)—
9.30 lbs. (4.22 kg) with wooden stock and 32 rounds
9.08 lbs. (4.12 kg) with metal stock and 32 rounds
0.45 ACP—8.95 lbs. (4.06 kg) with metal stock and 16 rounds
SIGHTS—Adjustable iron sights, flip aperture/post, graduations for 100 and 200 meters
SIGHT RADIUS—12.17 inches (30.9 cm)
EFFECTIVE RANGE—219 yards (200 m)
OPERATION—Blowback
TYPE OF FIRE—Selective, semi-, and full automatic
CYCLIC RATE OF FIRE—
600 rpm
.45 ACP—500 rpm

FEED DEVICE—
Removable 20-, 25-, and 32-round box magazines
.45 ACP—Removable 16-round box magazine
FEED DEVICE WEIGHT (EMPTY)—
.45 ACP—16 round—0.49 lb. (0.22 kg)
20-round—0.35 lb. (0.16 kg)
25-round—0.44 lb. (0.20 kg)
32-round—0.49 lb. (0.22 kg)
FEED DEVICE WEIGHT (LOADED)—
.45 ACP—16 round—1.23 lb. (0.56 kg)
20-round—0.89 lb. (0.40 kg)
25-round—1.12 lbs. (0.51 kg)
32-round—1.36 lbs. (0.62 kg)
MANUFACTURER—Israel Military Industries, Ramat Hasharon, Israel
SERVICE—In service with military and police units around the world
STATUS—In production
REFERENCES—Company literature

Skorpion submachine gun with holster and extra magazines. The weapon is loaded with a 20-round magazine while a 10-round is lying just below it. *Kevin Dockery*

NAME—Skorpion Vz-61
COMMON NAMES—Skorpion Model 61e

CALIBER—7.65×17 mmSR (.32 ACP)
OVERALL LENGTH—
10.63 inches (27 cm) with stock folded
20.35 inches (51.7 cm) with stock extended
8.75 inches (22.2 cm) suppressor
28.2 inches (71.6 cm) with suppressor mounted and stock extended
BARREL LENGTH—4.53 inches (11.5 cm)
RIFLING (TYPE AND TWIST)—6-groove, right-hand twist, 1 turn in 12 inches (30.5 cm)
LOAD—Ball
BULLET DIAMETER—0.312 inch (7.92 mm)
BULLET WEIGHT—74 grains (4.80 g)
MUZZLE VELOCITY—1,040 fps (317 m/s); 899 fps (274 m/s) with suppressor
MUZZLE ENERGY—178 ft./lb. (241 J); 133 ft./lb. (180 J) with suppressor
WEIGHT (EMPTY)—2.82 lbs. (1.28 kg)
WEIGHT (LOADED)—3.74 lbs. (1.70 kg) with 20 rounds; suppressor weight—0.75 lbs. (0.34 kg)
SIGHTS—Adjustable iron, aperture/post, settings for 75 and 150 meters
SIGHT RADIUS—5.79 inches (14.7 cm)
EFFECTIVE RANGE—
55 yards (50 m) as pistol
164 yards (150 m) with shoulder stock
OPERATION—Blowback
TYPE OF FIRE—Selective, semi-, and full automatic
RATE OF FIRE—
Semiautomatic—35 rpm
Full automatic—100 rpm
CYCLIC RATE OF FIRE—750 to 800 rpm
FEED DEVICE—Removable 10- or 20-round box magazines
FEED DEVICE WEIGHT (EMPTY)—
10-round—0.35 lb. (0.16 kg)
20-round—0.57 lb. (0.26 kg)
FEED DEVICE WEIGHT (LOADED)—
10-round—0.53 lb. (0.24 kg)
20-round—0.92 lb. (0.42 kg)
MANUFACTURER—Czech state ordnance factories

SERVICE—No present active military service

STATUS—Out of production

REFERENCES—Foss, Christopher F., and Gander, T. J., *Infantry Weapons of the World*; Hogg, Ian, *Military Small Arms of the 20th Century*, 7th Edition: Hogg, Ian, *Jane's Infantry Weapons: 1983–1984*: Defense Intelligence Agency DST-1110H-394-76 w/Change 1, *Small Arms Identification and Operation Guide: Eurasian Communist Countries*: USAREUR PAM No. 30-60-1, *Identification Handbook Soviet and Satellite Ordnance Equipment,* 6th Revised Edition, Part Two, June 30, 1966

The PM-63 submachine gun with the forward grip in the folded position and the slide forward. *Kevin Dockery*

NAME—Pistolet Maszynowy 63

COMMON NAMES—PM-63, Wz-63

CALIBER—9×18 mm

OVERALL LENGTH—

13.11 inches (33.3 cm) with stock folded

22.95 inches (58.3 cm) with stock extended

BARREL LENGTH—5.98 inches (15.2 cm)

RIFLING (TYPE AND TWIST)—6-groove, right-hand twist, 1 turn in 8 inches (20.3 cm)

LOAD—57-N-181S "PM" ball

BULLET DIAMETER—0.364 inch (9.24 mm)

BULLET WEIGHT—91 grains (5.9 g)

MUZZLE VELOCITY—1,058 fps (322 m/s)

MUZZLE ENERGY—226 ft./lb. (306 J)

WEIGHT (EMPTY)—3.25 lbs. (1.47 kg)

WEIGHT (LOADED)—4.14 lbs. (1.87 kg) with 25 rounds

SIGHTS—adjustable open iron flip aperture/blade, graduations for 100 and 200 meters

SIGHT RADIUS—4.4 inches (11.2 cm)

EFFECTIVE RANGE—

44 yards (40 m) without stock

216 yards (200 m) with stock extended

OPERATION—Blowback

TYPE OF FIRE—Selective, semi-, and full automatic

RATE OF FIRE—

Semiautomatic—40 rpm

Full automatic—75 rpm

CYCLIC RATE OF FIRE—650 rpm

FEED DEVICE—Removable 15- or 25-round box magazine

FEED DEVICE WEIGHT (EMPTY)—

15-round—0.23 lb. (0.10 kg)

25-round—0.34 lb. (0.15 kg)

FEED DEVICE WEIGHT (LOADED)—

15-round—0.56 lb. (0.25 kg)

25-round—0.89 lb. (0.40 kg)

MANUFACTURER—State arsenals

SERVICE—In limited service with reserve forces

STATUS—Production completed

The PM63 ready for firing. *Kevin Dockery*

REFERENCES—Foss, Christopher F., and Gander, T. J., *Infantry Weapons of the World*; Hogg, Ian, *Military Small Arms of the 20th Century*, 7th Edition; Hogg, Ian, *Jane's Infantry Weapons: 1983–1984*; Defense Intelligence Agency DST-1110H-394-76 w/Change 1, *Small Arms Identification and Operation Guide: Eurasian Communist Countries*; USAREUR PAM No. 30-60-1, *Identification Handbook Soviet and Satellite Ordnance Equipment,* 6th Revised Edition, Part Two, June 30, 1966

The Ingram M10 submachine gun. *Kevin Dockery*

NAME—Ingram submachine gun family

COMMON NAMES—

M10

M11

M11/9

CALIBER—

M10—.45 ACP

M10—9×19 mm

M11—.380 ACP (9×17 mm)

M11/9—9×19 mm

OVERALL LENGTH—

M10—10.51 inches (26.7 cm) without stock

10.59 inches (26.9 cm) with stock
telescoped

21.57 inches (54.8 cm) with stock
extended

31.42 inches (79.8 cm) with original
suppressor in place, stock extended

Original suppressor length—11.46
inches (29.1 cm)

M11—8.74 inches (22.2 cm) without stock

9.76 inches (24.8 cm) with stock
telescoped

18.11 inches (46 cm) with stock
extended

25.59 inches (65 cm) with original
suppressor in place, stock extended

26 inches (66 cm) with Viper suppressor
in place, stock extended

Original suppressor length—8.82 inches
(22.4 cm)

Gemtech Viper suppressor length—9.5
inches (24.1 cm)

M11/9—12.99 inches (33 cm) with stock
telescoped

22.99 inches (58.4 cm) with stock
extended

30.3 inches (77 cm) with Larand
suppressor in place, stock extended

30.88 inches (78.4 cm) with Viper
suppressor in place, stock extended

Larand suppressor length—8.92 inches
(22.7 cm)

Gemtech Viper suppressor length—9.5
inches (24.1 cm)

The Ingram M11 submachine gun with the MAC suppressor
in place on the barrel. *Kevin Dockery*

BARREL LENGTH—

M10—5.75 inches (14.6 cm)

M11—5.08 inches (12.9 cm)

M11/9—5.24 inches (13.3 cm)

RIFLING (TYPE AND TWIST)—

M10—5-groove, right-hand twist, 1 turn in
20 inches (50.8 cm)

M10 (9 mm)—6-groove, right-hand twist, 1
turn in 12 inches (30.5 cm)

M11—6-groove, right-hand twist, 1 turn in
12 inches (30.5 cm)

LOAD—

M10—M1911 ball

M10 (9 mm)—M882 NATO ball

M11—Ball

M11/9—M882 NATO ball

BULLET DIAMETER—

M10—0.452 inch (11.48 mm)

M10 (9 mm)—0.355 inch (9.02 mm)

M11—0.356 inch (9.04 mm)
M11/9—0.355 inch (9.02 mm)

BULLET WEIGHT—
M10—230 grains (14.90 g)
M10 (9 mm)—124 grains (8.04 g)
M11—95 grains (6.16 g)
M11/9—124 grains (8.04 g)

MUZZLE VELOCITY—
M10—918 fps (280 m/s)
M10 (9 mm)—1,200 fps (366 m/s)
M11—961 fps (293 m/s)
M11/9—1,200 fps (366 m/s)

MUZZLE ENERGY—
M10—430 ft./lb. (583 J)
M10 (9 mm)—396 ft./lb. (537 J)
M11—195 ft./lb. (264 J)
M11/9—396 ft./lb. (537 J)

WEIGHT (EMPTY)—
M10—6.26 lbs. (2.84 kg)
M10 (9 mm)—6.26 lbs. (2.84 kg)
M11—3.51 lbs. (1.59 kg)
M11/9—3.75 lbs. (1.70 kg)

WEIGHT (LOADED)—
M10—7.04 lbs. (3.19 kg) with 30 rounds
    7.59 lbs. (3.44 kg) with 30 rounds and suppressor
    Original suppressor weight—0.55 lb. (0.25 kg)
M10 (9 mm)—6.76 lbs. (3.07 kg) with 32 rounds
    7.31 lbs. (3.32 kg) with 32 rounds and original suppressor
    7.64 lbs. (3.47 kg) with 32 rounds and Viper suppressor
    Original suppressor weight—0.55 lb. (0.25 kg)
    Gemtech Viper suppressor weight—0.88 lb. (0.40 kg)
M11—4.63 lbs. (2.10 kg) with 32 rounds
    5.63 lbs. (2.55 kg) with 32 rounds and original suppressor
    Original suppressor weight—1 lb. (0.45 kg)

M11/9—4.83 lbs. (2.19 kg) with 32 rounds
    5.56 lbs. (2.52 kg) with 32 rounds and Larand suppressor
    5.71 lbs. (2.59 kg) with Viper suppressor and 32 rounds
    Larand suppressor weight—0.73 lb. (0.33 kg)
    Gemtech Viper suppressor weight—0.88 lb. (0.40 kg)

SIGHTS—Fixed, nonadjustable, aperture/post, set for 100 meters (M11—set for 50 meters)

SIGHT RADIUS—
M10—8.27 inches (21 cm)
M10 (9 mm)—8.27 inches (21 cm)
M11—7 inches (17.8 cm)
M11/9—9.06 inches (23 cm)

EFFECTIVE RANGE—
M10—27 yards (25 m)
M10 (9 mm)—27 yards (25 m)
M11—16 yards (15 m)
M11/9—27 yards (25 m)

OPERATION—Blowback

TYPE OF FIRE—Selective

RATE OF FIRE—
M10—
    Semiautomatic—40 rpm
    Full automatic—90 rpm
M10 (9 mm)—
    Semiautomatic—40 rpm
    Full automatic—96 rpm
M11—
    Semiautomatic—40 rpm
    Full automatic—96 rpm

CYCLIC RATE OF FIRE—
M10—1,145 rpm
M10 (9 mm)—1,090 rpm
M11—1,200 rpm
M11/9—1,200 rpm

FEED DEVICE—
M10—Removable 30 round box magazine
M10 (9 mm)—Removable 32-round box magazine

M11—Removable 16- or 32-round box
magazine
M11/9—Removable 15- or 32-round
polymer (Zytel) box magazine
FEED DEVICE WEIGHT (EMPTY)—
  M10—0.78 lb. (0.35 kg)
  M10 (9 mm)—0.50 lb. (0.23 kg)
  M11—
    16-round—0.13 lb. (0.06 kg)
    32-round—0.43 lb. (0.20 kg)
  M11/9—
    15-round—0.12 lb. (0.05 kg)
    32-round—0.21 lb. (0.10 kg)
FEED DEVICE WEIGHT (LOADED)—
  M10—2.16 lbs. (0.978 kg)
  M10 (9 mm)—1.30 lbs. (0.59 kg)
  M11—
    16-round—0.62 lb. (0.28 kg)
    32-round—1.12 lbs. (0.51 kg)
  M11/9—
    15-round—0.53 lb. (0.24 kg)
    32-round—1.08 lbs. (0.49 kg)
MANUFACTURER—Military Armament
Corporation, Powder Springs, Georgia (M10,
M11); SWD Incorporated, Atlanta, Georgia
(M11/9)
SERVICE—In service with limited special
operations units and government agencies
STATUS—Production completed, all models
REFERENCES—Archer, Denis, ed., *Jane's
Infantry Weapons: 1978*; Dockery, Kevin,
Compendium of Modern Weapons; company
literature

The MP5A4 with the fixed buttstock and 3-round burst
selector mechanism. *Heckler & Koch Defense*

NAME—Heckler & Koch MP5 series
COMMON NAMES—MP5

MP5A1
MP5A2
MP5A3
MP5A4
MP5A5
MP5 SFA2
MP5 SFA3
MP5-N
MP5-F
CALIBER—9×19 mm
OVERALL LENGTH—
  16.99 inches (43.2 cm) with receiver cap
(MP5A1)
  19.29 inches (49 cm) with stock collapsed
(MP5A3, MP5A5, MP5 SFA3, MP5-N)
  21.75 inches (55.2 cm) with stock
collapsed (MP5-F)
  25.98 inches (66 cm) with stock fully
extended (MP5A3, MP5A5, MP5 SFA3,
MP5-N)
  26.77 inches (68 cm) with fixed stock
(MP5A2, MP5A5)
  27.52 inches (69.9 cm) with stock fully
extended (MP5-F)
  33.06 inches (95.4 cm) with stock fully
extended and suppressor mounted (MP5-N)
  Suppressor length—7.75 inches (19.7 cm)
BARREL LENGTH—8.85 inches (22.5 cm)
RIFLING (TYPE AND TWIST)—Standard
profile, 6-groove, right-hand twist, 1 turn in
9.86 inches (25 cm)
LOAD—M882 NATO ball; 9 mm Mark 144
Mod 1 subsonic ball (MP5-N)
BULLET DIAMETER—0.355 inch (9.02 mm)
BULLET WEIGHT—124 grains (8.04 g)
  147 grains (9.53 g) (MP5-N with Mk 144 ball)
MUZZLE VELOCITY—1,312 fps (400 m/s)
  975 fps (297 m/s) (MP5-N with Mk 144 ball)
MUZZLE ENERGY—474 ft./lbs. (643 J)
  310 ft./lb. (420 J) (MP5-N with Mk 144 ball)
WEIGHT (EMPTY)—
  4.93 lbs. (2.24 kg) (MP5A1)
  5.59 lbs. (2.54 kg) (MP5A2, MP5A4, MP5
SFA2)

6.34 lbs. (2.88 kg) (MP5A3, MP5A5, MP5 SFA3, MP5-N)

6.70 lbs. (3.04 kg) (MP5-F)

7.57 lbs. (3.43 kg) with suppressor mounted (MP5-N)

Suppressor weight—1.25 lbs. (0.57 kg)

WEIGHT (LOADED)—All loaded with 30 rounds

6.23 lbs. (2.83 kg) (MP5A1)

6.79 lbs. (3.08 kg) (MP5A2, MP5A4, MP5 SFA2)

7.54 lbs. (3.42 kg) (MP5A3, MP5A5, MP5 SFA3, MP5-N)

7.90 lbs. (3.58 kg) (MP5-F)

8.85 lbs. (4.01 kg) with 30 rounds Mk 144 Mod 1 and suppressor (MP5-N)

SIGHTS—Open adjustable iron sights, aperture/post

SIGHT RADIUS—13.38 inches (34 cm)

OPERATION—Delayed blowback

TYPE OF FIRE—Various trigger groups are interchangeable between all the MP5 submachine guns. Available trigger groups include: single-fire (semiautomatic only); semiautomatic and 2-round burst only; semiautomatic and 3-round burst only; semiautomatic, 2-round burst, and full automatic; semiautomatic, 3-round burst, and full automatic; semi- and full automatic fire; as well as semi- and full automatic with ambidextrous controls (Navy group). The following are the standard groups that come with the specific model.

Semiautomatic only—MP5 SFA2, MP5 SFA3

Selective, semi-, and full automatic—MP5A1, MP5A2, MP5A3, MP5-F

Selective, semi-, and full automatic, ambidextrous—MP5-N

Selective, semiautomatic, 3-round burst, and full automatic—MP5A4, MP5A5

RATE OF FIRE—

Semiautomatic—40 to 50 rpm

Full automatic—100 rpm

CYCLIC RATE OF FIRE—725 to 800 rpm

FEED DEVICE—Removable 15- or 30-round box magazine

FEED DEVICE WEIGHT (EMPTY)—

15-round—0.26 lb. (0.12 kg)

30-round—0.38 lb. (0.17 kg)

FEED DEVICE WEIGHT (LOADED)—

15-round—0.67 lb. (0.30 kg)

30-round—1.20 lbs. (0.54 kg)

30-round—1.28 lbs. (0.58 kg) with 30 rounds Mk 144 Mod 1 subsonic ball (MP5-N)

MANUFACTURER—Heckler & Koch, Oberndorf, Germany, licensed manufacture in Greece, Iran, Mexico, Pakistan, and Turkey as of 2002

SERVICE—Military and commercial sales around the world

STATUS—In production

REFERENCES—Archer, Denis, ed., *Jane's Infantry Weapons: 1978*; Gander, Terry J., ed., *Jane's Infantry Weapons: 2001–2002*; Dockery, Kevin, *Special Warfare, Special Weapons*; company literature

The MP5A5 with the stock fully forward in the collapsed position. *Kevin Dockery*

COMMENTS—The French model of the MP5 series (MP5-F) is the most recent upgrade (1999) of the original basic weapon. Besides having an additional length in the buttstock as well as a thick rubber butt plate, the MP5-F has been strengthened internally to operate safely and extensively with a very high-pressure French military loading of the 9 mm round.

The U.S. Navy model of the MP5 (MP5-N) produced for the Navy SEALs has a short section of threaded barrel at the end of the muzzle, normally covered by a knurled steel sleeve. A special USN-adopted stainless steel suppressor threads onto the end of the barrel when the protective cap is removed. Though the suppressor can be fired with normal NATO ammunition, the Mk 144 Mod 1 subsonic 9 mm round was specifically designed for suppressed use in the MP5-N series of weapons. The subsonic loading of the Mk 144 produces no supersonic signature (crack) when fired and results in a very quiet weapon.

The MP5SD3 with a telescopic sight attached for suppressed sniping. *Kevin Dockery*

NAME—Heckler & Koch MP5 Schalldämpfer series

COMMON NAMES—MP5SD
  MP5SD1
  MP5SD2
  MP5SD3
  MP5SD4
  MP5SD5
  MP5SD-N

CALIBER—9 × 19 mm

OVERALL LENGTH—
  21.67 inches (55 cm) with receiver cap (MP5SD1, MP5SD4)
  23.97 inches (61 cm) with stock collapsed (MP5SD3, MP5SD6, MP5SD-N)
  30.42 inches (78 cm) with stock fully extended (MP5SD3, MP5SD6, MP5SD-N)
  30.42 inches (78 cm) with fixed stock (MP5SD2, MP5SD5)

BARREL LENGTH—5.73 inches (14.6 cm)

RIFLING (TYPE AND TWIST)—Standard profile, 6 groove, right-hand twist, 1 turn in 9.86 inches (25 cm)

LOAD—M882 NATO ball

BULLET DIAMETER—0.355 inch (9.02 mm)

BULLET WEIGHT—124 grains (8.04 g)

MUZZLE VELOCITY—935 fps (285 m/s)

MUZZLE ENERGY—241 ft./lb. (327 J)

WEIGHT (EMPTY)—
  6.17 lbs. (2.80 kg) (MP5SD1, MP5SD4)
  6.83 lbs. (3.10 kg) (MP5SD2, MP5SD5)
  7.50 lbs. (3.40 kg) (MP5SD3, MP5SD6, MP5SD-N)

WEIGHT (LOADED)—All loaded with 30 rounds
  7.37 lbs. (3.34 kg) (MP5SD1, MP5SD4)
  8.03 lbs. (3.64 kg) (MP5SD2, MP5SD5)
  8.70 lbs. (3.95 kg) (MP5SD3, MP5SD6, MP5SD-N)

SIGHTS—Open adjustable iron sights, aperture/post

SIGHT RADIUS—13.38 inches (34 cm)

OPERATION—Delayed blowback

TYPE OF FIRE—Various trigger groups are interchangeable between all the MP5 submachine guns. Available trigger groups include: single-fire (semiautomatic only); semiautomatic and 2-round burst only; semiautomatic and 3-round burst only; semiautomatic, 2-round burst, and full automatic; semiautomatic, 3-round burst, and full automatic; semi- and full automatic fire, as well as semi- and full automatic with ambidextrous controls (Navy group). The following are the standard groups that come with the specific model.
  Selective, semi-, and full automatic—MP5SD1, MP5SD2, MP5SD3
  Selective, semi-, and full automatic, ambidextrous—MP5SD-N
  Selective, semiautomatic, 3-round burst, and full automatic—MP5SD4, MP5SD5, MP5SD6

RATE OF FIRE—
 Semiautomatic—40 to 50 rpm
 Full automatic—100 rpm
CYCLIC RATE OF FIRE—725 to 800 rpm
FEED DEVICE—Removable 15- or 30-round box magazine
FEED DEVICE WEIGHT (EMPTY)—
 15-round—0.26 lb. (0.12 kg)
 30-round—0.38 lb. (0.17 kg)
FEED DEVICE WEIGHT (LOADED)—
 15-round—0.67 lb. (0.30 kg)
 30-round—1.20 lbs. (0.54 kg)
MANUFACTURER—Heckler & Koch, Oberndorf, Germany
SERVICE—Military and commercial sales around the world
STATUS—In production
REFERENCES—Archer, Denis, ed., *Jane's Infantry Weapons: 1978;* Gander, Terry J., ed., *Jane's Infantry Weapons: 2001–2002;* Dockery, Kevin, *Special Warfare, Special Weapons*; company literature
COMMENTS—The SD series includes an integral suppressor that is built around a ported barrel. The special ported barrel has an area just ahead of the breech that has thirty 2.5 mm holes drilled into the bore. These holes bleed off propellant gases, lowering the velocity of a standard round of ammunition to below the speed of sound. This makes the SD series the quietest of the MP5s when used with standard ammunition. The gas bleed-off system causes subsonic ammunition (such as the Mark 144 Mod 1) to lose so much velocity as the make the projectiles ineffective at anything but short ranges. Surrounding the barrel is a 12-inch-long suppressor tube that extends well out past the forearm of the weapon. The suppressor body screws onto a threaded portion of the receiver where it is sealed by a rubber O-ring.

The MP5KA1 version, the shortest of the MP5 series, this model comes with minimal sights for additional concealment. *Heckler & Koch Defense*

NAME—Heckler & Koch MP5 Kurz series
COMMON NAMES—
 MP5K
 MP5KA1
 MP5KA4
 MP5KA5
 MP5K-N
 MP5K-PDW
CALIBER—9 × 19 mm
OVERALL LENGTH—
 12.80 inches (32.5 cm) with receiver cap (MP5K, MP5KA1, MP5KA4, MP5KA5, MP5K-N)
 21 inches (53.3 cm) with receiver cap and suppressor mounted (MP5K-N)
 14.50 inches (36.8 cm) with stock collapsed (MP5K-PDW)
 23.75 inches (60.3 cm) with stock fully extended (MP5K-PDW)
 33.06 inches (95.4 cm) with stock fully extended and suppressor mounted (MP5K-PDW)
 Suppressor length—7.75 inches (19.7 cm)
BARREL LENGTH—4.5 inches (11.4 cm) (MP5K, MP5KA1, MP5KA4, MP5KA5)
 5.5 inches (14 cm) (MP5K-N, MP5K-PDW)
RIFLING (TYPE AND TWIST)—Standard profile, 6-groove, right-hand twist, 1 turn in 9.86 inches (25 cm)
LOAD—M882 NATO ball
 9 mm Mk 144 Mod 1 (MP5K-N, MP5-PDW)

BULLET DIAMETER—0.355 inch (9.02 mm)
BULLET WEIGHT—124 grains (8.04 g)
147 grains (9.53 g) (MP5K-N, MP5-PDW)
MUZZLE VELOCITY—1,230 fps (375 m/s)
962 fps (297 m/s) (MP5K-N, MP5K-PDW)
MUZZLE ENERGY—416 ft./lb. (564 J)
302 ft./lb. (410 J) (MP5K-N, MP5K-PDW)
WEIGHT (EMPTY)—
4.40 lbs. (2.00 kg) (MP5K, MP5KA1,
MP5KA4, MP5KA5)
4.61 lbs. (2.09 kg) (MP5K-N)
6.14 lbs. (2.79 kg) (MP5K-PDW)
5.87 lbs. (2.66 kg) with suppressor
mounted (MP5K-N)
7.40 lbs. (3.36 kg) with suppressor
mounted (MP5K-PDW)
Suppressor weight—1.26 lbs. (0.57 kg)
WEIGHT (LOADED)—All loaded with 30
rounds
5.60 lbs. (2.54 kg) (MP5K, MP5KA1,
MP5KA4, MP5KA5)
5.81 lbs. (2.64 kg) (MP5K-N)
7.34 lbs. (3.33 kg) (MP5K-PDW)
7.15 lbs. (3.24 kg) with 30 rounds Mk 144
Mod 1 and suppressor (MP5K-N)
8.68 lbs. (3.94 kg) with 30 rounds Mk 144
Mod 1 and suppressor (MP5K-PDW)
SIGHTS—
Open adjustable iron sights, aperture/post
(MP5K, MP5KA4, MP5K-N, MP5K-PDW)
Fixed, nonadjustable, square notch/bead
(MP5KA1, MP5KA5)
SIGHT RADIUS—
10.24 inches (26 cm) (MP5K, MP5KA4,
MP5K-N, MP5K-PDW)
7.48 inches (19 cm) (MP5KA1, MP5KA5)
OPERATION—Delayed blowback
TYPE OF FIRE—Various trigger groups are
interchangeable between the MP5K series.
The K series trigger groups are shorter than
the standard models and cannot be switched
with those of the standard MP5 series (full-
sized) guns. Available trigger groups include:
semiautomatic and 2-round burst only;

semiautomatic and 3-round burst only;
semiautomatic, 2-round burst, and full
automatic; semiautomatic, 3-round burst,
and full automatic; semi- and full automatic
fire, as well as semi- and full automatic with
ambidextrous controls (Navy group). The
following are the standard groups that come
with the specific model.
Selective, semi-, and full automatic—
MP5K, MP5KA1
Selective, semi-, and full automatic,
ambidextrous—MP5K-N, MP5K-PDW
Selective, semiautomatic, 3-round burst,
and full automatic—MP5KA4, MP5KA5
RATE OF FIRE—
Semiautomatic—40 to 50 rpm
Full automatic—100 rpm
CYCLIC RATE OF FIRE—900 rpm
FEED DEVICE—Removable 15- or 30-round
box magazine
FEED DEVICE WEIGHT (EMPTY)—
15-round—0.26 lb. (0.12 kg)
30-round—0.38 lb. (0.17 kg)
FEED DEVICE WEIGHT (LOADED)—
15-round—0.67 lb. (0.30 kg)
30-round—1.20 lbs. (0.54 kg)
30-round—1.28 lbs. (0.58 kg) with 30
rounds Mk 144 Mod 1 (MP5-N)
MANUFACTURER—Heckler & Koch,
Oberndorf, Germany, licensed manufacture
in Greece, Iran, Mexico, Pakistan, and Turkey
as of 2002
SERVICE—Military and commercial sales
around the world
STATUS—In production
REFERENCES—Archer, Denis, ed., *Jane's
Infantry Weapons: 1978*; Gander, Terry J.,
ed., *Jane's Infantry Weapons; 2001–2002*;
Dockery, Kevin, *Weapons of the Navy SEALs*;
company literature
COMMENTS—First introduced in 1978, the K
or Kurz (short) models are the shortest
members of the MP5 series of weapons. The
U.S. Navy model MP5K (MP5K-N), produced

The MP5K-N loaded with a 15-round magazine and with a stainless-steel suppressor in place on the muzzle. *Kevin Dockery*

for the Navy SEALs, has a short section of threaded barrel at the end of the muzzle. These threads are normally covered by a knurled steel sleeve. A special USN-adopted stainless steel suppressor threads onto the end of the barrel when the protective cap is removed. Though the suppressor can be fired with normal NATO ammunition, the Mk 144 Mod 1 subsonic 9 mm round was specifically designed for suppressed use in the MP5-N series of weapons and produces no supersonic signature when fired. The MP5K-PDW is a stocked version of the MP5K-N and as such can also mount a suppressor on the threaded end of its barrel.

The MP5KN-PDW. *Heckler & Koch Defense*

NAME—Heckler & Koch MP5 Plastic Training
COMMON NAMES—MP5 PT
MP5A4 PT
MP5A5 PT
CALIBER—9 × 19 mm
OVERALL LENGTH—
26.77 inches (68 cm) with fixed stock (MP5A4 PT)
19.29 inches (49 cm) with stock collapsed (MP5A5 PT)
25.98 inches (66 cm) with stock fully extended (MP5A5 PT)

BARREL LENGTH—8.85 inches (22.5 cm)
RIFLING (TYPE AND TWIST)—Standard profile, 6-groove, right-hand twist
LOAD—Plastic training ball
BULLET DIAMETER—0.355 inch (9.02 mm)
BULLET WEIGHT—6.5 grains (0.42 g)
MUZZLE VELOCITY—1,345 fps (410 m/s)
MUZZLE ENERGY—26 ft./lb. (35 J)
WEIGHT (EMPTY)—
5.60 lbs. (2.54 kg) (MP5A4 PT)
6.35 lbs. (2.88 kg) (MP5A5 PT)
WEIGHT (LOADED)—
6.13 lbs. (2.78 kg) loaded with 30 rounds (MP5A4 PT)
6.88 lbs. (3.12 kg) loaded with 30 rounds (MP5A5 PT)
SIGHTS—Open adjustable iron sights, aperture/post
SIGHT RADIUS—13.38 inches (34 cm)
EFFECTIVE RANGE—9 to 16 yards (8 to 15 m)
OPERATION—Gas-assisted blowback
TYPE OF FIRE—Selective, semiautomatic, 3-round burst, and full automatic; additional MP5 series trigger groups can be exchanged as desired by the user
RATE OF FIRE—
Semiautomatic—30 to 40 rpm
Full automatic—90 rpm
CYCLIC RATE OF FIRE—700 rpm
FEED DEVICE—Removable 15- or 30-round box magazine
FEED DEVICE WEIGHT (EMPTY)—
15-round—0.26 lb. (0.12 kg)
30-round—0.38 lb. (0.17 kg)
FEED DEVICE WEIGHT (LOADED)—
15-round—0.33 lb. (0.15 kg)
30-round—0.53 lb. (0.24 kg)
MANUFACTURER—Heckler & Koch, Oberndorf, Germany
SERVICE—Limited military and commercial sales
STATUS—Production completed
REFERENCES—Company literature
COMMENTS—Released in 1984, the MP5 PT

models were intended for training use only and cannot chamber or fire a normal ball round of ammunition. The only round used with the PT series is the Dynamit Nobel 9×19 mm training round that has an aluminum base holding a plastic casing with the 6.5-grain (0.42-gram) projectile cast as the front part of the round. When fired, the plastic separates at the mouth of the "case," and the projectile leaves the barrel. The entire round weighs about 34 grains (2.20 grams). The projectile is engraved by the rifling in the barrel and is accurate up to about 15 meters. The light projectile has a maximum range of 125 meters. To identify the PT series (besides markings on the top of the receiver), the cocking handle of the weapons are colored blue. Though the projectiles are light and relatively safe, the plastic training ammunition and the PT model weapons can be lethal within 8 meters or less. This makes the weapon applicable to situations where the range is limited, and danger to the surrounding area should be kept to a minimum (such as within an aircraft).

NAME—Colt 9 mm submachine gun
CALIBER—9×19 mm
OVERALL LENGTH—
     25.63 inches (65.1 cm) with stock collapsed
     28.88 inches (73.4 cm) with stock fully extended
     Buttstock can be locked in four evenly spaced positions, including fully closed and fully extended
BARREL LENGTH—10.5 inches (26.7 cm)
LOAD—M882 NATO ball
BULLET DIAMETER—0.355 inch (9.02 mm)
BULLET WEIGHT—124 grains (8.04 g)
MUZZLE VELOCITY—1,322 fps (403 m/s)
MUZZLE ENERGY—481 ft./lb. (652 J)
WEIGHT (EMPTY)—5.75 lbs. (2.61 kg)

WEIGHT (LOADED)—7.14 lbs. (3.24 kg) with 32 rounds
SIGHTS—Open adjustable iron, rear flip aperture (0 to 50m/50 to 100m)/post
SIGHT RADIUS—14.75 inches (37.5 cm)
EFFECTIVE RANGE—92 yards (100 m)
OPERATION—Blowback
TYPE OF FIRE—Varies according to model
     Model AR6451—Semiautomatic only
     Model RO635—Selective, semi-, and full automatic fire
     Model RO639—Semiautomatic and 3-round burst only
CYCLIC RATE OF FIRE—800 to 1,000 rpm; an optional hydraulic buffer is available from Colt that reduces the cyclic rate of fire by 100 to 200 rounds per minute
FEED DEVICE—Removable 20- or 32-round box magazine
FEED DEVICE WEIGHT (EMPTY)—
     20-round—0.40 lb. (0.18 kg)
     32-round—0.50 lb. (0.23 kg)
FEED DEVICE WEIGHT (LOADED)—
     20-round—0.95 lb. (0.43 kg)
     32-round—1.39 lbs. (0.63 kg)
MANUFACTURER—Colt Defense LLC, Hartford, Connecticut
SERVICE—Commercial sales, some U.S. government agencies, U.S. Marine Corps
STATUS—In production
REFERENCES—Company literature

NAME—Colt 9 mm DOE submachine gun
COMMON NAMES—Model RO633HB
CALIBER—9×19 mm
OVERALL LENGTH—
     21 inches (53.3 cm) with stock collapsed
     24.25 inches (61.6 cm) with stock fully extended
BARREL LENGTH—7 inches (17.8 cm)
LOAD—M882 NATO ball
BULLET DIAMETER—0.355 inch (9.02 mm)
BULLET WEIGHT—124 grains (8.04 g)

MUZZLE VELOCITY—1,200 fps (366 m/s)

MUZZLE ENERGY—396 ft./lb. (537 J)

WEIGHT (EMPTY)—5.41 lbs. (2.45 kg)

WEIGHT (LOADED)—6.36 lbs. (2.88 kg) with 20 rounds

SIGHTS—Open adjustable iron, rear flip aperture (0 to 50 m/50 to 100 m)/folding front post

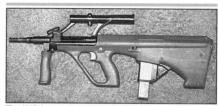

The AUG 9 mm submachine gun. *Kevin Dockery*

SIGHT RADIUS—11.54 inches (29.3 cm)

EFFECTIVE RANGE—92 yards (100 m)

OPERATION—Blowback

TYPE OF FIRE—Selective, semi-, and full automatic fire

CYCLIC RATE OF FIRE—

Model 633—700 to 900 rpm

Model 633HB—600 to 800 rpm

FEED DEVICE—Removable 20- or 32-round box magazine

FEED DEVICE WEIGHT (EMPTY)—

20-round—0.40 lb. (0.18 kg)

32-round—0.50 lb. (0.23 kg)

FEED DEVICE WEIGHT (LOADED)-

20-round—0.95 lb. (0.43 kg)

32-round—1.39 lbs. (0.63 kg)

MANUFACTURER—Colt Defense LLC, Hartford, Connecticut

SERVICE—Department of Energy and other agencies

STATUS—Limited production

REFERENCES—Company literature

COMMENTS—Reportedly, this very short model Colt 9 mm SMG was manufactured to the specifications of the Department of Energy for their security teams.

NAME—AUG 9 mm Para

COMMON NAMES—AUG/9 mm Carbine

CALIBER—9 × 19 mm

OVERALL LENGTH—26.18 inches (66.5 cm)

BARREL LENGTH—16.54 inches (42 cm)

RIFLING (TYPE AND TWIST)—6-groove, right-hand twist, 1 turn 9.8 inches (25 cm)

LOAD—M882 NATO ball

BULLET DIAMETER—0.355 inch (9.02 mm)

BULLET WEIGHT—124 grains (8.04 g)

MUZZLE VELOCITY—1,352 fps (412 m/s)

MUZZLE ENERGY—503 ft./lb. (682 J)

WEIGHT (EMPTY)—7.28 lbs. (3.30 kg)

WEIGHT (LOADED)—8.40 lbs. (3.81 kg) with 25 rounds

SIGHTS—Standard with optical sight built into handle with fixed notch/blade backup sights built into top of handle

SIGHT POWER—1.5 power magnification

SIGHT RADIUS—7.56 inches (19.2 cm) (backup sights)

OPERATION—Blowback

TYPE OF FIRE—Selective, semi-, and full automatic

CYCLIC RATE OF FIRE—650 to 750 rpm

FEED DEVICE—Removable 25- or 32-round box magazine

FEED DEVICE WEIGHT (EMPTY)—

25-round—0.44 lb. (0.20 kg)

32-round—0.53 lb. (0.24 kg)

FEED DEVICE WEIGHT (LOADED)—

25-round—1.12 lbs. (0.51 kg)

32-round—1.41 lbs. (0.64 kg)

MANUFACTURER—Steyr-Mannlicher GesmbH., Austria

SERVICE—Commercial sales

STATUS—Production as required

REFERENCES—Company literature

The removable barrel of the AUG system makes providing a suppressed version of the 9 mm submachine gun a simple matter as shown here. *Kevin Dockery*

COMMENTS—A conversion kit of parts exists to change the standard 5.56 mm Steyr AUG rifle over to the submachine gun configuration. Original parts on the rifles are exchanged for the kit's new, simplified 9 mm bolt assembly, barrel, magazine well adapter, and magazine. The magazine used in the AUG 9 mm version is the same magazine designed by Steyr for the MPi 69 and MPi 81 submachine guns.

The Mini Uzi with its stock folded. In this position, the stock can act as a front handgrip. *Kevin Dockery*

NAME—Mini Uzi

CALIBER—9 × 19 mm

OVERALL LENGTH—
14.17 inches (36 cm) with metal stock folded
23.62 inches (60 cm) with wooden or extended metal stock

BARREL LENGTH—7.75 inches (19.7 cm)

RIFLING (TYPE and TWIST)—4-groove, right-hand twist, 1 turn in 10 inches (25.4 cm)

LOAD—M882 NATO ball

BULLET DIAMETER—0.355 inch (9.02 mm)

BULLET WEIGHT—124 grains (8.04 g)

MUZZLE VELOCITY—1,155 fps (352 m/s)

MUZZLE ENERGY—367 ft./lb. (498 J)

WEIGHT (EMPTY)—5.94 lbs. (2.69 kg)

WEIGHT (LOADED)—7.06 lbs. (3.20 kg) with 25 rounds

SIGHTS—Adjustable iron sights, flip aperture/post, graduations for 100 and 200 meters

SIGHT RADIUS—9.17 inches (23.3 cm)

EFFECTIVE RANGE—91 yards (100 m)

OPERATION—Blowback

TYPE OF FIRE—Selective, semi-, and full automatic

CYCLIC RATE OF FIRE—
Standard Mini Uzi—950 rpm
Closed-bolt Mini Uzi—900 rpm
Heavy-bolt Mini Uzi—750 rpm

FEED DEVICE—Removable 20-, 25-, and 32-round box magazines

FEED DEVICE WEIGHT (EMPTY)—
20-round—0.35 lb. (0.16 kg)
25-round—0.44 lb. (0.20 kg)
32-round—0.49 lb. (0.22 kg)

FEED DEVICE WEIGHT (LOADED)—
20-round—0.89 lb. (0.40 kg)
25-round—1.12 lbs. (0.51 kg)
32-round—1.36 lbs. (0.62 kg)

MANUFACTURER—Israel Military Industries, Ramat Hasharon, Israel

SERVICE—In service with military and police units around the world

STATUS—In production

REFERENCES—Company literature

The Mini Uzi with its stock extended for shoulder firing. *Kevin Dockery*

The Micro Uzi with its stock extended. *Kevin Dockery*

NAME—Micro Uzi

CALIBER—9 × 19 mm (.45 ACP)

OVERALL LENGTH—

10.51 inches (26.7 cm) with metal stock folded

18.50 inches (47 cm) with metal stock fully extended

BARREL LENGTH—4.49 inches (11.4 cm)

RIFLING (TYPE and TWIST)—4-groove, right-hand twist, 1 turn in 10 inches (25.4 cm); 6-groove, left-hand twist, 1 turn in 16 inches (40.6 cm)

LOAD—M882 NATO ball; .45 ACP—M1911 ball

BULLET DIAMETER—0.355 inch (9.02 mm); .45 ACP—0.452 inch (11.48 mm)

BULLET WEIGHT—124 grains (8.04 g); .45 ACP—230 grains (14.90 g)

MUZZLE VELOCITY—1,148 fps (350 m/s); .45 ACP—787 fps (240 m/s)

MUZZLE ENERGY—363 ft./lb. (492 J); .45 ACP—316 ft./lb. (428 J)

WEIGHT (EMPTY)—4.20 lbs. (1.91 kg)

WEIGHT (LOADED)—5.09 lbs. (2.31 kg) with 20 rounds; .45 ACP—5.43 lbs. (2.46 kg) with 16 rounds

SIGHTS—Adjustable iron sights, flip aperture/post, graduations for 100 and 200 meters

SIGHT RADIUS—6.89 inches (17.5 cm)

EFFECTIVE RANGE—91 yards (100 m)

OPERATION—Blowback

TYPE OF FIRE—Selective, semi- and full automatic

CYCLIC RATE OF FIRE—1,250 rpm; .45 ACP—1,100 rpm

FEED DEVICE—Removable 20-, 25-, and 32-round box magazines; .45 ACP—removable 16-round box magazine

FEED DEVICE WEIGHT (EMPTY)—

.45 ACP—16-round—0.49 lb. (0.22 kg)

20-round—0.35 lb. (0.16 kg)

25-round—0.44 lb. (0.20 kg)

32-round—0.49 lb. (0.22 kg)

FEED DEVICE WEIGHT (LOADED)—

.45 ACP—16-round—1.23 lbs. (0.56 kg)

20-round—0.89 lb. (0.40 kg)

25-round—1.12 lbs. (0.51 kg)

32-round—1.36 lbs. (0.62 kg)

MANUFACTURER—Israel Military Industries, Ramat Hasharon, Israel

SERVICE—In service with military and police units around the world

STATUS—In production

REFERENCES—Company literature

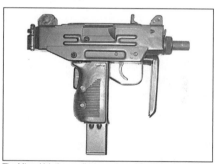

The Micro Uzi, the smallest member of the Uzi submachine gun family. *Kevin Dockery*

The HK53 submachine gun version of the HK53 rifle series.
Heckler & Koch Defense

NAME—HK 53 Submachine gun

COMMON NAMES—HK 53

CALIBER—5.56×45 mm

OVERALL LENGTH—
22.17 inches (56.3 cm) with stock
collapsed
29.72 inches (75.5 cm) with stock fully
extended

BARREL LENGTH—8.31 inches (21.1 cm)
without flash suppressor

RIFLING (TYPE and TWIST)—6-groove, right-
hand twist, 1 turn in 12 inches (30.5 cm)

LOAD—M855 ball

BULLET DIAMETER—0.224 inch (5.69 mm)

BULLET WEIGHT—62grains (4.02 g)

MUZZLE VELOCITY—2,461 fps (750 m/s)

MUZZLE ENERGY—834 ft./lb. (1131 J)

WEIGHT (EMPTY)—6.72 lbs. (3.05 kg)

WEIGHT (LOADED)—7.95 lbs. (3.61 kg) with
25 rounds

SIGHTS—Open adjustable iron sights,
aperture/post, range adjustments in 200,
300, and 400 meters

SIGHT RADIUS—15.35 inches (39 cm)

OPERATION—Delayed blowback

TYPE OF FIRE—Selective, semi-, and full
automatic; optional, semi-, 3-round burst,
and full automatic

RATE OF FIRE—
Semiautomatic—40 rpm
Full automatic—160 rpm

CYCLIC RATE OF FIRE—700 rpm

FEED DEVICE—Removable 25-round steel or
40-round aluminum box magazine

FEED DEVICE WEIGHT (EMPTY)—
25-round—0.55 lb. (0.25 kg)
40-round—0.35 lb. (0.16 kg)

FEED DEVICE WEIGHT (LOADED)—
25-round—1.23 lbs. (0.56 kg)
40-round—1.43 lbs. (0.65 kg)

MANUFACTURER—Heckler & Koch,
Oberndorf, Germany

SERVICE—Commercial sales

STATUS—Production completed

REFERENCES—Archer, Denis, ed., *Jane's
Infantry Weapons: 1978;* company literature

The rare HK54A1 submachine gun with the suppressor
unscrewed and lying below the weapon. This specimen is
loaded with the unique 50-round drum magazine developed
for this weapon. *Kevin Dockery*

NAME—Heckler & Koch 54A1

COMMON NAMES—HK54A1

CALIBER—9×19 mm

OVERALL LENGTH—
16.19 inches (41.1 cm) with stock
collapsed
23.5 inches (59.7 cm) with suppressor
installed and stock collapsed
24.25 inches (61.6 cm) with stock fully
extended
31.5 inches (80 cm) with suppressor
installed and stock fully extended
Suppressor length—13.13 inches
(33.4 cm)

BARREL LENGTH—7.06 inches (17.9 cm)

RIFLING (TYPE and TWIST)—Standard-
profile, 6-groove, right-hand twist, 1 turn in
9.86 inches (25 cm)

LOAD—M882 NATO ball
BULLET DIAMETER—0.355 inch (9.02 mm)
BULLET WEIGHT—124 grains (8.04 g)
MUZZLE VELOCITY—1,300 fps (396 m/s); 960 fps (293 m/s) with vent ports open for subsonic use
MUZZLE ENERGY—465 ft./lb. (631 J); 254 ft/lb. (344 J) with vent ports open for subsonic use
WEIGHT (EMPTY)—6.57 lbs. (298 kg); 7.49 lbs. (3.40 kg) with suppressor mounted
WEIGHT (LOADED)—9.42 lbs. (4.27 kg) with loaded 50-round drum; 10.34 lbs. (4.69 kg) with suppressor mounted and loaded 50-round drum
SIGHTS—Open adjustable iron sights, aperture/post
SIGHT RADIUS—12.75 inches (32.4 cm)
OPERATION—Delayed blowback
TYPE OF FIRE—Selective, semiautomatic, 3-round burst, full automatic, and locked breech
RATE OF FIRE—
  Semiautomatic—40 rpm
  Full automatic—100 rpm
CYCLIC RATE OF FIRE—800 rpm
FEED DEVICE—Removable 50-round polymer and alloy drum magazine
FEED DEVICE WEIGHT (EMPTY)—1.49 lbs. (0.68 kg)
FEED DEVICE WEIGHT (LOADED)—2.85 lbs. (1.29 kg)
MANUFACTURER—Heckler & Koch, Oberndorf, Germany
SERVICE—Evaluation, some limited combat use
STATUS—Samples only
REFERENCES—Dockery, Kevin, *Weapons of the Navy SEALs*

The HK54A1 with the stock extended to its full extent. *Kevin Dockery*

The JSSAP submachine gun with the suppressor dismounted. *Kevin Dockery*

NAME—Heckler & Koch SMG 94054
COMMON NAMES—JSSAP 6.3A SMG, SMG I
CALIBER—9×19 mm
OVERALL LENGTH—
  14.31 inches (36.3 cm) with stock collapsed
  21.63 inches (54.9 cm) with suppressor installed and stock collapsed
  22.69 inches (57.6 cm) with stock fully extended
  29.88 inches (75.9 cm) with suppressor installed and stock fully extended
  Suppressor length—10.81 inches (27.5 cm)
BARREL LENGTH—5.63 inches (14.3 cm)
RIFLING (TYPE and TWIST)—Standard-profile, 6-groove, right-hand twist, 1 turn in 9.86 inches (25 cm)
LOAD—M882 NATO ball
BULLET DIAMETER—0.355 inch (9.02 mm)
BULLET WEIGHT—
  124-grain (8.04 g) M882 NATO ball
  147-grain (9.50 g) OSP subsonic
MUZZLE VELOCITY—
  1,227 fps (374 m/s) M882 NATO ball
  1,017 fps (310 m/s) OSP subsonic
MUZZLE ENERGY—
  414 ft./lb. (562 J) M882 NATO ball
  338 ft./lb. (458 J) OSP subsonic

WEIGHT (EMPTY)—6.12 lbs. (2.78 kg)
7.87 lbs. (3.57 kg) with suppressor mounted
1.80 lbs. (0.82 kg) final model suppressor weight
WEIGHT (LOADED)—
7.1 lbs. (3.22 kg) with 30 rounds M882 NATO ball
8.95 lbs. (4.06 kg) with suppressor mounted and 30 rounds OSP subsonic
SIGHTS—Open adjustable iron sights, aperture/post, switch to change sights from supersonic to subsonic ammunition use
SIGHT RADIUS—12.5 inches (31.8 cm)
OPERATION—Blowback
TYPE OF FIRE—Selective, semiautomatic, and full automatic
RATE OF FIRE—
Semiautomatic—40 rpm
Full automatic—100 rpm
CYCLIC RATE OF FIRE—880 rpm
FEED DEVICE—Removable 30-round polymer box magazine
FEED DEVICE WEIGHT (EMPTY)—0.17 lb. (0.08 kg)
FEED DEVICE WEIGHT (LOADED)—
0.98 lb. (0.44 kg)—loaded with 30 rounds M882 NATO ball
1.08 lbs. (0.49 kg) loaded with 30 rounds OSP subsonic
MANUFACTURER—Heckler & Koch, Oberndorf, Germany
SERVICE—Evaluation
STATUS—60 units constructed
REFERENCES—Dockery, Kevin, *Weapons of the Navy SEALs*

The MP5/10 submachine gun with two magazines locked together side by side. *Heckler & Koch Defense*

NAME—Heckler & Koch MP5/40 and MP5/10
CALIBER—
MP5/40—.40 Smith & Wesson (10×22 mm)
MP5/10—10 mm Auto (10×25 mm)
OVERALL LENGTH—
19.29 inches (49 cm) with stock collapsed
25.98 inches (66 cm) with stock fully extended
26.77 inches (68 cm) with fixed stock
BARREL LENGTH—8.85 inches (22.5 cm)
RIFLING (TYPE and TWIST)—Standard-profile, 6-groove, right-hand twist, 1 turn in 15 inches (38 cm)
LOAD—
.40 S&W—Winchester Jacketed Hollow Point
10 mm Auto—Winchester Silvertip
BULLET DIAMETER—0.400 inch (10.16 mm)
BULLET WEIGHT—
.40 S&W—180 grains
10 mm Auto—175 grains
MUZZLE VELOCITY—
.40 S&W—990 fps (302 m/s)
10 mm Auto—1,473 fps (449 m/s)

MUZZLE ENERGY—
.40 S&W—392 ft./lb. (532 J)
10 mm Auto—843 ft./lb. (1143 J)
WEIGHT (EMPTY)—
5.88 lbs. (2.67 kg) with fixed stock
6.28 lb. (2.85 kg) with retractable stock
WEIGHT (LOADED)—All loaded with 30
rounds
MP5/40—7.22 lbs. (3.27 kg) with fixed
stock and 30 rounds .40 S&W
MP5/40—7.62 lbs. (3.46 kg) with
retractable stock and 30 rounds .40 S&W
MP5/10—7.36 lbs. (3.34 kg) with fixed
stock and 30 rounds 10 mm Auto
MP5/10—7.76 lbs. (3.52 kg) with
retractable stock and 30 rounds 10 mm Auto
SIGHTS—Open adjustable iron sights,
aperture/post
SIGHT RADIUS—13.38inches (34 cm)
OPERATION—Delayed blowback
TYPE OF FIRE—The MP5/10 and MP5/40
models may use all of the standard MP5
trigger groups. They most often come
equipped from the manufacturer with the
selective, semiautomatic, 3-round burst, and
full automatic trigger group mounted in
place.
CYCLIC RATE OF FIRE—800 rpm
FEED DEVICE—Removable 30-round
translucent polymer box magazine
FEED DEVICE WEIGHT (EMPTY)—
30-round—0.25 lb. (0.11 kg)
FEED DEVICE WEIGHT (LOADED)—
30-round—1.34 lbs. (0.61 kg) with 30
rounds .40 S&W
30-round—1.48 lbs. (0.67 kg) with 30
rounds 10 mm Auto
MANUFACTURER—Heckler & Koch,
Oberndorf, Germany
SERVICE—Commercial sales
STATUS—Production completed
REFERENCES—Gander, Terry J., ed., *Jane's
Infantry Weapons: 2001–2002;* company
literature

COMMENTS—The MP5/40 and MP5/10
models differ from each other only by the
caliber they are chambered for. Both
weapons were developed in 1991 to meet a
U.S. law enforcement demand for an MP5-
style weapon chambered for a more powerful
round than the standard 9 mm. The
translucent magazines have socket and lugs
cast into their sides to allow multiple
magazines to be securely stacked together
for quick reloading. A later model of
magazine constructed of carbon-fiber-
reinforced polymer has been produced in
replacement for the translucent model. The
carbon-fiber magazines require a magazine
clamp to be used to hold to magazines
together for a quick reload. A bolt catch
device was also included into the design, as
well as a threaded muzzle for the attachment
of a suppressor. The bolt catch will hold the
bolt to the rear on an empty magazine. It is
released by manipulating the button on the
catch or pulling back the cocking handle to
release the bolt.

The UMP45 submachine gun with the stock extended and a
suppressor locked in place on the muzzle. *Kevin Dockery*

NAME—Heckler & Koch Universal Machine
Pistol 45
COMMON NAMES—UMP45
CALIBER—.45 ACP (11.43×23 mm)
OVERALL LENGTH—
17.71 inches (45 cm) with stock folded
24.41 inches (62 cm) with stock folded and
suppressor mounted
21.17 inches (69 cm) with stock extended
33.86 inches (86 cm) with stock extended
and suppressor mounted

BARREL LENGTH—7.87 inches (20 cm)
RIFLING (TYPE AND TWIST)—6-groove, polygonal right-hand twist, 1 turn in 16 inches (40.6 cm)
LOAD—
  M1911 ball
  .45 +P JHP
BULLET DIAMETER—0.452 inch (11.48 mm)
BULLET WEIGHT—
  M1911 ball—230 grains (14.90 g)
  .45 +P JHP—185 grains (11.99 g)
MUZZLE VELOCITY—
  M1911 ball—853 fps (260 m/s)
  .45 +P JHP—1,257 fps (383 m/s)
MUZZLE ENERGY—
  M1911 ball—372 ft./lb. (504 J)
  .45 +P JHP—649 ft./lb. (880 J)
WEIGHT (EMPTY)—4.63 lbs. (2.10 kg)
WEIGHT (LOADED)—
  6.15 lbs. (2.79 kg) loaded with 25 rounds M1911 ball
  7.14 lbs. (3.24 kg) with B&T suppressor in place and loaded with 25 rounds M1911 ball
  B&T QC aluminum suppressor weight—0.99 lb. (0.45 kg)
SIGHTS—Adjustable open iron aperture/post; optional mountable MIL-STD-1913 rails available for the top of the receiver as well as the bottom and both sides of the forearm
SIGHT RADIUS—12.8 inches (32.5 cm)
OPERATION—Blowback
TYPE OF FIRE—Selective, semi-, and full automatic; optional semiautomatic-only and semi-/2-round burst trigger mechanisms available
CYCLIC RATE OF FIRE—
  M1911 ball—580 rpm
  .45 +P JHP—700 rpm
FEED DEVICE—Removable 10- or 25-round polymer box magazine
FEED DEVICE WEIGHT (EMPTY)—
  10-round—0.19 lb. (0.09 kg)
  25-round—0.38 lb. (0.17 kg)

FEED DEVICE WEIGHT (LOADED)—
  10-round—
    M1911 ball—0.66 lb. (0.30 kg)
    .45 +P JHP—.060 lb. (0.27 kg)
  25-round
    M1911 ball—1.52 lbs. (0.69 kg)
    .45 +P JHP—1.37 lbs. (0.62 kg)
MANUFACTURER—Heckler & Koch Defense, Oberndorf, Germany
SERVICE—Commercial sales
STATUS—In production
REFERENCES—Company literature

The UMP45 submachine gun with its stock folded to the right side. *Kevin Dockery*

The UMP9 submachine gun. *Kevin Dockery*

NAME—Heckler & Koch Universal Machine Pistol 9 mm and 40 S&W
COMMON NAMES—UMP9/UMP40
CALIBER—9 × 19 mm Parabellum/.40 Smith & Wesson (10 × 21 mm)
OVERALL LENGTH—
  17.71 inches (45 cm) with stock folded
  24.41 inches (62 cm) with stock folded and suppressor mounted
  21.17 inches (69 cm) with stock extended
  33.86 inches (86 cm) with stock extended and suppressor mounted
BARREL LENGTH—7.87 inches (20 cm)

RIFLING (TYPE AND TWIST)—6-groove, polygonal, right-hand twist

LOAD—

M882 9 mm NATO ball

.40 S&W 180 grain JHP

BULLET DIAMETER—

M882 ball—0.355 inch (9.02 mm)

.40 S&W—0.400 inch (10.16 mm)

BULLET WEIGHT—

M882 ball—124 grains (8.04 g)

.40 S&W—180 grains (11.66 g)

MUZZLE VELOCITY—

M882 ball—1,312 fps (400 m/s)

.40 S&W—1,174 fps (358 m/s)

MUZZLE ENERGY—

M882 ball—474 ft./lb. (643 J)

.40 S&W—551 ft./lb. (747 J)

WEIGHT (EMPTY)—4.63 lbs. (2.10 kg)

WEIGHT (LOADED)—

UMP9—5.83 lbs. (2.64 kg) with 30 rounds M882 ball

UMP9—6.67 lbs. (3.03 kg) with B&T suppressor in place and loaded with 30 rounds M882 ball

UMP40—6.24 lbs. (2.83 kg) with 30 rounds 180-grain JHP

UMP40—7.08 lbs. (3.21 kg) with B&T suppressor in place and loaded with 30 rounds 180-grain JHP

B&T QC aluminum suppressor weight—0.84 lb. (0.38 kg)

SIGHTS—Adjustable open iron aperture/post; optional mountable MIL-STD-1913 rails available for the top of the receiver as well as the bottom and both sides of the forearm

SIGHT RADIUS—12.8 inches (32.5 cm)

OPERATION—Blowback

TYPE OF FIRE—Selective, semi-and full automatic; optional semiautomatic-only and semi-/2-round burst trigger mechanisms available

CYCLIC RATE OF FIRE—745 rpm

FEED DEVICE—Removable 30-round polymer box magazine

FEED DEVICE WEIGHT (EMPTY)—0.38 lb. (0.17 kg)

FEED DEVICE WEIGHT (LOADED)—

M882 ball—1.20 lbs. (0.54 kg)

.40 S&W—1.61 lbs. (0.73 kg)

MANUFACTURER—Heckler & Koch Defense, Oberndorf, Germany

SERVICE—Commercial sales

STATUS—In production

REFERENCES—Company literature

The Jati Matic submachine gun. *Kevin Dockery*

NAME—GG-95 personal defense weapon

COMMON NAMES—Jati-Matic

CALIBER—9 × 19 mm

OVERALL LENGTH—14.76 inches (37.5 cm)

BARREL LENGTH—8.0 inches (20.3 cm)

RIFLING (TYPE AND TWIST)—6-groove, right-hand twist, 1 turn in 9.84 inches (25 cm)

LOAD—M882 NATO ball

BULLET DIAMETER—0.355 inch (9.02 mm)

BULLET WEIGHT—124 grains (8.04 g)

MUZZLE VELOCITY—1,312 fps (400 m/s)

MUZZLE ENERGY—474 ft./lb. (643 J)

WEIGHT (EMPTY)—3.64 lbs. (1.65 kg)

WEIGHT (LOADED)—4.41 lbs. (2.0 kg) with 20 rounds

SIGHTS—Open nonadjustable iron, notch/blade adjusted to point of impact (zeroed) at 100 meters

SIGHT RADIUS—11.42 inches (29 cm)

EFFECTIVE RANGE—165 yards (150 m)

OPERATION—Blowback

TYPE OF FIRE—Selective, semi-, and full automatic

CYCLIC RATE OF FIRE—600 to 650 rpm

FEED DEVICE—Removable 20- or 40-round box magazine

FEED DEVICE WEIGHT (EMPTY)—
20-round—0.22 lb. (0.10 kg)
40-round—0.33 lb. (0.15 kg)

FEED DEVICE WEIGHT (LOADED)—
20-round—0.77 lb. (0.35 kg)
40-round—1.43 lbs. (0.65 kg)

MANUFACTURER—Oy Golden Gun Ltd., Turku, Finland

SERVICE—No official service, commercial sales

STATUS—Ready for production

REFERENCES—Company literature

The P90 submachine gun. *FN USA, LLC*

NAME—P90

CALIBER—5.7 × 28 mm

OVERALL LENGTH—19.7 inches (50 cm)

BARREL LENGTH—10.35 inches (26.3 cm)

RIFLING (TYPE AND TWIST)—8-groove, right-hand twist, 1 turn in 9 inches (23.1 cm)

LOAD—SS190 ball

BULLET DIAMETER—0.220 inch (5.59 mm)

BULLET WEIGHT—31 grains (2.01 g)

MUZZLE VELOCITY—2,345 fps (715 m/s)

MUZZLE ENERGY—378 ft./lb. (513 J)

WEIGHT (EMPTY)—5.60 lbs. (2.54 kg)

WEIGHT (LOADED)—6.63 lbs. (3.00 kg)

SIGHTS—Optical 1/1 reflex sight with integral emergency nonadjustable iron sights; mounting points on sides of sight rail for sections of MIL-STD-1913 Picatinny rails

EFFECTIVE RANGE—165 yards (150 m)

OPERATION—Blowback

TYPE OF FIRE—Selective, semi-, and full automatic

CYCLIC RATE OF FIRE—900 rpm

FEED DEVICE—Removable horizontally mounted 50-round polymer box magazine with cartridge-rotating feed lips

FEED DEVICE WEIGHT (EMPTY)—0.37 lb. (0.17 kg)

FEED DEVICE WEIGHT (LOADED)—1.03 lbs. (0.47 kg)

MANUFACTURER—Fabrique Nationale Nouvelle, Herstal, Belgium

SERVICE—Commercial sales, military use with special operations forces, counterterrorism, and VIP protection units

STATUS—In production

REFERENCES—Company literature

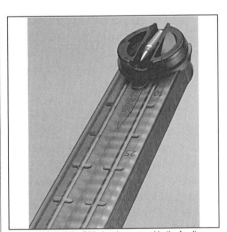

The magazine of the P90 showing a round in the feeding position. *FN USA, LLC*

COMMENTS—Additional accessories for the P90 include:

A sound suppressor that attaches over the standard flash suppressor without the use of tools. The suppressor weighs

0.88 lb. (0.40 kg), is 7.9 inches (20 cm) long, 1.6 inches (4 cm) in diameter, and reduces the sound signature by 30 decibels when used with the Sb193 subsonic ball (55-grain projectile, muzzle velocity 984 fps). Mounted in place, the suppressor adds 6.38 inches (16.2 cm) to the overall length of the weapon.

A 6-volt tactical flashlight weighing 0.52 lb. (0.24 kg) that can be mounted to either side of the sight rail.

A laser target designator that can be added to the inside of the front grip. The laser module is either a visible-light red dot version or an invisible infrared model for use with night vision devices. The laser module adds 0.31 lb. (0.14 kg) to the overall weight of the P90. The 3-volt lithium battery used by the lasers has a 10-hour combat life and puts out either 8 milliwatts with the visible laser or 5 milliwatts in the infrared laser. The lasers have a practical range of 100 meters with a 60 mm (2.3-inch) diameter spot at that range.

The MP7 personal defense weapon. *Kevin Dockery*

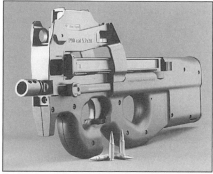

The P90. *FN USA, LLC*

NAME—Heckler & Koch MP7 personal defense weapon

COMMON NAMES—MP7 PDW

CALIBER—4.6×30 mm

OVERALL LENGTH—
   14.96 inches (38 cm) with stock retracted
   23.23 inches (959 cm) with stock extended

BARREL LENGTH—7 inches (18 cm)

RIFLING (TYPE AND TWIST)—Polygonal, right-hand twist, 1 turn in 6.3 inches (916 cm)

LOAD—4.6×30 mm ball

BULLET DIAMETER—0.18 inch (4.65 mm)

BULLET WEIGHT—26.2 grains (1.70 g)

MUZZLE VELOCITY—2,379 fps (725 m/s)

MUZZLE ENERGY—329 ft./lb. (446 J)

WEIGHT (EMPTY)—3.31 lbs. (1.50 kg)

WEIGHT (LOADED)—3.81 lbs. (1.73 kg) loaded with 20 rounds

SIGHTS—Adjustable folding iron sights, aperture/blade. MIL-STD-1913 (Picatinny) rail along top of receiver to accept additional sight systems. Normally fitted with Hensoldt Wetzlar quick detachable 24-hour red-dot reflex sight

SIGHT RADIUS—9.65 inches (24.5 cm)

EFFECTIVE RANGE—220 yards (200 m)

OPERATION—Gas

TYPE OF FIRE—Selective, semi-, and full automatic

CYCLIC RATE OF FIRE—950 rpm

FEED DEVICE—Removable 20- or 40-round polymer box magazines

FEED DEVICE WEIGHT (EMPTY)—
20-round—0.22 lb. (0.10 kg)
40-round—0.44 lb. (0.20 kg)
FEED DEVICE WEIGHT (LOADED)—
20-round—0.50 lb. (0.23 kg)
40-round—0.99 lb. (0.45 kg)
MANUFACTURER—H&K GmbH, Oberndorf,
Germany
SERVICE—In service with German KSK
special operations units
STATUS—In production
REFERENCES—Company literature

The Knight PDW. *Andre Dalla'u*

NAME—KAC PDW
CALIBER—6 × 35 mm
OVERALL LENGTH—
19.5 inches (49.5 cm) with stock folded
28 inches (71.1 cm) with stock fully
extended
BARREL LENGTH—10 inches (25.4 cm); 8
inches (20.3 cm)—optional compact barrel
LOAD—Ball
BULLET DIAMETER—0.243 inches (6.17 mm)
BULLET WEIGHT—65 grains (4.21 g)
MUZZLE VELOCITY—2,425 fps (739 m/s)
MUZZLE ENERGY—831 ft./lb. (1127 J)
WEIGHT (EMPTY)—4.5 lbs. (2.04 kg)
WEIGHT (LOADED)—5.52 lbs. (2.50 kg) with
30 rounds
SIGHTS—Open, folding, adjustable iron
sights, aperture/post, MIL-STD-1913 rail
along top of barrel and receiver, additional rail
sections along sides and bottom of forearm
SIGHT RADIUS—10.3 inches (26.2 cm)

OPERATION—Gas
TYPE OF FIRE—Selective, semi-, and full
automatic
FEED DEVICE—Removable 20- or 30-round
aluminum box magazine
FEED DEVICE WEIGHT (EMPTY)—
20-round—0.25 lb. (0.11 kg)
30-round—0.31 lb. (0.14 kg)
FEED DEVICE WEIGHT (LOADED)—
20-round—0.72 lb. (0.33 kg)
30-round—1.02 lbs. (0.46 kg)
MANUFACTURER—Knight's Armament
Company
SERVICE—Evaluation
STATUS—Development
REFERENCES—Company literature

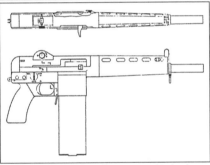

The 18.5 mm Rocket submachine gun assembly drawing.
AAI Inc

NAME: 18.5 mm submachine gun feasibility
model
TYPE: Personal defense weapon
CALIBER: 18.5 mm caseless (rocket)
OVERALL LENGTH—22.7 inches (57.7 cm)
BARREL LENGTH—11.5 inches (29.2 cm)
RIFLING (TYPE AND TWIST)—Right-hand
twist, 1 turn in 10 inches (25.4 cm)
LOAD—Scimitar flechette
BULLET (PELLET) DIAMETER—0.35-inch
thickness, 0.500-inch width
BULLET (PELLET) WEIGHT—16 grains
(1.04 g)

NUMBER OF PELLETS—14

MUZZLE VELOCITY—436 fps (133 m/s)

MAXIMUM VELOCITY—985 fps (300 m/s); 42 feet (12.8 meters) at burnout

MUZZLE ENERGY—233 ft./lb. (316 J); scimitars and sabot/rocket body w/fuel—552 grains (35.77 g) per projectile

MAXIMUM ENERGY PER PELLET—34 ft./lb. (46 J) per scimitar at maximum velocity

WEIGHT (EMPTY)—5.3 lbs. (2.40 kg)

WEIGHT (LOADED)—7.79 lbs. (3.53 kg)

SIGHTS—Open iron adjustable notch/blade

OPERATION—Retarded blowback

TYPE OF FIRE—Selective, semi-, and full automatic

CYCLIC RATE OF FIRE—850 rpm

FEED DEVICE—Removable 20-round box magazine

FEED DEVICE WEIGHT (EMPTY)—0.70 lb. (0.32 kg)

FEED DEVICE WEIGHT (LOADED)—2.49 lbs. (1.13 kg)

MANUFACTURER—AAI Company

SERVICE—None

STATUS—Prototype only

REFERENCES—Rottenberg, M. M., and Kudrick, J. R., *Prototype Development of Small Arms Rocket Ammunition Concepts Final Report*, AD529853, December 1973

GRENADE LAUNCHERS AND AREA WEAPONS

AREA WEAPONS

The individual explosive weapon, the grenade, was not invented during World War I, but it made its reappearance in a more modern, efficient form. The ability to attack an unseen target with an explosive bomb allowed soldiers going into the trenches on an assault to attack a target before they could see it directly. The next hole, trench, or bunker could be empty or hiding a number of soldiers lying in wait. Pitching a grenade into the trench or bunker and following the explosion with a quick, violent assault armed with a rifle or pistol became a commonly seen tactic on the battlefront.

The first hand grenades were little more than empty cans filled with explosive and surrounded with whatever fragmentation might be around: metal scraps, nails, bolts, etc. To fire the explosive, a burning-type fuse with an attached blasting cap would be inserted into the charge. Various kinds of mechanical grenade fuzes were developed during World War I until the Bouchon-type fuze with its safety lever and pull ring, was settled on by most of the allied forces including the United States. Fragmentation initially came from cast-iron grenade bodies, often deeply scored and serrated on the outside. The outside roughening of the grenade didn't control the fragmentation of the body at all; the blast usually blew the cast iron into several large chunks and a lot of relatively harmless dust. But the outside serrations on the body of the hand grenade did make the weapon easier to hold on to in the muddy, slippery confines of a trench. After World War II, it was discovered that by scoring the inside of a grenade body, the fragmentation could be controlled very closely. Other types of controlled fragmentation involved forming the fragmentation body from square cross-sectioned wire that was notched along its length and coiling that around the explosive filler. Such a wire fragmentation body was usually placed inside a sheet-metal grenade body for strength and sealing the explosive from the elements.

One of the problems with a hand grenade was that it could only be thrown so far. The strongest men could only put one out about forty

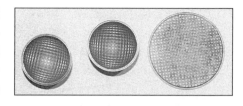

The flat engraved fragmentation body of the M67 hand grenade. The serrated round flat has been "coined" in a pattern that, when it is formed into the body of the grenade, will break up into controlled fragments.
Kevin Dockery

or fifty yards. To extend the range of such small bombs, the rifle grenade was developed. Either a modified existing hand grenade or a whole new design intended specifically for launching would have its hollow tail placed over a launcher attached to the muzzle of a rifle, or a rod attached to the bottom of the grenade slipped down the rifle's bore, or the grenade was just placed in a cup on the end of the rifle's barrel. Once a cartridge—either a special blank or a regular bulleted round depending on the grenade design—was fired, the explosive projectile would sail into the air, hopefully to come down on an enemy position. The launching of such grenades was hard on the rifles, and the accuracy of the weapon was not very good. But it was effective, and it was what was available to the individual soldier through World Wars I and II and the Korean War.

Tactically, the rifle grenade allowed the individual soldier to attack a target with an explosive weapon in the area between the longest distance that he could throw a hand grenade and the shortest distance a small mortar could drop a bomb close to him. The advantage of the weapon was that it could attack an area target—a group of men in the open or an emplacement—with a single round. The rifle and other projectile weapons could only strike at a direct target, something they could be aimed at, and the bullet would do the damage. With an area target, the fire might be indirect; the firer cannot see the enemy soldier, just the opening in a bunker wall or the window of a building. He would attack such a target indirectly, putting an explosive round through the window or into the area and allowing the blast and fragmentation to do the direct damage to the enemy. To conduct such an attack successfully, the soldier needed an individual weapon that he could aim and was considerably more accurate than the rifle grenade. The average rifle grenade was also quite large, being nearly a foot long and weighing several pounds, so the common soldier could only carry a few such munitions in addition to the rest of his regular combat load.

FORTY MILLIMETER GRENADES

The search for a new type of projected grenade for the use of the infantry soldier culminated in the creation of the 40 mm family of ammunition. The difficulty in launching a heavy projectile in a shoulder-fired weapon was one of recoil. Pushing out a heavy grenade at a reasonable velocity to give it range made for a serious kick being received on the part of the firer. It was suggested that most rifle grenades be launched with the butt of the rifle braced against the ground, keeping the recoil from the operator but also increasing the stress on the weapon. Shattered stocks often resulted from the launching of rifle grenades, and the accuracy from a difficult-to-aim, ground-braced weapon was not considered very good. A combination of design factors in the 1950s resulted in a very accurate, lightweight family of effective grenades being designed, as well as a number of weapons intended to launch them.

During World War II, the Rheinmetall-Borsig company of Germany developed a lightweight antitank weapon that used a very small charge of propellant for the size of the projectile it launched. The most important ballistic discovery of World War II was the "High and Low Pressure System," the *Hoch und Niederdruck* System, which took the propellant charge and fired it in a thick-walled cartridge case for complete combustion of the charge. The propellant gases produced were allowed to bleed through gauged holes in a thick metal plate before they could impinge on the projectile itself. Once the pressure on the round reached a certain level, a shear pin was cut, and the projectile left the muzzle under a smooth, even propulsion. The system allowed for a relatively light weapon to launch a large projectile with a smooth, even ballistic push from the propellant and relatively light recoil. The German weapon that used the system was the 8 cm Panzerabwehrwerfer 600 (PAW 600) that threw a modified 81 mm mortar shell out to a distance of 600 meters, where its shaped charge could punch through significant armor. Only about 250 of the PAW 600 weapons were produced before the end of the war, but the ballistic principle that allowed them to work was not forgotten by American ordnance engineers.

The discovery of controlled fragmentation allowed a very efficient fragmentation grenade to be built in a very small package. The

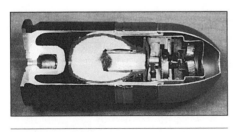

A cutaway 40 mm low-velocity high-explosive grenade. The spherical fragmentation body is filled with a white explosive simulant in this specimen.
Kevin Dockery

Honeywell corporation developed a precision fuze that was miniaturized to the point that it could fit inside a small shell and operate effectively at low firing pressures yet still remain inexpensive to produce. Finally, the high-low pressure principle was adapted to an aluminum cartridge case that could be made from extrusions in large numbers and still be able to launch a relatively fragile projectile that would be crushed if launched from a standard cannon. The combination of all of these factors resulted in the production of the 40 mm grenade, a self-contained shell that held a very small (on the order of 330 milligrams) charge of propellant that could launch a compact grenade that had an effective blast and fragmentation radius of five meters.

The heart of the 40 mm round of ammunition is the thick-walled, high-pressure chamber in the base of the cartridge case. When ignited by a standard percussion primer, the propellant charge burns very completely, creating a chamber pressure of about 35,000 pounds per square inch. When the pressure reaches a critical level, the thin alloy cup that separates the charge from the ports in the wall of the high-pressure chamber ruptures at each of the six precision ports. The propellant gas bleeds into the low-pressure chamber, where it reaches a working pressure of 3,000 psi. At that point, the projectile, the 40 mm grenade, breaks free of the seals and stake points that hold it to the aluminum cartridge case and begins traveling up the barrel. The pressure behind the projectile remains a constant 3,000 psi, giving a smooth level of acceleration to the grenade. The high-low propulsion system allows a relatively thin-walled, fragile projectile to be launched with very little stress on the projectile or the firing weapon.

The standard combat round of the 40 mm family into the 1970s is the M406 high-explosive fragmentation round. The compact M551 point detonating fuze of the M406 takes up about half of the internal volume of the projectile. Arming from both the setback inertia of firing and the centrifugal force of rotation from the rifling of the barrel, the M551 fuze delays its arming cycle until it has traveled a safe distance from the point of launch. The thirty-two-gram bursting charge of Composition B

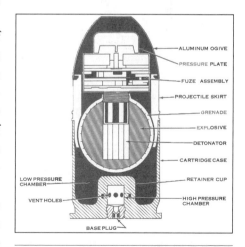

A cutaway drawing of the 40 mm low-pressure high-explosive grenade.
U.S. Army

explosive in the spherical grenade is enough to shatter its notched-wire body into hundreds of fragments. The fragments spread out to cover a circular area with a five-meter radius. Inside that radius, it is normally expected that 50 percent of any exposed personnel will become casualties. Much beyond that five-meter radius from the point of detonation, and the small fragments from the grenade have lost so much velocity that they quickly become harmless.

Another more universally useful 40 mm grenade was developed in the late 1960s and has become the more common combat round of today. The M433 high-explosive dual-purpose grenade has an internally scored fragmentation body surrounding the explosive core of forty-five grams of Composition A5. The explosive charge surrounds a cone-shaped copper liner that creates a shaped-charge effect within the grenade. The blast of the explosive shatters the body of the grenade into lethal fragments that cover a five-meter casualty radius. Additionally, the shaped-charge element of the grenade allows the copper cone to penetrate up to two inches (5.1 cm) of steel at the point of impact.

The 40 mm family of grenades has proven itself a very successful design. Dozens of payloads have been used to fill 40 mm projectiles, and they have been launched with the high-low propulsion system. Pyrotechnic rounds including flares, tear gas, signalling stars, smoke streamers, and ground markers have been produced in different colors and effects. A number of different explosive grenades have been designed, usually with different types of fillers, fuzes, or fragmentation bodies. Buckshot, flechette, target practice, and other even more exotic loads have been produced and issued.

M79

The first weapon that was fielded to utilize the new 40 mm ammunition was a short, thick-barreled, single-shot grenade launcher that greatly resembled a sawed-off shotgun. The M79 grenade launcher was designed at Springfield Armory in the late 1950s and adopted by the U.S. Army on December 15, 1959. Production difficulties, particularly those involving the complicated sight and the new type of barrel, prevented the M79 from reaching full production for several years. When it did reach the hands of the troops in numbers, it was very well received. The M79 is the first weapon in the U.S. arsenal to use an aluminum barrel. The low operating pressures of the 40 mm round allow the rifled barrel to be made from an aluminum extrusion. The overall weight of the M79 is relatively light, and it has proven a very accurate weapon in the hands of an experienced operator.

The low velocity and large projectile of the M79 cause the weapon to have a high, arcing trajectory. It takes an experienced grenadier to properly judge the distance to a target in order to drop a grenade in on it within the burst radius of the explosion. The generally accepted maximum range of the M79 for point targets, such as a window or bunker opening, is 150 meters. For an area target such as a group of men in the open, the effective range is considered to be 350 meters. A competent marksman with the M79 can place a round through a window at much more than 200 meters or hit a four-foot-square panel at the maximum range of the grenade, 400 meters. The projectile is sensitive to crosswinds that can easily blow it off target. While flying through the air, the big 40 mm grenade is so large and moving so slowly that it is common to be able to watch it in flight as it travels downrange.

In spite of its popularity, the M79 has several serious drawbacks. It is a single-shot weapon, which slows the rate of fire considerably. The requirement to open the weapon and extract the fired cartridge case manually before inserting a fresh round not only slows the rate of fire, it makes it difficult to correct the point of aim of a gunner when firing in wind or in otherwise difficult conditions. The weapon is also a dedicated one; the gunner is assigned to carry the M79 and trained in its use. While he is armed with the grenade launcher, he cannot normally use a rifle to add to the overall volume of fire of his unit. He is usually issued a sidearm for his own defense. The M79 is an excellent area-target weapon, but it has very limited point target capability.

M203

In January 1962, the Special Purpose Individual Weapon program was building up in importance. One of the new aspects of the SPIW weapon was the desire to combine the point target capability of the planned flechette-firing rifle with the area target effects of the newly fielded 40 mm grenade. The intention was to develop a weapon with the capability to fire both the flechette round and the 40 mm grenade as was stated in the objective in an official document on the weapon from March 1962. The document said that the intent was to "provide the individual soldier with a weapon system possessing the capability to engage point and area targets to a range of 400 meters." The plan was far too ambitious and was part of the reason the SPIW project failed to produce a viable weapons system. But the idea of combining a 40 mm grenade launcher with a rifle was considered a very good one.

In their production of the M16 family, Colt produced a 40 mm grenade launcher that mounted underneath the barrel of an M16 rifle by June 1964. The

Colt CGL-4 added only a few pounds to the overall weight of an AR15 or M16 and gave it the capability to accurately fire 40 mm grenades. The Colt weapon was eventually adopted on an experimental basis by the U.S. Army as the XM148 grenade launcher. The XM148 was tested in Vietnam beginning in December 1966, and it proved to be a worthwhile chunk of firepower, but it also showed itself to be a fragile design that didn't stand up to a combat environment.

A new proposal put out by the government in 1967 was for the submission of a Grenade Launcher Attachment Development (GLAD) device. Of the seventeen companies solicited for the project, seven showed a serious interest, but only three completed new designs that could be submitted for evaluation and approval. By far the most successful of these weapons was the pump-action launcher developed by AAI. The AAI Company had extensive experience with the SPIW project and the grenade launcher attachments that were a desired part of that weapon. Simplicity of design and operation had proved to be the watchword, AAI had learned during the SPIW work, and they applied that philosophy to the new grenade launcher attachment. The basic design of the AAI weapon was an aluminum-barreled, manually operated, single-shot launcher that mounted underneath the barrel of the M16 series of rifles with no modification to the host weapon other than changing the handguards. The muzzle of the 40 mm barrel did not extend much past the front sight base of the M16A1 rifle, so with very little modification it was also able to fit on the short XM177E2 weapon. The addition of a small stamped washer to go behind the front flash and noise suppressor of the XM177E2 was all that needed to be added in order to securely mount the AAI 40 mm design. Accepted by the Army for limited production and field trials, the AAI weapon received the designation XM203 40 mm grenade launcher.

Designed for right-handed users, the barrel latch of the XM203 is located right above the center of the barrel on the left side of the weapon. Grasping the barrel with his nonfiring hand, the operator can easily press in the barrel latch with his thumb and push the barrel assembly forward to its mechanical stop. If a fired cartridge case is in the chamber of the launcher, it is automatically extracted and ejected as the barrel goes forward. With the barrel in the fully forward position, a round of 40 mm ammunition can be slipped up and into the chamber. Pulling the barrel back seats and locks it in place.

The trigger is inside a spring-steel trigger guard that bears on the bottom lip of the magazine well to the M16. A rearward-curved part at the front of the trigger guard is the safety to the grenade launcher. With the safety in the on position, the firing mechanism is locked, and the weapon cannot fire. As an additional positive factor, when the safety switch is in the on position, it extends back into the trigger guard, blocking the trigger so that a finger can't be placed on it. By simply pushing the safety latch forward, the trigger is cleared, and the weapon is ready to fire.

The M203 grenade launcher with a round being loaded. *Colt Manufacturing*

The quadrant sight of the XM203 came from the development work done on the XM148 grenade launcher. The complex sight clamps securely in place on the carrying handle of the M16, where it extends out from the left side of the weapon. A folding aperture peep sight and front post can be extended out from the side of the quadrant sight for use and the whole assembly set for the proper range to the target. For a much faster to use but less exacting sight system for the XM203, an additional leaf sight is part of the upper handguard to the weapon. The leaf sight has a simple ladder system of indicator points on the inside of the rectangular folding metal leaf. The operator uses the proper set of points that match his range estimation to the target. The front sight post of the M16 rifle also acts as the front post for the leaf sight of the grenade launcher.

To use the XM203 grenade launcher, the gunner decides which sight system he is going to employ for the shot and simply shoulders the rifle. The magazine locked into the rifle acts as a grip for the firing hand to the XM203. By holding the magazine with his left hand and the pistol grip of the rifle with his right, the gunner can fire the grenade launcher or the rifle at will, allowing him to immediately engage either point or area targets as needed.

Production of the first 600 XM203 units was started by AAI in Baltimore in 1969. Production was soon switched over to the Colt company, who had the facilities to mass-produce the weapon to meet the government's demands. In January 1970, the M203 was declared the standard grenade launcher for the U.S. military and went into high-volume production. The weapon proved to be a tremendous success and has been used by a number of U.S. allies around the world. Probably the most significant honor shown to the success of the M203 design is that the proven concept of the underbarrel grenade launcher has been copied by a large number of countries and in several calibers. By the year 2000, over 300,000 M203 grenade launchers had been produced by the Colt company, and the weapon remains in production in a basically unmodified form.

To increase the tactical flexibility of the M203, in the 1990s, Colt produced

A Navy SEAL with an M203 on an M4 Carbine. The picture illustrates one of the drawbacks of the M203 as the trigger guard has slipped from its position on the magazine well and moved upward, blocking the trigger of the grenade launcher from being used.
U.S. Navy

a shoulder stock system that could be attached to the M203 to make it a stand-alone weapon. The use of such a weapon would be primarily for civil unrest situations were the appearance of heavily armed individuals could tip the balance into full-scale rioting. The Colt launcher system cuts back on that by allowing the M203 to be used as a tear gas gun or, with impact rounds, as a less-lethal weapon system. Both a fixed stock (length 27.75 inches, empty weight with launcher 6.5 lbs.) version and a carbine (sliding) stock version of the launcher system are made. The most unusual member of the launcher system family is the pistol grip version (length 18 inches, weight 5.5 lbs.) that has no stock at all.

M203A1

One of the most popular shoulder arms presently in use by U.S. forces is the M4 and M4A1 family of carbines based on the M16A2 rifle. The compact carbine is a direct descendant of the XM177E2 weapon produced during the Vietnam War. Like the XM177E2, the M4 series can mount the M203 grenade launcher. The adoption of the MIL-STD-1913 rail system (RAS—Rail Adapter System) for attachment to the M4 and M4A1 resulted in a modification of the mounting system for the M203 so that it could be quickly attached to the new rails. The barrel of the M203 was also shortened to nine inches and the weapon added to the SOPMOD package as the M203A1.

XM320

The adoption and fielding of the M203 grenade launcher in quantity proved out the concept of combining point and area fire capabilities in a single infantry weapon. For all of its success, the M203 had a number of drawbacks in its basic design that were not simple to address. The sights were a separate component from the grenade launcher itself, and they had to be rezeroed whenever they were removed or changed to another host weapon. In case of a misfire, the M203 could not be recocked without unlocking the breech and opening the weapon, a very unsafe procedure in the case of a hangfire, where there would be a long delay from the time that the trigger was pulled and the round actually fired. A hangfire is not a common malfunction in the case of fresh ammunition and a clean weapon, but after time in a combat environment, it can become considerably more common.

The pump-action method of operating the M203 restricted the ammunition that could be chambered in it to a maximum length of 5.5 inches. Limitations in the length of the rails that the barrel moved on prevented the barrel travel of the M203 from being extended to any great extent. The stamped-metal construction of some of the external parts of the M203 mechanism were a source of difficulty as was the method of attaching the launcher to the host weapon. The trigger guard in particular could slip up from its position against the magazine well of the host M16. When in the wrong position, the trigger guard could prevent the firer's finger from being able to reach the trigger until the problem was corrected.

In 2004, the Army posted a requirement for a new 40 mm Grenade Launcher Module to be obtained under the Soldier Enhancement Program. The intent of the solicitation was to obtain an off-the-shelf design for a grenade launcher that could be adapted to the needs of the Army with minimum modifications. The new weapon was to have a greater hit probability than that of the original M203. The minimum acceptable probability of a hit with the new weapon was to be a 20 percent chance of putting a grenade within 5 meters of a target at 400 meters—the maximum range of the low-velocity 40 mm ammunition. At 100 meters, the weapon was to have a 60 percent chance of a hit.

Heckler & Koch had been in production of a number of 40 mm grenade launchers since 1969. Their HK69 was one of the first grenade launchers produced outside of the United States to fire the low-velocity family of 40 mm ammunition. The HK69 could be mounted under the barrel of the standard German military rifle, the G3, but the assembly was difficult to use, and the product was dropped after a number of years. The modified Heckler & Koch grenade launcher, the HK69A1, was a stand-alone weapon with a sliding stock, compact enough to fit in a large hip holster. The HK69A1 was a much more successful variation of the original weapon and saw good sales for a number of decades.

The AG36 40 mm grenade launcher was produced by Heckler & Koch as a companion weapon for their G36 series of rifles. The AG36 has a prominent pistol grip with a double-action trigger. If the chambered round does not fire on the first primer hit, pulling the trigger again will once more strike at the percussion primer of the chambered round without having to open the barrel. The barrel

The XM320 mounted underneath an M4A1 carbine with the barrel of the grenade launcher swung out for loading.
Kevin Dockery

of the AG36 opens to the left side for loading. Pressing up on the breech release lever in the upper part of the trigger guard unlocks the spring-loaded barrel that snaps open to the left side of the weapon. If the firer is working from the prone position, he can see the open breech and the condition of the round in it without having to roll the weapon over on its side, which had to be done to conduct the same drill with the M203.

The modular design of the AG36 grenade launcher allows it to be easily changed to a stand-alone model (AG36/EGLM) with a sliding stock that could be detached for an even more compact weapon, or a model that could be mounted on the M4 carbine or M16 series of weapons (AG36-C).

Heckler & Koch Defense of the United States was awarded a production contract for a slightly modified version of the AG36-C on May 12, 2005, after the weapon was chosen from a competition of a number of commercial 40 mm designs. The new launcher has been designated the XM320 Grenade Launcher Module and is lighter and considered safer to use than the M203 it replaces. The design of the XM320 is such that it can be mounted on the M16A1 and M16A4 rifles, the M4 and M4A1 carbines, as well as the additional rifles and carbines that are under consideration for U.S. adoption such as the XM8 weapons system. The overall design of the XM320 makes it more accurate than the M203, and it has an attached ladder-type sight that does not have to be removed from the launcher to service it or to change from a host weapon to a stand-alone configuration. An additional reflex sight has been produced for the XM320 to increase the overall effectiveness of the weapon.

ENHANCED GRENADE LAUNCHER MODULE (EGLM)

To increase the overall value of the Special Operations Combat Assault Rifle (SCAR) weapon in both the heavy and light versions, a solicitation for a new 40 mm grenade launcher module was put out in addition to that of the rifle itself. The new grenade launcher was to replace the M203 with its leaf sight as well as the AN/PSQ-18A Grenade Launcher Sight, an infrared laser aiming device that allowed greater accuracy with the M203 during low light and night-time employment.

The new EGLM design will also be able to be upgraded with minimal changes to the basic launcher to take advantage of new programmable fuze technology as it becomes available as well as having a 25 percent greater probability of a hit as compared to the M203 with the AN/PSQ-18A. A stand-alone stock system is to be provided with the basic weapon, and the design must be able to chamber any length of 40 mm low-velocity round.

MILKOR MGL-140

The limitation for all of the under-barrel 40 mm grenade launcher designs is that they are single-shot weapons. The attempts to produce a semiautomatic or manually repeating mounted grenade launcher have failed due to the excessive weight of the weapon with the launcher attached. Stand-alone repeating 40 mm launchers have been attempted in the past with one design, the XM148 three-shot repeating launcher coming very close to adoption over that of the M79. The difficulty with the handheld repeating launchers has been one of accuracy and dependability; early repeating launchers had very poor round-to-round accuracy and were particularly sensitive to dirt and rough handling.

The South African–designed Milkor family of 40 mm repeating grenade launchers has proven itself a rugged and dependable weapon capable of standing up to severe conditions and remain functioning. The basic design of the Milkor grenade launcher is that of the revolver with a six-round cylinder. The weapon is lightweight, with a folding stock that allows it to be shoulder-fired or handheld.

The large ammunition cylinder of the Milkor weapon is spring-loaded. During the reloading process, the cylinder spring is wound, allowing the weapon to put out six rounds in three seconds. Operating at long ranges, the Milkor can put all of its rounds into the air before the first one has struck the target, saturating a target area twenty-two by eighty-two yards in size (twenty by sixty meters) with 40 mm grenades.

The rear section of the weapon swings out and away from the nonremovable cylinder for reloading. With the chambers filled and the cylinder spring wound, the rear of the weapon is rotated back and locked into place. When the double-action trigger is pulled, the firing pin is cocked and dropped on the chamber lined up with the barrel. Working independently of the trigger mechanism is the gas-operated cylinder system that advances the cylinder and locks the next chamber into alignment with the barrel. By using a manual override control, the operator can switch through the chambers in order to fire a particular round. Multiple types of ammunition can be loaded into the cylinder chambers at one time and be selected by the operator at will.

The sight used with the Milkor launchers is a reflex sight that can be quickly set to any range desired by the operator from 50 to 375 meters in 25-meter increments. A quadrant grid reticle on the sight allows the operator to quickly sight in on a target and adjust his point of aim with follow-on rounds without taking the weapon down from his shoulder.

After extensive testing, the U.S. Marine Corps adopted the Milkor MGL-140 in late October 2005 as the M32 Multiple Shot Grenade Launcher. The MGL-140 differed from other models of the grenade launcher in that its cylinder is long enough to accept 40 mm rounds 140 mm (5.5 inches) or less in length, which allows it to fire the standard family of U.S. 40 mm pyrotechnic ammunition. Modifications to the launcher to fit Marine Corps specifications included a special corrosion-resistant metal coating, attachment of MIL-STD-1913 rails to the top of the weapon and four sides of the barrel, as well as a thicker recoil pad and sliding (M4 carbine) style stock.

OBJECTIVE INDIVIDUAL COMBAT WEAPON (OICW)—XM29

Also known under the name Selectable Assault Battle Rifle (SABR) the OICW has been considered one of the most ambitious small arms programs ever undertaken by the U.S. military since the SPIW program of the 1960s. The OICW is the most advanced version to date of the concept of combining point and area target capabilities into a single weapon.

Prior to the completion of the Advanced Combat Rifle trials, the U.S. Army Infantry School at Fort Benning released their *Small Arms System 2000* paper, an analysis and prediction of what would be required for an advanced infantry weapons family. The document centered on the idea that the advancement of small arms had reached a developmental plateau. Not even the upcoming caseless and flechette technologies that were being examined as part of the ACR program would make it significantly easier for the soldier to hit his target in a combat situation.

The proposition from the Infantry School was that the only way to increase the hit probability of the weapons in a soldier's hands was to include the use of explosive projectiles and advanced sighting systems. With the use of smart fuze technology, an explosive projectile could be programmed to detonate in the area of a target, spraying it with fragmentation and blast effects rather than striking it with a single kinetic projectile such as a bullet. This would be a method of increasing the footprint of the projectile's effect. Rather than the idea of even a series of rapidly fired projectiles moving downrange in a swarm (the salvo and controlled burst concepts) to increase the chances of striking a target, an explosive projectile would only have to get near a target in order to spray it with hundreds of fragments. The burst of kinetic energy (penetrating) projectiles would cover an area only a few inches wide, less than a few feet at most, at one hundred meters while a single explosive projectile could cover an area— have a footprint—of at least several meters at the same range.

The use of such explosive projectiles would require a computerized sighting and programming system to set the fuze of the explosive rounds for the range to a specific target. This would have to be a very advanced sighting system in order to allow the soldier a quick and simple way to program the rounds he would be firing in the heat of combat.

Following shortly after the publication of the *Small Arms System 2000* paper, the U.S. Army Training and Doctrine Center (TRADOC) released their own paper in support of the concept. Released in 1989, the *Small Arms Master Plan* (SAMP) suggested that an entire family of new infantry weapons be produced to arm the soldiers of the twenty-first century. These "Objective" weapons included a personal defense weapon (OPDW) to arm support personnel, a crew-served weapon (OCSW) to succeed the existing heavy machine guns and machine grenade launchers, and the Individual Combat Weapon (OICW) that would be used to arm the combat soldier.

The new objective weapons would make use of the newest developments in computer technologies for both their sighting systems and the ammunition that they employed. Optical and electro-optical advancements would also have to be included in the development of the sighting systems for the OICW and OCSW in order for them to be truly day and night capable. To ensure that the new weapons would be lightweight for portability yet as strong as possible to survive the rigors of the combat zone, composite materials, polymers, and advanced alloys would be included in their construction as well as the most up-to-date principles of small arms operation.

The extremely ambitious ideas of the OICW and OCSW put forward on the pages of the SAMP included timelines for the development, production, and fielding of the new weapons systems as well as what their physical parameters should be and what they should cost. The weight and cost projections for the new weapons were far too ambitious for any practical results to meet them, much the same as had happened with the SPIW program more than twenty-five years earlier.

During the early part of the 1990s, a number of proposals for the OICW were examined in studies conducted by both military agencies and industrial groups. The basic layout of the OICW finally centered on a bullpup layout for the primary component, a magazine-fed 20 mm semiautomatic shoulder-fired cannon. The close-in defense mechanism of the OICW would be a conventional 5.56 mm round fired from a select-fire weapon that would mount underneath the high-explosive launcher. The over-under design was settled on after a number of layouts were examined and tested, including a side-by-side version that had the 20 mm and 5.56-caliber weapons lying parallel to each other, unified by a single trigger mechanism.

The development of the various components of the OICW, the fire control system, 20 mm ammunition and fuze, 5.56 mm weapon, and 20 mm launcher, would require a consortium of companies to bring all of the technologies required together to complete the project. The leading consortium varied its member companies over several years but settled on a general organization of four primary manufacturers. Providing the expertise to produce the 20 mm ammunition as well as the overall systems integration of the OICW would be Alliant Techsystems, with Heckler & Koch designing the basic weapon, Brashear LP developing the fire control system, and Octec the tracker.

The damage from the explosive 20 mm projectile would not come primarily from the energetic filler of the round but from the fragmentation of the shell body. The maximum efficiency of a fragmentation round came from being able to detonate it in an airburst over a target. With a shell detonating over a target rather than impacting with the ground, the majority of the fragments would spray down on the target area rather than just spend themselves in the dirt. Obtaining the airburst effect meant that the projectile had to be able to detect the range it had traveled from the point of launch, be programmed with the distance to the desired target, and the operator had to know the exact distance to the target in the first place.

The precise control of the point of explosion for the OICW high-explosive round was accomplished with the development of an electronic fuze that could sense the rotation of the projectile and count the number of revolutions as it flew through the air. Once a set number of revolutions were reached, the fuze would detonate the main charge, setting off the projectile as an airburst. The fuze was a major development of the weapon system, making all of the desired characteristics of the OICW possible.

The fire control system of the OICW project would set the fuze of a chambered round electronically just prior to it being fired. A laser range finder in the fire control system would detect the range to the target at a command from the operator, displaying the distance on an internal screen. By simply placing a red dot on the desired target and pressing a control, the computer system inside the fire control would detect and display the range, communicate the information to the fuze of the chambered round, and make the calculations necessary to give an adjusted aiming point on the visual display.

Looking into the sight, the operator of the OICW would see the range to the target and a red-dot-adjusted aiming point. All that would then have to be done is place the red dot over the target and decide to fire or adjust the detonation point of the high-explosive projectile. Pressing a plus or minus button with the trigger finger would allow the operator to add or subtract distance from the range set in the fuze by the computer. If the target was inside a room, pressing the plus button twice would add two meters to the distance the fuze would travel before detonation. If the target was in front of a wall but behind cover, pressing the minus button would take a meter off the range of the fuze setting. Pulling the trigger would then be all it would take to send the high-explosive projectile downrange, where it would detonate a few meters above the ground, sending out a spray of lethal fragments capable of penetrating body armor or a helmet. The rounds could also be set to point-detonate, exploding on contact with a target.

In the case of a close-combat situation, the operator could switch to the kinetic energy (5.56 mm) component of the OICW by flipping a selector switch. If desired, the 5.56 mm weapon could be detached from the 20 mm launcher and used as a stand-alone weapon for personal defense. Batteries to drive the complex electronics of the OICW would be contained in the buttstock of the 20 mm weapon.

Overall, the OICW system was intended to have a five-times-greater combat effectiveness at more than twice the range of the existing M16/M4/M203 weapons combination. The final designs of the OICW never reached their desired goals. The weapons system was too heavy, too large, and the lethality of the 20 mm projectile could not match what was needed to defeat the target. The overall price of the weapons system was also becoming a major factor with a 20 mm airburst round costing $25 each and the weapon and sights system reaching $10,000 per unit and rising.

The OICW was redesignated the XM29 Integrated Airburst Weapon, and production was suspended in late 2005. The year before, the decision had been made to develop the components of the XM29 as separate weapons systems. The 5.56 mm kinetic energy weapon was spun off to become the (OICW Increment I) XM8 rifle. The caliber of the grenade launcher was increased to 25 mm in order to aid lethality and increase commonality with other developing weapons systems, and it was spun off into the (OICW Increment II) XM25 airburst assault weapon. Once the XM8 and XM25 weapons were perfected, they would be combined as the (OICW Increment III) XM29 and its development resumed.

XM25 AIRBURST ASSAULT WEAPON

To eliminate some of the weight problems that caused the suspension of the XM29 Integrated Airburst Weapon, the stand-alone 25 mm XM25 airburst weapon was built of some very exotic materials that had not been used in a U.S. military small arm before. The receiver and stock of the bullpup weapon were built of carbon-fiber-reinforced composite materials, and the barrel was made of titanium with a rifled steel liner.

The increase in caliber from 20 to 25 millimeters gave an increased lethality to the projectile from the larger body. Even making the original 20 mm projectile from heavy metal such as tungsten could not give it the lethality envelope required by the military. The increased mass of the 25 mm projectile could supply the basic material needed to form enough fragments of a sufficient size to cover the burst area with a lethal spray.

The basic round of the XM25 shares the same projectile and fuze technology that is being developed for the XM307 Objective Crew Served Weapon but in a shorter and lighter package resulting in less recoil to the shoulder-fired XM25. An entire family of 25 mm rounds for both weapons is being planned, including the primary high-explosive airburst round, a high-explosive armor-piercing shell, a nonlethal impact round, an antipersonnel flechette shell, a door-breaching

The author holding a mockup of the XM25 airburst weapon with a round of 25 mm ammunition in his left hand.
Kevin Dockery

explosive round, and a fuel-air-explosive thermobaric projectile. The bulk of this ammunition is adaptations of existing designs to fit the smaller envelope of the 25 mm projectile. It is the air-bursting round that required the greatest development in addition to that done of the original OICW/XM29 project.

The revolution-counting fuze technology has proven itself the most effective means of detonating the projectile with a predictable airburst. It has been shown that at ranges under 2.5 kilometers, the turns-counting electronic system is less sensitive to round-to-round variations in muzzle velocity than a time fuze would be.

The fuze is activated on firing after having received its command programming from the fire control system. As a backup mode, there is a point detonating function for the fuze in case it is used without the fire control input, such as in the case of a dead battery. Additionally, there is a self-destruct feature that renders the projectile safe after a set time delay.

To program the fuze requires the use of the XM104 target acquisition/fire control system. The overall hit probability of the XM25 as well as the lethality of the ammunition it fires will be greatly increased by the use of the XM104 computerized sight, which is also one of the most complicated portions of the weapon to be developed. The sight will integrate a thermal-powered optical system for direct viewing of the target with a laser range finder, compass with an up or down angle detection system, and internal display with the ballistic computer and electronic fuze setter.

The controls used to initiate the laser range finder, select the sight modes, and to add or subtract a set distance to the fuze setter are a series of small buttons at the front of the trigger guard. Ejection of the spent cartridge case is selectable by the operator with a dust cover closing off the unused ejection window. The ejection system combined with the completely ambidextrous controls makes the XM25 easily able to be fired from either shoulder.

The detachable single-row magazine at the rear of the weapon holds six 25 mm rounds that can be quickly fired through the semiautomatic action of the launcher. This allows the operator to place multiple rounds on a downrange target without having to reload or unshoulder the weapon. A special recoil-mitigation system within the action of the weapon aids in a quick operator recovery between shots.

As planned, the XM25 provides a 300 to 500 percent increase in hit probability over existing shoulder-fired weapons systems out to a range of 500 meters. It is considered particularly well-suited for urban combat, where the enemy is often behind cover in the form of walls or inside rooms. By being able to set the projectile to within a few meters of an exact point of detonation, the airburst capability of the XM25 can defeat a target well beyond the maximum point target capability of a 40 mm M203 or XM320 grenade launcher. Present plans are to issue two XM25 systems per infantry squad, not replacing the 40 mm grenade launchers already organic to the unit but instead augmenting their firepower.

STK SQUAD SUPPORT WEAPON

The idea of the modernized point and area fire weapon making use of modern electronics has proven an interesting one to more organizations that just the U.S. military. In Singapore, an innovative company, Singapore Technologies Kinetics, has approached the problem of developing such a weapon, but without resorting to a new caliber of ammunition. The success of the 40 mm low-velocity rounds has been well proven all over the world, and several companies in Singapore produce their own versions of both 40 mm grenade launchers and the ammunition. As the fuze technology matures for a dependable airburst round, a new launcher would need to have the capacity to adapt to that new technology. That was what ST Kinetics planned into the concept of their new weapon.

The ST Kinetics weapon is the Squad Support Weapon (SSW), and it is intended for military operations in urban terrain (MOUT). It is a dual-caliber weapon, primarily a grenade launcher but with a built-in select-fire weapon for close-in defense of the gunner. The semiautomatic launcher holds four 40 mm grenades in a tubular magazine that can be reloaded by the operator with loose rounds to top up the magazine during a lull in a combat situation.

The concept weapon already has the fire control technology built into the system to utilize 40 mm grenades with an electronic fuze system. But it can also be fielded with the standard family of high-explosive grenades and still be more effective and accurate than standard grenade launchers. The effectiveness of the launcher comes from its electronic fire control system (FCS) that is a miniaturized version of those used on large crew-served weapons. The FCS combines a ballistic computer with a display screen and laser range finder to increase the first-round hit probability of the grenade.

Operating much as the XM25 airburst weapon is said to, the gunner of the SSW places the red-dot reticle on the display screen of the sight onto the target and triggers the laser range finder. Once the distance has been determined and displayed on the screen, a secondary aiming point is shown, calculated according to the round being fired, the local conditions, and the range and angle to the target. The operator then has to just place the aiming point on the target and pull the trigger. Up to four grenades can be fired in rapid succession should the situation warrant it.

For close-in defense, up to about 200 meters if necessary, a 5.7×28 mm weapon is also part of the SSW. If desired by a customer, the PDW portion of the SSW can also be chambered for the German 4.6×30 mm round. Either caliber is fed from a twenty-round magazine into the PDW, which is operated with the same trigger mechanism as that of the grenade launcher.

The ST Kinetics weapon is a conceptual design; an operational model is expected to be ready for testing in 2009 or 2010. Variations on the basic design include a magazine-fed 40 mm grenade launcher and a stand-alone launcher that does not incorporate a PDW weapon as part of the design.

FN HIGH-IMPULSE WEAPON SYSTEM

As a means of increasing the range and payload for a handheld 40 mm grenade launcher, Fabrique Nationale de Herstal has adapted a shoulder-fired launcher to use the high-velocity family of 40 mm grenades. Developed in the early 1960s for helicopter-mounted grenade launchers, the high-velocity 40 mm round utilizes the standard high-low pressure system to launch its projectile, but it has a much larger charge of propellant to launch a much heavier projectile than those used in the M79 or M203 grenade launchers.

The low-velocity 40 mm ammunition is identified as the 40×46 mm SR (semirimmed) round. The high-velocity grenades have a longer cartridge case to keep the much higher-pressure rounds from being chambered in a standard shoulder-fired launcher. These grenades are identified as the 40×53 mm SR rounds and launch a more than half-pound projectile at around three times the muzzle velocity of the standard 40 mm rounds. The operating pressure of the high-velocity 40 mm ammunition would normally shatter a standard grenade launcher. And the recoil to the operator would cause serious injury. But the FN weapon, also called the High Velocity 40 (HV-40) as well as the more formal High-Impulse Weapon System, is designed to fire both the high- and low-velocity family of grenades from the shoulder and with no modifications to the launcher.

By allowing the barrel to move

A cutaway specimen of a high-velocity 40 mm grenade. The very thick walls of the cartridge case can be seen, surrounding the central high-pressure chamber.
Kevin Dockery

back for a long length against increasing resistance, the recoil of firing a heavy projectile is spread out over a much longer time than normal, mitigating its effect on the operator. The action of the HV-40 is a simple bolt-action mechanism with the breech located near the center point of the receiver. When the trigger is pulled, the entire barrel assembly moves to the back of the receiver. Recoil is still very heavy when compared to a standard 40 mm grenade launcher, but the maximum range of the high-velocity ammunition is 2,200 meters with a point target effective range of 600 meters.

The overall accuracy of the HV-40 is considered excellent, enough so that the weapon is being developed further. Additional design work on the stock system will aid in reducing the severe but manageable recoil of the prototype weapon. Firing the HV-40 with standard low-velocity grenades was simply a matter of chambering the ammunition; no other modifications had to be done to the weapon.

SEVENTY-SIX MILLIMETER URBAN WARFARE WEAPON

The long barrel movement system of recoil mitigation has also been used in a much larger weapon, the Lacroix Samourai 76 mm Urban Warfare Weapon from France and marketed by FN of Belgium. The Lacroix launcher puts out a three-inch projectile from a shoulder-fired weapon with none of the backblast or other recoil-reducing methods that would prevent it from being used in an enclosed area. The recoil of the more than three-pound projectile is absorbed into the 600 millimeter rearward travel of the barrel as it moves against increasing resistance in the receiver tracks. When the barrel reaches the end of its travel, the empty cartridge case is automatically ejected.

The 76.2 mm Lacroix launcher being held by the author.
Kevin Dockery

The fin-stabilized round of the Lacroix is still being developed but has room for a considerable warhead. The projectile can carry a payload weight of 0.65 kilograms, sufficient for a large blast-type warhead with fragmentation or a high-explosive armor-piercing charge.

In spite of the recoil mitigation system, the Lacroix weapon has a heavy recoil and requires some consideration when it is fired. The operator must put his weight behind the weapon, leaning in to the recoil; otherwise it is more than capable of knocking even a large-sized man off his feet. The present configuration of the weapon cannot be fired from the prone position without the possibility of injury to the shooter. In spite of the present limitations to the system, it has shown considerable promise as an area or point target weapon and is being further developed. It is also known as the 76 mm High-Impulse Weapon System (76-HIWS).

The XM140 RAW in firing position.
Brunswick Manufacturing

RIFLEMAN'S ASSAULT WEAPON

Developed by Brunswick Defense, the Rifleman's Assault Weapon or RAW is a unique rocket-propelled spherical grenade that carries a large explosive charge. Fired from a small launcher that attaches to the muzzle and bayonet lug of an M16-series rifle, the RAW is spin-stabilized, giving it a very flat trajectory for its size. The rocket has a straight, line-of-sight flight path out to several hundred meters while having a relatively small launch signature and no felt recoil to the operator.

The RAW rifle launcher frame is a disposable launcher that slips over the flash hider on the end of an M16 rifle and is secured in place by a latch that snaps over the bayonet lug. The 140 mm–diameter spherical warhead and short rocket body hangs on a minimum-length launching rail underneath the frame of the weapon. The rifle can continue to be fired with the RAW launcher in place with no serious effects on either the launcher or the rifle. Using tracers, the host rifle can be used to indicate the impact point for the RAW munition out to a range of about 200 meters.

To fire the RAW, the safety/arming switch on the center of the launcher frame is set to the fire position. The next round that is fired from the rifle will also launch the RAW rocket. The forward support of the launcher frame taps off a small amount of the propellant gases that would otherwise escape from the muzzle of the weapon. The gases are guided into the firing mechanism on the frame of the RAW, where they impinge on the firing pin that in turn ignites the rocket motor on the munition. A turbine assembly bleeds off some of the rocket exhaust to spin up the projectile and stabilize it for flight. There is very little backblast from the launch, and a small shield on the launcher frame protects the operator from any of the rocket's exhaust gases.

A general warhead for the RAW is a high-explosive squash head (HESH), where the payload is a large charge of plastic explosive. When the projectile strikes the target, the warhead flattens out, pancaking itself against the surface of the target. When the fuze at the base of the warhead detonates the explosive charge, the blast can cause spalling on armor plate, a condition where the shock wave of the explosion drives a section of the armor on the inside of the plate to break off and go flying into the compartment of a vehicle or bunker at high speed.

The more common target for the RAW rocket has been against walls during urban combat. The RAW warhead can blast a hole over a foot wide in a thick concrete wall or an even larger hole though a brick or cinder block wall. This makes the weapon useful for standoff breaching of a target, one of the reasons the RAW was adopted by the U.S. Marine Corps.

The fuze on the RAW warhead arms through the actions of spin and the setback of firing. A mechanical delay inside of the fuze mechanism retards the arming procedure until the round has traveled about thirty meters from the point of launch. This delay helps ensure the safety of the operator from the blast of his own projectile. For direct fire, the RAW has an effective range of about 200 meters. For that type of firing, the standard sights of the host weapon or any attached optical or electronic sights can be used to aim the RAW rocket. When held to a high angle and fired indirectly at a target, the RAW rocket can travel up to 2,000 meters with some accuracy. Very little special training is necessary for an infantry soldier to be able to use the RAW weapon, as the system operates from the standard service weapon with no modifications.

SCORPION

A second version of a rifle-mounted rocket weapon was the Scorpion Multipurpose Individual Munition produced by the McDonnell Douglas Corporation in the mid-1980s. The advantage of such rifle-launched rockets is that they would have little recoil and could be employed with relatively little training. Such weapons are issued as a round of ammunition and given out to soldiers as determined by their immediate leadership or unit standard operating procedures. The rocket propulsion system for such weapons allows a significant warhead to be fired with little or no effect on the host weapon. That allows a rifleman to remain a rifleman at all times while also giving him the capability of taking on a much larger target than he otherwise would be capable of, the classic effect of a force-multiplier weapon.

The unique aspect of the Scorpion weapon is that the launch tube would mount underneath the barrel of an M16-series rifle in much the same manner as an M203 grenade launcher. The fiberglass tube is a disposable, one-shot weapon and contains its own firing mechanism for the Scorpion rocket munition. The rifle acts as a support to hold the Scorpion when it is being fired as well as supplying the sights of the host rifle to aim the rocket. Tracers fired from the rifle also act as spotting rounds out to about 300 meters. When the track of the tracers impacted on the desired target, the Scorpion rocket could be fired, and the operator could be fairly certain of a hit.

To develop a repeating 40 mm grenade launcher to increase the firepower available to the infantry man, this 40 mm pump-action weapon was made during the Vietnam War for the use of special operations forces. The rare weapon has been put back into limited production, not just for collectors but also with an eye to supplying the military with a "future" weapon that is a resurrection of the past.

Kevin Dockery

The exhaust ports for Scorpion's rocket propulsion are located at the front of the rocket motor, angling off to either side of the munition itself. The angled ports allow the munition to be launched from a relatively short tube attached to a rifle while not putting the operator at any risk from the rocket exhaust. Slots on both sides of the Scorpion's launch tube clear the rocket exhaust as it leaves the weapon. Spring-loaded fins at the base of the round extend when the munition has exited the launcher to maintain stability during flight. Once fired, the launch tube to the Scorpion is removed and discarded by the operator. A carrying tube has been designed for transporting the Scorpion by a sling that the operator can place over his shoulder. The weapon is able to be quickly removed from the carrying tube and attached to a host weapon for use in well under a minute.

The high-explosive warhead of the Scorpion could blast a hole through a twelve-inch-thick brick wall or an eight-inch-thick reinforced concrete wall. Several rounds could blast a man-sized hole through a normal building wall, and the minimal backblast of the rocket allowed it to be fired from inside an enclosure such as the room of a building.

■ Area Weapons Data ■

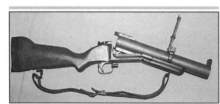

The M79 grenade launcher, its barrel open for loading.
Kevin Dockery

NAME—M79 grenade launcher
COMMON NAMES—Thumper
CALIBER—40×46 mm SR
OVERALL LENGTH—28.78 inches (73.1 cm)
BARREL LENGTH—14 inches (35.7 cm)
RIFLING (TYPE and TWIST)—6-groove, right-hand twist, 1 turn in 48 inches (122 cm)
LOAD—M406 high-explosive fragmentation
ROUND WEIGHT—0.5 lb. (0.23 kg)
PROJECTILE DIAMETER—1.626 inches (4.13 cm)
PROJECTILE WEIGHT—0.38 lb. (0.17 kg)
MUZZLE VELOCITY—247 fps (76 m/s)
PROJECTILE EFFECT—Ground burst blast and fragmentation
AREA OF EFFECT—5.5 yards (5 m)
WEIGHT (EMPTY)—5.95 lbs. (2.7 kg)
WEIGHT (LOADED)—6.45 lbs. (2.93 kg)
SIGHTS—Open, leaf-type, square-notch/blade, adjustable 75 to 375 meters in 25 meter increments
SIGHT RADIUS—6.14 inches (15.6 cm)

MINIMUM RANGE—45 to 90 feet (14 to 27 m)
EFFECTIVE RANGE—383 yards (350 m)
MAXIMUM RANGE—437 yards (400 m)
OPERATION—Manual break-open
TYPE OF FIRE—Single shot
RATE OF FIRE—6 rpm
FEED DEVICE—Single round
FEED DEVICE WEIGHT (LOADED)—0.5 lb. (0.23 kg)
MANUFACTURER—Various; primary military contractor TRW
SERVICE—Previous service with all U.S. military forces, found worldwide in some military and paramilitary forces
STATUS—Obsolescent
REFERENCES—Dockery, Kevin, *Weapons of the Navy SEALs*

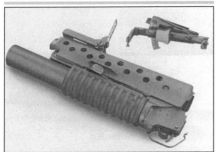

The M203 40 mm grenade launcher unmounted. The quadrant sight is at the upper right corner. *Colt Manufacturing*

NAME—M203 grenade launcher; M203A1 grenade launcher

CALIBER—40×46 mm SR

OVERALL LENGTH—15.3 inches (38.9 cm); M203A1 SOPMOD—12.3 inches (31.2 cm)

24.7 inches (62.8 cm)—Stand-alone mount with launcher with stock collapsed

28 inches (71.1 cm)—Stand-alone mount with launcher with stock extended

BARREL LENGTH—12 inches (35.7 cm); M203A1 SOPMOD—9 inches (22.9 cm)

RIFLING (TYPE and TWIST)—6-groove, right-hand twist, 1 turn in 48 inches (122 cm)

LOAD—M406 high-explosive fragmentation

ROUND WEIGHT—0.51 lb. (0.23 kg)

PROJECTILE DIAMETER—1.626 inches (4.13 cm)

PROJECTILE WEIGHT—0.38 lb. (0.17 kg)

MUZZLE VELOCITY—235 fps (71 m/s); 217 fps (66 m/s)—M203A1 SOPMOD

PROJECTILE EFFECT—Ground burst blast and fragmentation

AREA OF EFFECT—5.5 yards (5 m)

WEIGHT (EMPTY)—3.60 lbs. (1.63 kg); 2.81 lbs. (1.27 kg)—M203A1

WEIGHT (MOUNTED AND LOADED)—12.64 lbs. (5.73 kg) w/loaded M16A1, sight assemblies, and 40 mm M406; M203A1 SOPMOD—9.83 lbs. (4.46 kg) with loaded M4 carbine, sight assemblies, and 40 mm M406; stand-alone mount with carbine stock—6.6 lbs. (3.0 kg) with M406 round

TYPE OF MOUNT—M16 family of shoulder arms, stand-alone mount and mounts for additional weapons available

WEIGHT OF MOUNT—M16A2—8.54 lbs. (3.87 kg) with 30 rounds M855 ball

M4 carbine—6.23 lbs. (3.05 kg) with 30 rounds M855 ball

Stand-alone mount with carbine stock—3.11 lbs. (1.41 kg)

SIGHTS—Two sights issued with grenade launcher: open, folding ladder-type short range, indicator post, adjustable, graduated to 250 meters, secured to upper handguard; and open, folding long-range quadrant aperture/post adjustable graduated to 400 meters, secured to carrying handle of weapon

1.10 lbs. (0.50 kg)—Quadrant sight weight

0.35 lb. (0.16 kg)—Leaf sight weight

MINIMUM RANGE—45 to 90 feet (14 to 27 m)

EFFECTIVE RANGE—383 yards (350 m)

MAXIMUM RANGE—437 yards (400 m)

OPERATION—Manual pump action

TYPE OF FIRE—Single shot

RATE OF FIRE—6 to 8 rpm

FEED DEVICE—Single round

FEED DEVICE WEIGHT (LOADED)—0.51 lb. (0.23 kg)

MANUFACTURER—Colt Manufacturing Company, Inc.

SERVICE—In service with all U.S. military forces, found worldwide in over thirty military organizations

STATUS—In production

REFERENCES—Dockery, Kevin, *Weapons of the Navy SEALs*

COMMENTS—M203A1 has adapter rail and quick-release bracket for mounting on M4 carbine. M203A1 SOPMOD has 9-inch barrel and mounting brackets.

The XM320 40mm grenade launcher in place on an M4A1 carbine. *Kevin Dockery*

NAME—XM320 grenade launcher module (GLM)

CALIBER—40×46mm SR

OVERALL LENGTH—13.70 inches (34.8cm)

BARREL LENGTH—11.02 inches (28cm)

RIFLING (TYPE and TWIST)—6-groove, right-hand twist, 1 turn in 47.2 inches (120cm)

LOAD—M433 high-explosive dual purpose

ROUND WEIGHT—0.51lb. (0.23kg)

PROJECTILE DIAMETER—1.626 inches (4.13cm)

PROJECTILE WEIGHT—0.39lb. (0.18kg)

MUZZLE VELOCITY—259fps (79m/s)

PROJECTILE EFFECT—Penetrates 2 inches (5.1cm) of steel with fragmentation around the point of impact approximately equal to the M406 HE rounds' effects

AREA OF EFFECT—5.5 yards (5m) burst radius

WEIGHT (EMPTY)—3.30lbs. (1.5kg)

WEIGHT (LOADED)—3.81lbs. (1.73kg) w/M406 40mm grenade

WEIGHT (MOUNTED)—10.04lbs. (4.55kg) w/M4A1 Carbine, 30rds M855 ball, rear sight/carrying handle assembly, and M406 40mm grenade

TYPE OF MOUNT—M16-series rifle or carbine equipped with MIL-STD-1913 rail on underside of forearm

SIGHTS—Open, folding ladder-type sight on launcher, indicator/post, adjustable 50 to 350 meters in 50-meter increments

SIGHT RADIUS—5.83 inches (14.8cm)

MINIMUM RANGE—45 to 90 feet (14 to 27m)

EFFECTIVE RANGE—383 yards (350m)

MAXIMUM RANGE—437 yards (400m)

OPERATION—Manual, side-opening

TYPE OF FIRE—Single shot

RATE OF FIRE—6 to 8rpm

FEED DEVICE—Single round

FEED DEVICE WEIGHT (LOADED)—0.51lb. (0.23kg)

MANUFACTURER—Heckler & Koch Defense

SERVICE—Entering service with U.S. military

STATUS—In production

REFERENCES—Company literature, PEO Soldier Portfolio

The Milkor MGL MK1L 40mm grenade launcher. *Kevin Dockery*

NAME—Milkor MGL, Mk1L; MGL-140

COMMON NAMES—M32 Multiple Shot Grenade Launcher; MGL-140

CALIBER—40×46mm SR, maximum round length 5.5 inches (14.0cm)

OVERALL LENGTH—
26 inches (66.5cm) with stock folded
27 inches (68.6cm) with stock folded (MGL-140)
30 inches (76.5cm) with stock extended
31 inches (78.7cm) with stock extended (MGL-140)

BARREL LENGTH—14 inches (35.7cm)

RIFLING (TYPE and TWIST)—Progressive twist, final rate 1 turn in 48 inches (122cm)

LOAD—M406 high-explosive fragmentation

ROUND WEIGHT—0.5lb. (0.23kg)

PROJECTILE DIAMETER—1.626 inches (4.13cm)

PROJECTILE WEIGHT—0.38lb. (0.17kg)

MUZZLE VELOCITY—247fps (76m/s)

PROJECTILE EFFECT—Ground burst blast and fragmentation

AREA OF EFFECT—5.5 yards (5 m)

WEIGHT (EMPTY)—13.2 lbs. (5.99 kg)

WEIGHT (LOADED)—16.2 lbs. (7.35 kg)

SIGHTS—Trijicon Armson Occluded Eye Gunsight (OEG) collimating aim point
    4 MIL-STD-1913 rail sections on top, bottom, and sides of barrel (MGL-140)

SIGHT POWER—1/1 red-dot reticle

MINIMUM RANGE—45 to 90 feet (14 to 27 m)

EFFECTIVE RANGE—383 yards (350 m)

MAXIMUM RANGE—437 yards (400 m)

OPERATION—Manual spring-loaded revolver

TYPE OF FIRE—Semiautomatic

RATE OF FIRE—6 rounds in 3 seconds maximum; 18 rpm sustained fire

FEED DEVICE—Six-round nonremovable cylinder

FEED DEVICE WEIGHT (LOADED)—3 lbs. (1.36 kg)—6 rounds

MANUFACTURER—Milkor, South Africa/Milkor USA

SERVICE—U.S. Marine Corps as M32, international military use

STATUS—In production

REFERENCES—Company literature

COMMENTS—Can saturate an area 66×196 feet (20×60 meters) with six 40 mm rounds in three seconds.

The Milkor grenade launcher with the rear of the weapon swung open for loading. *Kevin Dockery*

One of the early operational OICW prototypes. *Kevin Dockery*

NAME—Objective Individual Combat Weapon (OICW)

OTHER NAMES—XM29 Integrated Airburst Weapon System, Selectable Assault Battle Rifle (SABR)

CALIBER—
    5.56×45 mm (kinetic energy: KE)
    20×28 mm B (high-explosive: HE)

LOAD—M855 (5.56 KE)

AVAILABLE LOADS—
    20 mm high-explosive airburst
    20 mm target practice

WEIGHT (LOADED)—18 lbs. (8.2 kg) with 20 rounds 5.56 and 6 rounds 20 mm; 15 lbs. (6.8 kg)—Target weight

SIGHTS—Optical fire control system with laser range finder, video, compass, tracker, ballistic computer, and fuze programmer, with red-dot reticle; backup iron sights

SIGHT POWER—Up to 6×optical magnification

MINIMUM RANGE—55 yards (50 m) (20 mm HE)

EFFECTIVE RANGE—
    328 yards (300 m) (5.56 mm KE)
    547 yards (500 m) (20 mm HE)
    1,094 yards (1000 m)—Target range (20 mm HE)

OPERATION—Gas (5.56 mm KE)

TYPE OF FIRE—
    Semiautomatic (20 mm HE)
    Select fire, semi-, and 2-round burst (5.56 mm KE)

RATE OF FIRE—
    85 rpm—5.56 mm KE weapon
    10 rpm—20 mm HE weapon

FEED DEVICE—
20- or 30-round removable box magazine
(5.56 mm KE)
6-round removable box magazine
(20 mm HE)
MANUFACTURER—Heckler & Koch/Alliant
Techsystems/Brashear LP
SERVICE—Evaluation
STATUS—Development suspended
REFERENCES—Company literature

A display mockup of the M25 airburst weapon. *Kevin Dockery*

NAME—XM25 airburst weapon system
CALIBER—25 × 39 mm B
AVAILABLE LOADS—
High-explosive air-bursting
Antipersonnel (flechette)
Nonlethal (blunt impact)
Training/target practice
Armor-piercing
Door-breaching
WEIGHT (LOADED)—About 14 lbs. (6.35 kg)
SIGHTS—XM104 target acquisition/fire
control with thermal powered direct-view
optical viewing system laser range finder,
compass, ballistic computer, and fuze setter
SIGHT POWER—2× optical and thermal
magnification
EFFECTIVE RANGE—547 to 766 yards
(500 to 700 m)
TYPE OF FIRE—Semiautomatic
FEED DEVICE—6-round box magazine
MANUFACTURER—Heckler & Koch
(weapon), L-3 Brashear (fire control), Alliant
Techsystems (ammunition)
SERVICE—Evaluation

STATUS—Developmental
REFERENCES—Company literature

A conceptual mockup of the SK Technologies Squad
Support Weapon. *Kevin Dockery*

NAME—SKT Squad Support Weapon
COMMON NAMES—SSW
CALIBER—40 × 46 mm SR and 5.7 × 28 mm
OVERALL LENGTH—27.76 inches (70.5 cm)
LOAD—M406 high-explosive fragmentation
(40 mm); PDW LOAD—SS190 ball
ROUND WEIGHT—0.5 lb. (0.23 kg) (40 mm)
PROJECTILE DIAMETER—1.626 inches
(4.13 cm) (40 mm); PDW bullet diameter—
0.220 inch (5.59 mm)
PROJECTILE WEIGHT—0.38 lb. (0.17 kg)
(40 mm); PDW bullet weight—31 grains (2.01 g)
MUZZLE VELOCITY—247 fps (76 m/s)
(40 mm); PDW muzzle velocity—2,345 fps
(715 m/s); PDW muzzle energy—378 ft./lb.
(513 J)
PROJECTILE EFFECT—Ground burst blast
and fragmentation
AREA OF EFFECT—5.5 yards (5 m)
WEIGHT (EMPTY)—11.25 lbs. (5.10 kg)
WEIGHT (LOADED)—13.67 lbs. (6.2 kg) with 4
rounds M406 HE and 20 rounds 5.7 mm
SS190 ball
SIGHTS—Electronic fire control system with
laser range finder and ballistic computer with
automatic chambered ammunition
recognition function, red-dot reticle; battery
life 168 hours (planned)
SIGHT POWER—1/1 reflex
MINIMUM RANGE—45 to 90 feet (14 to 27 m)
(40 mm)

EFFECTIVE RANGE—383 yards (350 m) (40 mm); 219 yards (200 m) (5.7 mm)

MAXIMUM RANGE—437 yards (400 m) (40 mm)

TYPE OF FIRE—Semiautomatic (40 mm); selective fire, semi-, and full automatic (5.7 mm)

RATE OF FIRE—8 to 12 rpm (40 mm)

FEED DEVICE—4-round tubular magazine (40 mm); removable 20-round box magazine (5.7 mm)

FEED DEVICE WEIGHT (EMPTY)—0.15 lb. (0.070 kg) (5.7 mm)

FEED DEVICE WEIGHT (LOADED)—
2 lbs. (0.91 kg)—4 rounds M406 (40 mm)
0.42 lb. (0.19 kg)—20 rounds (5.7 mm)

MANUFACTURER—ST Kinetics, Singapore

SERVICE—None

STATUS—Conceptual model

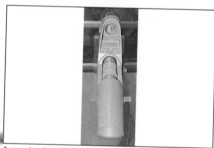

A rear view into the control panel and unusual 40 mm magazine of the SKT SSW. *Kevin Dockery*

REFERENCES—Company literature

The HV-40 mm grenade launcher. *Kevin Dockery*

NAME—HV-40 mm grenade launcher

CALIBER—40×53 mm SR and 40×46 mm SR

OVERALL LENGTH—31 inches (78.7 cm)

LOAD—M384 high-explosive fragmentation

ROUND WEIGHT—0.76 lb. (0.34 kg)

PROJECTILE DIAMETER—1.626 inches (4.13 cm)

PROJECTILE WEIGHT—0.54 lb. (0.24 kg)

MUZZLE VELOCITY—722 fps (220 m/s)

PROJECTILE EFFECT—Ground burst blast and fragmentation

AREA OF EFFECT—16-yard (15m) burst radius

WEIGHT (EMPTY)—17 lbs (7.71 kg)—Planned weight reduction to 15 lbs

WEIGHT (LOADED)—17.76 lbs. (8.06 kg) with 1 round M384 HE

SIGHTS—Proposed day/night reflex sight with tritium (beta) element

MINIMUM RANGE—59 to 118 feet (18 to 36 m)

EFFECTIVE RANGE—656 yards (600 m)

MAXIMUM RANGE—2,187 yards (2000 m)

OPERATION—Manual bolt action

TYPE OF FIRE—Single shot

RATE OF FIRE—6 to 8 rpm

FEED DEVICE—Single round

FEED DEVICE WEIGHT (LOADED)—0.76 lb. (0.34 kg)

MANUFACTURER—FN Herstal

SERVICE—None

STATUS—Developmental

REFERENCES—Company literature

76.2 mm launcher. *Kevin Dockery*

NAME—Lacroix 76.2 mm Samouraï Urban Warfare (SUW) Weapon

COMMON NAMES—HIWS-76 High-Impulse Weapon System

CALIBER—76×250 mm R
OVERALL LENGTH—40.5 inches (103 cm)
BARREL LENGTH—37.3 inches (94.7 cm)
RIFLING (TYPE and TWIST)—Smoothbore,
fin-stabilized
LOAD—3-inch HIWS Universal Cargo Round;
1.43 lbs. (0.65 kg) available for cargo
ROUND WEIGHT—3.3 lbs. (1.50 kg)
PROJECTILE DIAMETER—3 inches
(76.2 mm)
PROJECTILE WEIGHT—2.2 lbs. (1.0 kg)
MUZZLE VELOCITY—328 fps (100 m/s)
WEIGHT (EMPTY)—16 lbs. (7.26 kg)
WEIGHT (LOADED)—19.3 lbs. (8.75 kg)
SIGHTS—Reflex sights fitted for
development
SIGHT POWER—1/1
EFFECTIVE RANGE—300 yards (274 m)—
direct fire; 731 yards (800 m)—indirect fire
OPERATION—Manual
TYPE OF FIRE—Single shot
RATE OF FIRE—2 to 3 rpm
FEED DEVICE—Single round
FEED DEVICE WEIGHT—3.3 lbs. (1.50 kg)
MANUFACTURER—Lacroix Defense,
France/FN Herstal, Belgium
SERVICE—Evaluation
STATUS—Developmental
REFERENCES—Company literature

7.62 mm round cargo projectile with cutaway cartridge case.
Kevin Dockery

140 mm RAW launcher with rocket projectile. *Kevin Dockery*

NAME—140 mm Brunswick Rifleman's
Assault Weapon
COMMON NAMES—XM140 RAW, USMC
Rifleman's Breaching Weapon
CALIBER—140 mm
OVERALL LENGTH—12 inches (30.5 cm)
LOAD—High-explosive squash head
(HESH)—2.8 lbs. (1.27 kg) of high-explosive
ROUND WEIGHT—8.5 lbs. (3.86 kg)
PROJECTILE DIAMETER—5.5 inches
(14 cm)
MAXIMUM VELOCITY—568 fps (173 m/s) at
200 meters
PROJECTILE EFFECT—Blasts a 14-inch
(36 cm) hole through 8 inches (20 cm) of
double-reinforced concrete
WEIGHT (EMPTY)—1.93 lbs. (0.88 kg)—
launcher body
WEIGHT (LOADED)—10.43 lbs. (4.73 kg)
WEIGHT (MOUNTED)—18.97 lbs. (8.60 kg) on
M16A2 rifle with 30 rounds M855 ball
TYPE OF MOUNT—M16-series rifles
SIGHTS—Uses sights of host weapon,
spotting round with 5.56 mm tracers
MINIMUM RANGE—33 yards (30 m)
EFFECTIVE RANGE—328 yards (300 m)
MAXIMUM RANGE—2,187 yards (2000 m)
OPERATION—Manual, fires from discharge
of host weapon
TYPE OF FIRE—Single shot, disposable
FEED DEVICE—Single round prepackaged
on launcher
MANUFACTURER—Brunswick Corporation
Defense Division

SERVICE—U.S. Marine Corps

STATUS—In production

REFERENCES—Company literature

COMMENTS—Normal accuracy—5 mils dispersion around point of aim

The 140 mm RAW launcher in place on the muzzle of an M16A2 rifle resting on a bipod. *Kevin Dockery*

The Scorpion underbarrel rocket launcher in place on an M16A2 rifle. *Kevin Dockery*

NAME—Scorpion Multipurpose Individual Munition

CALIBER—66 mm

OVERALL LENGTH—30.5 inches (77.5 cm); 32 inches (81.3 cm) Scorpion packaged for carry

BARREL LENGTH—30 inches (76.2 cm)

RIFLING (TYPE and TWIST)—Smoothbore, projectile stabilized with 6 spring-loaded folding fins

LOAD—Rocket projectile

ROUND WEIGHT—7.5 lbs. (3.4 kg)

PROJECTILE DIAMETER—66 mm

PROJECTILE WEIGHT—5.68 lbs. (2.58 kg)

LAUNCH VELOCITY—225 fps (69 m/s)

MAXIMUM VELOCITY—1,350 fps at 82 feet (411 m/s at 25 m)

PROJECTILE EFFECT—Shaped charge penetrator or high explosive fragmentation loads under development

WEIGHT (EMPTY)—1.5 lbs. (0.68 kg)

WEIGHT (LOADED)—8.99 lbs. (4.08 kg)

WEIGHT (MOUNTED)—17.53 lbs. (7.95 kg) on M16A2 rifle with 30 rounds M855 ball

TYPE OF MOUNT—M16-series rifles

SIGHTS—Uses sights of the host weapon, tracers act as spotting rounds

MINIMUM RANGE—11 yards (10 m)

EFFECTIVE RANGE—328 yards (300 m)

OPERATION—Manual

TYPE OF FIRE—Single-shot disposable

FEED DEVICE—Single round prepackaged in launcher

FEED DEVICE WEIGHT (LOADED)—9.90 lbs. (4.49 kg) packaged for transport

MANUFACTURER—McDonnell Douglas Astronautics Company

SERVICE—None

STATUS—Prototype, development suspended

REFERENCES—Company literature

ENERGY WEAPONS

All weapons perform their function by delivering energy on the target. This can be kinetic energy in the form of a projectile, chemical energy as produced by an explosive, or the much more exotic directed energy of a laser.

Of all of the possible future weapons, none raises the general level of interest or excites the imagination as much as those that use directed energy. Whether a ray gun or a laser beam, directed, controlled energy has been the stuff of science fiction for one hundred years and more. The phaser and blaster have been in popular entertainment for decades, but they have yet to be developed in any practical manner. They were thought to have finally found a means of existing in the discovery of a unique process, light amplification by the stimulated emission of radiation, known everywhere now as the laser.

The laser as a device is less than sixty years old. In that time it has grown from a laboratory curiosity to a common device that is used every day in grocery store checkout lanes, DVD and CD players, even simple pointers used in classrooms. These are all low-energy lasers that operate by projecting coherent light, extremely pure light of a single wavelength, that can be precisely and carefully controlled.

Tremendous levels of power can be transmitted by the laser. Beams of coherent radiation in a wide range of wavelengths, from the visible to the infrared, have blasted through steel blocks, alloy targets, and even ripped missiles in flight from out of the sky miles away from the laser generators. But all of these applications have a serious drawback; the laser is terribly inefficient in converting the energy fed into it into energy that comes out of it in the form of laser light.

Hugely powerful lasers do exist. The high-energy lasers (HEL) of the airborne ballistic missile system, designated the YAL-1A by the United States Air Force, is one such powerful laser. Produced by a system known as the chemically pumped oxygen-iodine laser or COIL, the HEL of the airborne laser (ABL) system can pump out a laser beam of such power that it can destroy a

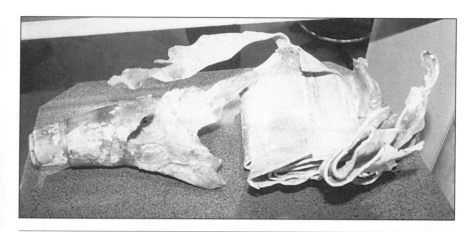

The remains of a Soviet-made Katyusha rocket, ripped from the sky during a test of the Theater High Energy Laser (THEL), a joint U.S./Israeli project for a tactical missile defense.
Kevin Dockery

ballistic missile as it burns its way through the atmosphere during the boost phase of its launch. And the ABL can destroy that missile at a range of hundreds of kilometers.

The drawback of the ABL system's COIL lasers is that the module that is needed to produce a single beam is about the size of a panel van and weighs over two tons. The laser tube that generates the beam is nearly the full length of a 747 aircraft, the vehicle that carries the ABL system. But the value of being able to destroy a missile while it is still over the territory of the country that launched it is of such value that the Air Force has spent years and countless man-hours perfecting the ABL system and preparing it for use. Within a very short time, the first of the converted 747 aircraft that carry the COIL laser and the ABL system may be protecting the country from the possibilities of a missile launch from a rogue country.

The multimegawatt power of the COIL laser on the ABL system cannot be duplicated in a small device that could be held by a single operator or even mounted in a medium-sized van. The power that has to be generated to overcome the inefficiency of the laser is too large for easy portability. Low-energy lasers (LEL) are the common versions that can be powered by a battery small enough to fit in a watch, yet they project a red dot that can be seen clearly at some distance. They are the common applications of the laser principle that have found their use in the military.

Low-energy lasers have myriad uses in range finders, electronic devices, and even aiming devices that are used to direct more powerful weapons. The

AN/PEQ-2A and AN/PEQ-5 are laser aiming devices that mount on rifles and other weapons to direct their aim at night through the use of an invisible beam of infrared light. The laser beam is plainly visible to the shooter who is looking through a night vision device. But the first warning that the enemy would know that he has been laser-targeted would be when he felt the impact of the bullet.

Visible light lasers have also found their use in the military as target designators. The bright red dot that indicates the impact point of a projectile can help a soldier aim a weapon when he is in a bad position or just isn't able to properly use the sights. Another aspect of the visible laser designators is that they have been found to prevent a soldier from even having to fire his weapon. When a civilian protester refuses to leave an area, and the situation looks as if it will quickly escalate, the red dot of a laser has been found to have a suddenly calming effect on the individual doing the instigating.

These indicating lasers are referred to as Class IIIb power devices. That means they project a beam with power levels in the fifty milliwatt and greater range. This power level is considered an acute direct exposure hazard to the eyes and skin, but particularly the eyes. To be considered eye-safe (Class I), a laser has to put out a beam that has a maximum power level of less than a milliwatt. Most military laser devices are much more powerful than that, but they are considered a secondary danger when compared to all of the other hazards of the battlefield and are not an antipersonnel weapon.

What have been considered as weapons are lasers that are powerful enough to blind anyone looking at them or injure someone who has been struck in the eye by the beam. Focused on the retina of the eye by the lens, a powerful laser will burn the inside of the eyeball, scarring the delicate surface of the retina and damaging it irreparably. Immediately or eventually, this type of laser can cause blindness.

The idea of a weapon whose sole purpose is to cause blindness on the part of the soldiers who face it is so repugnant that the development and fielding of such devices is banned by international agreements. Even before such agreements were formally in place, the United States suspended a number of laser devices from further development. Such intentional restraint has not been universal in the development of such weapons.

In the mid-1990s, the Chinese government offered for international sale the ZM-87 Portable Laser Disturber. The ZM-87 weighed seventy-three pounds complete with its battery supply and small tripod. It was sold in 1994 as a weapon that could damage the sensor systems of enemy equipment or the soldiers manning that equipment. The power level put out by the ZM-87 laser was more than enough to do instant and permanent damage to an observer's eye. While being sold at an arms exhibition in the Philippines in 1995, one of the capabilities of the ZM-87 was announced to be the ability to blind enemy soldiers.

Few details are available on the ZM-87; it was not on the market for very long, and few specimens have been examined. The specifications of the device list the effective range for eye damage from the laser as 2,000 to 3,000 meters. If observing through an optical device with a magnification of seven or greater, the effective range for damage to that eye from the ZM-87 laser is 5,000 meters. The laser beams from the ZM-87 were reported as being pulsed and selectable from between two different frequencies and fired at a power level of fifteen megawatts. That power level would give the ZM-87 a dazzling (flash blinding) range of 10,000 meters. That would be distance enough to injure the eyes of a pilot flying at over 32,000 feet altitude. And reports have the ZM-87 being sold to a number of rogue countries and terrorist groups before sales were suspended. It was the first laser weapon sold that had the tactical mission of being used against human targets.

Several laser devices for use against humans as nonlethal weapons have been fielded by the U.S. military. One of the devices, the Saber 203, has seen field use in subduing crowds before they could become violent. The Saber 203 is a laser illuminator that fits in the chamber of an M203 grenade launcher while the triggering transmitter unit wraps around the outside of the barrel. When triggered, the Saber 203 projects a dazzling, disorienting laser light that is safe for up to a ten-second exposure. The mechanics of laser eye injuries are complex, and the possibility of damage to the eyes of a civilian population with the Saber 203 had caused it to be withdrawn from use while additional testing and development is conducted.

One laser device that is being presently developed is the Personnel Halting and Stimulation Response (PHaSR). The PHaSR is a man-portable laser "rifle" intended to disorient and disable personnel through the use of two beams produced by low-power diode-pumped lasers. One beam would be in the visible spectrum while the other is a mid-infrared wavelength that is invisible to human sight.

A large, riflelike weapon, the PHaSR can be handled by one

The PHaSR laser device set up on a small bipod.
U.S. Air Force

man and fired from the shoulder or from its folding bipod while on the ground. The device weighs less than twenty pounds and can be manipulated as a large, shoulder-fired weapon. Development of the prototype PHaSR device is being conducted in 2006 with the objective being to attach an eye-safe laser range finder into the circuitry of the device. The laser range finder would automatically adjust the power level of the PHaSR's beam to prevent it from being permanently damaging to a specific target.

Another very well-developed directed-energy weapon actually produces its effect through the application of kinetic energy to the target. The electromagnetic launcher uses twin rails to conduct a very powerful electric current through them to accelerate projectiles to much higher velocities than could be reached with chemical propellants. The rails used in these devices are the source of their common names: rail guns.

Like the powerful lasers used as weapons, the rail guns are power-hungry monsters. A ten-foot-long rail gun can send a fin-stabilized long-rod penetrator out of the muzzle at velocities of 2,000 meters per second (over 6,500 feet per minute) or better. At those velocities, a long rod penetrator can cut through the thickest armor than can be placed on a tank and still be capable of movement.

But to launch that projectile from the rail gun takes a surge of power measured at up to 4.5 million amps and 5,000 volts. That means a power supply the size of a small building. And the recoil of such a launcher is tremendous. Once perfected, it would take a heavy armored vehicle to stand up to the kick of a powerful rail gun. Making such a device into a weapon the size of a rifle might be possible with the development of high-density power storage and generation, but the physics of the rail gun would mean that the recoil would probably seriously injure the shooter if it didn't just kill him outright.

INDEX

Page numbers in *italic* indicate photographs or illustrations; those in **bold** indicate tables.